CULTURAL STUDIES

Series Editors

Janice Radway, Duke University
Richard Johnson, University of Birmingham

Viewing, Reading, Listening: Audiences and Cultural Reception
edited by Jon Cruz and Justin Lewis

The Madonna Connection: Representational Politics, Subcultural Identities, and Cultural Theory edited by Cathy Schwichtenberg

Dreaming Identities: Class, Gender, and Generation in 1980s Hollywood Movies Elizabeth G. Traube

Enlightened Racism: The Cosby Show, *Audiences, and the Myth of the American Dream* Sut Jhally and Justin Lewis

FORTHCOMING

Frameworks of Culture and Power: Complexity and Politics in Cultural Studies Richard Johnson

An Introduction to Media Studies edited by Stuart Ewen, Elizabeth Ewen, Serafina Bathrick, and Andrew Mattson

Art and the Committed Eye: Culture, Society, and the Functions of Imagery Richard Leppert

MTV Jack Banks

Body Politics: Disease, Desire, and the Family edited by Michael Ryan and Avery Gordon

VIEWING, READING, LISTENING

Audiences and Cultural Reception

edited by
Jon Cruz
University of California–Santa Barbara

Justin Lewis
University of Massachusetts–Amherst

Westview Press
Boulder • San Francisco • Oxford

Cultural Studies

Copyright © 1994 by Westview Press, Inc.

Published in 1994 in the United States of America by Westview Press, Inc., 5500 Central Avenue, Boulder, Colorado 80301-2877, and in the United Kingdom by Westview Press, 36 Lonsdale Road, Summertown, Oxford OX2 7EW

Library of Congress Cataloging-in-Publication Data
Viewing, reading, listening : audiences and cultural reception /
   [edited by] Jon Cruz, Justin Lewis.
     p.   cm. — (Cultural studies)
   Includes bibliographical references.
   ISBN 0-8133-1537-9. — ISBN 0-8133-1538-7 (pbk.)
     1. Mass media—Audiences.   2. Popular culture.   I. Cruz, Jon.
II. Lewis, Justin, 1958– .   III. Series.
P96.A83V54   1994
302.23—dc20   93-25969
                                                                               CIP

Printed and bound in the United States of America

   The paper used in this publication meets the requirements
   of the American National Standard for Permanence of Paper
   for Printed Library Materials Z39.48-1984.

10   9   8   7   6   5   4   3   2   1

Contents

Acknowledgments

This collection of essays grew out of the intellectual spirits involved in the Audience Studies Group located at the University of Massachusetts, Amherst, and the invited colleagues who shared their research with that group through public forums. James Der Derian and Ellen McCracken lent their energies and critical commentary to our endeavors to further critical research on audiences and reception. We extend our gratitude to David Maxcy, who assisted us in taping and transcribing. We especially thank Dean Glen Gordon of the University of Massachusetts for his generous support enabling us to invite and gather many of the chapters presented in this book.

Jon Cruz
Justin Lewis

About the Contributors

Ian Angus is associate professor in the Department of Anthropology and Sociology at Simon Fraser University in Canada. He has written widely on philosophy, culture, and contemporary social theory and is the coeditor of *Cultural Politics in Contemporary America* (Routledge, 1989).

Denise Bielby is professor of sociology at the University of California, Santa Barbara. Her research interests are popular culture, gender, and work. Currently she is studying, with William Bielby, social networks and careers in the television industry. Among their recent publications is *The 1993 Hollywood Writers' Report,* published by the Writers' Guild of America, West. She and C. Lee Harrington are exploring the coproduction of meaning between viewers and producers of television series.

Elizabeth Cole is assistant professor of psychology and ethnic studies at Northeastern University. Her research includes the analysis of pro-life and pro-choice women's interpretations of the abortion issue and the study of midlife political involvement of African American and white women who came of age during the late 1960s and early 1970s.

Jon Cruz is assistant professor holding a joint appointment in sociology and Asian American studies at the University of California, Santa Barbara. He has written on the blues, health depictions in mass media, conservative populism, Filipino community formation, and multiculturalism. He is author of a forthcoming study on the discovery of African American music by white cultural elites in the nineteenth century (Princeton University Press).

Stuart Hall is professor of sociology at the Open University in Great Britain. He is former director of the highly influential Centre for Contemporary Cultural Studies at the University of Birmingham and is the doyen of British cultural studies.

C. Lee Harrington is assistant professor of sociology and anthropology at Miami University of Ohio. Her research areas include cultural studies and emotions, and she is currently working on a book about fan communities with Denise Bielby.

Sut Jhally is associate professor in the Department of Communication at the University of Massachusetts and is director of the Foundation for Media Education. He has published works on many aspects of U.S. media and culture, including *Codes of Advertising* (Routledge, 1987) and, with Justin Lewis, *Enlightened Racism:*

The Cosby Show, Audiences, and the Myth of the American Dream (Westview, 1992).

Ron Lembo is assistant professor of sociology and anthropology at Amherst College. He has written on cultural studies criticism and the analysis of the television-viewing process. He is completing a book-length study on how television viewers incorporate television into everyday life.

Justin Lewis is associate professor in the Department of Communication at the University of Massachusetts. He has written widely on British and U.S. media and popular culture. His recent work includes *The Ideological Octopus* (Routledge, 1991) and, with Sut Jhally, *Enlightened Racism:* The Cosby Show, *Audiences, and the Myth of the American Dream* (Westview, 1992).

Elizabeth Long is associate professor of sociology and anthropology at Rice University. She is currently involved in an ethnographic study of book-reading groups. Her publications include *The American Dream and the Popular Novel* (Routledge, 1985) and numerous essays on the ethnography of reading groups and cultural studies.

David Morley is a reader in media studies, Goldsmiths' College, University of London. He is one of the pioneers in introducing a British cultural studies approach to media use and reception. His most recent book is *Television, Audiences, and Cultural Studies* (Routledge, 1992).

Andrea Press is assistant professor in the Department of Communication at the University of Michigan. She has published widely on topics of feminist theory and television's representation of abortion politics. She is author of *Women Watching Television: Gender, Class, and Generation in the American Television Experience* (University of Pennsylvania Press, 1991).

Janice Radway is professor in the literature program at Duke University. In addition to *Reading the Romance: Women, Patriarchy, and Popular Literature* (University of North Carolina Press, 1984), she has published widely in the areas of cultural studies, reception studies, and feminist theory.

Cathy Schwichtenberg teaches in the Department of Speech Communication at the University of Georgia. She has edited *The Madonna Connection* (Westview, 1992) and is the author of *Approaches to Popular Culture* (Sage, 1993).

Introduction

JON CRUZ AND JUSTIN LEWIS

What is an "audience?" How does it come into being? Are audiences more than receptacles for cultural content? Are they just sometimes, or are they always, more than passive consumers assimilating and accommodating what they are given by the marketplace? What is the relationship between externally produced cultural goods and individual, group, race, class, and gender identities? Under what conditions do audiences become actors engaged in struggles over the meanings of the cultural goods that help constitute them as "audiences" in the first place? How do the cultural practices of audiences affect the production of cultural products? And whether it be reading, listening, attending, buying, watching, or in general using an externally produced commodity or communication, how do we, as analysts, proceed from the specific practices of cultural appropriation to the broader parameters established by history, society, and culture in general?

These may seem to be basic questions, but not long ago such questions were of relatively little concern to media sociologists, communication researchers, and humanist scholars. If they were entertained, they were quickly reframed and dispensed with in terms of media effects, persuasion, and public opinion theories. Today, questions about audiences (and related notions like interpretive communities, reading formations, reception, and identity formations) loom large within cultural studies. And these concerns, which surface in overlapping fashion across the social sciences and humanities, challenge us to reconceptualize audiences.

Much of the new interest in audience studies has come about through cross-disciplinary convergences among the social sciences and the humanities. Today it is common for analysts trained in one disciplinary field to seek out kindred debates in other fields. Cross-disciplinary cultural analysis now requires a relative openness, in which the capacity to move beyond narrowly defined intellectual borders is both a necessity and a virtue. The mutual exchange of theories and methods is, perhaps, reminiscent of the late nineteenth century when intellectuals looked broadly toward the "human sciences" (before twentieth-century scientism purged the plurality of knowledges and equated legitimate inquiry with highly calibrated systems of measurement).

The growing number of cultural analysts no longer content to stay within traditional intellectual boundaries is not simply a gathering of a few smart people with strong intellectual wills. Rather, the scramble for interdisciplinarity is symptomatic of a crisis in the politics of knowledge after poststructuralism. Nowhere is this condition more obvious than in the debates that surround theories of representation and reception. Departments of Communication, Literature, Sociology, History, and other disciplines across the humanities and social sciences have, in many cases, been forced to consider broad questions of representation that cut across their traditional boundaries. The stability of disciplinary canons has been called into question by broader inquiries into ideology and epistemology, inquires that have forced researchers to think reflexively about their own work. People writing about history, culture, and society have begun to look at the ideological and cultural assumptions embedded in their own disciplines—to look at how history, culture, and society have been represented and defined.[1]

These questions have produced substantive transformations in some of the more traditional disciplines. Some English departments, for example, have made strides to take on characteristics of ethnic studies programs, now that hitherto silenced texts from the racial and cultural margins have been more widely admitted; and this has come in tandem with a recognition that the cherished master canons never actually transcended the presumably banal social categories of race, class, and gender but, on the contrary, had much to do with such matters in their very installation, their manner of institutionalization, and how they were read. The newer disciplines (such as ethnic studies and women's studies), on the other hand, have, at least in part, been created out of this interdisciplinary focus on representation. They begin with the premise that traditional forms of inquiry have been constructed with deeply ideological assumptions that have excluded whole categories of thought and activity. How women or ethnic groups have been represented by high culture or popular culture has thus been a growing critical concern. The issue of representation as problematic has opened the way for the examination of a whole cultural process: the process whereby representations are produced, received, and interpreted. This, in turn, has prompted new ways of thinking about audiences.

Many of these interdisciplinary developments have been associated with cultural studies, in which assumptions about culture and ideology have been confronted head-on. Yet with so many different sensibilities coming together, these intellectual endeavors resemble more a cacophony of critical voices than some unified chorus singing from a single score.[2] Their different concerns, subject matters, and lexicons make any attempt at an overall synthesis an extremely messy business. It is not our intention, therefore, to argue for an overarching, grand theory of audiences, representation, or reception. On the contrary, we feel that the crisis surrounding representation and reception has virtue in that it opens up sorely needed intellectual debate, unfreezes what disciplines have historically fixed, facilitates fresh engagements, and unties the skills and capacities needed in the critical appraisal of how to rethink the problems of audience analysis.

Theoretical Shifts and the Problem of Reception

The theoretical crisis in the analysis of representation impinges upon cultural analysis in general and audience studies in particular. But the challenges and pressures leading to the reconceptualization of audiences have been building for quite some time. By the end of the 1920s and continuing throughout the 1930s, a critique of orthodox Marxism was unfolding in the writings of Karl Korsch, Georg Lukacs, and Antonio Gramsci; the analytical shift introduced new possibilities for rethinking culture within a framework of historical determination and for conceptualizing it as more than simply a product of an economic system. The notion of history following along inexorable laws that would produce a particular historical subject, the proletariat, was difficult to sustain in the context of modernity. The twin triumphs of authoritarian-bureaucratic state socialism and a profoundly successful consumer capitalism (gently regulated by welfare states) checked rather than delivered the progressive class-conscious proletariat. These forces challenged Marxist historical teleology and eclipsed the vision of a collective subjectivity automatically produced by historical forces.

Much of the early work of reassessing the problems associated with the cultural turn proceeded along a number of intellectually vibrant fronts. Breaking from orthodox or "party" Marxism, Western Marxism began to reinstate the importance of ideology and culture in the social sciences. By the mid-1950s the exiled Frankfurt School theoreticians (Max Horkheimer, Theodore Adorno, Herbert Marcuse, and Leo Lowenthal) had merged cultural Marxism with psychoanalytic and Nietzschean theory to produce an analysis of how mass culture was able to set new conditions governing the cultural consciousness of modern individuals.[3] Jurgen Habermas, critiquing the early Frankfurt School yet extending its core theoretical concerns, continued the legacy through the attempt to retrieve modernity's frustrated promise of a rationally invested critical public sphere in which modern political subjects could achieve freedom from class domination.[4]

In the United States, New Left intellectuals merged the insights of Western Marxism (and "left Weberianism") and its critique of mass culture with the research produced by revisionist historians during the 1960s and 1970s. Revisionist historicism readdressed the problem of advanced capitalism by exploring the ties among corporate, political, and military power as a distinctly modern social formation (corporate liberalism) and its relation to American politics.[5] Building on the critical traditions of revisionist historicism and the analysis of forms of social domination, but adding a cultural component to its corporatist critique, social scientists began to bring issues of race, class, gender, and mass media into the picture of social and cultural historiography.[6]

In France the rise of structuralism and semiotics introduced a major reorientation in cultural analysis. The central importance of symbolic systems was given its first structuralist treatment in the work of Ferdinand de Saussure. From this perspective stem some direct routes to structural anthropology and semiotic theory. Claude Levi-Strauss drew upon the Saussurian notion of language, pressing it into service as an analytic metaphor. For Levi-Strauss, the Saussurian model for a science of signs (semiology) provided a new foundation for cultural analysis. Culture could be seen to operate as language did. The linguistic model was seen as applicable to the study of culture for two general but related reasons. First, social and cultural phenomena were more than material objects or events; they were objects and events with particular meanings. And this also made them signs. If such human activity was to have meaning, it must rest on some underlying system of distinctions and relations (or a structure) that could make meaning possible. Second, social and cultural phenomena were not to be grasped as isolated and discrete events possessing an essence all to themselves; instead, they were to be defined through the underlying network of rules and practices—just as languages were.

Adding to the structuralist project of developing a new taxonomy of cultural meanings was Roland Barthes's elaboration of semiology.[7] Language, artifacts, representations, cultural practices, and social events could be analyzed in terms of how they enabled the production of meanings based on their relation to underlying systems through which they were generated. Within the purview of structuralism, cultural objects or activities were thus understood partly through their position within the overall structure of the system.

At this theoretical juncture additional challenges emerged. If, as Barthes argued, language did not simply represent a verifiable reality but instead produced ideology or myth, then the whole rational edifice upon which inquiry was based was in jeopardy. And this is precisely the point where Michel Foucault's work in discourse theory, circulated in the 1970s and early 1980s, entered the picture. How could rational minds inescapably mired in the myth-making tools of language ever prove the existence of underlying structures? If ideas in general—including scientific notions of structure as well as reason, nature, and truth—were symbolic constructs, then the problem was not to take the content of representations at face value but rather to interrogate the systems that produced regimes of representations themselves. In this reorientation, the very concept of *structure,* at least as a fixed and specifiable entity discoverable through the excavating tools of a neutral language, became suspect. This emerging distaste for the concept of structure ushered in a new host of issues that by the late 1970s hovered under the umbrella of poststructuralism. Rejecting the concept of structure gave symbolic production more autonomy. And with this newly claimed autonomy, cultural analysis could be approached as discourse analysis and the study of discursive practices.

In the mid-1970s the emergence of cultural studies, associated with the Centre for Contemporary Cultural Studies in Britain, was launched within the very juncture of Western Marxism's crisis around class politics, working-class histories, and traditional as well as emergent forms of popular culture. The attempt to rethink the importance of signification and political economy played a major role in the formation of British cultural studies. Here, the broader problems of Western Marxism were extended through the theoretical contributions of the Italian political theorist Antonio Gramsci and the structural Marxism of Louis Althusser. The cultural sphere, in all of its sprawling manifestations, was seen as the key terrain upon which politics, power, and domination were mediated. Some of the notable achievements of British cultural studies at this point were the remappings of media analysis and working-class cultures. Integrating insights from Gramsci and Althusser, Stuart Hall helped to frame the theoretically innovative approaches that combined the analysis of the relations of classes, subcultures, race, gender, and mass media. Ethnographic assessments of everyday life within the sphere of larger institutional and social structures characterized these class-specific ethnographies.[8] Such syntheses in the cultural analyses of the center's formative years were responsible for launching a widespread interest in this form of cultural studies, and the influence on ethnographic work has been significant.

As cultural studies expanded in the late 1970s and early 1980s, the integration of theoretical considerations was extended in new and critical ways. These went beyond British Marxist labor historicism and structural Marxism to include poststructuralism, semiology, and psychoanalytic theory. Much of this work focused on media analysis and was published in the journals *Screen* and *Screen Education*. However, the absorption of poststructuralism within British cultural studies did not produce a rejection of Marxist theory (as did deconstructionism in the United States). Class and economic issues as well as race and gender were not disregarded, nor was the importance of ideology or the state dismissed. Given that cultural studies had roots in social theory, these elements were retained as important in grasping key (but not ontologized or essentialized) configurations of social relations.[9] What poststructuralism invigorated was a critical rereading of Marx salvaged from orthodox Marxism and an illumination of the cultural blind spots found in class and/or economic reductionism. By the late 1970s the centrality of gender theorizing appeared as an additional critique of social and cultural theories. It was as this juncture that historiography, psychoanalytic (Lacanian) theory, and subculture studies began to incorporate as well as transform feminist theorizing in ways that, in turn, challenged and transformed the contours of cultural studies.[10]

The cultural orientation within Western Marxism, the American critique of corporate liberalism, the linguistic turn in French structuralism, the elaboration of subculture and media analysis conducted by the Centre for Contemporary Cultural Studies, and the fields of semiotic theory and poststructuralism helped to open up the study of signification and its relation to ideology, institutions, cultural practices, and modes of social exchange. In various combinations, these developments bequeathed the now sprawling intellectual terrain of cultural studies. In this regard, the very cracks opened by Western Marxism's critique of economism and problematizing culture became chasms that were filled with the crisis of representation and the new complexities of cultural production.[11]

Related to these theoretical shifts were developments in literary theory and textual interpretation. The rise of reader-response theory emerged as a direct challenge to New Criticism by rejecting the analytic assumptions that the meanings of texts were contained in the texts themselves. Reader-response theory argued for a restoration of the importance of readers, and the problems of interpretation shifted toward investigation of the formation of identity by focusing on the reader. In highlighting the act of reading texts and not simply the facticity and objectivity of texts themselves, reader-response theory repositioned the problem of cultural production within literary studies. Stanley Fish's notion of interpretive communities endorsed the centrality of the reader by arguing that interpretive conventions govern reception; thus authorial intent—what authors and producers of texts want to convey—mattered less than the interpretive strategies readers bring to texts. Shifting attention to the practices of reading did not mean abandoning texts but instead repositioning texts and their interpretation, and this, in turn, forced literary theory toward social theory. The return of the reader in literary theory facilitated moves that shared a set of interpretive analytics having considerable overlap with the developments that inform contemporary cultural studies. Indeed, the importance given to the analysis of cultural practices and cultural production has facilitated the vibrant ties between social theory and literary theory.[12]

From Markets to Politics

At the turn of the century, popular literature, newspapers, and magazines had already found their niche in well-established markets. By the mid-1920s, cinema, the recording industry, and radio broadcasting were well on their way toward becoming large-scale media institutions. The rise of mass culture, so central to the modern form of democratic capitalist consumer society, was profoundly unsettling to earlier and more traditional institutions of cultural authority. Social scientists, humanists, religious leaders, and lay critics were increasingly compelled to respond to the new conditions of mass culture. In the United States, modern social science research in mass communications evolved hand in glove with the industrial spread of mass media. In the decades between 1920 and 1960, broadcasting was institutionalized and rationalized. In the emerging academic focus on mass communication, the notion of audience rapidly became formalized within social science.

A number of related developments in this era were important. Economic calamity and social upheaval during the depression of the 1930s raised the question of managing governmental legitimacy with the challenges of social control. President Roosevelt's "fireside chats" with the American radio audience reflected the new recognition of the functional ties among broadcasting, the public, and government. Two major wars, World War II and the Korean War, encompassing the 1940s and 1950s, added new dimensions to the cultural relations between mass media and the state. Industrial expansion, the growth of suburbs, and the rise of radio and television broadcasting helped to expand and deepen the institutionalization of modern consumer society as publics became addressed as audiences for consumer goods. As publications were transformed by new technology and new markets, so were the publics that consumed them. In a society increasingly solidified through mass communication, audiences became ever more important to political, industrial, educational, and broadcasting interests. Not surprisingly, the analysis of audiences developed along with new approaches in the social sciences: the emergent fields of public opinion, propaganda analysis, techniques of persuasion, public relations, and market research. The links forged between the various social science subfields and media research culminated in the dominance of the market-centered study of mass culture and audiences. Todd Gitlin's essay on the "dominant paradigm" was one of the first attempts to explore the systematic development of how American media sociology came into being, in relation to the pressures industrialization placed on scientific inquiry. Tracing the theoretical, intellectual, and social roots of mass communication analysis, Gitlin revealed how the theories, models, and methods that characterized much of sociology's communication research were forged in and compromised with the rise of the industrialization of media itself.[13]

While the rise of media studies in the first half of the twentieth century had deep ties to the industrialization of culture, the questions being asked were not only in response to industry's needs. Mass culture was met with responses that ran the gamut from consumerist glee to apprehension and dread. A number of significant examples illustrate the clash between market and moral imperatives. As an important form of leisure for the urban white ethnic working class, nickelodeons were frowned upon. Disapproval turned to scorn when more and more members from middle and upper-middle classes began to attend the movies that were viewed as corrosive to moral conduct.[14] In a similar fashion, the dance craze of the 1920s, with white youth finding pleasure in the music and dances emanating from African American enclaves, engendered much apprehension. To this chronology we might add the famous Payne Fund studies on movies and their association with juvenile delinquency in the early 1930s. The debates over mass culture and youth carried forward into the mid-1950s with major Senate hearings on television and an invigorated investigation by social scientists.[15] In addition, comic books, rhythm and blues, and rock and roll were indicted for their corrosive effects on youth. Ironically, moral and political panics surrounding popular culture coincided with well-designed foreign policy programs launched by the national security strategists who went to great length to promote abroad the same aspects of popular culture vilified at home. Demonized in the popular press, African American music was fit for export through "goodwill" tours to Soviet-bloc and nonaligned Third World nations, whose populations were perceived to be politically exploitable through the weaponry of American popular culture.

These examples marked highly contentious relations between market-driven incursions into popular culture and the attempts by cultural and moral gatekeepers to put a brake on cultural commodification and to resist the market's capacity to flood particular communities with new forms of leisure. Indeed, the rise of media-effects research in media social science was shaped, in part, by the cultural battles between the pressures of market expansion and the moral responses concerned with the market's perceived detrimental effects. Besides the questions that dominated early research on media effects and those singularly focused on the effects of advertising or political campaigns, many concerns were symptomatic of broad anxieties about the emerging mass culture: Did the media influence political attitudes, or, alternatively, did they create forms of deviancy?

Consistent with the ambiguity and anxiety that surrounded the new social order, the emerging conceptions of audiences were constructed primarily on either moral or market-based scaffolding—and sometimes on both. On the one hand, audiences were understood as social entities (communities, youth, women, and so on) in need of protection from an overpowering set of external cultural forces (mass media) that overrode the local family or community. On the other hand, audiences were viewed as targets for market-centered campaigns geared to expand and streamline consumer society. The attention to mass media thus had a double function: It absorbed the threats to social norms, and it helped further normalize and deepen consumerism. Both perspectives promoted distinct ways in which audiences were conceptualized.

Within this market-versus-morals framework, the meaning of the audience came to rest, always tendentiously, on a simple presupposition: "Audience" assumed an assembly of passive yet malleable listeners whose attention was devoted to an externally produced communication, a view rooted in the earlier debate over the new industrially dependent mass society during the early twentieth century. Nevertheless, while the concerns of market engineers and social guardians were similar (both saw the new mass audience as a function of the new mass media), they worked within very different conceptual frameworks. To the guardians of public morals or tastes, the audience was cast in the role of victim, molded by media to conform to certain ways of thinking and behaving. For the advocates of consumerism, on the other hand, the audience could be not be regarded simply as putty to be shaped in the privacy of corporate boardrooms. The ideology of consumerism—particularly when pitted against a communist system in which the public was portrayed as witlessly manipulated by state propaganda—was sold by embracing the notion of consumer choice. The concept of mass audiences sat uncomfortably with the ideology of individual freedom on which the consumer society was supposed to be predicated.

It was, perhaps, ironic in this regard that the media-effects tradition that dominated early research suggested (rightly or wrongly) that the media were more influential in promoting consumerism than in instituting more general moral, political, or behavioral change.[16] To many researchers at the time, in other words, the effects of advertising campaigns were more demonstrable than the effects of media on political attitudes or behavior. The ideology (rather than the operation) of free market consumerism required research models that spoke very differently about audiences. The rise of "uses and gratifications" theory in the late 1950s was, in this sense, far more compatible with the self-effacing public identity of corporate capitalism. The new perspective self-consciously reversed the roles in the media/audience relationship: No longer the victim of media, the "free" audience was seen as the determining force that shaped the form and content of media to its own needs and interests. The debate about audiences thus became (and remains) enshrined within debates about free market capitalism. We can find common political threads between free market theorists and those who see audiences as groups of active individuals who can mold the meaning of mass media to suit their particular interests.[17] The political forces on the other side of this equation are more disparate: Marxists and McCarthyites alike represented a tendency to see media as all-powerful and the mass audience as too witless or feeble to defend itself from its rampaging hegemonic influence.

Since the 1950s and 1960s, audience theories on the Right and on the Left have followed very different paths. The Right remains caught between two contradictory positions: on the one hand asserting the power of consumers in a free market to get the media they want (a capitalist version of democracy in which wallets and purses, as the vessels of consumer choice, replace the sacred symbol of the ballot box), and on the other berating the media for causing a decline in moral values. Thus, in the last days of the Bush administration, Vice President Dan Quayle, the son of a newspaper magnate, was able to blame the "liberal" media for its failure to reflect the "true" values of the majority of Americans, while simultaneously expressing faith, like a good free marketeer, in the corporate world's ability to do just that. The contradictions here are profound: To put it bluntly, if the free marketeers are correct and the media are liberal, it can only be because the audience prefers it that way.

The Right has, in the last two decades, offered some interesting intellectual interventions in a number of areas, but audience research is not one of them. This is an area in which the right-wing intelligentsia are conspicuous by their absence, and the theories of media and audience that are still fashionable on the Right have remained bogged down in conception that the more sophisticated branches of social science abandoned many years ago. The Left, on the other hand, has sought to come to terms with some of its own contradictions. The levels of determinacy in the media/audience relationship thus have been reconceived in order to retain the notion of the mass media as a powerful ideological apparatus while granting au-

diences distinct degrees of agency and identity. There are many important moments in this theoretical history.

The work of Gramsci and subsequent reworkings of the theory of hegemony
saw the mass media as a site of ideological struggle, a place where different claims
over the meaning of things (including the media) were fought out. This perspective thus envisioned the ideological role of the media while seeing audiences as active bearers of ideologies that engaged with media messages, creating either con-
sent or resistance. Stuart Hall's encoding/decoding model (discussed in the final
chapter) was a methodological expression of this more complex formulation of
the media/audience relationship. At the same time, the meaning of messages (or
texts) themselves was opened up by work from structuralist, poststructuralist,
and semiotic perspectives, allowing a conception of audience whose meaning was
seen as, on the one hand, potentially open and contested and, on the other, culturally specific. The theory of the sign in semiotics implied an approach to meaning in which both message (the realm of the signifier) and audience (the realm of
the signified) were interactive in the ideological process of meaning construction
(the realm of the sign). Feminist critiques of Marxism also made it clear that the
audience was not a homogeneous entity but a complicated place where different
identities and ideologies interplayed. The delicate and difficult consequences of
this realization favored more ethnographic or qualitative forms of audience research, which seemed more capable of avoiding traditional assumptions about
the role of media and the audience.

Most of these inquiries were also informed by an epistemology that no longer
saw audiences as stranded between media (or ideology) and reality, forced to
choose between two straightforward accounts of the world. Rather, audiences
were seen as surrounded by (and constructed by) different histories and accounts,
in a world in which the media competed with the other representations, practices,
and experiences that shaped people's lives. Simple notions of media effects were
replaced by theories of "cultivation," in which the power of media stories were
measured against stories told elsewhere.[18]

It is not surprising, given the range of theoretical approaches brought to bear
on the media/audience dynamic, that the contemporary field of audience research
is decidedly untidy, with diverse combinations of older theoretical traditions as
well as new theories scattered across it. If we could once talk of theoretical ortho-
doxies defining audience research, we can no longer. In this collection, therefore,
we do not seek to lead the reader in any particular direction; we seek only to provide a fairly up-to-date map of this field. Like all maps, needless to say, much will
inevitably be left out.

*   *   *

The essays in this collection open up and explore a number of issues. The
approaches of the contributors are wide ranging; they vary in the questions
posed, the domains explored, the medium of cultural texts investigated, the prac-

tices analyzed, and the institutional and historical settings against which they un-fold. The contributors mobilize a diverse set of theoretical, analytical, and meth-odological orientations. By providing a wide range of approaches to the notion of audiences, the essays point toward the need to broaden and extend the arenas of inquiry, and they encourage us to expand the parameters of audience research. There is no presumption here that the essays highlight an overarching and grand theory of "the audience" or "reception" in general. Nor do they display any sense of theoretical and epistemological uniformity. Many of the essays are parts of larger inquiries in progress. But in their diversity they affirm the importance of recognizing the juncture in which the study of cultural production, reception, and interpretation now finds itself. Their collective meaning is to demonstrate that the horizons of audience research have profoundly and irrevocably shifted.

The problem of signification and of its inseparable ties to meaning is funda-mental to the critical assessment of cultural production, representation, and re-ception. One of the key theoretical tools cultural analysts have at their disposal is semiology—the study of meaning. The opening essay by Justin Lewis highlights semiology and its tremendous importance to cultural analysis and interpretation. Lewis is critical of the way in which semiology is reduced to a set of technical aids to deconstructing a text outside of the cultural and historical specificity in which it appears. When semiology is thus employed in an institutional and historical vacuum, it loses its radical potential to tell us about how cultural products and cultural meanings work. The radical break with linguistics implied by semiology, Lewis argues, has often been overlooked or misunderstood. The theory of the sign should be seen as invoking the audience, not as departing from it. Lewis argues for a retrieval of the linkage between media and audiences and makes the case that semiology has theoretical and methodological power to enable the analytic and interpretive bridge between cultural production and systems of meaning. He demonstrates his case with reference to his own empirical audience research.

Delving into the problem of meaning and exploring the concept of television interaction, Ron Lembo critiques several contemporary approaches to conceptu-alizing the television-viewing process for being far too general and, in many ways, simple. Drawing on ethnographic research, Lembo shows how the relations be-tween the viewer and television programming are multifarious. Television view-ing is broken down into three stages: the preparations involved in the turn to tele-vision, television interaction, and the ways in which television viewing fits back into everyday life. Each of these phases of viewing is shown to be composed of many varying levels, modes, and forms of engagement with television. In sympa-thetic yet critical contrast to most theories of viewing that circulate as cultural studies perspectives, Lembo draws upon social psychological and hermeneutic traditions of self-formation and distills from his larger work a detailed and com-pelling argument that television interaction is a unique cultural form and yet con-tains patterns of self-formation similar to more traditional arenas of cultural life. This orientation builds toward a theory of the viewer's mindfulness toward television in ways that highlight new approaches to rethinking how individuals and groups use mass media, the negotiations of structures of meaning, and the links between notions of self-formation and ideology.

Andrea Press and Elizabeth Cole provide a nuanced look at how images of gender and class are perceived and negotiated by working-class women. In an examination of television portrayals of abortion issues, responses of working-class women are assessed in relation to their self-perceptions of class location and class identifications. Press and Cole show how working-class women differ in how they think of themselves as class subjects. These class identities are seen as crucial in shaping the reception of cultural representations of women in general and abortion issues in particular. Working-class women who see themselves as "working-class identified" or "middle-class identified" thus diverge in their reception and evaluation of televised abortion content as well as how they see class images of women on television in general.

The essay by Denise Bielby and C. Lee Harrington and the one by David Morley shift from the immediacy of television program reception to an examination of how individuals and groups use secondary forms of communication technology to augment their social lives. Bielby and Harrington trace the ways in which fans of particular television programs seek out one another by creating and tapping into forms and modes of gossip, news, speculation, queries, and reactions. An analysis of how viewers use secondary resources such as electronic bulletin boards to enhance their understandings of cultural texts by participating in dialogues with other fans opens up largely unexplored ways in which individuals form cultural connections around programs. By focusing on the ways in which viewers use their interests in programming to interact with one another, Bielby and Harrington highlight the social bonds that facilitate an important tier of reception strategies not tapped by survey and interview techniques that isolate the viewer as a respondent.

Building on his investigations of families and television, David Morley explores the way in which the progressive penetration of traditional media (radio, newsprint, television) and the ensuing expansion of new information and communication technologies (ICTs)—satellite/cable TV, teleshopping, interactive services, telebooking, and so on—open up hitherto unexplored complications and contradictions that go beyond the notion of reception. By focusing on ICTs, Morley presents a persuasive argument that cultural reception deserves to be expanded beyond the problem of grasping the meanings individuals, groups, and classes bring to and derive from their encounters with media. The growing potential of ICTs suggests the need to consider how they may be reconstituting institutional structures—in this case the family. While the new ICTs have an enhancing effect upon families as consumers and media resource users, they are also new forms of social technologies that transgress and break down the traditional notion of the family as a private sphere by opening it to increased public-technological penetrations.

Turning to music, Jon Cruz and Sut Jhally present quite different approaches to the notion of audiences and reception. Rather than beginning with already developed cultural forms, Jon Cruz backs up historically to explore how African American music was discovered, accessed, interpreted, and thus transformed into goods useful to white cultural leaders and intellectuals during the second half of the nineteenth century. Prior to and continuing throughout the Civil War, abolitionists transformed black oral culture into literary texts for white consumption. After the Civil War, and with the failure of Reconstruction and the rise of white ethnic working-class antagonisms in the North, the elite reception of African American music shifted increasingly toward a new interpretive formation led by the emerging social scientific canons of professional folklore. As abolitionist and folkloristic "discoveries," the narratives and Negro spirituals are shown to be important in helping white elites frame their tensions with modernization and their growing sense of cultural erosion. Cruz illustrates how elite interpretive formations of marginalized cultures were socially, politically, and culturally installed. He argues for a need to look more carefully at the development of interpretive formations and how such formations shift.

Whereas Cruz's essay focuses on midnineteenth-century precapitalist and precommodified cultural forms that were initially produced at the racial and cultural margins, Sut Jhally explores his attempt to produce a critical pedagogical video that draws on the core imagery of today's mass culture. As the producer of *Dreamworlds: Desire/Sex/Power in Rock Video,* Jhally chronicles the making of a video based on MTV images that would intervene into this now pervasive form of popular culture. Jhally recounts the different stages of selection, rearrangement, and renarration involved in the making of *Dreamworlds* and relays the responses it elicited from students, professional media critics, and others involved in viewing and discussing earlier versions as well as the final form of *Dreamworlds.* Jhally describes how he inscribed the responses of his target audience into the production process. It is a unique reflection and assessment of cultural production and audience interpretation from a producer's point of view and illustrates the complex relations between the variety of ways a cultural text can be organized (in this case edited) and its corresponding multiple readings. The essay is also an argument about the meaning of rock video in contemporary culture.

Extending the problem of feminist reassessments of audience studies, Cathy Schwichtenberg draws attention to the problems encountered when gender is seen primarily as sexual difference. Such conceptualizations reproduce and stabilize a priori sexual categories that, Schwichtenberg argues, preclude assessments of multiple, contingent, and variant-gender identities. Schwichtenberg proposes that the pairing of gender and genre in feminist audience research be destabilized and reconceptualized in order to open up analytic possibilities for grasping the wider range of multiple gender readings of self and culture. Drawing on the recent work of Wendy Chapkis and Holly Devor, Schwichtenberg illustrates how multiple gender identifications operate as difficult processes of cultural negotiation. Most feminist approaches to audience and reception studies elide these dimensions of gender blending. Schwichtenberg suggests research strategies relevant to the study of variant-gender identities.

Shifting to the problem of collective strategies of cultural reception, Elizabeth Long explores ethnographic approaches to reading groups. Long critiques reader-response theories for their nonsociological premises that share a long history privileging the view of the isolated reader. This view is corroborated by illustrative examples of the iconography of the autonomous reader captured in art. In contrast, Long argues that reading and writing are socially formed, and we must grasp the social infrastructure that gives these actions their social and cultural forms. Drawing from observations taken from among approximately seventy-five known reading groups located in the Houston, Texas, area, Long illustrates how reading groups are formed, how they select and interpret their reading material, and how they devise collective strategies for each of these steps. Long theorizes how the aesthetic reflections are negotiated by group members who, in turn, are embedded in much larger discursive aesthetic fields. Long's essay presents a novel slant on how groups use reading to forge new sociocultural identities.

Janice Radway's pioneering study of women romance readers helped clarify how this popular literary genre operated as a key site for feminine subjectivity and sexuality. In her essay, Radway pushes these issues further by arguing that the romance refracts important struggles over feminism as well. Radway revisits the cultural context of romance critique of the 1970s in which fantasy was regarded with suspicion (a perspective Radway shared with others critical of the genre). What has ensued over the last fifteen years is significant change within the academic feminist community and among romance writers; both quarters now defend the critical and utopian cultural work enabled through the romance's feminist fantasy. Radway illustrates how these new configurations of cultural alliance are being sketched in the interplay among contemporary romance texts, feminist critics, and changes in the dispositions of romance readers, which Radway attributes to the impact feminist discourse has had upon white middle-class women. As a cultural site, the romance harbors new potential for cultural realignments among feminist critics, romance writers, and readers.

Moving toward the problem of audiences and democracy, Ian Angus explores the limits that modern communications systems impose upon audiences. Reciprocity—the capacity to speak as well as listen—does not take place under modern communication systems. Audiences are constituted as listeners, but the opportunities for them to participate in democratic turn-taking are severely truncated. Communications systems tend to sever audiences from reciprocating in the production of social knowledge and decisionmaking. Audiences are rendered as listeners and denied the grounds to become speakers. Contemporary assessments that emphasize pluralist identity formations and active audience theories are correct to point out the variations of reception. But what is underemphasized in the new pluralism within contemporary cultural studies,

Angus argues, is that audiences are blocked from developing equally plural relations to media. The emphasis on multiple modes of media reception leaves unaddressed the shriveled access to and opportunities for communicative reciprocation. Any critical theory of audiences within democracy must address the monopolization of communications and the cultural strategies necessary to ensure audiences the right to move from being listeners to being speakers.

Completing the contributions is an interview with Stuart Hall. Twenty years ago Stuart Hall published a short essay entitled "Encoding and Decoding in the Media Discourse." This seminal essay was very influential in the moves to rethink the dominant paradigm of media studies and the problems of production and reception within cultural studies. Much of Hall's ensuing work has both complemented and challenged his earlier concepts. The interview enables Hall to reflect on the "Encoding and Decoding" essay, the context in which it was written, and the theoretical stakes involved. Reflecting on this early work allows Hall to trace how some of his views on cultural studies, representation, and reception shifted in the appraisal of new theoretical developments and challenges during the 1980s. Hall's reflections are highly relevant to the theoretical tensions the field of cultural studies encounters today.

Notes

1. Traditional epistemological assumptions have been radically critiqued by analysts who place emphasis on the problems of representation. The reorientation in the humanities and social sciences can be observed, for example, in the critiques of historiography, literary theory and interpretation, and sociological and cultural theory. Exemplary debates in these fields can be found in Lynn Hunt, ed., *The New Cultural History* (Berkeley: University of California Press, 1989); H. Aram Veeser, ed., *The New Historicism* (New York: Routledge, 1989); James Clifford and George E. Marcus, eds., *Writing Culture: The Poetics and Politics of Ethnography* (Berkeley: University of California Press, 1986); Scott Lash, *Sociology of Postmodernism* (London: Routledge, 1990); and Steven Seidman, "The End of Sociological Theory: The Postmodern Hope," *Sociological Theory* 9:2 (Fall 1991), pp. 131–146.

2. See Carey Nelson and Lawrence Grossberg, eds., *Marxism and the Interpretation of Culture* (Urbana: University of Illinois Press, 1988); and Lawrence Grossberg, Carey Nelson, and Paula A. Treichler, eds., *Cultural Studies* (New York: Routledge, 1992).

3. The key work is Adorno and Horkheimer's *Dialectic of Enlightenment*, trans. John Cumming (New York: Seabury Press, 1972 [1944]). In the United States the journals *Telos* and *New German Critique* played major roles in disseminating the interpretive traditions of critical theory.

4. Habermas's attempt to provide a more nuanced historical scaffolding for critical theory can be found in his *The Structural Transformation of the Public Sphere: An Inquiry into Category of Bourgeois Society,* trans. Thomas Burger (Cambridge, Mass.: MIT Press, 1989). See also the important engagements with poststructuralist and postmodern theory in *The Philosophical Discourse of Modernity: Twelve Lectures,* trans. Frederick Lawrence (Cambridge, Mass.: MIT Press, 1987), and "Modernity Versus Postmodernity," *New German Critique* 22 (Winter 1981), pp. 3–14.

5. The work of C. Wright Mills was central to the New Left critique of American society. Mills's classic works, which include *The New Men of Power: America's Labor Leaders* (New York: Harcourt, Brace, 1948) and *The Power Elite* (New York: Oxford University Press, 1956), prepared the ground for the reception of critical theory. In this context a text like Herbert Marcuse's *One Dimensional Man: Studies in the Ideology of Advanced Industrial Society* (Boston: Beacon Press, 1964) could be appreciated for its scathing indictment of corporatism and cultural domination. In historiography, parallel critiques of class and corporate power were provided by William Appleman Williams, *The Contours of American History* (Cleveland, Ohio: World Publishing, 1961); Gabriel Kolko, *The Triumph of Conservatism: A Reinterpretation of American History, 1900–1916* (New York: Free Press, 1963); and James Weinstein, *The Corporate Ideal in the Liberal State, 1900–1918* (Boston: Beacon Press, 1968).

6. The scholarship that combines critical race, class, gender, and media analysis is sprawling, and the theoretical accents and analytic tropes are extensive as well as diverse. We cite here only examples. For race, see Philip Foner, *Organized Labor and the Black Worker, 1619–1973* (New York: Praeger, 1974), and Ronald Takaki, *Race and Culture in 19th-Century America* (New York: Oxford University Press, 1990 [1979]). Drawing on labor historiography but moving in distinctly culturalist directions privileging working-class agency are Roy Rosenzweig's *Eight Hours for What We Will: Workers and Leisure in an Industrial City, 1870–1920* (Cambridge: Cambridge University Press, 1983) and Kathy Peiss's *Cheap Amusements: Working Women and Leisure in Turn-of-the-Century New York* (Philadelphia: Temple University Press, 1986). In media analysis, Herbert Schiller's *Communication and Cultural Domination* (White Plains, N.Y.: International Arts and Sciences Press, 1976) and *Information and the Crisis Economy* (Norwood, N.J.: Ablex Publishing, 1984) place stark emphasis on corporate domination of mass media. Important social and cultural histories of media formation are presented in Michael Schudson, *Discovering the News: A Social History of American Newspapers in New York* (Boston: Basic Books, 1978), and Lary May, *Screening Out the Past: The Birth of Mass Culture and the Motion Picture Industry* (New York: Oxford University Press, 1980). Todd Gitlin's *The Whole World Is Watching: Mass Media in the Making and Unmaking of the New Left* (Berkeley: University of California Press, 1980) was one of the first book-length studies of American media to attempt an interpretive synthesis informed by critical theory, British cultural studies media theory, and Gramscian hegemony theory.

7. See Roland Barthes, *Mythologies,* trans. Annette Lavers (New York: Hill and Wang, 1972 [1957]); *Elements of Semiology,* trans. Annette Lavers and Colin Smith (New York: Hill and Wang, 1964); *Image-Music-Text,* trans. Stephen Heath (New York: Hill and Wang, 1977); and *S/Z* (New York: Hill and Wang, 1974 [1970]).

8. The theoretical writings of Stuart Hall and the ethnographic case studies of Paul Willis are exemplary. See Stuart Hall, "Culture, the Media, and the 'Ideological Effect,'" in J. Curran et al., eds., *Mass Communication and Society* (Beverly Hills, Calif.: Sage, 1978), pp. 315–348; "Cultural Studies: 'Two Paradigms,'" *Media, Culture and Society* 2 (1980), pp. 57–72; "The Rediscovery of 'Ideology': Return of the Repressed in Media Studies," in M. Gurevitch, T. Bennett, J. Curran, and J. Woollacoot, eds., *Culture, Society and the Media* (London: Methuen, 1982), pp. 56–90; "Popular Culture and the State," in T. Bennett, C. Mercer, and J. Woollacoot, eds., *Popular Culture and Social Relations* (London: Milton Keynes/Open University, 1986); Stuart Hall, J. Clarke, T. Jefferson, and B. Roberts, "Subcultures, Cultures and Class: A Theoretical Overview," *Working Papers in Cultural Studies,* no.

7/8, pp. 9–74, 1976; and Stuart Hall and T. Jefferson, eds., *Resistance Through Rituals: Youth Subcultures in Post-War Britain* (London: Hutchinson, 1976). A most ambitious example of the new cultural studies drawing upon collective efforts can be found in the comprehensive study of the mediating links among race, social problems, mass media, and the state published in Stuart Hall, Chas Critcher, Tony Jefferson, John Clarke, and Brian Roberts, *Policing the Crisis: Mugging, the State, and Law and Order* (London: Macmillan, 1978).

Paul Willis's contributions to some of these theoretical and analytic issues can be found in *Profane Culture* (London: Routledge and Kegan Paul, 1978); "Shop Floor Culture, Masculinity and the Wage Form," in J. Clarke et al., eds., *Working Class Culture: Studies in History and Theory* (London: Croom Helm, 1979); *Learning to Labor: How Working Class Kids Get Working Class Jobs* (New York: Columbia University Press, 1977) [Morningside Edition, 1981]; and "Orders of Experience: The Differences of Working Class Cultural Forms," *Social Text* 7 (Spring/Summer 1983), pp. 85–105; and Paul Willis and Philip Corrigan, "Cultural Forms and Class Mediations," *Media, Culture and Society* 2 (1980), pp. 297–312.

Angela McRobbie extends the working-class ethnographic approach of cultural studies to women in "Working Class Girls and the Culture of Femininity," in Women's Studies Group, ed., *Women Take Issue* (London: Hutchinson, 1978), pp. 96–108; and "Just Like a *Jackie* Story," in Angela McRobbie and Trisha McCabe, eds., *Feminism for Girls* (London: Routledge, 1981), pp. 113–128. See also Elizabeth Long's helpful comparative assessment in "Feminism and Cultural Studies: Britain and America," *Critical Studies in Mass Communication* 6:4 (1989), pp. 427–435.

9. In this context, see Robert F. Berkhofer, Jr., "A New Context for a New American Studies?" *American Quarterly* 41:4 (December 1989), pp. 588–613, for an insightful discussion of the recent "sociological turn" in contemporary American studies.

10. Christian Metz's influential *The Imaginary Signifier: Psychoanalysis and the Cinema* (Bloomington: Indiana University Press, 1982) remains the classic book-length synthesis of Lacanian theory and film analysis. Robert Allen, ed., *Channels of Discourse: Television and Contemporary Criticism* (Chapel Hill: University of North Carolina Press, 1987) contains Sandy Flitterman-Lewis's "Psychoanalysis, Film, and Television" and E. Ann Kaplan's "Feminist Criticism and Television." Both provide helpful introductions and include annotated bibliographies. The introduction to Andrea Press's *Women Watching Television: Gender, Class, and Generation in the American Television Experience* (Philadelphia: University of Pennsylvania Press, 1991) can be profitably read as an assessment of how British cultural studies and feminist theory converge in ethnographic approaches to gender analysis and mass culture. An excellent critical summary of shifting theoretical and research orientations can be found in David Morley, "Changing Paradigms in Audience Research," in Ellen Seiter et al., eds., *Remote Control: Television, Audiences, and Cultural Power* (London: Routledge, 1989), pp. 16–43.

11. Examples of the attempt to integrate social analysis, the new attention to symbolic arenas, and historical interpretation can be found in Lynn Hunt, ed., *The New Cultural History* (Berkeley: University of California Press, 1989).

12. See Wolfgang Iser, *The Act of Reading: A Theory of Aesthetic Response* (Baltimore: Johns Hopkins University Press, 1978), and *Prospects: From Reader Response to Literary Anthropology* (Baltimore: Johns Hopkins University Press, 1989); Robert Holub, *Reception Theory: A Critical Introduction* (London: Methuen, 1984); and Stanley Fish, *Is There a Text in This Class? The Authority of Interpretive Communities* (Cambridge, Mass.: Harvard University Press, 1980). For a survey of reader-response issues, see Jane P. Tompkins, ed.,

Reader-Response Criticism: From Formalism to Post-Structuralism (Baltimore: Johns Hopkins University Press, 1980); Elizabeth Freund, *The Return of the Reader: Reader-Response Criticism* (New York: Methuen, 1987); and Robert C. Allen, "Reader-Oriented Criticism and Television," in Robert C. Allen, ed., *Channels of Discourse: Television and Contemporary Criticism* (Chapel Hill: University of North Carolina Press, 1987), pp. 74–112. See also the debates collected in Ellen Spolsky, ed., *The Uses of Adversity: Failure and Accommodation in Reader-Response* (London: Associated University Presses, 1990).

13. Todd Gitlin, "Media Sociology: The Dominant Paradigm," *Theory and Society* 6 (November 1978), pp. 205–253. On the earlier cultural dimensions relevant to emergence of democratic consumer society, see Michael Schudson, *Discovering the News: A Social History of American Newspapers* (New York: Basic Books, 1978), and Jackson Lears and Richard Wightman Fox, eds., *The Culture of Consumption: Critical Essays in American History, 1880–1980* (New York: Pantheon Books, 1983). An expanded critique of the market-centric orientation, especially as it applies to television audiences, can be found in Ien Ang, *Desperately Seeking the Audience* (London: Routledge, 1991).

14. One of the earliest social scientific assessments of movies and social problems can be found in Herbert Blumer and Philip Hauser, *Movies, Delinquency, and Crime* (New York: Macmillan, 1933). The rise of cinema and its association with social crisis are presented in Lewis Erenberg, *Steppin' Out: New York Nightlife and the Transformation of Culture* (Westport, Conn.: Greenwood Press, 1981).

15. For an example of an investigation that came on the heels of the Senate hearings, see Wilbur Schramm et al., *Television in the Lives of Our Children* (Stanford, Calif.: Stanford University Press, 1961).

16. See C. I. Hovland, "Reconciling Conflicting Results Derived from Experimental and Survey Studies of Attitude Change," *American Psychologist* 14 (1959), pp. 8–17.

17. This is not to suggest that uses-and-gratifications or other research models that emphasized audience self-determination deliberately justified a conservative economic agenda. However, aspects of these research traditions could be conveniently appropriated by free market theorists.

18. See George Gerbner, Larry Gross, Michael Morgan, and Nancy Signoreilli, "The 'Mainstreaming' of America: Violence Profile No. 11," *Journal of Communication* 30:3 (1980), pp. 10–29, and "Living with Television: The Dynamics of the Cultivation Process," in Jennings Bryant and Dorf Zillman, eds., *Perspectives on Media Effects* (Hillsdale, N.J.: Lawrence Erlbaum Associates, Inc., 1986), pp. 17–40.

ONE

The Meaning of Things:
Audiences, Ambiguity, and Power

JUSTIN LEWIS

The Status of Audience Research

I would like to begin by identifying two types of media criticism. The first is speculative and literary; it uses forms of textual analysis to explore the possibilities of media messages. In this enterprise, all analysis (whether Marxist, existential, psychoanalytic, or postmodern) is legitimate: As Roland Barthes pointed out, to deny any one of them would be to deny the ambiguity of messages (or, in their literary designation, "texts"). The second is more overtly political; it sees media analysis as a way to understand the nature of the media's power and influence in contemporary society. The range of possibilities, in this endeavor, is necessarily confined by the limits of history and society.

Most literary critics have known for some time that there is no "correct" way to interpret a text, whether it's "The Cosby Show" or *Hamlet*. We may choose to focus on Hamlet's existential meanderings or on the complexities of his relationship with his parents. The conflicting interpretations we produce simply add to the richness of Shakespeare's text. The literary critic is, in this sense, an intellectual free agent, unconfined by the need to iron out ambiguity. Whether people in theaters are moved by the strands of meaning discovered by the critic is not relevant—critical interpretations do not need to be validated by theatergoers to be legitimate.

If, however, we want to evaluate the meaning of *Hamlet* for specific audiences (whether Elizabethan or contemporary), we find ourselves engaged in a very different exercise: We are suddenly forced to play our literary game by the rules of social science. This approach not only confines our evaluation but also transforms it: We are no longer exploring the art of the possible but the realm of historical specificity. We lose our literary license because we are forced to address how a message or a text fits within the ideologies that infuse or upset a society's power structure. The specificity of meaning takes on social significance—it matters.

Although both these types of media criticism may overlap, we should not confuse them. The second requires sociological evidence to make its case, the first does not. Without evidence, in other words, a textual analysis (no matter how ingenious) tells us little about how media influence people. Or as Janice Radway puts it, it is only by understanding the meanings constructed by audiences that we can "understand how that (cultural) form functions within the larger culture" (Radway 1986). This understanding, in turn, is the only effective basis for political intervention to change that culture. Media criticism that fails to address this point may be intellectually stimulating, but it is politically insignificant.

If media criticism is to engage in politics, it must consider the audience, which, in turn, necessarily means doing audience research, although we should not be too literal about what such a task involves. We can study audiences by asking them questions or by monitoring how they express themselves or how they behave, which are the traditional methods. We can also study audiences, however, by analyzing culture in a more general sense. Cultural forms do not drift through history aimlessly; they are grounded in an ideological context that gives them their historical significance. The meaning of a TV program may be partly revealed by looking at other TV programs, at a range of popular cultural products, or at the phrases politicians use to get elected (what has been called a "discursive formation").

So, for example, if we are interested in the contemporary meaning of a pop video, we might usefully look at the range of related cultural products consumed by the people that watch it: magazines, posters, albums, concerts, TV interviews, and so on (see Goodwin 1987). We might also want to ask people questions, but we do not have to—the search for the audience can be made in a number of different places. John Fiske makes the same point when he refers to the "secondary and tertiary texts" that surround the media product we choose to analyze:

> When Madonna's primary texts are "linked" to the subordinate culture of young girls in patriarchy they "speak" quite differently from when they are "linked" with the sexist masculine culture of *Playboy*. Reading the secondary and tertiary texts can help us see how the primary text can be articulated into the general culture in different ways, by different readers in different subcultures (Fiske 1987, p. 126).

As Fiske says, the cultural objects that surround Madonna at a particular moment in history give us an insight into her cultural and political significance.

Audience research is, in this broad definition, the accumulation of evidence about the meaning of things. The question we should put to textual analysis that purports to tell us how a cultural product "works" in contemporary culture is simple: Where's the evidence? Without evidence, everything is merely speculation.

This is not to dismiss what I have characterized as literary criticism but merely to acknowledge its function. Moreover, the distinction I am making is one of status rather than style. The techniques of literary (textual) criticism have taught us a great deal about how messages may or may not work; an appreciation of these techniques allows us a far more sophisticated understanding of the relation between messages and audiences than hitherto. The question is not about technicalities but about the purpose and context of our analysis. As analysts, we need to be clear about what we are doing when we are doing what we are doing—to put it another way, it is because I am interested in politics that I am interested in audiences.

The Use and Abuse of the Sign

One of the more celebrated theoretical links between modern literary criticism and media studies is semiology. Semiology, the study of meaning, has opened up whole new vistas in both disciplines. In particular, the theory of the sign forces us to consider not only how messages are constructed but how they are consumed. Unfortunately, semiology has, at best, been robbed of its radical potential and, at worst, been misunderstood or abused.

Semiology is often characterized by both critics and advocates as a way of exploring messages. It has encouraged analysts to borrow the complexities of literary criticism, with its focus on form, metaphor, and poetics, and apply it to the study of nonliterary messages, from fashion to football to film. This is all well and good, but the problem arises when semiology is treated (or dismissed) as simply a bright new box of tricks with which to take a message apart and put it together again, thus demonstrating, as we might with a car engine, how it works. It has now become commonplace for analysts, having reduced semiology to a set of technical aids for deconstructing and reconstructing, to criticize semiology for its ahistoricism and for its failure to invoke the role of audiences in the construction of meaning. This criticism may be fair commentary on the contemporary use of semiology, but it completely misses the innovative thrust of the semiological endeavor.

If we treat semiology merely as a glorified form of linguistics, we are missing its radical potential. Although semiology states that to analyze texts we must analyze audiences, the contemporary use (or abuse) of semiology has actually diverted people's gaze from audiences toward an exclusive focus on messages. Semiology invokes the audience, yet few semiologists do so.

This is not to say that early semiologists, like de Saussure, have a theoretical purity that others have misunderstood; de Saussure was as unsure (and understandably so) about how to cope with his theory of the sign as were others after him. What has been lost is the insight implicit in the theory of the sign: the perception that meaning is neither fixed nor transcendental but the product of historical processes.

According to semiology's founding principle (the signifier + the signified = the sign), meaning is not the property of or reducible to objects or subjects; it is socially constructed and historically specific. The signifier (the object) signifies nothing on its own but requires somebody to interpret it (in semiological language, to give it a signified). This, in turn, creates a whole new realm in the study of meaning: the sign. The sign gives a name to an activity—signification—that is reducible to neither of its constituent parts.

The term that has been most frequently misused in critical or semiotic literature is "the signified." The signified is the concept we use to understand or interpret a signifier. It is what we (or any other animal species, for that matter) think in response to a thing. The signified, as opposed to the signifier, is never material; it must be converted into something else (a signifier, like a word or a gesture) before it can be displayed. Unless we believe in what has been called the "transcendental signified" or in the ability to read people's minds, we cannot communicate without returning to the level of the signifier.

Unfortunately, the signified is often discussed as if it refers to the reality that signifiers refer to (thus the word "dog" is the signifier while the signified is the dog itself) rather than to the concept of that reality. Since the signified is always conceptual and never material (beyond the materiality of our little gray cells!), this is a serious misconception: The object that a word refers to (like the dog itself) is in this sense merely another signifier, no more or less a part of reality than the word associated with it. We make sense of the world by relating signifiers (we connect the word "dog" to the dog itself), thereby constructing coherent social (and historically bound) systems of truth and knowledge in which the material world is a constituent but dependent part.

Semiologists have distinguished between iconic (or motivated) signs, where the signifier and the signified bear some properties in common (a dog is likely to have something in common with what we think of when we see it, such as four legs and a tail), and symbolic (or unmotivated) signs, where they do not. Words are put in the second category, since the word "dog," composed of three letters, is seen to have nothing whatever to do with what we think of when we read or hear it. Language is described as an arbitrary sign system, in which each word could be substituted by another (hence different languages use completely different linguistic signifiers to refer to the same signified). This is likely to be true, but we should not assume that it is inevitably so. We may read the letters d-o-g and think of those three letters carved into a mountainside rather than of a friendly domestic quadruped. In this case, the signifier shares some properties with the signified, and the relation between them is not arbitrary.

This point is less pedantic than it may appear. The failure to acknowledge the possibility of an iconic linguistic sign is part of a more general failure to appreciate fully what constitutes the realms of signifier and signified. The assumption that language is symbolic while objects or photographs are iconic is potentially misleading because it allows us to assume that the nonlinguistic object (like a dog or a picture of a dog) is inevitably closer to the signified (of dog) than the linguistic object (d-o-g). This then creates the tendency to confuse the nonlinguistic signifier (the dog or picture of a dog) with the signified.

This confusion is compounded by the concept of the "referent," a term used in semiology to designate the object that a word refers to (so the referent of d-o-g is a living, four-legged, tail-wagging dog). The concept of the referent is a perfectly legitimate one, but it is, I believe, unhelpful because it seems to encourage a perception that the referent is not a signifier (hence we need a new name) when in fact it is no more or less a signifier than the word that relates to it. Meaning comes when we relate one to the other.

Semiology, indeed, should enable us to see that meaning is a product of the relation between signifiers and/or signifieds. This meaning is derived not only through difference between signifiers (as semiologists have stressed) but through their association. A baby may understand the signifier "mother" by distinguishing between her absence and presence but will do so also by establishing associations, such as mother/breast/food. The meaning of a thing, in other words, derives from what it is like as well as what it is not like.

Because we are used to equating some objects (signifiers) and our conception of them (signifieds), we sometimes assume that the relation between signifier and signified can be direct and unambiguous. Semiology dispels this cultural illusion. Objects do not automatically represent themselves to us—they have no essential meaning for us to discover. What is the essence of an apple? What meaning lies at its core? There is none. If an apple means "a sweet, juicy, edible object," that is because we know the apple predominantly through the practice of eating. If we came from another culture, we might think of an apple as an object to throw at people we dislike. In both instances we are constructing a relationship between two signifiers: an object and a practice. Terence Hawkes makes this point briefly and succinctly: "The true nature of things may be said to lie not in things themselves, but in the relationships we construct, and then perceive, between them" (Hawkes 1977, p. 17). We are not free to determine these relationships as we please; we are part of a prearranged semiological world. From the cradle to the grave, we are encouraged by the shape of our environment to engage with the world of signifiers in particular ways.

This deterministic environment includes everything from the words and objects offered by parents, teachers, and friends to the way a shopping center is designed. The structure and layout of a supermarket, for example, is something we take for granted, and yet, like everything else in our environment, it shapes our perceptions and our actions. As Eco puts it, it "frames" our cognition: "The supermarket frame would involve virtually the notion of a place where people enter to buy items of different types, pick them up without mediation from any vendor, pay for them all together at a terminal counter, and so on. Probably a good frame of this sort also involves a list of all the commodities one can find in a supermarket (brooms: yes; cars: no)" (Eco 1979, p. 21). Our view of shopping and the world of commodities is, therefore, highly coded by these signifying structures. As we learn more, we slip into familiar routines and practices, and this carefully constructed world begins to seem natural and inevitable. Each culture is, in this way, able to generate a common stock of shared meanings.

Semiology thereby enables us to overcome an epistemological hurdle that has plagued the study of ideology and culture. This is the notion of ideology as either a misrecognition of the world (as in "false consciousness") or an inescapable condition distancing us from the real world. The first of these notions, critics have pointed out, lapses into empiricism, with reality as a self-disclosive entity that, once free of ideological blinkers, is instantly recognizable. The second notion has been more burdensome to modern social theory. It has led to fruitless attempts to theorize the relation between "the discursive" (the realm of ideology) and "the real," the conclusion being that since we can only know the real through the discursive, we are always one step away from reality.

Once we begin to adopt an intangible notion of reality, we have ingeniously bamboozled ourselves to a position where our terms of reference are no longer useful. If reality, as an organizing principle, is no longer capable of distinguishing between itself and its opposite (what is real and what is unreal), it is little more than an article of faith or, at best, something that makes sense at a given moment, something you would bet your money but not your life on. Even more confusing, such a logic assumes, at some point, that the discursive is not part of the real and vice versa—a misleading and untenable assumption.

Semiology, in contrast, gives us a notion of discourse with reality as part of the package rather than some absent entity lurking worrisomely in the distance. The sign is the product of our interaction with the real world. The real is the level of the signifier, and its activity in the construction of the sign is as tangible as is our own (the level of the signified). The real, in this semiological definition, is as much a word as the thing a word refers to. It is both discourse and objects. Moreover, the real does not need to enter into the world of signification (in other words, it need not become a sign).

The tree falling in the forest that nobody hears and nobody sees still falls, and it still makes sound waves when it does so. But it has no meaning. This is quite different from saying it has no existence. It is simply a signifier without a signified.

Semiology, like other theories of social construction, acknowledges the futility of attempts to behold an essential truth or an essential reality (an attempt critics have labeled "essentialism"). Unlike other theories of social construction, it collapses distinctions between discourses (composed of signs) and reality (composed of signifiers): Discourses are real, and the real is discursive. Reality is a construction, rooted in history and society, but it is no less true or real for that. We experience the real through signification, and we give it meaning accordingly. The real, whether it comes in the form of a word or the object that word refers to, is simply a sum of the fragments of meaning we ascribe to it, no more, no less. The sign, the category of meaning, is an entity that links us in our subjectivity (the signified) to the outside world (the signifier).

In this sense, semiology is more than a set of tools for deconstructing messages; it is a way of understanding the relationship between media and audience. Semiology does not, as some have suggested, deny the activity of audiences but rather relies upon it. Audiences construct the signifieds, and without audiences there is existence but no meaning. This is not to say that audiences determine the meaning of media messages but only that they are simply a necessary part of a process—a process, moreover, in which the message (or signifier) necessarily plays a determining role. The sign, be it Madonna or "The Cosby Show," is overdetermined—by the signifier, the signified, and the activity that combines them.

The founding principle of semiology (the signifier + the signified = the sign) gives us a more comprehensive and systematic understanding of this sometimes chaotic world. It establishes the status of meaning itself, enables us to appreciate the nature of ambiguity, and provides us with an analytical framework for investigating why things mean what they mean. We can begin the search for the source of meanings on a surer footing.

The consequences of this semiotic analysis for the study of TV viewing are profound. We can now define the nature of the relationship between the viewer (signified) and the screen (signifier). The meaning of the television message is not fixed, but neither is it arbitrary. It is determined by the viewer's semiotic environment, which includes the viewer's history, neighborhood, and class and of course television itself. It takes us beyond the confines of "effects" and "uses and gratifications" to enable us to evaluate the process whereby television signifiers become television signs. These signs, held in place by the juxtaposition of media and audience, can then be taken apart in order to see what binds them together.

As cultures become more complex and sophisticated, the range and diversity of semiological systems increase the permutations available and cause meanings to fragment. Twentieth-century postindustrial societies are usually described in this way. Meaning becomes a battleground between and among folk cultures, class subcultures, ethnic cultures, and national cultures; different communications media, the home, and the school; churches and advertising agencies; and different versions of history and political ideologies. The sign is no longer inscribed within a fixed cultural order. The meaning of things seems less predictable and less certain.

Ambiguities

Nothing, semiology tells us, is unambiguous. Something as intricate as a TV program is seeped in potential ambiguity, or what semiology calls "polysemy" (many meanings). This should not surprise us—indeed, the televisual message is so extravagantly coded that it is amazing any two people should respond to it in the same way. That people do is a testimony to our tightly controlled cultural horizons.

Even something as simple and innocent as a close-up shot can operate as a highly coded sign, signifying—to those with access to the appropriate cultural codes—different things in different televisual contexts. In the TV interview, an extreme close-up may signify that the person being interviewed is probably hiding something, the camera "interrogating" his or her face for clues (see Brundson and Morley 1979 or Campbell 1991). In the TV drama, it may signify depth of feeling (the camera forcing us to consider the meaning of the smallest facial expression as significant) or the point of view of another character who is within an intimate distance. To someone who has never seen a photographic image, it may simply signify that a character's face has, mysteriously, grown extremely large. These ambiguities then intertwine with the many different meanings we may have already given the subject of the extreme close-up. A whole minute of interchanging images and sounds increases the number of permutations still further. During an hour-long TV program, the chance of our coming up with the same reading as the person we are watching it with would seem to be as remote as our chance of winning a national lottery.

And yet, despite the almost infinite complexity of the televisual discourse, many of us will routinely experience television in much the same way. Not only will most of us find our way out of the labyrinth of sounds and images, but we may well choose roughly the same path through it. Semiology teaches us that nothing has a fixed or inexorable meaning—commonality is rooted only in culture. We have, it would appear, been well trained. The capacity of societies to create such levels of cultural uniformity is remarkable.

The problem with a society that nurtures and guides its citizens toward common meanings is its tendency to suppress not only the ambiguity of things but the very idea of ambiguity. We behave as if the meaning of things were natural and inevitable. The failure to come up with the socially agreed meaning is often interpreted as stupid or troublesome. In many societies, the very act of digression from this semiological control is seen as subversive and, because it challenges the fixity of the sign, threatening. Herein lies the resistance to cultural diversity and, by degrees, the breeding ground for racial or religious intolerance.

Our reluctance to accept ambiguity has had profound consequences in the study of television. It would have been logical (or, more accurately, semiological) to start with the premise of polysemy, so that we might trace the social roots of commonality. The history of television audience research has done precisely the opposite: Commonality of meaning has been assumed; ambiguity has had to be explained. So, if something meant the same to X, Y, and Z, it remained uninterrogated. Only when X, Y, and Z responded differently were questions asked.

The corollary of this approach is that the nature and roots of television's ambiguity have only recently been explored. Some of the more interesting studies have rooted the analysis of ambiguity in cultural difference. In particular, the global distribution of TV programs and commercials has inevitably raised a number of questions about the ambiguities of TV messages across different cultures. As Katz and Liebes put it: "Consider the worldwide success of a programme like 'Dallas.' How do viewers from another culture understand it?" (Katz and Liebes 1985, p. 187). Their analysis of discussions among groups from five different ethnic/cultural backgrounds (Israeli Arabs, new immigrants to Israel from Russia, immigrants from Morocco, kibbutz members, and North Americans from Los Angeles) explores the culturally generated ambiguities of "Dallas."

One of the many cultural differences in the way the varied groups talked about the program concerned the cultural location attributed to the world of "Dallas." The non-Americans saw it as a story about the United States, generating a stream of specific cultural references that were less likely to occur to the North Americans. The non-Americans were consequently more willing to interpret the program as realistic, while the North Americans were far more playful in their interpretations. Ien Ang's study of Dutch attitudes to the program (Ang 1985) suggests that viewers in the Netherlands were closer to the North American readings than the ethnic groups studied by Katz and Liebes. From the cultural position of the Dutch, it would appear, the world of "Dallas" seemed less culturally specific and closer to home. This allowed them to develop the playful responses that Ang describes in her book.

This point is developed by Hodge and Tripp (1986) in a slightly different way. They discovered that Australian aboriginal children were able to identify with particular representations of black Americans on television by transforming them into Australian aboriginals. In so doing, these children were able to transcribe their own disadvantaged ethnic minority position onto the black characters in U.S. TV shows and to interpret them accordingly.

If the ambiguities revealed by these cross-cultural studies are not especially surprising, we should not forget their semiological implication. Ambiguity is not simply added onto a straightforward message by people from different cultures; it is there already, waiting to be discovered. The meaning of "Dallas" to a group in Los Angeles is as culturally defined as it is to a group of Israeli Arabs.

Meaning is potentially endless and historically fixed. As students of contemporary culture, we must acknowledge its potential but explain its fixity. What, in our recent history, are the ideological forces that freeze the flow of ambiguity? What cultural glue binds so many of us together in clusters of common interpretation?

Before answering this question, we should be aware of what our answer might mean. The existence of ambiguity has often been used to argue that the power of television in our society is weak. If meaning fragments into a series of different interpretations, then we assume its impotence. Ambiguity is thus equated with audience freedom. This assumption has dominated audience studies in recent years, and yet it is profoundly flawed. The presence of ambiguity tells us only that our culture is not completely totalitarian or homogeneous. If we assume that a message's ideological power is solely dependent upon lack of ambiguity, we are lapsing back into the presemiological notion that meaning is naturally fixed in messages. If messages come inscribed with unitary meanings, then ambiguity is indeed subversive. Once we understand ambiguity as a consequence of a message's cultural potency (rather than its instability), then we can understand ambiguity not as something that weakens a message's ideological power but as something that complicates it.

Suppose, for example, a TV program means different things to people within a culture and that the difference is related to, say, a viewer's class or race. The power of that program is not necessarily diminished by its various semiotic inflections; it is simply diversified. The power of the message, such as it is, is located in a range of cultural locations rather than in any presupposed center in the message itself. In some cases, a message's cultural power might be because of (rather than in spite of) its ambiguity: A TV program may be influential because it is able to reach different audiences in different ways and because in so doing, it demonstrates its potency in a variety of cultural contexts.

Similarly, we should not assume that the encoded meaning of a message (the meaning constructed by those who produced it) is the measure of a message's power. A news program, for example, may be completely misinterpreted (from the producer's point of view) and still shape the way people think.

The Power of Ambiguity and Misunderstanding

To assume that an ambiguous message shifts power away from the message to the audience is to simplify and misconstrue the process of decoding. This realization gradually dawned on me during various attempts to interpret qualitative audience data (usually interview transcripts). In retrospect, it is now clear to me that audience research, if it is to make sense of the material it generates, must rid itself of a number of assumptions.

The first of these regards the nature of ambiguity. It is easy, sometimes, to confuse ambiguity on a general social level with more individual forms of ambiguity. If a TV program means one thing to viewer X and another to viewer Y, we call that message ambiguous—and so it is. But it may not be ambiguous as far as viewer X or viewer Y is concerned. Indeed, both X and Y may dismiss each other's interpretations as "wrong." This means that we, as audience researchers, can describe the message as ambiguous, but we must at the same time acknowledge that the audience may respond to it as if it were not.

During research on "The Cosby Show," for example, it became apparent that middle- and upper-middle-class viewers tended to see the show as class-specific (i.e., a show about people like them), while working- and lower-middle-class viewers often referred to the show as classless and universal (i.e., also about people like them). This diversity suggests that the signifiers about class on the show are, on a cultural level, ambiguous. At the same time, this ambiguity was not experienced by the viewers themselves. The success of "The Cosby Show" in appealing to both sets of viewers (within a more general discourse of the American dream) relies not upon the program's ambiguity across classes but upon its lack of ambiguity within them.

This example raises a second point about the nature of ambiguity. It is easy to see how ambiguity might diminish a message's ideological power, but we should also appreciate that it does not necessarily do so. On the contrary, it is possible that ambiguity (present within the culture but suppressed by the individual viewer) may help to reinforce the ideological power of "The Cosby Show."

The show was generally interpreted by respondents as yet another proof of the idea that anybody in the United States, black or white, can "make it" (see Jhally and Lewis 1992). "The Cosby Show" thereby forms part of a television argument against affirmative action or any other social program that tries to redress inequities in opportunity. But it is sustained, in so doing, by two very different discourses. The middle- and upper-middle-class viewers enjoy the references to class-inflected tastes and actions (such as appreciating high art or sending your kids to private colleges) because they share them. The Huxtables' privileged class position, like their own, can therefore be seen as deserved because the Huxtables have what it takes culturally to make it.

For working-class viewers to interpret the show in the same way would exclude them from this particular version of the American dream because they do not share these class-inflected tastes and actions. These features must therefore become unimportant if working-class viewers are to identify with the Huxtables and with the American dream they exemplify.

The show "thirtysomething," on the other hand, can be seen as failing to appeal to the same kind of mass audience because of its lack of ambiguity. The acutely class-conscious realism of "thirtysomething" ran counter to the ideology of the American dream because it clearly portrayed class position as linked to a set of cultural norms that many viewers do not share. The implication of this class consciousness is precisely that anyone lacking the right upbringing or education cannot make it. The fact that the show was so repeatedly described as a "yuppie" drama reflects not the social position of its characters (which was no more privileged than the great majority of TV characters) but its unambiguous, killjoy class consciousness. Ambiguity, in this instance, does not dilute the ideological power of "The Cosby Show" but extends it.

Part of the failure of contemporary audience research to fully appreciate this point lies in a particular interpretation of the notion of the "preferred meaning." There are many versions of this idea, and they revolve around the principle that a message is ambiguous but only partially so. A message cannot be said to have one meaning, frozen in time and culture, but neither is its meaning arbitrary. It can, in this sense, prefer but not guarantee the communication of certain meanings.

This notion is, in one form or another, at the heart of most innovative contemporary audience studies and rightly so (particularly in its semiological formulation that understands the structure of the preferred meaning as contingent on both the message and its audience). The problem arises when we use a definition of preferred meaning that cannot accommodate ambiguity—when the meaning being preferred is so monolithic that it can only be accepted, partially accepted, or rejected. In the case of "The Cosby Show," one of the preferred meanings (an endorsement of the American dream) depends upon the way the show encourages different readings (one class-conscious, the other not).

Another difficulty arises when we equate a message's ideological power with the ability of its authors—consciously or unconsciously—to infuse programs with a preferred meaning. My work on audience interpretations of television news suggests that although unforeseen aspects of the decoding process can play havoc with the producer's preferred meanings, they do not necessarily give the audience any more power or, alternatively, lead to a tepid string of ambiguous or aberrant decodings.

The structure of news, I discovered, can make it very difficult for viewers to understand most of the meanings preferred by the program producers. Unlike most popular television, "hard" news items on TV ignore most of the conventions of popular narrative: They reveal events in sequences that are hierarchical (the most important first and so on, a model borrowed from print journalism) rather than chronological or developmental, and they do not move, as most popular narratives do, from enigma to resolution (see Lewis 1991). This structure makes it hard for many viewers to follow what they are being told, which in turn leads to a tendency to focus on brief isolated moments of a news item and to interpret them within what appears to be an appropriate ideological framework.

The structure of news items, in other words, leads the audience in directions that neither newsmakers nor news analysts would have anticipated. News items are not communicating the messages they seem to convey. This does not mean, however, that news has no influence or that its viewers are empowered to choose their own meaning.

The news producer may have relinquished control, but the news discourse works semiotic spells of its own. Audiences are still guided (albeit by default) toward the construction of certain meanings, and these meanings have ideological consequences.

A good example of this process concerns a news item about the West Bank shown to respondents. The item contained a number of pieces of information: It reported (although not in this order) that Israel had sacked a number of Palestinian mayors in the West Bank, that Israel had come under international criticism for so doing, that Israeli administrators justified the sackings with allegations that the mayors were members of the PLO (and hence terrorists), that some Palestinians had reacted to the sackings with street demonstrations, and that Israeli troops had clamped down hard on these demonstrations leading to clashes between troops and protesters. All most respondents actually remembered, without any of the contextual information, was the street sparring between Israelis and Palestinians.

For most of these viewers, the meaning of this item was based on the meaning of this one isolated moment. This moment was placed in a commonly shared framework about trouble spots around the world and the uncivilized behavior of the foreigners who inhabited them. Placed in this context, the news item reinforced a clear and unambiguous meaning: that inhabitants of the various trouble spots around the world share a common and foreign inability to act in a rational or civilized manner. This casually racist response cannot be discounted as unintended or based upon a misreading of the news item. On the contrary, since it was the reading constructed by most viewers in the survey, we should take such a response—and the specific decoding processes that inform it—very seriously indeed.

The failure of a message's producers to communicate a preferred meaning is not, in this instance, a failure to communicate altogether. The narrative structure of the item played a very specific role in rendering most of the item incomprehensible and thereby, in conjunction with ideological assumptions held by the audience, encouraging particular interpretations. Ambiguity, in this instance, lies in the gap between encoding and decoding. The ideological consequences, however, are not ambiguous at all.

In a more general sense, the structure of news appears, often quite unintentionally, to engender a deeply ahistorical view of the world. This limited perspective is not so much a failure of omission as a breakdown in communication: Even when historical context is provided, it is inserted into the narrative in such a way as to render it almost completely silent for many viewers. This ahistoricism is not ideologically innocent; it is a fertile breeding ground for political mythology. News becomes myth, and as Barthes puts it: "Myth deprives the object of which it speaks of all History. In it, history evaporates. It is a kind of ideal servant: it prepares all things, brings them, lays them out, the master arrives, it silently disappears: all that is left for one to do is to enjoy this beautiful object without wondering where it comes from" (Barthes 1988, p. 151). Ideas are freed from the constraining logic of our social history. Problems like crime, unemployment, poverty, or pollution are dislodged from the social, cultural, and economic conditions that created them. Politicians thus are able to offer solutions without ever referring to these conditions.

Even if the semiology of decoding media messages is often much simpler than this, we should not mistake that simplicity for a general rule. If audiences react differently or unpredictably, they do so for reasons that must be understood rather than discounted under the heading of ambiguity. In the case of differences in interpretation, just because audience research affords us a glimpse at these different interpretations does not mean audiences are granted the same right. An ambiguous TV program can be just as manipulative as an unambiguous one.

Similarly, a program that prefers meanings that have little to do with the message as a whole still prefers meanings.

The use of semiology in audience research is often taken to be an act of political anarchy or, worse still, a digression from politics. Unfortunately, in the service of certain kinds of literary or cultural criticism, this is what it has become. The plea I am making here is, instead, for semiology as an act of political precision, as a way to grasp the complexity of contemporary meaning. With this approach, it may be that we end up appreciating how very powerful certain media messages are in shaping or reinforcing remarkably monolithic (and, in its profoundly political sense, remarkably dominant) ideologies.

References

Ang, I. 1985. *Watching Dallas,* London: Methuen.

Barthes, R. 1974. *S/Z,* New York: Hill and Wang.

———. 1977. *Image-Music-Text,* Glasgow: Fontana.

———. 1988. *Mythologies,* New York: Noonday Press.

Brunsden, C., and D. Morley. 1979. *Everyday Television—Nationwide,* London: BFI.

Campbell, R. 1991. "Securing the Middle Ground: Reporter Formulas in *60 Minutes*," in L. Vande Berg and L. Wenner, eds., *Television Criticism,* New York: Longman.

Eco, U. 1981. *The Role of the Reader,* London: Hutchinson.

Fiske, J. 1987. *Television Culture,* London: Methuen.

Goodwin, A. 1987. "Music Video in the (Post) Modern World," *Screen,* vol. 28, no. 3.

Hawkes, T. 1977. *Structuralism and Semiotics,* London: Methuen.

Hodge, R., and D. Tripp. 1986. *Children and Television,* Cambridge: Polity Press.

Jhally, S., and J. Lewis. 1992. *Enlightened Racism: Audiences, "The Cosby Show," and the Myth of the American Dream,* Boulder, Colo.: Westview Press.

Katz, E., and T. Liebes. 1985. "Mutual Aid in the Decoding of *Dallas*," in P. Drummond and R. Paterson, eds., *Television in Transition,* London: British Film Institute.

Lewis, J. 1991. *The Ideological Octopus: An Exploration of Television and Its Audience,* New York: Routledge.

Radway, J. 1986. "Identifying Ideological Seams: Mass Culture, Analytical Method, and Political Practice," *Communication,* vol. 9.

TWO

Is There Culture
After Cultural Studies?

RON LEMBO

The perspectives of cultural studies represent the most sophisticated of contemporary approaches to the issue of television's influence. The strength of these perspectives lies in deepening our understanding of how the power of television works to privilege some ideologies over others and some textual interpretations over others. These perspectives reveal how negotiated and oppositional interpretations prevent the preferred encodings from achieving total dominance in social life. Fiske, Morley, and others who study television argue that television viewers interpret the text of programming in different ways because differing locations in the social structure give rise to distinct material interests, resulting in differing strategies of interpretation (Fiske 1987, 1986b; Morley 1980; Press 1992). Oppositional interpretations of the text depend on a viewer's subordinate status. Through continued readings of television texts, oppositional interpretations become a source of cultural resistance and provide a basis for political empowerment. Particular studies of television (and of mass culture more generally) differ in emphases, but proponents of cultural studies perspectives assume a clear correlation among social location, cultural resistance, and political empowerment.

As Stuart Hall has pointed out, cultural studies in its variety of forms takes as its point of departure the analysis of cultural objects and meanings as situated (Hall 1980, 1975). Although initially concerned with capitalist power relations and class-based conceptions of identity and cultural practice, those working from critical cultural perspectives have recently broadened this concern to include the power relations of patriarchy and the racial and ethnic divisions that characterize industrial society. Feminist and poststructuralist theory and research have moved audience research even further, conceptualizing discursive forms of power and the dynamic and complex negotiation of meaning by socially situated audiences.

It is difficult to conceive of cultural studies as a singular paradigm, due in part to its interdisciplinary origins. Yet there are what may be termed working assumptions underlying the various perspectives that loosely or otherwise comprise cultural studies. These assumptions, I find, include at least the following: (1) Society is divided into dominant and subordinate groups that differ in terms of their access to social power; (2) dominant groups assert their power in cultural as well as in political and economic domains; (3) cultural meanings are linked to the social structure and, consequently, to power relations, and such meanings can only be understood if the history of the social structure and power relations is made explicit; (4) the creation of cultural meanings by those who use the media is relatively autonomous from the institutional production of media objects; (5) this relative autonomy in the creation of meanings in media use can serve as a basis for oppositional politics.

In focusing on the adequacy of cultural studies–based conceptions of television culture and the nature of audience research in the United States, Stuart Hall (1975), David Morley (1986, 1980), Ien Ang (1985), and in particular John Fiske (1987) come to the forefront in their work.[1] Much of their research offers insight into the dynamics of ideological interpretation, an important issue in understanding how people locate themselves vis-à-vis television and, as a result, what real power there is in the hegemonic process of television viewing.

Certain problems, however, arise when we try to understand and explain the experience of television viewing using the working assumption of the television as a text (as programming has come to be called) and textual interpretation (or reading). The sophistication of cultural studies–based conceptions takes the researcher only part of the way toward explaining the meaningful nature of television viewing in the United States. With the emphasis on text and textual interpretation, the conceptual insight into ideological power dynamics that has proved so valuable in advancing audience research begins to obscure important features of television viewing. These features of viewing, I am convinced, are distinctive to the American scene. Simply stated, the distinctiveness has to do with understanding corporate culture as a process of dissociation and recombination of images that enables the power of images to take multiple forms: television as an object of consumption comparable to other objects of consumption and other leisure activities; television as a normative (or ideological) frame of reference; and television as a fragmented form of social experience. Our conception of television culture in the United States needs to allow for and help explicate the complex and dynamic relations of corporate culture to the social self.

Two key problems with the cultural studies perspectives need to be addressed. First, there is, at the outset, an inability to capture the distinctiveness of television as an object of social experience in the United States, which includes the necessity of locating the text as a form of social power in a more inclusive framework of what I term corporate culture. The second problem involves how cultural studies conceives of the self; the conception favors the already constructed as opposed to emergent qualities of the self, even in perspectives that seek to validate difference.

This essay is an attempt to bring to cultural studies a perspective that takes into account the multiple forms of corporate power and the multiple levels of viewers' mindful and emotional relationship to them. My strategy here is first to identify and examine two interrelated problems in the group of perspectives that could be called cultural studies and its de facto approach to understanding television's influence. I then conclude by outlining some new directions for the study of the U.S. television audience.

Problems with Cultural Studies

The Distinctiveness of Television in the United States

The emphasis that cultural studies perspectives place on ideological power and the contestation of that power needs to be located amid a broader conception of corporate culture if such theory and research intend to capture the multiple forms of influence characteristic of television programming in the United States. Television is first and foremost an object mass-produced and distributed in a national market to realize exchange value and serve consumption needs. Television is one of a variety of objects available for leisure activity, and at this level of analysis, its particular textual features do not come into play in assessing its significance in U.S. culture. By focusing on issues of ideological power, cultural studies neglects to analyze television as an object of people's social experience. Interestingly enough, this kind of analysis has figured more prominently in more scientistic accounts of television use. Comstock and others (1978), for example, present numerous empirical studies that document the displacement effect of television in the United States. In "uses and gratifications" research, comparative data focusing on the social-psychological dimensions of media use have accrued over the years, yielding significant insights into distinctive needs, motivations, uses, and gratifications that pertain to television use[2] (Katz, Gurevitch, and Haas 1973). Yet as Blumler (1979) has pointed out, the charting and profiling of needs and uses of different media must be taken further, so that the relationship between the unique grammar of different media and the particular requirements of audience members is addressed.

In cultural studies perspectives, terms such as "system of objects," "consumption culture," or the "ideology of consumption" are often invoked and carry an explicit reference to the broader historical influence of television in the organization of leisure time, a focus the scientistic approaches typically fail to consider. Although this approach preserves a sense of power relations inscribed in capitalist commodity relations, for the most part it avoids the more concrete task of empirically situating this power of television amid other objects of consumption and, significantly, amid other nonconsumption-related activities. Omitted are accounts of the ways people become mindfully engaged during periods of leisure and especially how they decide to engage in one activity as opposed to another.[3] What is needed, then, is a more adequate conceptualization of television as an object of the viewer's social experience. To grasp the concrete nature of its influence, television as an object of consumption must be conceptualized in terms of the mindful qualities of the viewer's self-experience.

Cultural studies perspectives tend to focus their attention beneath this broader level of consumption culture, purporting to understand and explain the particular ways that social experience is mediated by the television text. Yet this ends up being a selective and unnecessarily limited conceptualization of television's representational forms and, consequently, of the potential for mindful engagement on the part of the audience. By focusing on television as a text (which is no doubt linked to power relations), cultural studies misrecognizes what is a deeper social logic of corporate broadcast institutions, a logic that is responsible for generating not only texts but images as well. Misperceived is the principle intrinsic to the workings of corporate culture in the United States: the dissociation of images from real-life cultural forms and their recombination as televisual discourses.

In modernist terms, culture is social, shared, and sustained through close and continued interpersonal contact. Culture in these terms also takes the form of symbolic objects that serve as referents for shared meanings that people can identify as their own. Culture persists over time, often emerges in localized contexts (quite apart from the marketplace), and as cultural studies reminds us, under certain circumstances can emerge in opposition to dominant culture. Culture, then, in such modernist terms, is a kind of raw material for the industrial production of entertainment value. Creative people and corporate decisionmakers base their conceptions of programming on some version of culture that they think will resonate with the audience (Gitlin 1983). The subject matter, settings, characters, story lines, and so on carry meaning precisely because they represent some version of real life for viewers.[4] In these corporate versions, entertaining images of real-life cultural forms are mass-produced to generate exchange value. These images are a partial and invariably sanitized (some would say co-opted) version of the real-life cultural forms to which they refer. But the entertaining version predominates. It is dissociated from other (perhaps more meaningful) versions that would be likely if one were located within the culture itself. For example, "The Cosby Show" is an entertaining image of an upper-middle-class black family precisely because (among other things) the stresses and strains of professional work for Claire and Cliff are rarely represented, the impact of work life on family interactions is seen to be negligible, and family interactions are invariably snappy in order to keep the laughs coming at a quick enough pace. While viewers may find varying degrees of plausibility in "The Cosby Show," virtually all of them would recognize that this is indeed a representation of black families that exist in real life.

Once dissociated, images of real life are recombined to form televisual discourses. In the process, two irreconcilable tendencies of corporate culture emerge.

That is, the process of dissociation and recombination results in patternings to programming that privilege dominant, or mainstream, values (Gerbner et al. 1986; Gerbner et al. 1979; Gitlin 1983, 1979, 1978). This occurs even when (and perhaps especially when) the real-life cultural forms are oppositional in nature (or potentially so). This tendency of corporate culture lends coherence to the self-experience of audience members by centering their experience in these dominant representations. To the extent that people make dominant (and even negotiated) readings of the text, the orientation is the basis of television's legitimating function in advanced capitalism.

The second tendency arising from the separation of images from real-life cultural forms is less familiar to audience research per se but is a focal point of poststructuralist-based theories about television: the tendency toward fragmentation of meaning in the viewing culture. This tendency is based, as is the hegemonic tendency, in the expansionary principle of the market as a basis for the production and distribution of programming. The logic, however, is different. The former is one of coherence, the latter of fragmentation. From the logic of fragmentation, television can be seen as a continual flow of images across numerous broadcast and cable channels. This flow generates a world (or system, as some would call it) of images that becomes increasingly difficult for viewers to render coherent at the level of meaning. The images are simply too vast, ever-changing, and lacking in coherence always to be made coherent by viewers. From this perspective, meaning becomes based on dissociated images that do not necessarily add up to a more unified understanding of real life. Corporate culture works to fragment cultural meanings and even block the formation of coherent ideas about the self and collective experience. This power need not be intentionally produced; rather it is more likely to be collective, or institutional, in nature. This lack of coherence that television promotes is similar in its logic to what David Harvey (1989) calls "the condition of postmodernity." He refers to the postmodern as a world in which "we cannot aspire to any unified representation of the world, or picture it as a totality full of connections and differentiations," nor can we sustain "historical continuity in values, beliefs, or even disbeliefs" (Harvey 1989, pp. 52, 54). It is a world that is "depthless," one in which there is a "fixation with appearances, surfaces, and the instant impacts that have no sustaining power over time" (Harvey 1989, p. 58).

In the United States, then, television takes multiple objective forms as a product of corporate culture. Its power works in different ways, only one of which is textual (the hegemonic tendency). In contrast, by conceptualizing television as an object of consumption and as a fragmented flow of imagery, we focus attention on corporate forms of power that are not explicitly textual.

Thus, taken together, these three tendencies (television as object, text, and image) account for a multiplicity of forms of corporate power in the United States. As a multiplicity, the different tendencies are not reducible to one another; they do not add up to any single unified form of cultural power. With regard to cultural studies, this characteristic means that television does not—indeed, cannot—add up to the power of the text alone or to the limited focus on the negotiation of textual power by the audience. Furthermore, these multiple tendencies cannot be reconciled with one another. In fact, they generate entirely different meaningful qualities in the audience experience (as I hope to demonstrate later in this chapter), and they do not provide any overall sense of unity to the television audience experience in corporate culture.

Conceptualizing the Self

The problems posed by the lack of a conceptualization of corporate culture in cultural studies perspectives are compounded by a concomitant limited idea of the self. In an approach that corresponds to the conception of television as text, the viewer is understood as a socially located interpreter of the text. The capabilities for interpretation derive from already constructed social locations: In the cultural studies perspectives, these are typically locations of class, race, gender, and ethnicity. My own research, however, points to viewing patterns that do not fit with this conceptualization of the audience but are in fact obscured by it.

For example, I found that viewers routinely recognize the formulaic nature of television programming, and that this phenomenon—recognition of formula—is not properly understood as an ideological reading of the text (Lembo 1989; Lembo and Tucker 1990). Instead, it is a case of viewers seeing through the ideological representation of real-life cultural forms to uncover the corporate form of television entertainment, a form that underlies virtually all of the particular ideological encodings of programming. The text, as a product of corporate culture, is more than the ideology encoded there. Additionally, in the United States at least, the text is a representation of corporate requirements for the production and distribution of entertainment value. Therefore, textual interpretation cannot encompass the entire range of ways in which viewers make programming meaningful.

My research also indicates that recognition of formula does not originate in already existing social locations, such as class, race, gender, and ethnicity. Instead, it originates in television culture or in corporate culture more broadly (Lembo 1989). Seeing through the commodification of meaning in television programming is a form of knowledge that emerges through the repeated practice of viewing. This practice has become ritualized and now serves as a social location in its own right.

Another feature of television culture that bears on the issue of the emergence of self is the fact that the programming text is often not the exclusive focus of viewers' attention. Viewers often treat the entire set of offerings known as programming as a set of movable images (Lembo 1989). Some viewers use television as background noise with voices and sounds providing companionship, or they treat it as an anchor of sorts when they haven't decided or don't want to decide to do any one thing. They use it as a focal point for attention, an approach enabling them to create a space in which to think about things completely unrelated to what's on the screen. Viewers can move in and out of mindful engagement with programming as a text, shuffling across different narrative contexts of action, ignoring ideological segments encoded there, and often abandoning the need to interpret textual meanings altogether. I refer to this phenomenon as image-based viewing and find that it takes multiple forms.

In one type of image-based viewing, "simultaneous viewing," people typically watch television while engaged in any number of other activities, ranging from housework, preparing meals, and talking to reading, doing crossword puzzles, writing letters, and completing ongoing hobbies, crafts, or other household projects. When viewers engage in "channel switching," they are regularly moving between at least two but sometimes three or four different programs, and once again, significant segments of the ideology encoded in one program are ignored as attention turns to an alternative program. I have found that this movement in and out of particular programs is sustained and constitutes a viewing relation in its own right, though it is not without ideological effect or meaning. Sometimes viewers have a difficult time focusing on any text, and instead they continually flip through the channels, occasionally giving sustained attention to a particular program. In a third type of image-based viewing, "image play," viewers once again treat programming not as a text but as a discrete image or series of images with which to link their own experiences. Viewers use the imaginative space of programming to create brief excursions in which their own actions play off of televised representations or are interrelated with other media representations, or they move into an imaginary space of their own making, quite apart from a relationship with media imagery of any kind. On a simpler but no less profound level, viewers play with the colors, contrasts, and movements of images, which I have found often brings them into momentary but intensely felt experiences with the visual myths of the dominant culture. This pattern is quite common in the viewing of music television and commercials with fast-paced editing. These moments of mythic experience do not appear to involve an explicit reading (dominant or negotiated) of programming as text, and for this reason, I hesitate to call them ideological. In fact, they seem to occur quite independently of any recognition of the ideology of programming or the narrative development of action and correspond more closely to what Deleuze and Guattari (1983) refer to as interruptions and flows of desire.

In image-based viewing, primacy is not given to sustaining textual interpretation, and as a result, it does not exhibit the closure characteristic of more narrative-based viewing. This does not mean, however, that ideology ceases to be significant as a form of social power in the viewing culture. My observations and the interview accounts indicate that during image-based viewing, textual interpretation, if it occurs, shifts from the overall development of narrative action to hyperritualized scenes of social action that occur within the narrative. For example, in simultaneous viewing, viewers attend intermittently to game shows, news, or talk shows and, as a result, often ignore significant portions of the ideology encoded in these programs. Only particular scenes, for one reason or another, register with them in meaningful terms. This is a profoundly important shift because it suggests that viewers' knowledge of the world is now much more compressed and dissociated. This distinction in the temporal quality of textual interpretation, as well as in the very existence of image-based viewing, is not conceptualized in the cultural studies account of television culture. It may be true that in documenting dominant (or, for that matter, oppositional or negotiated) textual interpretations, those analysts working within cultural studies perspectives are not necessarily conceptualizing ideological reproduction as narratively based or claiming that the interpretive process is a coherent one. Instead, they may be identifying a more disrupted interpretive process. It seems, however, that such distinctions, if they are salient, need to be accounted for.

At stake here is an understanding of the way hegemonic ideology works in particular instances. What kind of discursive space do people inhabit in television culture? Do they participate in the imaginative re-creation (reproduction) of ideology in a setting that unfolds over half-hour, one-hour, and two-hour time periods? Do they grasp the ideological import in the more discrete hyper-ritualized segments that characterize image-based viewing? Do viewers experience ideology as a consistency of meaning generated in sustained attention to the narrative development of action or as a disassociation of meanings generated by the segmentation of programming and its continual flow over the course of typical viewing experiences? These questions cut to the heart of debates about the ideological role of television. Depending on which of these empirical tendencies predominates, we as analysts come away understanding the ideological role of television in very different ways. Does television center viewers' ideological experience, or does it fragment and block ideological consistencies from emerging at all and thus shape the meaning of viewing in an explicitly nonideological form? What implications does this difference have for the nature of viewers' mindful participation in culture as a whole?

The documentation of viewers' recognition of formula and of their formation of image-based viewing relations points to an inadequacy in the conception of the viewer found in cultural studies perspectives. This inadequacy and the problems related to the conceptualization of corporate culture stem, I believe, from the Marxist, neo-Marxist, structuralist, and poststructuralist assumptions about the primacy of power in television culture. These assumptions link the viewer's interpretive activity too closely with power and have the unintended consequence of denying the viewer any capabilities of self that are not tied to power. The strategy that proponents of cultural studies have shown in documenting textual interpretations has taken shape from an interest in locating political resistance through audience members' subcultural identities—identities that, at least objectively, enable oppositional interpretations to emerge in the viewing culture. The practical knowledge of viewers is ultimately derivative of preexisting discursive structures:

the text and, more important, subcultural location. This conception is problematic because it fails to consider that viewers can actualize capabilities of self that are not in a strict sense based on already existent identity. As Mead (1938, 1932), Blumer (1969), Dewey (1934), Winnecott (1971, 1965), and a host of others have pointed out, the social self is also a reflexive form of engaging with already existent identities and discursive structures. This notion seems to be the basic premise in a general cultural studies conception of resistance rooted in a reflexive engagement with dominant ideology. If such is the case, why restrict this reflexive engagement to subcultural locations?

In image-based viewing situations mentioned earlier, viewers make judgments about what to pay attention to in the flow of television imagery; they recognize scenes, settings, and characters as occurrences of everyday life; they intersperse thoughts and emotions about their own lives with those of the characters and scenes represented; and they "space out" by thinking of things completely unrelated to what's on the screen. These are typical instances of mindful activity that, although not presupposing a self-identification with characters, scenes, or the development of narrative action or constituting explicit opposition to such textual features of programming, give meaningful form to the activity of television viewing. In these cases, it is self-reflexivity and not self-identity that provides the meaningful form of activity.

The conceptualization of the self in cultural studies is also problematic because the act of viewing is an emergent and therefore unique level of social reality that provides a space for intersubjectivity that is between (to use Deleuze's [Deleuze and Parnet 1987] term) the text (and its power) and resistance-based (or any other) social locations. It is in this space that recognition of formula and image-based viewing relations emerge. These are meaningful forms of the viewing culture that cannot be derived from television as ideological text and subcultural identity. Television culture takes new forms by virtue of the meeting between corporate cultural forms and capabilities of audience members to act as social selves. As yet, cultural studies has not adequately conceptualized such relations.

Locating the Audience in U.S. Television Research

To address the previously outlined problems associated with a cultural studies approach, I now propose a different path for conceptualizing the U.S. television audience. Some of the ideas are specific to my research; others are more general concepts that ought to be considered in any investigation of television use in the United States. I focus more on the latter. Likewise, some of the considerations I raise are issues that inform my methods of research, and others are ideas that primarily concern the analysis of interview material.

As a product of corporate culture, television is constitutive of a social domain that manifests several possible cultural forms at once: television as object in consumption culture (the choice of television viewing among other leisure-time activities), as hegemonic ideology (television as text), and as an image flow (image-based viewing). These multiple forms are part of a complex, multilayered audio-visual discourse. Likewise, viewers can be conceptualized as social selves—as persons capable of a range of mindful and emotional engagement with the object world and able to take their own social experience as the object of subsequent action.

Whether or not any of the cultural forms of television present themselves to the viewer is, obviously, dependent first on the viewer's decision to turn on the television. Beyond that, the viewer's movements among the different meaningful possibilities shape in important ways which cultural forms of power will become important for that viewer. As a product of corporate culture, then, television must be located in the viewer's context of choice.

Given an understanding of the multiple cultural forms of television, the analyst must suspend these notions and move toward empirical documentation of the particular viewing contexts. This focus allows one to reconstruct particular cultural forms from within the experience of viewers and to see how viewers bring the object into their lives, a multilayered and complex experience. The complexity of the viewer's context of choice involves multiple, often overlapping, social locations (of viewers) and decisions about watching television and sustaining involvement (of whatever quality) with it.

The researcher must enter television culture through the lives of particular viewers. The analytical reconstruction of the viewing experience, however, must begin with a conceptualization of the typical patterns in which viewers encounter television as an object of consumption culture in the first place. This first step begins, I have found, by identifying categories of viewers within the broader context of society. The work/leisure distinction, as an inherent characteristic of advanced capitalist society, plays a pivotal role in the analysis. In my research, the basic analytic categories consist primarily of working people, students (including children), retired people, homemakers, and so on. It is around these most basic of social locations—work, school, and home—that viewers orient their daily activities, including their encounters with television. These locations must be taken into account in the initial reconstruction of the audience experience, and the assessment must analytically occur prior to the conceptualization of subcultural locations that figure so importantly in cultural studies–based accounts of the audience because at this point, the text and textual interpretation have not yet emerged as salient factors. (If these subcultural social locations do come into play here, it is in terms of their contribution to the organization of daily life in relation to leisure-time activity.) At this point, the analyst merely makes explicit the perspectivism inherent in empirical research.

Next, the conception of television culture must be made concrete by considering typical patterns of television use by particular viewers. The researcher must reconstruct the meeting ground between the cultural forms of television as an object and the capabilities of persons as social selves. The primary sociological task here is to identify specific, patterned ways that viewers make their use of television meaningful. Following the conception of Langer, Blank, and Chanowitz (1978), I use the idea of viewers participating with a range of "mindfulness." Mindful orientations to television exist and can be documented at various points throughout the experience that is television culture. The viewer's mindfulness in television culture is itself affected by numerous social and psychological background factors. So, in conceptualizing television use, it is important to account for class, age, gender, race, ethnicity, religion, education, and occupation. Other factors can be important as well, including use of print media, participation in other creative leisure-time activities, and viewers' sense of community (their connectedness with other people).

I then analytically distinguish among viewers' initial turn to television, their interaction with programming per se, and the fit of television back into their daily lives. The basic conceptual components of television culture thus are

1. Television as an object of corporate culture (includes a prior conceptualization of the representational forms of programming)
2. The turn to television and to other activities
3. Television interaction
4. Leaving television and placing it back into the context of daily life

The remainder of this essay offers a brief outline of what within the components analysts may need or wish to consider regarding this meeting ground between the objective forms of television and the socially located self. Although this discussion is drawn from my analysis of working people's lives, I believe that the empirical documentation of a range of mindfulness in the lives of other viewers is basic to overcoming the limitations of cultural studies perspectives.

The Turn to Television

Typically, individuals must come to television from some other aspect of their lives; similarly, they must turn off the set and fit television back into their lives. This progression—from turning to television, to interacting with it, to leaving it and fitting it back into life—is the basic pattern of television use. In defining each stage, it is important to clearly identify empirical patterns in the viewer's mindful relationship to particular features of television.

The turn to television is the category that reveals how the broader context of a person's life shapes the mindfulness with which he or she chooses television viewing as an activity. When a person thinks about watching television, it is usually in a specific situation and often has something to do with the way that person is feeling. Also of consequence are the other possible nontelevision activities someone could engage in. In the turn to television, then, an important initial component of the symbolic processes that underlie television use can be identified. And this information has the merit of being grounded in the typical, recurring behavior patterns of daily life.

There are at least five aspects of the turn to television that I investigated: (1) situational contexts of television use, composed of objective situations and feeling states; (2) the mindfulness in turning to activities (including television); (3) the mindful potential of activities (including television); (4) activities other than television chosen under the same or similar conditions; and (5) programming watched.

For each situational context, the mindfulness typically involved in turning to activities and in the activities themselves can be identified. Because of the inherently complex nature of these situations, a researcher needs to tailor the situational context selected for the particular groups to be studied. I focused on working people. Consequently, I found that television may be one activity among a number of alternatives that a person considers in certain recurring situations such as, say, being at home after work. By identifying objective situations, the analyst provides a means of relating the larger social context of viewers' lives to their turn to television. The category of feeling states is a more social-psychological construct designed to capture a range of significant differences in terms of how individuals experience themselves emotionally. For example, a range can include being tired, bored, relaxed, lonely, and so on.

Both the objective and subjective sources of variation can be combined to identify typical situational contexts of television use. Depending on the particular location of viewers being researched, relevant situational contexts can be selected and used as a point of departure for documenting the turn to television. Because my focus was on people who work, I concentrated my analysis of the interview accounts on the following situational contexts: (1) tired after a hectic day at work; (2) relaxed after a good day at work; (3) relaxed at home in the evening, with dinner or responsibilities out of the way; (4) relaxed at home during the day on the weekends.

The second aspect of the turn to television is the mindfulness involved in the individual's turn from these situational contexts to other activities, including television. In this context, mindfulness refers to the cognitive process involved in how people think about doing things or decide to do things, not the cognitive quality of the resulting activities themselves. By identifying differences in mindfulness at this level of behavior, we are able to capture an important meaningful dimension of television culture: the presence of mind that individuals have in turning to television as compared with other activities. Based on preliminary research, I identified qualities typically involved in decisions to engage in activities and thus included some preconceptualized (i.e., based on previous participant observation) ranges of choice in my otherwise open-ended interviews. In one instance, characterization choices referring to qualities of mind ranged from habitual to escapist to playful to a more explicitly reflective quality of mind.

Television viewers often display or express knowledge of having engaged in decisionmaking processes that fall within this range of mindfulness in orienting themselves to activities from particular contextual starting points. Depending on the quality of mindfulness expressed, this construct will identify the extent to which individuals utilize their capacity to act as a self in turning to activities, and direct comparisons between turning to television versus turning to other activities can be made.

Television viewers I've interviewed have repeatedly made a distinction between the way they decide to engage in activities in the first place and the nature of their actual involvement in the activities themselves. The mindfulness of their orientation to television may carry implications for the way they actually become involved with programming imagery. But each specific activity may have a potential for mindful expression different from others. If a person comes to an activity with an orientation of "play," for example, and that activity only has the potential for a much lower level of symbolic interaction, then the person is likely to end up engaged in an activity in a way that is much different from the mindfulness displayed at the outset. Similarly, a person may wish to escape from a situation and may typically do this by, say, watching television or doing yardwork around the house. By choosing television or yardwork, however, the person ends up in a potentially different activity (from the standpoint of mindfulness) that is quite independent of the turn to it. For reasons such as these, it is important to distinguish between the mindfulness of the turn to activities and the mindful potential of the activities themselves. I have identified four aspects of the mindful potential of activities pertinent to the study of television: (1) whether the participation is active or passive; (2) whether participants can control the pace of the activity; (3) whether there is a developmental course to the activity, which indicates that individuals are able to integrate participation in it from one occasion to the next; and (4) whether there is possibility for insight, which refers to the likelihood that individuals are able to reflect on and gain insight about themselves, their society, or the broader environment while engaged in an activity (including television). Taken together, participation, pace, developmental course, and possibility for insight represent the four dimensions of the mindful potential of activities. Using them allows the analyst to identify and compare the social nature of activities, including television.

Television Interaction

Once television is turned to as an activity, the real-life context that may have shaped the turn does not recede completely into the background. Yet the image and text of television programming tend to become the focal points of the viewer's attention. In conceptualizing television interaction, I try to identify the way in which hegemonic and fragmenting tendencies of programming are made meaningful by viewers.

The idea that there are different patterns of viewing and that they exhibit a range of mindfulness emerged from earlier interviews and observations of viewing behavior. I found a good deal of variation in the ways a viewer's capability to act as a self emerged in relation to programming and, in the case of group viewing, in relation to other viewers as well. In some cases, as I mentioned earlier, people related to television as an object, using it simply for background noise or to have some company in the house. In other cases, I found that the viewer's imaginative or reflective capacities of self were consistently brought to bear in ways that most fully realized the meaningful potential of television as both image and text. In these more mindfully engaged patterns, particularly the textually based ones, viewers typically applied some standard of interpretation—either artistic, technical, or a standard derived from life experience—to position what was viewed within a larger, socially meaningful context, such as knowledge of realist film conventions, experience with work, family, romantic relationships, and so on. Furthermore, I found that the same viewer could indeed engage in different levels of mindful interaction in relation to both television imagery and other viewers, and that it was quite common for this to occur within a single viewing situation. Sometimes, attention would be riveted to the screen, the viewer closely following in his or her mind the dialogue and interaction among characters as the story unfolded. Other times the same viewer's attention to dialogue and interaction would fade and be replaced by a more superficial kind of recognition of what was taking place, during which time the viewer may or may not have been engaged in some other activity as well. Despite the simplicity of much television programming and the taken-for-granted presence of at least one set in virtually every U.S. household, the viewing culture is a complex symbolic world, one not easily understood without entering into the mindful experience that viewers actually inhabit.

When trying to discern the degree of mindfulness that viewers apply when watching television, it is necessary to allow for a broad range of possibilities, given the wide range of possible viewing situations. One overall category of situations is solitary viewing. This framework limits the scope of the problem somewhat, but there are still many ways of interacting with the television while alone. In solitary situations, viewers can interpret (or fail to interpret) any number of representational features that pass by during the program. They may intermittently attend to what is on the screen, following only the most exciting scenes and then quickly becoming distracted by other things. Sometimes viewers sit in the room and look at the screen but fail to watch in what could be called an attentive manner a good portion of the program. Certainly they are watching television, but it is difficult to say that they are consistently engaged in an ideological reading of programming.

Viewing occurs in solitary situations and in group situations. Like solitary viewers, viewers in group situations can interpret (or fail to interpret) a range of representational features in programming or, for that matter, the communicative actions of other viewers. At one extreme, the relation of each viewer to the television is of primary importance, and the analyst is faced with the task of determining the significance of the separate relationships of self to programming for each of the viewers present. At the other extreme, programming and the communicative actions of viewers can be so well integrated with each other that the viewing situation becomes a highly organized social world in its own right. In my research, I have come upon what some viewers call "the game of television" (Lembo 1989). It begins with different viewers voicing their opinions about what they are seeing on television in order to elicit comments from others and get discussion started (the show is one regularly watched in common). The give-and-take of conversation around specific textual features of programming allows shared meanings to emerge, and viewers actually develop a common culture through television. Most of the time, however, group viewing lies somewhere between these two extremes. Sporadic conversation interrupts attention to the screen. Sometimes it is focused on interpretations of the program and sometimes not. One by one, viewers become distracted by other things and then return to watching once again. In many instances, the flow of imagery and periodic interruptions of this flow through conversation form the basis of the viewing patterns.

Because each viewer can engage in this entire range of viewing relations in solitary and group situations, the task of understanding how television affects the self becomes very complicated. With all these possible relationships and endless programming variations, how does the analyst determine the way a viewer maintains his or her presence of mind or the net effect that programming has? Are viewers able to create a meaningful context for a specific feature of a program by interpreting its significance in light of what has come before and what will follow—a symbolic capacity attributed to the functioning of a "self"? Is this a self located within dominant ideology or one consistently critical of it? When viewers develop more image-based viewing patterns in which consistent ideological readings (whether dominant, negotiated, or oppositional) are interspersed with engagement in other activities, are those readings simply less important as a function of the limited attention to the screen? What consequence does image-based viewing have for the development of the self, and what part does the ideology of programming play? These profoundly important questions lie at the center of a cultural study of the audience. At this time, there is no overall conception that can link what goes through the viewer's mind with the multiple representational forms of programming. But by conceptualizing television viewing in terms of particular self-object relations, we can identify patterns that show the mindful quality of these relations to assess how the viewer's capability to act as a self emerges in television viewing and how the different tendencies of programming may exert influence. For a preliminary stage in conceptualizing differences in the mindfulness television viewing, I have derived the following range of viewing relations (patterns) from preliminary interviews to create a profile of viewers.

1. The set is just "on" with voices and sounds providing some companionship. Sometimes people become interested and watch, but they are usually doing other things—housework, dinner preparation, chores, and so on.

2. People actually sit down to watch TV, but they don't pay attention all the time; they get up often to do other things—read the paper, eat, talk on the phone—and then come back to watching again. The TV is just a good focus when they haven't decided to do any one thing.
3. People watch what's on the screen, but they are not really thinking too deeply or getting too involved in anything. The images are interesting and stimulating, and viewers just like to watch things go by and see what happens.
4. People get interested in the story, the action, or the characters. They like to see how things are put together, to follow the scenes or what the characters do, and to see why things come out as they do.
5. People become very involved in the story, the action, or the characters, and these seem real to them. They feel they are in the situation and almost a part of what's happening; they may think about what the characters should do next or how they might act in the situation.
6. People get very involved in what they are watching, but they don't simply accept everything they see. They think about what's on, and if something doesn't make sense, they react to it and question whether it's plausible or not.
7. People become very involved in what they are watching and see connections with other things they've watched on TV, seen in films, or had happen to them.
8. People become seriously engaged in a show, closely watching it as they would other artistic performances. They think about its technical or artistic merit and try to interpret it against the standards set by similar performances; sometimes they can reflect on their own lives and enrich the understanding they have about the kind of world they live in.

The concept of television interaction was developed to take explicit account of the particular ways viewers give meaningful form to the multiple tendencies represented in television programming. I treat the concept as a separate component of television culture in order to isolate viewers' relationships with programming per se from the broader context that shapes the turn to television and its fit back into daily life. In television interaction, the possible ideological effects of television programming are conceptualized as one aspect of a more fundamental process of self-formation with the medium. This aspect is reflected in my conception of a range of mindful interaction patterns applicable to both solitary and group viewing situations. Taken together, these conceptual constructs provide a solid basis for developing an empirical profile of viewers' interaction patterns.

The Fit of Television Back into Daily Life

This component refers essentially to the symbolic process that underlies the integration of television imagery back into viewers' lives when the set is off. It includes consideration of the sense of self that viewers have after watching, the particular features of television that are retained, and the mindful and emotional quality of this experience.

One part of analyzing the sense of self that viewers have after watching is to assess the degree of self-control they exercise in leaving television. In my research, I have found that viewers exhibit a number of different patterns of self-control in turning off the set. For example, on one end of the scale are viewers who in watching television continue to find the best of what's on until something better to do comes along or until there is something else they have to do. In the middle are viewers who, after whatever they were watching is over, will watch some uninteresting shows for a while and then turn off the set. At the other end of the scale are viewers who know when they will turn off the set even before they start to watch and who (almost) always keep to their plans.

A second aspect of analyzing the sense of self after watching is the quality of the viewers' emotional state as they turn off the set and move into other activities and whether viewers feel in control of their emotions as they leave television. This analysis indicates the extent to which the emotional level of their interaction with programming has been resolved in a mindful way.

The exercise is important because much of television programming is designed to appeal to viewers on the emotional level. Making such assessments, however, is difficult, particularly because the more unresolved aspects of this emotional level of involvement may be beyond the capacity of viewers to recognize and report on. In part, this is captured by the range of self-control exhibited in leaving television, but an explicit focus on viewers' emotions can help clarify the different ways that interaction with programming in fact stays with viewers at the conclusion of viewing and affects their capacity to act as selves. Viewing diaries and in-depth interviews can be used to explore this area systematically and provide a clearer indication of what the relevant categories may be.

Analyzing the actual fit of television imagery back into daily life is also difficult, primarily because there are so many ways that features can be integrated into the viewer's life. At the behavioral level, there is the question of how viewers enter into conversation with others concerning what they watch. Does conversation occur regularly, with the same people? Is it about favorite shows and characters watched in common? Or is conversation more random and infrequent, limited to comments about special shows such as particular sporting events or miniseries? Distinctions such as these are important because they indicate the extent to which viewers use programming as a basis of reciprocal interaction in discussing and reinterpreting their understanding of what is seen. As a result, the significance of particular symbolic features, such as characters, exciting stories, and settings, can be determined as much by the symbolic interaction outside of viewing as by the initial way that individuals may have viewed them. In the long run, conversations outside of viewing may change the very way that viewers watch television—what they choose to watch, what they find plausible or implausible, and so on. And it is in this analysis that the reliance cultural studies places on subcultural locations becomes most salient in the conceptualization of leaving television.

At the level of ideology, television imagery clearly has an influence. But when viewers accept particular television presentations of, say, Dallas oil barons or inner-city police as plausible, does this have a direct bearing on how they understand oil barons or inner-city police in the real world? The interpretations of programming can be determined at the level of interaction, but their actual integration into viewers' knowledge of the world is much more difficult to assess.

There is also a more practical level of ideology to consider. Do viewers find some things they see on television helpful in dealing with problems or personal issues in their lives? Do the ways that particular, well-liked characters deal with fictional issues, such as family problems, relations with superiors at work, alcoholism, and so on, become incorporated into viewers' handling of these issues? These ideological considerations play an important role in the determination of television's possible standardizing effects in that a limited range of ideas and images provides the basis for interpreting the infinitely varied situations in which millions of viewers find themselves.

The fit of television also encompasses a consideration of fantasy. Are certain types of viewers more likely than others to daydream about some things they see on television? Do viewers picture themselves as particular characters? If so, which ones? Do they imagine themselves in particular settings? If so, are they romantic settings, action-adventure settings, or high-status settings depicting consumption-oriented lifestyles?

Conclusion

In this essay, I have outlined a conception of television viewing that explicates the mindful dynamics underlying the viewer's relationship with the medium at three distinct stages: the turn to television, television interaction, and the fit of television back into daily life. The mindful qualities of the viewer's involvement with the representational forms of television are central to this analysis. This involvement can be understood as a unique form of culture in that patterns of self-formation with television are similar to patterns of self-formation in more traditional arenas of cultural life.

This conception of television culture has a more general applicability to other communication media. It identifies, I believe, basic components involved in the use of other objects of mass communication and can be used to establish patterns in their cultural use. In all cases, individuals must turn to a medium, they must become involved in specific ways with particular features of its form and content, and they must eventually leave the object and fit it back (symbolically), in some way, into their daily lives afterward. We can conceptualize a medium's different symbolic features and the individual's different mindful forms of involvement with it to explicate the underlying symbolic process in a fashion similar to that found in studying television culture. In this way, it becomes possible to examine the broader culture of mass communication through methods based on similar constructs of mindfulness that provide a systematic level of comparison.

We must treat audience reception in cultural terms but do so in a way that treats the self's relationship to the medium or object in question as a distinctive form of culture. There is in television use a "formation of the social" that is not reducible either to the preexisting discursive forms of programming or to textual interpretations made from preexisting social locations (class, race, gender, ethnicity) or other locations relevant for particular viewers. The acts of turning to television and of viewing exhibit patterns in which people give meaningful form to their activity in ways that lie beyond preestablished structures of meaning.

Notes

1. See also Lull (1990, 1980); Radway (1984); Grossberg (1987); and Press (1992).

2. See also Katz and Foukes (1962); Katz, Blumler, and Gurevitch (1973); and Blumler (1985, 1979).

3. The conception of mindfulness is adopted from the work of Langer, Blank, and Chanowitz (1978); in the context of television culture, it refers to the cognitive quality of people's engagement in activities, including television viewing. In my research, I conceptualized mindfulness as ranging from a routine or habitual orientation to a purposive or self-directed one. This conception is dealt with later in the chapter.

4. A qualification is in order here. Gitlin (1983) argues that much television programming is recombinant—that is, based on already successful television versions of real life. It is certainly true that viewers can at times recognize those features of television programming that derive from previous programming. I would argue, however, that to the extent that such programming is plausible to viewers, they would continue to understand it in terms of its representing some version of real life.

References

Ang, Ien. 1985. *Watching "Dallas": Soap Opera and the Melodramatic Imagination*. London: Methuen.

Aronowitz, Stanley, and Henry Giroux. 1991. *Postmodern Education*. Minneapolis: University of Minnesota.

Barthes, Roland. 1972. *Mythologies*. New York: Hill and Wang.

Baudrillard, Jean. 1981. *For a Critique of the Political Economy of the Sign*. St. Louis, Mo.: Telos.

———. 1983. *Simulations*. New York: Semiotexte.

Bauman, Zygmunt. 1973. *Culture as Praxis*. London: Routledge and Kegan Paul.

Blumer, Herbert. 1936. "Social Attitudes and Non-Symbolic Interaction." *Journal of Educational Sociology* 9:518–520.

———. 1969. *Symbolic Interactionism*. Berkeley: University of California.

Blumler, Jay. 1979. "The Role of Theory in Uses and Gratifications Studies." *Communication Research* 6:9–36.

————. 1985. "The Social Character of Media Gratifications," in Karl Rosengren, Lawrence Wenner, and Philip Palmgreen, eds., *Media Gratifications Research: Current Perspectives.* Beverly Hills, Calif.: Sage.

Blumler, Jay, and Elihu Katz. 1974. *The Uses of Mass Communication: Current Perspectives in Gratifications Research.* Beverly Hills, Calif.: Sage.

Carey, James. 1988. *Media, Myths, and Narratives.* Beverly Hills, Calif.: Sage.

————. 1989. *Communication as Culture.* Boston: Unwin Hyman.

Comstock, George, Steven Chaffee, Nathan Katzman, Maxwell McCombs, and Donald Roberts. 1978. *Television and Human Behavior.* New York: Columbia University.

Deleuze, Gilles. 1991. *Empiricism and Subjectivity.* New York: Columbia University.

Deleuze, Gilles, and Felix Guattari. 1983. *Anti-Oedipus: Capitalism and Schizophrenia.* Minneapolis: University of Minnesota.

Deleuze, Gilles, and Claire Parnet. 1987. *Dialogues.* New York: Columbia University.

Dewey, John. 1934. *Art as Experience.* New York: Capricorn.

Dunn, Robert. 1991. "Postmodernism: Populism, Mass Culture and the Avant-Garde." *Theory, Culture and Society* 8:111–135.

Fiske, John. 1986a. "Television: Polysemy and Popularity." *Critical Studies in Mass Communication* 3(4): 391–408.

————. 1986b. "British Cultural Studies and Television," in Richard Allen, ed., *Channels of Discourse: Television and Contemporary Criticism.* Chapel Hill: University of North Carolina.

————. 1987. *Television Culture.* London: Methuen.

Fiske, John, and John Hartley. 1978. *Reading Television.* New York: Methuen.

Gerbner, George, Larry Gross, Michael Morgan, and Nancy Signoreilli. 1986. "Living with Television: The Dynamics of the Cultivation Process," in Jennings Bryant and Dolf Zillman, eds., *Perspectives on Media Effects.* Hillsdale, N.J.: Lawrence Erlbaum.

Gerbner, George, Larry Gross, Nancy Signoreilli, Michael Morgan, and Marilyn Jackson-Beeck. 1979. "The Demonstration of Power: Violence Profile No. 10." *Journal of Communications* 29(3): 177–196.

Gitlin, Todd. 1978. "Media Sociology: The Dominant Paradigm." *Theory and Society* 6(2): 205–254.

————. 1979. "Prime-Time Ideology: The Hegemonic Process in Television Entertainment." *Social Problems* 26(3): 251–256.

————. 1983. *Inside Prime Time.* New York: Pantheon.

————, ed. 1986. *Watching Television.* New York: Pantheon.

Grossberg, Lawrence. 1987. "The In-Difference of Television." *Screen* 28:28–45.

————. 1988. "It's a Sin: Postmodernity, Popular Empowerment and Hegemonic Popular." Paper presented at Rice University Conference on the Sociology of Television, Houston, Tex.

Grossberg, Lawrence, Cary Nelson, and Paula Treichler, eds. 1992. *Cultural Studies.* New York: Routledge.

Hall, Stuart. 1975. "Television as a Medium and Its Relation to Culture." Stenciled Occasional Paper, Centre for Contemporary Cultural Studies, Birmingham, England.

————. 1980. "Cultural Studies: Two Paradigms." *Media, Culture, and Society* 2:57–72.

Hall, Stuart, Dorothy Hobson, Andrew Lowe, and Paul Willis, eds. 1980. *Culture, Media, Language.* London: Hutchinson.

Hall, Stuart, and Tony Jefferson, eds. 1976. *Resistance Through Rituals: Youth Subcultures in Post-War Britain.* London: Hutchinson.

Hall, Stuart, Ian Connell, and Lydia Curti, eds. 1976. "The Unity of Current Affairs Television." *Working Papers in Cultural Studies* 9.

Harvey, David. 1989. *The Condition of Postmodernity.* Oxford: Basil Blackwell.

Hebdige, Dick. 1985. *Subculture: The Meaning of Style.* London: Routledge.

Hobson, Dorothy. 1982. *"Crossroads": The Drama of a Soap Opera.* London: Methuen.

Hoggart, Richard. 1966. *The Uses of Literacy.* Boston: Beacon.

Horkheimer, Max, and Theodor Adorno. 1969. *Dialectic of Enlightenment.* New York: Seabury.

Jameson, Fredric. 1983. "Postmodernism and Consumer Society," in Hal Foster, ed., *The Anti-Aesthetic: Essays on Postmodern Culture.* Port Townsend, Wash.: Bay Press.

———. 1991. *Postmodernism, or, The Cultural Logic of Late Capitalism.* Durham, N.C.: Duke University.

Johnson, Richard. 1986. "What Is Cultural Studies Anyway?" *Social Text* 16:38–80.

Katz, Elihu, and David Foukes. 1962. "On the Use of Mass Media for Escape: Clarification of a Concept." *Public Opinion Quarterly* 26:377–388.

Katz, Elihu, Jay Blumler, and Michael Gurevitch. 1973. "Uses and Gratifications Research." *Public Opinion Quarterly* 37:509–523.

Katz, Elihu, Michael Gurevitch, and H. Haas. 1973. "On the Uses of Mass Media for Important Things." *American Sociological Review* 38:164–181.

Langer, Ellen, A. Blank, and B. Chanowitz. 1978. "The Mindlessness of Ostensibly Thoughtful Action: The Role of 'Placebic' Information in Interpersonal Interaction." *Journal of Personality and Social Psychology* 36(6): 635–642.

Langer, Suzanne. 1957. *Philosophy in a New Key.* Cambridge: Harvard University.

Lembo, Ron. 1989. *The Symbolic Uses of Television: Social Power and the Culture of Reception.* Unpublished doctoral dissertation. Department of Sociology, University of California, Berkeley.

Lembo, Ron, and Ken Tucker. 1990. "Culture, Television, and Opposition: Rethinking Cultural Studies." *Critical Studies in Mass Communication* 7:97–116.

Lull, James. 1980. "Family Communication Patterns and the Social Uses of Television." *Human Communications Research* 7(3): 319–334.

———. 1990. *Inside Family Viewing: Ethnographic Research on Television's Audiences.* New York: Routledge.

Mead, G. H. 1932. *The Philosophy of the Present.* Chicago: University of Chicago.

———. 1934. *Mind, Self and Society.* Chicago: University of Chicago.

———. 1938. *The Philosophy of the Act.* Chicago: University of Chicago.

Morley, David. 1980. *The Nationwide Audience.* London: British Film Institute.

———. 1986. *Family Television and Domestic Leisure.* London: Comedia.

Press, Andrea. 1992. *Women Watching Television.* Philadelphia: University of Pennsylvania.

Radway, Janice. 1984. *Reading the Romance.* Chapel Hill: University of North Carolina.

Streeter, Thomas. 1984. "An Alternative Approach to Television Research: Developments in British Cultural Studies at Birmingham," in Donald Rowland and Bruce Watkins, eds., *Interpreting Television: Current Research Perspectives.* Beverly Hills, Calif.: Sage.

Swanson, Guy E. 1965. "On Explanations of Social Interaction." *Sociometry* 28(2): 101–123.

———. 1970. "Toward Corporate Action: A Reconstruction of Elementary Collective Processes," in Tamotsu Shibutani, ed., *Human Nature and Collective Behavior*. Englewood Cliffs, N.J.: Prentice-Hall.

Williams, Raymond. 1974. *Television, Technology, and Cultural Form*. London: Fontana.

———. 1982. *The Sociology of Culture*. New York: Schocken.

———. 1983. *Culture and Society*. New York: Columbia University.

Willis, Paul. 1977. *Learning to Labor*. London: Saxon House.

———. 1978. *Profane Culture*. London: Routledge, Kegan Paul.

Winnecott, D. W. 1965. *The Maturation Processes and the Facilitating Environment*. Madison, Wis.: International Universities Press.

———. 1971. *Playing and Reality*. New York: Tavistock.

THREE

Women Like Us: Working-Class Women Respond to Television Representations of Abortion

ANDREA PRESS AND ELIZABETH COLE

In this study, our goal is to articulate discourses of gender and class used by groups of working-class women in the contemporary United States. First, in studying discourses of gender and class characterizing dominant media representations of the abortion issue, we attempt to establish the cultural background against which women's ideas about this issue in particular and gender and class more generally are conceived and expressed. Second, by examining variations and nuances within the discourse of particular groups of women and differences among groups, we seek to illustrate the complexity and fluidity of women's discourses and to emphasize both their resonance with and resistance to mass media discourse. The ultimate goal of the work is to use the example of abortion to promote a rethinking of the notion of media hegemony and, more specifically, of the relation of women to social class and gender identities and political discourse in the contemporary United States.

Theoretical Context

Recent studies of the mass media audience, influenced by postmodernist critiques of the concept of the subject and by developments in feminist theory and research, have exposed the communication field's traditional attempts to construct

Special thanks to Renee Anspach, Linda Blum, Margaret Somers, and especially to Bruce A. Williams for comments on earlier versions of the chapter.

scientific studies of the popular cultural audience (Willis 1978; McRobbie 1978, 1981, 1984; Morley 1980; Hobson 1982; Radway 1984; Long 1986, 1987; Lull 1987; Seiter et al. 1989; Seiter 1990; Liebes and Katz 1990; Press 1991). Critiques have identified such studies as yet another academic and political effort to subject the populations studied to the hegemonic structuring already taking place in their very constitution as media audiences. In contrast, newer studies have emphasized "resistances" to power occurring at individual and small-group levels.

Widespread criticism of traditional audience studies has altered the research techniques and theoretical orientations that predominate in the field. For example, many recent studies tend to feature qualitative rather than quantitative methodological approaches. Some have embraced critical historical methods (May 1980; Rosenzweig 1983; Peiss 1986; Gabler 1988) to ask new questions about the ways historically specific audiences have created and used popular cultural forms to structure and restructure their own identities as critical subjects.

Others, interested in more current practices, have turned to ethnographic methodologies (Bacon-Smith 1992; Brown 1991a, 1991b; Press 1991; Radway 1984, 1988). Ethnographic researchers face the paradox of studying the subject in an age of postmodernist insights that challenge the existence of unified, reflective subjects in any traditional sense, substituting instead a more diffuse (but less easily researchable) notion of constructed subjectivity (Baudrillard 1988; Radway 1988; Scott 1988; Lyotard 1984).[1] Yet unlike the abstract theorizing that marks postmodernist texts, ethnography requires a level of faith in the possibility of creative activity at the level of the subject and in the potential of ethnographers to come to understand their subjects, which is often difficult to maintain in the face of theoretical challenges to our customary notions of the subject. This paradox has led to an unfortunate and growing split in the field between those most deeply affected by the postmodernist critique and those more interested in practicing the new research techniques spawned in its wake.

This seeming contradiction between theory and method has particularly affected scholars using ethnographic techniques to study the popular cultural audience. Most centrally, the question of the way mass media audiences constitute and reconstitute themselves as subjects who at times resist cultural hegemonies and at others accommodate them has preoccupied researchers in this field, continually posing challenges to traditional notions of the subject (Radway 1988; Grossberg 1988, 1989; Fiske 1989a, 1989b, 1990). Increasingly, in these studies, scholars eschew notions of a unified subject, thereby accommodating the postmodernist critique. As a result, newer studies contrast sharply in form and theoretical orientation with slightly older studies in the field (e.g., Morley 1980; Hobson 1982; Radway 1984). In fact, it has proved difficult to alter the actual working notion of subjectivity that informs most current work, particularly if one is to maintain the political thrust inspiring most cultural studies of the audience. Those in the vanguard have produced theoretical critiques of earlier works, theoretical tracts, and research proposals for ethnographic work based on these new ideas, but little actual audience research has itself been produced based on these critiques. Feminist scholars have been particularly affected by this paradox, as ethnographic methodologies have been attractive to feminist researchers looking specifically at the female audience (McRobbie 1978, 1981, 1984; Hobson 1982; Radway 1984; Press 1991).[2]

The new direction in feminist cultural studies is toward more historically and geographically specific studies of particular groups of women. The pitfalls of essentialism are effectively avoided as studies become increasingly specific in scope.[3] The theoretical disadvantage of such studies from the perspective of more traditional feminist aims is the perhaps unavoidable fact that it is impossible to generalize about "the female audience" or the popular cultural subject at all. Researchers now seek to examine different groups of women for their increasingly differentiated political dialogue; they construe the media as similarly political and multivocal. Although the terms of postmodernist theorizing have been useful in pointing out the fluid, shifting nature of group identities, this approach often seems to depoliticize such studies by emphasizing only the fluidity of boundaries rather than the actual positions they represent and the actors who constitute them. Most feminist research, inspired by political concerns and in search of political actors, stops short of totalizing deconstructions of the subject and retains an affinity for ethnography for these reasons. It is in this tradition that we locate the study discussed in the remainder of this chapter.

Abortion, Television, and Social Class

In this study, we try to incorporate some of the insights of the postmodernist critique of the subject in specifying the way the political perspective and identity of two groups of working-class women resonate with and resist the dominant political discourses and the construction of a particular political subject they confront in the mass media. To accomplish this, we focus on the moral, intellectual, personal, and political issue of abortion.

Current mass media organs often discuss the issue of abortion. In addition, most women have at least thought about the issue of abortion in relation to their own experience or to that of family and friends. One of the few political issues almost universally experienced at both the private (or personal) and the public (or political) level, abortion is especially useful for examining how specific groups of women constitute themselves as political and intellectual actors in the contemporary United States.

The relationship between our cultural thinking about abortion and social class issues has long been a theme in feminist defenses of the pro-choice position (Ginsburg 1989, Luker 1984)[4] but has never explicitly entered more popularly accessible discussions of abortion from either the pro-choice or pro-life sides of the abortion debate. Others have analyzed in great depth the conventions marking abortion rhetoric in our culture's literature and mass media (Condit 1990). Nevertheless, the social class issues that implicitly riddle the representations of abortion in mass media have been virtually ignored, as has the potential impact this feature may have on both pro-life and pro-choice constituencies. On prime-time television, for example, the medium we examine here, images of economically needy women seeking abortions predominate over images of middle-class women in similar circumstances, despite the fact that large numbers of middle-class women seek abortions as well (Condit 1990; Petchesky 1990; Luker 1984). The abortion-seeking subject on television is a working-class, female subject, articulated by a series of signifiers typical of television's portrayal of working-class women.

Television representations are produced at every level—writers, producers, actors, directors—by the middle class. In fact, television representations of the experience and identity of working-class women in our culture represent a middle-class cosmology or perspective on working-class experience. These representations may or may not correspond to the representations and interpretations working-class women themselves might create were they given the opportunities for expression they currently lack in our culture. On a more obvious level, representations of the working class on television falsely unify experiences differentiated in fact by ethnic, geographical, religious, and employment-related factors.

In this chapter, we examine working-class women's responses to the working-class subjects characterized in two abortion scenarios aired on prime-time television. The first is an episode of the police drama "Cagney and Lacey," the second a fictionalized account of the real-life Norma McCorvey (alias Jane Roe in real life, Ellen Russell in the fictionalized version) broadcast in the made-for-television movie *Roe vs. Wade*. In particular, we compare responses to these programs made by several groups of pro-choice[5] working-class women. These groups, composed of nonactivist women, were chosen specifically to fill the gap in the feminist literature about abortion with information about "ordinary" women's views.

Our findings build on conclusions made in Press's recent book (1991). In research for that work, Press found that working-class women accept television's depiction of middle-class life as normal and as normative, in that many view achieving a middle-class lifestyle as a goal of their own lives. In contrast to middle-class women, working-class women value what they define to be "realism" in television. But often they define realism as images of middle-class life rather than middle-class constructions of their own lives and experience. When television does portray the working class, women become extremely critical of its images, which allegedly lack the realism they seek. In this chapter, we seek to extend Press's research by drawing more finely the distinctions and trends that occur within working-class women's discourse, including about television.

At one level, our study seeks to afford working-class women the opportunity to respond to and criticize middle-class representations of their own experience. At another, broader level, we seek to explicate pro-choice working-class women's implicit articulation of a more general critique of the pro-choice subject as essentially a middle-class subject, the outgrowth of a discourse rooted in middle-class representations of working-class experience in our culture. Normally the pro-choice position is defined simply as one of a bipolar set of opinions characterizing the abortion debate. In general, this view excludes mention of the different types of subject positions possible under the rubric of "pro-choice."

Abortion on Prime Time

Over the last two decades, television entertainment's representation of abortion decisions has coalesced around a norm of what one scholar terms "generally acceptable abortions" (Condit 1990). What this means, in effect, is that on television, middle-class or upper-class women can legitimately abort only in cases of rape or incest, to save the life of the mother, or if genetic testing reveals a severely deformed fetus. Aborting to further a woman's career or to maintain a middle-class level of comfort for the family is not morally condoned in these representations. Single middle-class women may seek abortions, but in general these are portrayed as the selfish solution to a problem having other possible resolutions. Although middle-class women may be seen to agonize over abortions contemplated for these reasons, in television treatments they are customarily spared the consequences of such decisions by acts of nature (sudden miscarriage or the realization of false pregnancy) relieving the necessity for choices the dominant media find unacceptable. Usually, it is poor or working-class women only who actually obtain abortions in the end.

These norms did not always characterize television representations of abortion. They evolved, in part, in response to public protest over earlier, more liberal representations. For example, in two episodes of "Maude" broadcast on CBS in 1972, the lead character opted for an abortion primarily because she felt too old to raise another child. The network was flooded with angry calls and letters from viewers objecting to this rationale for abortion (Montgomery 1989). Future network programming responded to this history by aiming toward explicitly balanced representations of the issue. Ultimately this approach meant that women's ability to choose abortion freely would no longer be morally sanctioned or could be sanctioned only under very specific circumstances, such as in the case of women who face mitigating economic circumstances. Only women who are too poor to care properly for a child or are for whatever reason economically unstable are permitted on prime-time television to have morally approvable abortions. Even for these women, evidence of the responsibility of their decisions must be made abundantly clear. Either they must acknowledge the irresponsibility of their actions, or they must demonstrate that obtaining an abortion will contribute to their efforts to raise themselves out of their economically unstable situation into the boundaries of the middle class.

Television depictions of the abortion issue articulate our society's general ambivalence toward the issue. By depicting abortions only in cases of apparently extreme hardship, television attempts to offer a balanced representation. In this way, the medium captures the issue as it is contested and resolves it in a way that a majority finds palatable or at least reasonably inoffensive.

We have chosen two separate abortion stories that fall under this prime-time umbrella of acceptable representations of the issue. One, an episode of "Cagney and Lacey" originally broadcast in 1985, offers an immigrant Hispanic heroine who seeks an abortion to allow her to finish school and better her family circumstances. The other, a made-for-television movie broadcast in 1990 entitled *Roe vs. Wade,* details the struggles of the real-life woman Norma McCorvey who unsuccessfully sought an abortion in Texas in 1970 and ultimately challenged the legality of prohibitive abortion laws in the landmark case decided by the U.S. Supreme Court in 1972.

The "Cagney and Lacey" episode used in this study embodies television's characteristic pro-choice slant (although pro-life elements are present for balance) and pictures a prototypically acceptable abortion scenario. The main plot involves police sergeant Christine Cagney and her partner police officer Mary Beth Lacey (who is five months pregnant in the episode) being called upon to protect a Latina (and by implication, Catholic) woman, Mrs. Herrera, who is intimidated by angry antiabortionists while attempting to enter an abortion clinic. Soon after, someone bombs the clinic, inadvertently killing a transient old man. Cagney and Lacey are assigned to uncover the bomber and ultimately discover that a somewhat crazed member of the picketing right-to-life group is responsible.

Mrs. Herrera is depicted as poor (her husband is on disability). While she is conflicted about the abortion, Mrs. Herrera is convinced that her dreams of becoming a well-paid court stenographer will be unattainable should she give birth to a child now. She mentions in particular her fear of going on welfare and her belief that she will be forced to drop out of school if she has the child. Mrs. Herrera's plight makes one of television's strongest arguments in favor of abortion: that the lives of poor women will be ruined beyond repair by the burden of an unwanted child. Another strong argument in favor of abortion is made when Lacey, talking to her husband in bed, tells of her frightening experience as a teenager seeking an illegal abortion, which led her to fly to Puerto Rico to obtain one legally, an expense that, as a self-supporting student at the time, she could ill afford. Lacey also mentions in an argument with Cagney the plight of rape and incest victims. The abortion clinic doctor bemoans the clinic's bombing by referring to twelve-year-olds who have sought abortions there because they had nowhere else to turn.[6] But the logic that abortion is most legitimate and necessary in the case of poor women predominates on the show.

In their desire to avoid inflaming activists on either side as the "Maude" episodes had done years earlier (Montgomery 1989), producers of this "Cagney and Lacey" episode consciously sought to achieve a balanced presentation of the abortion issue. Several characters clearly articulate different sorts of pro-life as well as pro-choice arguments (Condit 1990). Balance is also attempted through the presence of an articulate pro-life spokesperson, Mrs. Crenshaw, a white middle-class woman who is head of the pro-life organization sponsoring the demonstration. We also hear Cagney's father, a retired Irish-Catholic police officer who believes abortion is murder.

Despite the overt attempts at balance, the show represents abortion as an acceptable choice but only after careful consideration and under specific conditions, which are present in the case of Mrs. Herrera. The show favors women's right to safe, legal abortions more so than it does arguments in support of the pro-life perspective. This view is supported by Condit (1990) and most of the groups, both pro-choice and pro-life, whose members viewed the tape in our study. Yet Mrs. Herrera's abortion is framed in a particular way. She is not an independent, well-employed, middle-class woman as is the Barnard-educated Cagney. Although arguments in favor of the latter's right to abortion are made on the show, the actual abortion subplot it contains concerns a working-class woman rather than the middle-class Cagney, and even her desire for an abortion is portrayed as morally ambiguous. While in the end it appears that Mrs. Herrera has chosen abortion, the act is left unseen; her ambivalence and fears are highlighted, perhaps to maintain viewer sympathy with her. Choice is legitimated but only just: In extreme or seemingly extreme circumstances, a woman may legitimately opt for abortion, provided it is a last resort for one who feels herself emotionally and— possibly most significant—*financially* backed against the wall.

The television movie *Roe vs. Wade* presents a working-class heroine who, unlike the respectable Mrs. Herrera, doesn't play by the rules. Ellen Russell lives a defiantly anti–middle-class lifestyle and takes no recognizable steps toward achieving middle-class status. Unstable, with little family support, no good options for employment, and no history or anticipation of a stable relationship with a man, Ellen is a relentlessly nonconformist figure with few if any prospects for attaining middle-class status. Hard-drinking and rough-talking, Ellen defies conventional family values in telling us "I'm a loner; I don't mess with nobody and I don't want nobody messing with me." Her lack of prospects for conventional family life are fully matched by the lack of promise in her employment history. Traveling with a carnival when we meet her, Ellen quits the job upon learning that she is pregnant for reasons that are not altogether clear to us. She unsuccessfully searches for another job all during her pregnancy; her failure to find anything at all mandates the necessity of giving away her child, although Ellen makes it clear throughout her pregnancy that she feels herself financially incapable of supporting a child in any case.

Ellen's earlier first pregnancy had led her to marry a man who beat her for alleged unfaithfulness when he learned she was pregnant. The marriage ended abruptly after the abuse. Ellen's extremely critical mother forced her to sign away daughter Cheryl's care in the best interests of the child. Ellen's mother became guardian of Cheryl, Ellen moved away, and now, living a transient life, Ellen rarely sees her daughter. Ellen found the experience of giving up her child extremely painful. She thought constantly of Cheryl and felt she could not live through the experience of giving away another child. Yet she could not see her way clear to keeping her second child either, in part because of her guilt at giving up Cheryl ("If I could afford it, wouldn't I be raising Cheryl?"). Ellen's mother makes it clear that she is unwilling to raise a second child for her, thus eliminating that option as an end to the pregnancy.

Ellen's only way out of her dilemma, as she sees it, is to have an abortion. Yet in 1970 abortion is illegal in Texas. She could obtain one legally in New York or California but lacks the money to travel to either state. She tries to obtain an illegal back-alley abortion but is frightened away by the conditions of the operating room. She asks a doctor to help her obtain an abortion but he refuses ("I'm not going to break the law"). He will only refer her to a lawyer to help arrange an adoption. This lawyer also refuses her request to refer her to a doctor willing to perform the abortion. Instead, he introduces her to two attorneys interested in challenging Texas laws prohibiting the performing of abortion. Ellen cooperates with the attorneys, telling them "You ladies are my last hope." She believes or at least hopes that their suit will be settled in time for her to obtain an abortion. Although they are ultimately successful—and in 1972 antiabortion statutes are overturned nationwide—the final decision comes too late for Ellen. In the end, she goes through with her pregnancy and gives the baby up for adoption. We see a heartbreaking scene in the delivery room, where the nurses will not allow her even once to hold or look at her child. Following the experience, Ellen becomes so depressed that she attempts suicide. She is unsuccessful, however, and the movie ends with her reading in the newspapers that her case has succeeded when brought to the Supreme Court. Despite her momentary anger toward the lawyers for not making her abortion possible, in the end Ellen is grateful to have participated in so momentous a lawsuit.

Unlike Mrs. Herrera, Ellen does not play by the rules of middle-class society. Even if Texas laws could have been changed in time for her to obtain it, her abortion would not have helped her enter into the middle class or even become a more stable member of the working class. It would merely have spared her the pain of giving up yet another child, a pain already felt very keenly every time Ellen's thoughts turned to her daughter Cheryl. We are told nothing of her plans to further her education or obtain job skills or even of her resolve to attain steady employment. Yet Ellen is portrayed in a heroic light, a pioneer of the feminist fight against restrictive abortion laws. Her story is meant to be uplifting. Sympathetically drawn, Ellen remains spunky despite the many obstacles she faces in her life, restrictive abortion laws among them. She and other women like her, the movie implies, are victimized by these laws. Ellen's story is meant to offer some justification for the feminist struggle to change them and for the continuing fight to uphold the *Roe v. Wade* decision.[7]

Methodology

To date we have conducted focus-group interviews with twenty-nine groups of two to five women, usually in the home of one of the respondents; the total number of respondents to date is eighty-eight.[8] Of these, four working-class pro-choice groups, four working-class pro-life groups, and two middle-class groups from each perspective viewed *Roe vs. Wade;* four working-class pro-choice groups, two working-class pro-life groups, four middle-class pro-choice groups, and two middle-class pro-life groups viewed "Cagney and Lacey."[9] Interviews began with a series of questions about the respondents' activities as a group, their typical pattern of discussion about moral issues, and their television viewing habits. Later we asked them to describe and discuss their experiences with either their own decisions about unwanted pregnancies or those of friends or relatives. They were encouraged to talk about the considerations that women they know made in order to reach their reproductive decisions and to give us their thoughts as well on the topic. The respondents then viewed either a thirty-minute version of the "Cagney and Lacey" abortion episode from which subplots and commercials had been edited or the first thirty-five minutes of the *Roe vs. Wade* television movie (using identical wording, we told each group how the story ended following this segment). After viewing the tape, the women were asked specific questions about their reactions to the positions expressed by the characters in the show. Prior to each interview, respondents completed a questionnaire concerning basic demographic information, media-use habits, and general opinions about abortion. The sessions generally lasted from two and a half to three and a half hours. All group interviews were taped and later transcribed and coded.

Pro-Choice Working-Class Responses

Generally, working-class women reject television images of women making abortion decisions, permeated as they are with television's particular focus on the experiences and problems of working-class women seeking abortions. Although responses from each of the groups we explore in the study excerpted here vary, all resist the terms prime-time television uses to define the abortion issue. Pro-life women, for example, are distanced from television in a very general way. Their vision of the world includes utopian hopes for the ability of families and communities to come together and support women, particularly women in need. Because the terms of this vision are essentially absent from television, these women by definition feel excluded by its images, as they are in so many ways excluded from mainstream society in the United States.

Working-class pro-choice women are also alienated from television representations of abortion but in a more complicated way given that the pro-choice perspective does predominate on the medium. Both the middle-class–identified and the working-class–identified pro-choice working-class groups object to the victimization of working-class women in television portrayals; neither group accepts that these women are powerless or even very disadvantaged. But middle-class–identified women feel the relatively powerless ought to pay for their faults, that they should not be free to depend on others or on the state to solve problems they themselves have created. Their support for the pro-choice perspective is qualified by this fear of granting irresponsible women too much freedom and support. In contrast, working-class–identified women focus their criticisms on the authorities and corrupt professionals whom they partially blame for their own difficulties. Their pro-choice position is based in part on objections to any policies that might further the authority of the state.

Working-class pro-choice groups are unified in their almost universal affection for and support of Mrs. Herrera, the lead character in the "Cagney and Lacey" episode. Mrs. Herrera, it seems, is a relatively uncontroversial heroine of a television abortion story. Pregnant within marriage, working hard in school, worried about her husband, and troubled over the morality of abortion, Mrs. Herrera faces her abortion decision in a way that makes her as acceptable to these women as she is to middle-class pro-choice women and even to some pro-life women. Working-class pro-choice women particularly find it easy to identify with Mrs. Herrera's struggle to be upwardly mobile. Yes, they agree, it is difficult to finish school while caring for a child and receiving welfare. One woman even recalls her social worker's advice to delay schooling until her children are of school age:

> **Respondent 1**: Well, in her situation I could see why she'd want to do it. She'd be
>   better off doing it than to have the baby and have to give up everything and
>   then, you know, not be able to take care of her kids in the future. It's really, really
>   hard to go to school when you have kids and people try to make it look like
>   there's a chance and there isn't. There's almost this much chance. … One in a
>   million people make it. I'm trying right now to go to beauty school and get help
>   from the state, and the lady's just telling me, "Don't even try it." The lady from
>   the welfare office, she's saying, "You won't be able to afford to pay the babysitter,
>   you won't be able to do this." I don't want to give you such a negative aspect, but
>   they told me not to do it.

Other working-class pro-choice women mention the fact that the disabled Mr. Herrera might need care as well, worrying that Mrs. Herrera will be unable to meet the needs of her husband as well as her child. They see her desire for an abortion as understandable in this light. In all, reactions to Mrs. Herrera are relatively untroubled and supportive. Women in these groups find that her situation presents a strong argument justifying legalized abortion.

In contrast, Ellen Russell's situation provokes a more troubled reaction. Ellen is received by pro-choice working-class women on a continuum ranging from lukewarm approval to extreme disapproval. While women do not tend to condemn

Ellen's right to abortion, they disapprove more generally of her lifestyle and the circumstances that led to this unwanted pregnancy in particular, as in these comments:

> **Respondent 3:** She was not the type to raise a child, definitely. No, her lifestyle was not that. ... I don't think it would be conducive to raising a child. Of course there are a lot of children who live with carnivals and things of that nature who are truly remarkable people. Her own personal lifestyle, however, leaves something to be desired there. She's rather loose there.

> **Respondent 4:** She needs to get a little more responsible with where she's sleeping around or what she's doing while she's there though. A little more responsible sex.

Some women object explicitly to the fact that Ellen's case was used to illustrate abortion. Why not invoke the image of middle-class women in abortion clinics?

> **Respondent 4:** But that's not true [that it's only women like Ellen who have abortions]. Doctors' wives can have one. Attorneys' wives, you know. You can be a well-to-do woman and still want an abortion. You don't have to be a street person, and they made it look like only the bad people. ... Well, this kind of made me feel like that because she was from a rough part of town or she acted rough and tough and she liked to hang out in bars and all this. ... That's not reality. In reality any woman could need an abortion whether she's on the streets, in a fifty-thousand- or four-hundred-thousand-dollar home.

We suspected that women as audiences would receive and construct television images according to the way they construe their identities and their relationship to dominant groups. Thus we expected women's responses to these two quite distinctive heroines to vary according to women's sense of their own identity in relationship to other groups in the broader society. In fact, these expectations were largely confirmed in our results. In contrast to the less controversial Mrs. Herrera, who aspires to middle-class status, Ellen Russell is depicted as a working-class woman who appears to have no real prospects of leaving her class, nor does she actively seek them. Among pro-choice working-class groups, there are two different sets of responses to her character that emphasize the multivocality of working-class discourse and identity in our culture. These two discourses mark deep divisions within working-class women's experience and in their attitudes toward middle-class life and societal authority. The first group we term "middle-class–identified"; these women embrace middle-class values and sharply criticize working-class women they see on television. The other group we term "working-class–identified"; these women identify themselves as outsiders vis-à-vis more mainstream society and are more apt to sympathize with the problems attributed to working-class women and their lives on television.[10] Women's evaluations of Ellen vary in relation to how working-class–identified versus middle-class–identified women are themselves. Initial pretelevision interviews indicate that women vary widely along this dimension. We will consider the responses to the character of Ellen in particular and to *Roe vs. Wade* in general made by members of one prototypical group chosen to represent each category.

Working-Class–Identified Women

While some working-class women see themselves as no different from and/or aspiring toward the middle class, others construct a very different self-identity, one more working-class–identified. The latter is well encapsulated by the words of one woman who asked us what groups we were interviewing. Wanting to respond honestly but unwilling to use explicitly the terminology of social class, we rather euphemistically responded that we were sampling different occupational groups. Our subject responded "Oh, you mean high class, middle class, and no class, like us!" Another woman, from another working-class–identified pro-choice group, explained that we could feel free to use her first name (though as a matter of policy we do not), since "No one who was a professor would know who I was." This lack of concern for anonymity contrasts sharply with middle-class–identified women's attitudes; they were so concerned with anonymity that they took false names from the very beginning of the interview tape, a position uncommon among the women interviewed. The former quotation acknowledges that women of the working-class–identified group neither identify with nor necessarily aspire to membership in the middle class. The speaker emphasizes the assured sense of anonymity and invisibility women in this group experience based on the feeling of discontinuity from other social groups. In the discussion that follows, we choose the group from which the former quote originated as our prototype representing the working-class–identified category.

Working-class–identified women tend to be suspicious of middle-class authority in ways middle-class–identified women are not. Their speech is littered with references to their distrust of middle-class (and, by extension, societal) authority. For example, this group strongly criticizes Ellen's attorneys for "using" her to further their careers. On the show, the attorneys tell us they have not been entirely honest with Ellen, in that they never told her this was their first case. Indeed, after the first verdict, Ellen accuses them of misleading her into thinking the case would be decided in time for her to have an abortion (the show leaves the facts surrounding this issue somewhat ambiguous). However, in the show a balancing attempt is made to depict attorney Sarah Weddington's concern for Ellen in their conversations.

The group responds to this situation as follows:

AP: What did you think of how the women lawyers handled their contacts with her? The way they treated her?

Respondent 4: I don't think they were very fair and honest with her right up front. I think they misled her. I don't think she realized in the beginning how long it really would take.

Respondent 3: Well, they didn't tell her either [that it would take] two months.

Respondent 4: And then here you see her all of a sudden and she's got this big old belly. And I think they took this case on ... they believed in it and they believed in woman's choice, but I think they did it to set their career off. I think it was done selfishly on their part, because like they both said, "We're not telling her the truth—neither one of us has ever litigated."

AP: So you thought the women lawyers were sort of misleading her?

Respondent 3: I think so, I think they were just trying to further themselves. I don't think they really came down to the bottom line with her, and I don't think she was really smart enough to question them thoroughly enough on the situation.

Respondent 1: It was just any light of hope.

Respondent 2: They told her in May and it was March, she was just like ...

Respondent 4: She was in limbo, she didn't know what to do. She was just believing what they told her.

Respondent 3: Since there was nothing available at that point in time in Texas, that they would give her some alternatives. But they didn't even suggest anything. I think they did it to further their own careers, and they're probably rich wealthy lawyers now.

The group goes on to agree that the lawyers should have helped Ellen obtain a legal abortion in New York and mentions several other ways the attorneys might also have helped Ellen once they realized their case would not be resolved in time for her to obtain an abortion:

AP: Do you think they should have given her the money to go to New York to get the abortion?

Respondent 2: You know, that crossed my mind, that if they would have really cared, you know, they could have probably done that. They looked like they ...

Respondent 4: Had they have done that, wouldn't that have just thrown the case right out the window and they—wouldn't that have thrown the case right out the window? Wouldn't that have stopped all court procedures had they done something like that?

Respondent 1: How would they know?

Respondent 3: She was using a fictitious name anyway.

Respondent 4: Well, that's true, that's true.

Respondent 3: Why couldn't she have gone to some abortion clinic or Planned Parenthood or however they did it at that point in time in New York and used another fictitious name? Who's to say where the money came from? How would anybody know where the money came from? Unless one of the three said something.

Women in this group are much more effusive in detailing the possible ways her attorneys might have helped Ellen than are women in other pro-life and pro-choice groups, even though most agree that the attorneys used Ellen to further their own goals and careers. This is consistent with the group's generally critical attitude toward professionals and authorities of any kind.

In contrast to their critical attitude toward authority, working-class–identified women are less critical of Ellen herself than are any other working-class women interviewed. One woman, for example, praises Ellen's unwillingness to go on welfare, attributing it to her pride and independence. These women find Ellen's pride and stubbornness admirable.

Working-class–identified women are also more inclined than others to identify with Ellen, finding that her character and situation have parallels for them or others in their families or friend groups. One woman in the group, after viewing the show, retells the story of her niece she had mentioned in the pretelevision discussion, noting at several points her similarity to Ellen. Like Ellen, her niece as a teen had one child whom relatives had (almost entirely) raised; the niece became pregnant again soon after the birth. Our respondent had paid for her niece's abortion of the second pregnancy. The experiences of women in this group and their family connections lead them to accept the way *Roe vs. Wade* portrays Ellen's lack of resources. In contrast to pro-life women in particular, who as explained elsewhere (Press 1992) insist that Ellen has not fully tapped all family resources available to her, these women feel that at times such resources do not exist.

In sum, what marks the distinctive perspective of working-class–identified women is not necessarily their experiences but their interpretations of these experiences. They view themselves as not altogether unlike Ellen. Thus they reject what they perceive to be Ellen's powerlessness in favor of a more empowered embrace of her identity. They identify with Ellen and see many of her positive qualities.

Middle-Class–Identified Women

In contrast, working-class women who are middle-class–identified see themselves as essentially members of the middle class already. Unlike working-class–identified women, they take great pains to construct a picture of themselves as completely separate from the members of their class, who don't work responsibly, don't have drive and ambition, take drugs or drink heavily, are "drifters," and have sex irresponsibly. One woman characteristically differentiates herself from those "others" who would accept public assistance as follows:

> **Respondent 2:** Many of us may have been in a situation at one time or another where we've struggled, and we've made real hard attempts to avoid using those sources or may have been denied those sources for various reasons.

In the following discussion, we rely on the remarks of a group we've chosen to represent the prototype of the middle-class–identified pro-choice perspective.

In contrast with their working-class–identified counterparts, middle-class–identified women are relentlessly critical of Ellen's character. Many of Ellen's unconventional traits directly offend women in this group. For example, unlike women in the working-class–identified group, these women interpret Ellen's unwillingness to go on welfare as evidence of ignorant "Texican" attitudes about who is trash and who isn't.

Women in the middle-class–identified group fill in the narrative's unsaid elements, completing Ellen's character sketch with details that ultimately make her an even more striking object of disapproval. One often criticized but only sketchily drawn aspect of Ellen's situation, for example, is the circumstances under which she became pregnant. We are not told anything about the baby's father or her relationship with him. All Ellen tells us is that he is "not interested," presumably in helping her either to raise the child or to obtain an abortion.

One member of the middle-class–identified group, however, articulates in some detail her belief that Ellen probably sleeps around: "I don't sleep with a man three days after I meet him," she ventures, implying that Ellen does precisely this (although there is no evidence to this effect on the show except a similar unsupported accusation made by Ellen's mother). This woman and others in the group are quite willing to fill in the details of Ellen's character with a series of negative qualities not necessarily intended in the television portrayal:

> **Respondent 4**: She obviously did not want to be pregnant. Obviously. She didn't seem to be in a long-term relationship. It sounded like it was just some guy passing through town or one of the other carnies. … OK, I've known him for a month or two months or however long. Personally, I don't go to bed with somebody three days after I meet them, but that's just me [laughs]. It just seemed it wasn't that she was in this long-term involved, stable relationship. [It was] not even necessarily long term—it seemed like it was just like a one-night stand basically. Oops, I got pregnant. You've got to be a little more careful, you know.

> **Respondent 3**: She even said to her father and mother he was just a guy. That's too bad.

> **Respondent 2**: I think it seemed like she was constantly in an environment where drinking might be available. She might have been drunk at the time of the pregnancy, you don't know.

The women in the group jump off from their discussion by using their construction of Ellen's character to rationalize their plan to sterilize women who have had too many abortions, thus draining either government money or bleeding insurance companies dry. Such irresponsible behavior, they reason, should be stopped, particularly when their taxes or health care costs are affected by it or when it wastes doctors' valuable time:

> **Respondent 4**: Those are the people who line up frequently, using abortion as birth control. There's a whole lot easier, cheaper, less painful ways to have birth control than to keep getting abortions. We have people at work that [say things like] "I think I'm pregnant again, I don't think I can go through my fourth abortion." "You're twenty-two, what do you mean your fourth abortion?" "Well, I didn't

want to go to the drug store." "Well, then cross your legs and go home!" [Several jokes are made by group members here.]

AP: Do you think that people like that should also have access to abortions?

Respondent 4: I think they should have access to voluntary sterilization.

Respondent 3: Precisely.

Respondent 4: Have sex three times and you're out of here. ... No, I ... [laughter].

Respondent 3: There has to be some kind of control. We need a national computerized system here. Get an abortion in Boone, Kentucky, ... and then if they move to Ypsilanti, Michigan, to get another abortion—that's it, chick. Twice and you're out! I'm serious, OK? *We are the government* [emphasis added], we have a responsibility to stop all this endless waste. It's a waste of money, it's a waste of good professional time. Why should some doctor spend all the time aborting some woman? I know one who has had seven abortions! I'm ahead of you. Why should some doctor spend good medical time and taxpayers' money or anybody's money to keep aborting the same person over and over again?

These women recoil from a situation in which abortions are too free and easy to obtain, constructing a vision that would rely on centralized authorities to promote responsible behavior by limiting women's access to them. Members of this group show no hesitation in invoking societal authorities to discipline women they feel are too free and easy. In fact, they identify with these authorities explicitly in their speech, insisting that "We are the government."

Most strongly criticized by these women generally is Ellen's lack of self-reliance. Ellen is a woman "looking for a handout," the very type of person most likely to end up with a free ride from the welfare system—and probably the least deserving of it. They find Ellen's job search and her continual complaint that she cannot find work unconvincing: "She kept saying she kept trying to find a job, that there wasn't any work. Yet she could go out and have fun with her friends." Ellen gets no credit, as she did from the working-class–identified women, for her reluctance to go on public assistance (although somehow, given the group's attitude, it seems that she should). For this group, her other irresponsible qualities completely override this virtue.

Most telling of the group's particularly accepting attitude toward authority, and in sharp contrast to their working-class–identified counterparts, is the way middle-class–identified women characterize Ellen's relationship with the middle-class attorneys who take her case to the Supreme Court in an attempt to legalize abortion. Whereas working-class–identified women criticize the attorneys for using Ellen to get ahead, this group simply acknowledges this situation matter-of-factly. When asked if they thought her attorneys ought to have flown Ellen to New York to obtain a legal abortion, they chant an indignant "no" in a unison that rarely occurs in group interviews of this nature. They argue that Ellen did not "contract" in advance with her lawyers for this kind of help. Perhaps had she been shrewd enough to demand it in the beginning, she might deserve it. Rather than garnering their sympathy through her naïveté, Ellen in their view ought to pay for her lack of sophistication and strategy. Her attorneys owed her no help, nor did she deserve any. In fact, the group reacts with some disbelief that anyone would take this position; it seems to offend their most basic convictions in the importance of individual self-reliance. In contrast, working-class–identified women express compassion for Ellen's inability to look out for her own interests more successfully.

Overall, the middle-class–identified group's criticisms of Ellen help the members construct their own identities in opposition to hers. The women's tendency to separate themselves from Ellen's character and social group is emphasized by their reconstruction of the experiences of a child of one of their members, in marked contrast to the working-class–identified woman's tale of her niece described in the preceding section. In this case, a group member's daughter, Arlene, had become pregnant while still in high school, causing her to drop out of school and have an abortion. (All names attributed in the context of respondents in this study are pseudonyms.) Shortly thereafter, she became pregnant again and decided to keep the baby, although she remained unmarried. She later married the father briefly and was now divorced. She was currently working, caring for her daughter, and planning to attend school part-time in the future.

Members of the group collectively assume an unusual, almost reverent tone when discussing this girl's experience. The attitude is particularly remarkable when compared to the tone they later assume to discuss and evaluate Ellen's character, as in these passages:

> **Respondent 3**: Arlene is a very mature young lady, always has been. Her actions at that time may not have been considered mature, but her decisions were correct for her at that time.
>
> **Respondent 2**: She has an unusual confidence and responsibility. I think a lot of that comes from the support that she's received. It's an unusual circumstance in that she has a real friendship I think with her mom and with Pete [her stepfather].

Group members repeat several times "Arlene is an exceptionally mature individual" and variations thereof. No one criticizes Arlene's character, despite her actions. Ellen, on the other hand, disliked strongly by all group members, is criticized as morally loose and irresponsible for actions strikingly similar to those of Arlene.

While the group's regard for her mother's feelings certainly accounts in part for their reluctance to criticize Arlene, what comes across in their discussion is the feeling that the women strongly believe what they are saying. Our interpretation could of course be mistaken, but the women really seem to like Arlene and to admire her strength in surviving and making the best of difficult circumstances. We conclude that the divergence in these women's feelings toward Arlene and Ellen may be accounted for by their desire to separate themselves from media images of "those immoral" working-class people like Ellen.

This interpretation is strengthened by the group's view of welfare abusers. The women strongly disapprove of the "lazy, irresponsible" people who receive government assistance—who use food stamps to buy "lobster dinners" for all their friends. The system is flawed, people have no incentive to work, and ultimately the women would like to see it wiped out altogether. These abstractly expressed opinions on the subject, however, contrast sharply with the women's descriptions of the actual people on welfare that they meet at work. One woman, for example, takes job applications at her place of employment (a large discount supermarket-hardware establishment). She sympathetically describes applicants coming to her who "should have been paid yesterday," single fathers whose children haven't eaten in days, and others in extreme need of aid. She and the group strongly agree that these people are in need of assistance. When discussing them, the women criticize the welfare system for not being generous enough, for not meeting the needs of such people quickly enough. The woman in charge of hiring such applicants goes on to describe the decisions she must make regarding their work abilities. Often such people "need a chance," as she puts it; they could be efficient workers despite their lack of experience, high school degrees, or other paper qualifications. These attitudes toward the actual people she encounters in the course of her job, many of whom end up as her co-workers, contradict the way she and her friends characterize the scheming masses on welfare—and also the way they seem to place Ellen in this category despite her insistence on remaining off welfare. Again, such contrasts might be explained by the women's desire to separate themselves and those they work with from the bulk of working-class and poor people "out there," thereby strengthening their construction of and identification with a middle-class–identified subject position. Alternately, the women may actually be interested in separating themselves from media representations of the working class that are imposed from above and manufactured by the middle class. In sum, in this instance working-class women in our middle-class–identified group put aside their personal experience in favor of expressing more abstract commitments to principles often untouched by their own specific experience. Mass media are often evaluated similarly, with reference to their commitment to principle rather than their own experience with reality. When experience and principle conflict, the conflict is often decided in favor of the latter rather than the former.

Conclusion

Working-class pro-choice women's responses to the television characters of Mrs. Herrera and Ellen Russell may be divided into two main prototypes. In contrast to their essentially sympathetic response to Mrs. Herrera, working-class women's responses to Ellen question rather than assume the perspective of Ellen's middle-class creators who sympathize with her while creating a narrative that disempowers her almost entirely. What unifies both sets of pro-choice working-class women's responses is that each group resists this disempowering presentation of Ellen's self, objecting to its fundamental terms and logic. To working-class pro-choice women in both groups, Ellen can take charge—or at least can assume more control—of her life more so than she is pictured as capable of doing. One of the reasons Mrs. Herrera fares so well in comparison with Ellen is precisely because she is interpreted as in control of her destiny, while Ellen is not. Neither group of women is willing to relinquish this vision of control. Perhaps in the end, they identify too strongly with television's working-class women and refuse to concede a lack of control in their own lives, as they do in Ellen's.

Class and group differences in these responses correspond to the different languages invoked in defense of the pro-choice position by members of these two groups. Preliminary data indicate that middle-class pro-choice women embrace a uniformly liberal language to justify their support of an individual's right to make her own private decisions (Press 1992). This language is qualified, however, in the case of pro-choice working-class women, as their responses to its mass media incarnations illustrate. Media afford them the opportunity to respond to middle-class perspectives on working-class life and to resist them by putting forth their own interpretations and evaluations of such experiences. In this way an alternative working-class identity is constructed—their own.

Middle-class–identified working-class women resist the sympathetic middle-class constructions of their own identity that pepper the mass media. Rather than acknowledge the limitations of class, these women steadfastly deny the existence of any limits at all. They resist the liberal, therapeutic[11] worldview that acknowledges with sympathy the personal problems and handicaps faced by many and that Ellen's portrayal automatically calls up in our study's middle-class respondents. Instead, they embrace more conservative threads in our culture. They oppose the welfare state, insisting that we are all equal and that government ought to be limited, allowing us to obtain what we deserve by dint of our own hard efforts and perseverance. This belief in a low profile for government also leads this group to embrace generally pro-choice tenets concerning abortion. Yet the group's adherence to the pro-choice perspective is a qualified one. The right to abortion ought not to justify an irresponsible freedom for women. Women giving evidence of exercising their freedom irresponsibly ought to have that freedom curtailed. In addition to the rhetoric of rights, then, the group members invoke notions of the good as well in their moralistic interpretation of Ellen and in their prescriptions concerning the ways in which immoral behavior ought to be curtailed. This is the "communitarian" strain in their thought (Sandel 1984). Communitarianism contrasts community-based notions of what is "good" to the Kantian liberal rhetoric of "rights" most often used to support the pro-choice position in our public political discourse. A qualified, communitarian pro-choice perspective better describes the group's position than does our more customary, undifferentiated use of the pro-choice label to construct a pro-choice political subject. The women envision a hierarchical community in which the smarter and more able must care, however unwillingly, for those less intelligent and responsible. In this view, the latter ought to pay for their burdensome qualities: The danger of abortion, welfare, and unemployment benefits is that things may become too easy for them, threatening the triumph of the sensible—themselves and the authorities with whom they feel interchangeable.

For working-class–identified women, in contrast, the dangers are reversed: More restrictive abortion laws may mean that central control of women might become too easy for the authorities who reign, persons whose interests are inevitably at odds with their own. Working-class–identified pro-choice respondents also resist media portrayals of their condition. Like their middle-class–identified counterparts, women in this group dislike Ellen; they find her irresponsible and irritatingly—but unconvincingly—helpless. Yet rather than blame Ellen for her plight, they are suspicious of both the professional and familial authorities—the doctor, her lawyers, and her mother. Television's benevolent professionals do not impress them in the least. Ellen's salvation lies not in obeying authority and conforming to society's rules but in learning to navigate these rules to the best of her ability, as do these women in the course of their lives. For this group, criticisms of television focus on articulating and exposing its sanctioning of authorities and the rights of authorities to interfere in women's lives.

Whether or not these women personally condone abortion (and often by their own admission they do not), women in this group are reluctant to invoke societal authority to outlaw it. They remain unconvinced that they should support the authorities who rule their society and communities. In their experience, such authorities are more likely to persecute them than to work to secure their rights. The group's propensity, then, is to support policies designed to limit the authorities' reach, as is the case with the pro-choice stance on abortion. Unlike the middle-class–identified group, working-class–identified women do not put their faith in notions of the good that then must be supported by societal and community authorities. Consequently, their liberal support for the right to free choice is more unqualified, as they are reluctant to allow authorities any more personal power over their lives than the considerable and sufficient amount that, in their view, is already exercised.

Television readily captures both a moralistic attitude toward abortion as well as a rights-oriented defense of the pro-choice position in its portrayal of "generally acceptable abortions." Both characters, Mrs. Herrera and Ellen Russell, are painted sympathetically as poor women who find they must make the extremely difficult decision to abort unplanned children. Middle-class–identified women accept these portraits at face value, whereas working-class–identified women do not.[12] Instead, working-class women make distinctions and judgments within these television images of their own group.

Some judgments result from aspirations of these women toward middle-class identity and consequent rejection of a fixed working-class identity for themselves or any other members of their class. If easy access to abortion for all women must be somewhat sacrificed in the construction of this alternative identity, the middle-class–identified women are willing to pay this price, in part because they believe it won't affect "sensible" people like themselves. The responses of middle-class–identified women to television images in these instances can be seen as evidence that they resist hegemonic interpretations of abortion dilemmas and hegemonic constructions of their own identities as subjects. But the basis for this resistance is an ultimate conformity to hegemonic notions of what upward mobility, middle-class identity, and middle-class membership really mean. In this sense, then, working-class women in this subgroup are ultimately thwarted in their attempt to truly resist dominant meanings and definitions of their identities and actions and the parameters of their world.

Pro-choice working-class–identified women offer a different order of critique. They reject not only images of themselves created by the middle class but those created to portray the middle class as well. Their overall skepticism of television maintains a distance from it that is absent for their middle-class–identified counterparts. These women more successfully maintain their guard in the face of mass media's efforts to define their self-identities. Their constructions do not match the public incarnations of the pro-choice subject to which the media have helped inure us. As Glendon notes, public "political rhetoric has grown increasingly out of touch with the more complex ways of speaking that Americans employ around the kitchen table, in their schools, workplaces, and in their various communities of memory and mutual aid" (1991, xii). Our study illustrates some of the differences between the way the pro-choice political subject is constructed in our public political rhetoric, as incarnated in the mass media, and the ways in which pro-choice subjectivity is constructed by members of two groups of pro-choice working-class women. Glendon's observation is well illustrated by our findings. We hope through this study to achieve a more sophisticated view of the ways in which concrete political subjectivities are constituted in our society in response to their more undifferentiated incarnation in dominant media forms.

This study offers an example of the new tradition of feminist research studying the popular cultural audience. Unlike more traditional audience research, the methodologies employed here allow women to speak for themselves and with each other in the context of television viewing, questionnaire answering, and in-depth interviewing. The focus-group methodology allows women to engage in semipublic discourse during the interview, which enables us to observe and interpret differences between this type of discourse as it occurs in the presence and absence of television. Our focus on social class differences among women (and racial differences in the larger study) adds a dimension to feminist audience research that has too often either overgeneralized from white middle-class samples or ignored class and racial differences among women altogether. It challenges the customary pro-life/pro-choice dichotomy that excludes explicit reference to the ways members of different social classes articulate their positions on abortion differently. Our research indicates that "pro-choice" as we commonly define it indeed derives from middle-class conceptions of the world, of individuals, of the experience of haves and have-nots, and of pregnancy and childbearing and women's related dilemmas.[13] The information presented here may shed light on some of the difficulties the pro-choice movement has experienced in presenting a unified political front during recent and ongoing abortion struggles.

Information about the ways in which different groups of women form and express their identities as subjects against the background of hegemonic cultural and media discourses will, we hope, help us to develop more fully notions about the forms of subjectivity that characterize postmodern society. Perhaps further awareness of these forms will lead increasingly to more effective ways of coming to know and understand the varieties of subjectivity we continually encounter in our work and in our lives.

Notes

1. This approach has been written about extensively in the anthropological literature; see, for example, Rabinow (1977); Geertz (1983, 1988); Clifford and Marcus (1986); Marcus and Fischer (1986).

2. See Long (1989) for a detailed overview of the work currently being done in feminist cultural studies.

3. Essentialism is defined by some as the abstract and ahistorical construction of "the female subject." Feminist cultural studies that emphasize concrete historical or current studies of a specific and situated female popular cultural audience have generally led away from essentialism on one level, stressing as they do the study of concrete, historically situated cultural subjects. Yet on another level, the temptation of constructing an equally essentialized, resisting female subject that can be effectively contrasted to the male subject more customary in cultural theory has been a continuing problem, if only because such language often seems central to feminist problematics. Missing in this work is a sense of the socially and historically situated nature of the subjects studied; somehow the terms of feminist theory have made these details seem, at times, superfluous luxuries, not really essential to the political thrust of these works. See Harding (1991) and Long (1989) for a good discussion and critique of essentialism. Also, see Scott's (1988) review of several then-current works in feminist theory whose authors she criticizes for this tendency.

4. Both Ginsburg (1989) and Luker (1984) have noted that the social class constituencies of pro-life and pro-choice activist groups differ, pro-life groups appearing more working class in character.

5. The categories of "pro-life" and "pro-choice," as we argue elsewhere (Press and Cole 1992), falsely dichotomize working-class women's actual positions on abortion. Interviews reveal that women often disagree with the basic presumptions behind the existence of these two opinion categories. We retain use of these two categories, however, for descriptive purposes.

6. Our analysis of this episode is indebted to Condit's (1990) discussion.

7. *Roe vs. Wade* was broadcast at an extremely critical time in the politics of abortion in the United States. It coincided with an increase nationwide in state-level struggles to pass laws prohibiting the use of public funding for poor women's abortions. Ellen's story certainly serves as an example to those campaigning for restrictions against state-funded abortions of the difficulties poor women seeking abortions might face in the absence of available state funds.

8. See Krueger (1988), Glick et al. (1987-88), Basch (1987), and Watts and Ebbutt (1987) on the methodology of focus-group interviews. Most women interviewed to date have been white, although some groups include black women as well.

9. Women's class membership is not always easy to assess; see Rubin (1979) for a discussion of the difficulties involved. She discusses her difficulties in determining the class status of women as opposed to that of men or families. She found that "In some instances, a husband's status still clearly determines the wife's; in others, it clearly does not. Those are the easy ones. But that leaves the cases where there is no clarity" (1979, 216). Like Rubin, we found it necessary to make some judgments, using background questionnaire data on each participant. In general, working-class women were employed in a blue- or pink-collar position (Howe 1978), and/or had two years of college or less, and/or were married to a man fitting these characteristics.

10. These labels are coined primarily from tendencies exhibited in women's pretelevision discussions. In these rather far-ranging discussions, women answered several general questions concerning their patterns of media use and their attitudes about politics, morality, and abortion. Working-class women's answers to these questions can be grouped into two main categories based on their relationship to authority. The first are women who seem comfortable identifying with reigning authorities in our social and political system, themselves primarily middle or upper class ("middle-class–identified" women). These women identify themselves as the same as middle-class women, although by our measures they would be considered in the working class. In the second group are antiauthoritarian women who do not identify with middle-class authorities ("nonmiddle-class– or working-class–identified"). These women hold views that are not generally supportive of social authorities in the United States. Posttelevision discussions reveal that they do not identify themselves in the same category with the middle-class characters on the television shows we showed them.

Women in the two groups we discuss here happen to occupy different positions within the working class. The middle-class–identified group is composed of low-level managers. Members of the working-class–identified group work in positions likely to be classified as "below" those occupied by the other group; their connection to the more stable working-class group is more tenuous, with some women supporting themselves with relatively transient work. Of course, one must be careful of generalizing this link between ideology and position based on the small sample the study includes.

11. See Bellah et al. (1984) for a fuller description of middle-class worldviews in our culture. In particular, Bellah and colleagues describe the therapeutic perspective and the origins of liberalism in middle-class outlooks generally.

12. See Press (1992) for fuller explication of data on middle-class women's responses to these characters.

13. See also Press and Cole (1992) on dissonance within the pro-choice discourse and on the inability of this category to articulate adequately a particular political discourse and subject position.

References

Agar, Michael H. 1980. *The Professional Stranger: An Information Introduction to Ethnography.* New York: Academic Press.

Bacon-Smith, Camille. 1992. *Enterprising Women.* Philadelphia: University of Pennsylvania Press.

Basch, Charles E. 1987. "Focus Group Interview: An Underutilized Research Technique for Improving Theory and Practice in Health Education." *Health Education Quarterly* 14(4): 411–448.

Baudrillard, Jean. 1988. *Selected Writings.* Stanford, Calif.: Stanford University Press.

Bellah, Robert N., Richard Madsen, William M. Sullivan, Ann Swidler, and Steven M. Tipton. 1984. *Habits of the Heart: Individualism and Commitment in American Life.* Berkeley: University of California Press.

Brown, Mary Ellen. 1991a. "Knowledge and Power: An Ethnography of Soap-Opera Viewers." Pp. 178–197 in *Television Criticism,* ed. Leah Vande Berge and Lawrence Wenner. New York: Longman.

_____. 1991b. "Soap Opera as a Site of Struggle: The Politics of Interpretation." *Media Development* 2:23–26.

Clifford, James, and George E. Marcus. 1986. *Writing Culture.* Berkeley and Los Angeles: University of California Press.

Condit, Celeste Michelle. 1990. *Decoding Abortion Rhetoric: Communicating Social Choice.* Urbana and Chicago: University of Illinois Press.

D'Acci, Julie. 1987. "The Case of *Cagney and Lacey.*" Pp. 203–225 in *Boxed in: Women and Television,* ed. Helen Baehr and Gillian Dyer. New York: Pandora Press.

Fiske, John. 1987. *Television Culture.* London and New York: Methuen.

_____. 1989a. *Reading the Popular.* Boston: Unwin Hyman.

_____. 1989b. *Understanding Popular Culture.* Boston: Unwin Hyman.

_____. 1990. "Ethnosemiotics: Some Personal and Theoretical Reflections." *Cultural Studies* 4(1): 85–97.

Flax, Jane. 1987. "Postmodernism and Gender Relations in Feminist Theory." *Signs* 12(4): 621–641.

Fonow, Mary Margaret, and Judith A. Cook, eds. 1991. *Beyond Methodology: Feminist Scholarship as Lived Research.* Bloomington: Indiana University Press.

Gabler, Neal. 1988. *An Empire of Their Own: How the Jews Invented Hollywood.* New York: Crown.

Geertz, Clifford. 1973. *The Interpretation of Cultures.* New York: Basic Books.

_____. 1983. *Local Knowledge: Further Essays in Interpretive Anthropology.* New York: Basic Books.

_____. 1988. *Works and Lives: The Anthropologist as Author.* Stanford, Calif.: Stanford University Press.

Ginsburg, Faye D. 1989. *Contested Lives: The Abortion Debate in an American Community.* Berkeley: University of California Press.

Glendon, Mary Ann. 1991. *Rights Talk: The Impoverishment of Political Rhetoric.* New York: Free Press.

Glick, Deborah C., Andrew Gordon, William Ward, et al. 1987-88. "Focus Group Methods for Formative Research in Child Survival: An Ivoirian Example." *International Quarterly of Community Health Education* 8(4): 298–316.

Grossberg, Lawrence. 1987. "The In-Difference of Television." *Screen* 28(2): 28–45.

———. 1988. "Wandering Audiences, Nomadic Critics." *Cultural Studies* 2(3): 377–391.

———. 1989. "On the Road with Three Ethnographers." *Journal of Communication Inquiry* 13(2): 23–26.

Harding, Sandra. 1991. *Whose Science? Whose Knowledge? Thinking from Women's Lives.* Ithaca, N.Y.: Cornell University Press.

Hobson, Dorothy. 1982. *Crossroads: The Drama of a Soap Opera.* London: Methuen.

Howe, Louise Kapp. 1978. *Pink Collar Workers: Inside the World of Women's Work.* New York: Avon.

Krueger, Richard A. 1988. *Focus Groups: A Practical Guide for Applied Research.* Beverly Hills, Calif.: Sage.

Liebes, Tamar, and Elihu Katz. 1990. *The Export of Meaning: Cross-Cultural Readings of "Dallas."* Oxford and New York: Oxford University Press.

Long, Elizabeth. 1986. "Women, Reading, and Cultural Authority: Some Implications of the Audience Perspective in Cultural Studies." *American Quarterly* 38:591–612.

———. 1987. "Reading Groups and the Crisis of Cultural Authority." *Cultural Studies* 1(2): 306–327.

———. 1989. "Feminism and Cultural Studies: Britain and America." *Critical Studies in Mass Communication* 6(4): 427–435.

Luker, Kristin. 1984. *Abortion and the Politics of Motherhood.* Berkeley: University of California Press.

Lull, James, ed. 1987. *Popular Music and Communication.* Newbury Park, Calif.: Sage.

Luttrell, Wendy. 1989. "Working-Class Women's Ways of Knowing: Effects of Gender, Race, and Class." *Sociology of Education* 62 (January): 33–46.

Lyotard, Jean Francois. 1984. *The Postmodern Condition: A Report on Knowledge,* trans. Geoff Bennington and Brian Massumi. Minneapolis: University of Minnesota Press.

Maguire, Patricia. 1987. *Doing Participatory Research: A Feminist Approach.* Amherst, Mass.: Center for International Education.

Marcus, George E., and Michael M.J. Fischer. 1986. *Anthropology as Cultural Critique.* Chicago and London: University of Chicago Press.

May, Larry. 1980. *Screening Out the Past: The Birth of Mass Culture and the Motion Picture Industry.* New York: Oxford University Press.

McDonnell, Kathleen. 1984. *Not an Easy Choice: A Feminist Re-examines Abortion.* Boston: South End Press.

McRobbie, Angela. 1978. "Working-Class Girls and the Culture of Femininity." Pp. 96–108 in *Women Take Issue,* ed. Women's Studies Group. London: Hutchinson.

———. 1981. "Just Like a *Jackie* Story." Pp. 113–128 in *Feminism for Girls,* ed. Angela McRobbie and Trisha McCabe. London: Routledge.

———. 1984. "Dance and Social Fantasy." Pp. 130–162 in *Gender and Generation,* ed. Angela McRobbie and Mica Nava. New York and London: Macmillan.

Montgomery, Kathryn C. 1989. *Target: Prime Time.* New York: Oxford University Press.

Morley, David. 1980. *The Nationwide Audience: Structure and Decoding.* London: British Film Institute.

———. 1986. *Family Television.* London: Comedia.

Nicholson, Linda. 1986. *Gender and History: The Limits of Social Theory in the Age of the Family.* New York: Columbia University Press.

Peiss, Kathy. 1986. *Cheap Amusements: Working Women and Leisure in Turn-of-the-Century New York.* Philadelphia: Temple University Press.

Petchesky, Rosalind Pollack. 1990. *Abortion and Woman's Choice: The State, Sexuality, and Reproductive Freedom.* Boston: Northeastern University Press.

Press, Andrea. 1991. *Women Watching Television: Gender, Class, and Generation in the American Television Experience.* Philadelphia: University of Pennsylvania Press.

————. 1992. "Mass Media and Moral Discourse: The Impact of Television on Modes of Reasoning About Abortion." *Critical Studies in Mass Communication* 8:421–441.

Press, Andrea, and Elizabeth R. Cole. 1992. "Pro-Choice Voices: Discourses of Abortion Among Pro-Choice Women." *Perspectives on Social Problems* 4:73–92.

Rabinow, Paul. 1977. *Reflections on Fieldwork in Morocco.* Berkeley and Los Angeles: University of California Press.

Radway, Janice. 1984. *Reading the Romance: Women, Patriarchy, and Popular Literature.* Chapel Hill: University of North Carolina Press.

————. 1986. "Identifying Ideological Seams: Mass Culture, Analytical Method, and Political Practice." *Communication* 9:93–123.

————. 1988. "Reception Study: Ethnography and the Problems of Dispersed Subjects." *Cultural Studies* 2(3): 359–376.

Reeves, Jimmie L., and Richard Campbell. 1991. "The Politics and Poetics of Drug Transgression: Crusading Journalists on Crack Street." Paper presented at the November meetings of the Speech Communication Association, Atlanta, Georgia.

Roberts, Helen, ed. 1981. *Doing Feminist Research.* London: Routledge and Kegan Paul.

Rosenzweig, Roy. 1983. *Eight Hours for What We Will: Workers and Leisure in an Industrial City, 1870–1920.* Cambridge: Cambridge University Press.

Rubin, Lillian. 1979. *Women of a Certain Age: The Midlife Search for Self.* New York: Harper and Row.

Sandel, Michael J., ed. 1984. *Liberalism and Its Critics.* Oxford: Basil Blackwell.

Sanjek, Roger, ed. 1990. *Fieldnotes: The Makings of Anthropology.* Ithaca, N.Y., and London: Cornell University Press.

Scott, Joan Wallach. 1988. *Gender and the Politics of History.* New York: Columbia University Press.

Seiter, Ellen. 1990. "Making Distinctions in TV Audience Research: Case Study of a Troubling Interview." *Cultural Studies* 4(1): 61–84.

Seiter, Ellen, Hans Borchers, Gabriele Kreutzner, and Eva-Maria Warth, eds. 1989. *Remote Control: Television, Audience, and Cultural Power.* London and New York: Routledge.

Watts, Mike, and Dave Ebbutt. 1987. "More than the Sum of the Parts: Research Methods in Group Interviewing." *British Educational Research Journal* 13(1): 25–34.

Willis, Paul. 1978. *Profane Culture.* London: Routledge and Kegan Paul.

FOUR

Reach Out and Touch Someone: Viewers, Agency, and Audiences in the Televisual Experience

DENISE BIELBY AND C. LEE HARRINGTON

Bringing in Audiences

Scholarship on American television broadened in the early 1980s to include critical, humanist, and literary approaches to the medium, counterbalancing orthodox social science concerns and approaches. Until these developments took hold, the dominance of the "uses and gratifications" and "mass culture" models of the effects of media essentially foreclosed a close look at the social construction of audiences' meanings, consumption, and preferences—in short the practices that underlie audiences' cultural engagement with televisual texts.

A significant development during this period was Hall's work (1980 [1974]) on television's communicative process. Hall introduced an alternative to conventional explorations of cultural uses of the medium by drawing attention to the encoding and decoding of television texts and the class, cultural, and gender specificity of audiences' negotiated readings of those texts (Morley 1980, 1981). Kaplan's anthology *Regarding Television* (1983) subsequently called attention to television aesthetics, to how meaning is produced, and to television's functioning as an ideological institution that shapes cultural meanings. Allen (1983, 1985), Feuer (1984, 1987, 1989), and others advanced this line of theorizing by incorporating the literary categories of genre, text, and reader to analysis of the televisual experience.

Recent work has continued to lament the lack of research on how audiences fill "the gaps between text, meaning and representation, or more broadly, the gaps between production, texts and consumption, or between interests, practices, and effects" (Grossberg 1987, p. 36). Grossberg's comments apply equally to those ana-

81

lytical approaches that concentrate on the political economy of production and to those that address the construction of narrative, production codes, and texts. In response, scholars are using ethnographic and other anthropological methods to seek audiences' negotiated readings of the televisual text, letting audiences speak for themselves about relevant meanings and the social bases of individual and categorical differences in those readings (Seiter et al. 1989).

However, advocates of televisual textual analysis and the study of audiences have become engaged in a disciplinary turf war. For example, textual analysts warn of "exuberance over the discovery of 'real' audiences, the danger of lapsing into a happy positivism in our methodologies, and an overreading of points of resistance" (Seiter et al. 1989, p. 7). Seiter and colleagues note how "attacks on audience studies have been mounted by some who see this kind of work as implicitly and necessarily collusion—simply doing the industry's market research for it" (p. 6). In our view, some caution is warranted but not for these reasons. Rather, a more serious risk comes from oversubscribing to the ever-diminishing returns from describing historical, ideological, and gender-situated audiences, especially when those descriptions become ends in themselves. These descriptions risk reifying essentialist categories and distracting from efforts to advance theoretical explanations for audience readings, response, and engagement.

Despite its shortcomings, audience studies has overcome serious limitations of conventional analyses of television. For example, scholars no longer presume that the preferred readings of television producers are monolithically transcribed into the psyches of viewers who are indistinguishable from one another. Moreover, scholars now attend to the cultural bases for viewers' readings of televisual texts and their construction of meanings and preferences. In short, without the conceptual advances stemming from audience studies, viewer agency would be largely excluded from understanding the televisual experience.

While debate continues over conceptualizing the audience, we focus specifically upon the social construction of audiences as constituted by viewers themselves in response to televisual texts. We are particularly interested in the process of audience emergence and formation around particular televisual texts. We address how viewers, as part of that process, personally and socially identify their preferences, thereby defining the popular. Our approach contrasts with earlier work on audiences that relies upon viewers' reports to interviewers or upon ethnographers' observations of the viewing process. As a result, our approach minimizes the problems inherent in interviewer intervention, including concern over the politics of the analyst's interpretation (Ang 1989).

Our work builds upon two concepts. First, we draw upon the fact that television is popular—that it is widely enjoyed. We examine how television confirms the experience of the viewer and how that confirming is negotiated among viewers themselves (Nye 1971). We explore how enjoyment is recognized and dispersed. We are especially interested in how the dispersion of popularity constitutes audiences, just as audiences define television as a cultural object through appropriation of its texts.

Second, our work recognizes that viewers exhibit agency. Following Shibutani (1991, p. 1), we define agency as the ability of socially embedded individuals to initiate and control behavior. In earlier work, we found that television viewers as social agents generate meaning by establishing social bonds with each other (viewer-viewer), with television characters (viewer-character), and with producers (viewer-producer) (Bielby and Harrington 1992). The concept of agency has not been fully explored in existing scholarship on audiences and viewers. As typically conceived, a television audience is composed of isolated viewers who have little or no contact with one another. In fact, audiences can be "virtual communities," actively constructed through social bonds. Yet existing work has failed to capture the social dynamic implied by viewer agency (Fiske 1987).

The means through which viewers as agents become communities remain to be identified. Our approach builds upon the concept of "idioculture," which consists of knowledge, beliefs, behaviors, and customs that group members can refer to and use as the basis for subsequent interaction (Fine 1979). Fine (1979; Fine and Kleinman 1979) has elaborated how idioculture is located in the organization of emergent interaction among members of a group and is revealed by the kinds of information transmitted within and between subgroups. In this view, cultural objects are experienced through the communication system of small groups, even though the cultural objects themselves may be widely known. Thus, by analyzing networks of interaction, we can explore how groups construct meanings by drawing upon gossip, news, speculation, queries, and reactions. By isolating the elements viewers refer to in discussions about their televisual experiences, we should be able to identify what is culturally meaningful to them.

Our approach analyzes how selected cultural resources are appropriated by viewers to generate meaning during reception, recognized by viewers as significant, and shared among viewers. First, we analyze the structural means through which viewers disseminate those cultural resources by examining their communication with one another to understand how their interaction functions. We focus specifically upon commentary, speculation, requests, and diffusion of information as forms of interaction among viewers. Second, we identify cultural resources viewers use to interpret their experiences, including the following: viewers' awareness of production processes; claims about viewer agency; discussion around the viewer-viewer, viewer-producer, and viewer-character bonds; and finally, viewer pleasure. We conclude by considering the contribution of our work to current issues and debates in the area of audience studies.

Exploring Viewer Interaction

Our materials are drawn from a variety of sources. Some of the information about television series, viewers, and audiences is drawn from electronic or print media that report on the television industry, including televised promotionals, fan magazines, news programs, newspapers, and media-industry trade journals. Most of our materials come from transcripts of messages and announcements posted by subscribers of two national electronic bulletin boards. Through either a monthly subscription fee or on-line charges, members can correspond with all other subscribers of the service at any time of the day or night, seven days a week. Members have access to each other through a variety of file topics, including prime-time television series, daytime serials, celebrity gossip, and media-industry information. Under each file topic they may post public messages and reply to one another. In most cases, interaction occurs between individuals who are not, at least initially, acquaintances. However, some subscribers develop ongoing communication with one another that offers evidence of sustained viewer-viewer interaction.

Electronic bulletin boards are used by viewers who are sufficiently literate to operate a personal computer in a forum of quasi-anonymous public interaction that invites subscribers to join in. Messages are typically posted under one's name and are announced by topic within a given file or category. Interaction is sequential and can be immediate but differs from typical conversational interaction in that it is not conducted face-to-face. As such, it does not carry with it the identity markers (such as age, ethnicity, social class, and so forth) that affect conversational dynamics (Boden and Bielby 1983, Stone 1990, Zimmerman and West 1975). Instead, members initially interact as equals and build credibility and identity through the content they share. The majority of members engage in an exchange with a purpose in mind, either to give or receive information on a given topic. This process differs somewhat from ordinary conversation, which may or may not be directed toward eliciting or offering specific information. Our materials also differ from what one would find through naturalistic observation because they are drawn from a forum wherein all types of people interact with one another, not just those of one's own social category. Thus, our materials allow us to examine viewer interaction and audience formation in a context that is relatively unconstrained by social location.

There was an abundance of information from which to select our materials. Among messages exchanged about prime-time series, interaction tended to focus on serialized dramas, although an entirely separate file existed solely for interaction over daytime serial dramas. We sampled from members' exchanges, seeking comments on specific characters, series, or related topics that illustrated dynamics relevant to viewer interests and audience formation. The sampled interactions are reasonably representative of the interactions among members on the topics of prime-time television and daytime dramas.

Findings: What Viewers Say to Each Other

The messages on electronic bulletin boards (EBBs) reveal how viewers interactively construct meaning from televisual products. The messages are important in terms of both structure (i.e., how the messages function) and content (i.e., what the messages reveal about the interpretive process, particularly the cultural resources that viewers draw upon to make meaning).

Structure

Messages serve four possible functions: commentary, speculation, request for information, and diffusion of information. While each message functions in at least one of these ways, some messages serve multiple functions.

Commentary. In most cases, messages that function as commentary consist of opinions or statements by viewers of what they find pleasurable, displeasurable, satisfying, or irritating about a given aspect of a televisual product, including character, set design, plot, authenticity, and so on. For example:

- I think the Eckerts are kinda dull. I don't like that Jenny Eckert at all. She seems to believe that the ends justify the means—she'll "borrow" stuff from a department store just so that she can look good or something. She really bugs me.
- There really have been NO high points lately, unless you count the scene this week when Jack smiled and nodded in agreement after Jenn "informed" him that he loves her. Give me a BREAK!!! When will he finally say it HIMSELF?? After the wedding? This is really getting tiresome.
- Kuzak is turning into (or maybe he always was and I just didn't notice) such an A**hole. I am liking him less and less. I'll be glad to see him off the show.

Each of these quotations reveals viewers' opinions in the form of recognized pleasure or displeasure about various aspects of a cultural object. Commentary functions to show both the interpretation viewers have made of an object and how they share that interpretation with others.

Speculation. A second, related function of electronic messages is that of speculation, or a "dynamic oral culture" (Fiske 1987, p. 80) that interacts with the culture of television. Speculation is essentially gossip about a given program in terms of character development, story-line potential, plot twists, and so forth. Gossip establishes an active relationship between viewers and programs and between and among viewers themselves. It is important in the generation of meaning in cultural objects in two ways: "It constructs audience-driven meanings and it constructs audience communities within which those meanings circulate" (Fiske 1987, p. 80).

The examples that follow concern one specific plot development on "Days of Our Lives" and viewers' speculation around that development. One EBB member put forth her ideas about the story line, which elicited appreciative responses from several other members. In the following interaction between two EBB members, note how speculation serves to construct both cultural meaning and a bond between the two viewers:

Viewer 2: Debbie, the Cal theory is brilliant, and I think Kathy's [another EBB member] tie-in with Johnny makes it almost plausible, given Cal's continued manipulation of the doctor even when in prison.

Viewer 1: So you like the Cal theory, huh? There are still a few bugs in it, but I'm working on chasing them out. For instance, hasn't Cal been in jail all this time? How did he get out to kill Nick? ... Cal could have paid Johnny to kill Nick ... perhaps Johnny was in cahoots with Johnny's previous "employer," Ernesto Toscano.

Viewer 2: Now, as to the development of the Cal theory—remember, Steve's coffin was stolen from the graveyard and replaced with a presumably empty one. ... Maybe Steve, seeking revenge, is pulling the strings but going through Cal because he doesn't want anyone to know he's alive. ... Nah, I still like the Cal-Johnny connection, but I really can't imagine Johnny, louse that he is, killing his own brother. ... Oh, well, I'll keep working on this.

Speculation (or gossip) focuses not only on the primary text but on secondary texts as well (for explanations of texts, see Fiske 1987). Much of the speculation revealed on one EBB concerns pieces of "outside" information. At times a member will post information that has been learned from newspapers, magazines, fan-club newsletters, the production staff, or other sources (the function of diffusion, discussed later) that will generate speculation among other EBB members. In the following examples, note how speculation can be generated not by events on the programs themselves but by secondary-source information that impacts viewer interpretation.

Example 1
- My feeling is that something will happen between Abby and CJ and then the following week, CJ will go out and find herself a gorgeous date as an act of denial. ... I know for fact that she will have a date with a gorgeous guy as my cousin Bill is to be the dish. My aunt said the episode would air in a few weeks.

- Thanks for the inside scoop. Are you a major "L.A. Law" fan? What are your predictions for the season finale?

Example 2
- I've heard that one of the reasons Wagner is splitting GH is to distance himself professionally from Kristina.

- Thanks for the news. I had not heard this. That would be quite interesting.

As Fiske suggests (1987), part of the function of speculation or gossip is the creation of audience communities. We see that clearly in our materials, as members seek interaction with others who view the same programs. Members can quite literally tap into a specific audience by posting a message about a particular program or story line. Speculation generated by the message is, in effect, viewer-to-viewer interaction that underlies audience formation. We also see how groups form around particular interests in a given series, a process that reveals the diversity of interests among subgroups composing the larger audience.

Request. A third function of electronic messages is that of request. Bulletin boards such as the ones surveyed here serve as a forum by which members can request information on a variety of issues: events of missed episodes, the history or "backstory" (see Allen 1983) of a character or story line, information about news from secondary sources that might impact story lines, and so on.

- I can't recall who Molly is. … Is she a very new character? I'm still two weeks behind on my "Days" tapes. Or is she the one who works at the police station?
- What exactly IS Anna's secret?
- I think Jack Wagner's contract is up in the summer, and I was wondering does anyone know if he is leaving?
- Please help me. Due to a family crisis … I was not only unable to watch Monday's episode, but I couldn't even tape it. I would love for someone to give me a brief synopsis of what exactly happened. I can only get bits and snatches from all the bulletins so far. … Thanking all in advance.

The variety of information requested by EBB members reveals several important things. First, it indicates the interactive nature of creating meaning. Viewers perceive that it is necessary (or desirable) to have certain information in order to enjoy or interpret what is happening on a program, and they turn to other viewers for help.

Second, the requests for information reveal the importance of intertextuality in the generation of cultural meaning. The principle of intertextuality holds that any one text is necessarily read in relationship to others and that the reader brings prior textual knowledge to the reading of a text (Fiske 1987, p. 108). Intertextual knowledge preorients the reader by drawing on some meanings rather than others.

Fiske suggests that there are three types of texts that work together to generate meaning on television: primary texts (the television programs themselves), secondary texts (those that refer explicitly to the primary text—fan magazines, newsletters, commercials for a series, and so forth), and tertiary texts (gossip, oral culture, and letters from fans). We observe viewers utilizing intertextual knowledge in the EBB materials as they draw on a wide range of sources (both primary and secondary texts) to interpret a given character, event, or story line and rely on other members for that information as well (tertiary texts).

Finally, the requests for information reveal how viewers perceive themselves as members of a definable audience and draw explicitly on that audience in the interpretive process. That viewers request information about a specific series suggests that they recognize each other as members of a specific group. Moreover, requests for information suggest, first, that viewers assume others will identify with the requester's need for information and, second, that membership entitles the requester to access to the group as a resource for creating culturally relevant meanings.

Diffusion. A final and perhaps most important function of electronic messages is diffusion of information. The bulletin boards contain a rich detail of information that has either been directly solicited by a request or has simply been posted voluntarily. An interesting string of messages concerns an episode of "Northern Exposure" in which viewers lost portions of the program due to technical difficulties. The initial request for information stated:

- Help! On 4/14 show, when Chris opened Maggie's door to leave, there was a cut to a freeze of Fleischman's face, a blackout, another cut to F's frozen face, another blackout. … Did our local station do some sloppy editing or what?

The diffusion of information from other viewers was immediate. Responses came in from viewers in New York City, Philadelphia, Cincinnati, Washington, D.C., Indianapolis, and elsewhere.

- Nah, it looked like a CBS-feed screwup that probably affected at least all of Eastern and Central time zones.
- All East Coast got the same freeze. We're waiting for some West Coasters to fill us in if the later runs of it were unfrozen. Look under Nort Exp 4/15 SOS for more feedback. Are you in the Eastern time zone too?
- Same thing happened to me in Indianapolis. We need someone from the West Coast to H*E*L*P us.

This communal request for information from viewers in the Central and Eastern time zones was soon resolved by several West Coast viewers, who provided brief summaries of the missed portion of the episode. This interchange reveals the interactive nature of the diffusion of information as well as the reciprocity extended to others in the group. It also reveals the importance of diffusion to the interpretive process and how audiences emerge from small groups linked together through individualized interests and experiences.

Also clearly revealed is the importance viewers place on information diffusion, particularly on their role as a diffuser. One viewer responded to requests for information about the serial "Days of Our Lives" with a long stream of detailed inside information. Although she did not reveal her source, her message ended "That is all of the new information that I have at the moment. When I get more I will pass it along here to everyone." Clearly, this viewer perceives the importance of her role as diffuser to others' interpretation of the given program.

Most of the information diffused on electronic bulletin boards comes directly from other viewers. That is, one viewer informs another about something that occurred on the primary text, was gathered from secondary sources, or was learned from a third viewer. Occasionally, however, someone directly involved with media production posts a message on an EBB that provides other members with inside information. One example was already mentioned: A viewer could offer informed speculation on future developments of "L.A. Law" because she knew that her cousin was appearing in an upcoming episode.

A more striking example, however, is the regular appearance on one of the EBBs of one of the assistant directors of "Northern Exposure," who provides audience members with detailed information on the production of the program.

- We got a 24 share in the Nielsens, number one in the time slot (over big-drawing movies), and number one in all demographics for the whole night. Let's hope we keep it up. Next two episodes are killers.
- Good news!! CBS Promo department had us shoot some "grab" shots of our cast members lip-syncing to the CBS Fall Promo song, so looks like someone thinks we'll be back.

The involvement on an EBB of someone directly involved with the production of "Northern Exposure" allows its viewers access to inside information in the meaning-making process and reveals how producers perceive an audience for a given object.

These four functions of EBB messages (commentary, speculation, request, and diffusion) show how viewers interactively negotiate the meaning of a televisual product. By providing opinions, gossiping about potential developments, and requesting and receiving information, viewers reveal their idioculture wherein they identify common interests and create an audience that becomes an interpretive community through which meaning is continually regenerated (Fine 1979).

In addition to describing how electronic bulletin boards are structured, we must also pay attention to what the messages themselves reveal about the interpretive process. By examining the content of messages, we are able to uncover elements that viewers recognize as culturally meaningful and thus popular to them.

Content

The content of the messages is extremely varied, due in part to the different functions that each message can serve. For our purposes, we focus on five aspects of EBB messages that seem most important to the interpretive process. These include the following: viewers' awareness of the production process, claims about viewer agency (both of these aspects are crucial to the viewer-producer bond), the viewer-character bond, the issue of viewer pleasure, and the viewer-viewer bond (see Bielby and Harrington 1992).

Viewers' Awareness. The content of the messages is important in revealing how viewers actively and communally generate cultural meaning. We argue, as Cantor and Cantor (1986) and others have asserted, that viewers are not passive victims of the production process but rather are actively involved in the generation of meaning of cultural objects. Viewers are knowledgeable about various aspects of media production and utilize and share that knowledge in defining what interests them and thus in making meaning.

One way in which viewers display awareness of the production process is through intertextuality (Fiske 1987). As was argued previously, viewers draw on various texts in the interpretive process: the primary text, secondary texts, and tertiary texts. Electronic bulletin boards are an interesting phenomenon in that one can readily trace the diffusion of information from a source in the production industry (such as the messages from the assistant director of "Northern Exposure") to corroboration from secondary sources (e.g., "I read in *Soap Opera Digest* that …") to the gossip and speculation generated by the information. Through intertextuality, viewers actively draw on multiple resources in interpreting a televisual product.

In addition to their reliance on intertextuality, viewers also display agency in accepting, rejecting, or questioning the production of a televisual object. Messages consistently reveal sophisticated knowledge of the complex codes that are read by viewers in the interpretive process, including genre boundaries, set design, lighting, the economics of production, backstory, and so on (see Allen 1983), all of which they draw upon for acceptance or rejection of a viewing experience.

- Gloria & Co. [the new producer of "General Hospital"] really are making some very unwise choices as far as who should stay and who should monopolize the show.
- I do like the new camera angles on "General Hospital." They had some different ones other than the standard straight-on ones. Like when Robert, Anna, and Mac were on the train, they have some shots that made it seem like you were looking down from the corner of the ceiling of the train. … It made it seem more hectic and realistic.
- There is a lack of good, likeable characters [on "Days of Our Lives"]. There is no one on this show that I am really rooting for. The characters I used to love have all become boring through loss of love interest and bad writing.
- Remember the S&M case with the twins [on "L.A. Law"]? I wonder if there'd have been more of a payoff to that one if that season hadn't been shortened by the writers' strike.
- I think the editing bothered me the most. Normally, I love the fast pace of the show ["The Simpsons"], but on that show there was no room to breathe.

These messages show how viewers use their knowledge of production codes and processes to identify their pleasures and displeasures and then use that knowledge as a resource in the interpretive process. Knowledge of codes also appears as viewers speculate with one another about a given character or story line. An understanding of production constraints aids viewers in making informed guesses about what might occur. A convoluted story line on "Days of Our Lives" drew the following response from a disgusted viewer:

- Maybe we'll figure out the resolution before the writers, 'cause they sure look like they haven't got a clue how to end this.

And the planned cancellation of ABC's controversial "Twin Peaks" elicited a long string of messages on an EBB, including the following comment and response:

- I'm really disappointed by the cancellation. "Twin Peaks" was a very unique show, in an industry full of your basic run-of-the-mill sitcoms that just don't cut it.
- Well, it shows that the days of network dominance by ABC, CBS, and NBC are coming to an end. The effects of strong independent stations and cable television are finally beginning to take hold.

Viewer Agency. Closely related to viewers' awareness of the production process is their claim to agency in that process. Viewers are not passive victims of television production but rather are actively involved in the generation of meaning in televisual products. Viewers regularly respond through letters, petitions, and so forth with opinions, suggestions, complaints, and praise. These tertiary texts (Fiske 1987) are then fed back into the production process. As Brown suggests, "It is possible that producers and sponsors take [viewers'] suggestions under consideration when writing [television programs]" (1989, p. 168).

Materials from one EBB contain a great deal of evidence of viewer agency. One long string of messages informed members of a group called Viewers for Quality Television, which supports certain programs by writing to producers, directors, and others in production roles that affect program decisions. The information diffused about the group sparked much interest in other viewers. Other examples of audience agency abound.

- C.O.O.P. has started to stop ABC from cancelling ["Twin Peaks"]. C.O.O.P. is an acronym for Citizens Opposed to the Offing of "Peaks." I am serving as president of the Greensboro, NC, chapter. ... This is a nationwide campaign which will be a unified effort to return "Peaks" to the air.
- I don't know when "China Beach" will be back, but I am waiting VERY impatiently. I have written to ABC, but I need to get another letter out soon. We really have to fight for the quality shows.
- As well as writing to the cast and crew, I recommend you also write CBS telling them just how much we all love this show ["Northern Exposure"] and that you want to see it back in the fall. Ratings are great, but one fan letter counts for about ten thousand, so you can make a big impact.

- Let's try to keep this topic on the Arts BB as long as possible and maybe stimulate some real interest among the [BB] users.

One EBB message revealed not only evidence of viewer agency but also some evidence that producers are aware of and heed opinions and efforts by viewers. The woman dispersing information about Viewers for Quality Television stated "Network execs listen to VQT," and the assistant director of "Northern Exposure" urged viewers to write the producers, indicating that producers do, in fact, pay attention to fan letters.

These two components—viewers' awareness of the production process and viewers' claims to agency—support the existence and strength of the viewer-producer bond. As we suggested in an earlier essay: "[Viewers] carry ... agency beyond viewing and into not only the construction of readings and meanings derived from the televisual experience, but also into the social bonds that emerge ... between viewers and those whose products they consume" (Bielby and Harrington 1992, p. 14). On one EBB, evidence for this bond is seen most clearly in the messages of the "Northern Exposure" assistant director, who at times makes explicit promises to the viewer about the quality of upcoming episodes. One promise, "Next two episodes are killers," elicited a response several days later from a viewer who stated, "You were right. 'One Who Waits' episode is a killer ... can't wait for the next one!" The producer made an additional promise: "Next week, a 256-year-old spirit visits Ed. Week after, Holling gets a circumcision for Shelley. Hold on to your hats, folks, it does get better!" This message reveals not only producers' involvement in the diffusion of information to viewers but also producers' perception of what viewers will find enjoyable or pleasurable.

Evidence for the viewer-producer bond indicates that each negotiates with the other in the generation of televisual meaning. In recent years, the resurrection of such popular (but low Nielsen-rated) programs as "Beauty and the Beast" and "The Days and Nights of Molly Dodd" (as well as the furor over the cancellation of "Twin Peaks") indicates the power of the viewer in the production process and the strength of the viewer-producer bond.

Viewer-Character Bond. In addition to the viewer-producer bond, EBBs provide evidence for the existence of a bond between viewers and characters (Bielby and Harrington 1992). Through repetitive viewing, audience members perceive a similarity between televisual characters and real-world people (that is, a character's authenticity) or can, in fact, come to perceive characters as "intimates" (the latter seems especially likely for daytime serial viewers, due to particular characteristics of the genre; see Allen 1983). How viewers experience these elements of the televisual process is tied to their social context.

Discussion of character's authenticity was recently emphasized with the emergence of the prime-time "humanistic ensemble dramas," including programs such as "thirtysomething," "L.A. Law," and "Northern Exposure" (and the defunct "Hill Street Blues" and "St. Elsewhere"). These programs support "solid values" (DuBrow 1991) that elicit response from viewers revealing their comprehension of the elements of emotional maturity and character authenticity that mark the boundaries of this genre. Since "thirtysomething" premiered and television critics labeled the characters "whiners" (Rosenberg 1991), their authenticity has been closely monitored. Note responses from EBB subscribers:

- Sure, it gets a bit whiney sometimes, but so do real people. I'm 32, newly married, and the characters do remind me of lots of my friends. I grew up in Ohio, have lived on the East Coast for a while, and recently moved. ... I can relate to the characters, at most times.

- Maybe because I'm in my mid-30s, with a couple of kids, a house constantly undergoing remodeling ... some of the characters sound very much like people I know.

As essential elements in the humanistic ensemble genre, the emotional maturity and authenticity represented are also seriously evaluated. Note the discussion between two viewers of "thirtysomething":

Viewer 1: I find that I can often identify with the emotions that the characters (some of them) go through. It seems very real.

Viewer 2: Thanks ... and my feelings about the show are similar, even though I've been married longer. I've gone through some phases of identifying very strongly with Elliott and Nancy [characters on the series] too.

Viewer 1: Well, I may be nothing more than a sentimental slob, but I know of no other TV program that can bring me to tears with the parallels I find in my life.

Those who have disliked the series also draw upon a comparison of their social position with that of the characters. One viewer drew upon the perspective of another, older generation to interpret the criticism leveled at the series. She asserts:

- The people who seem to really hate it are the parents of the 50s and 60s. My mother-in-law watched it once and said she couldn't believe Hope [a character] needed to get a babysitter once a week ... because she "needed to get out of the house and away from her child for awhile." ... That's one reason why this show is misunderstood; older people see the characters as spoiled.

Further evidence for the viewer-character bond exists in many of the messages that function as commentary. As noted earlier, these messages often contain viewers' complaints, praise, irritation, and so forth about the characters of their favorite programs, responses that reveal viewers' perception of intimacy with the characters. Avid viewers can recognize appropriate and inappropriate behavior by characters, just as in real life our intimate knowledge of someone tells us when the person is behaving falsely. In the following messages, two viewers interact over the development of Michael Kuzak, a key character who served as an up-and-coming young lawyer on NBC's "L.A. Law," by noting the constraints of the production process on his evaluation:

> **Viewer 1:** I agree with what you say about Michael. My point was that he sort of threatened to go public with what he had figured out, thus breaking lawyer/client confidentiality. THAT would be illegal, although perhaps the moral thing to do. Michael has been playing fast and loose with the law for a long time. If I were writing it, he'd finally go too far and get disbarred.

> **Viewer 2:** About Michael, what would be the point of telling the world that Rikki [a short-term character] had killed her husband? ... But you are right that he has been "playing fast and loose with the law" lately. However, there is still time to have him do something else to be disbarred.

> **Viewer 1:** Maybe Michael will leave unscathed, but I sort of hope not. It seems un-realistic to me that he manages to follow his own convictions, even when they cause him to ignore the law.

Viewer Pleasure. Closely related to the concept of the viewer-character bond is that of viewer pleasure. It has long been debated what viewers are connecting with in particular televisual genres. Pleasure for daytime serial viewers, for example, is argued to lie not in narrative realism but rather in emotional realism (Ang 1985). What is recognized as real by the viewer is not knowledge about the world but rather a familiar and subjective experience of the world—a "structure of feeling" (Ang 1985, pp. 41–45).

Pleasure among viewers of daytime and prime-time serials has been widely studied, and research on it documents how predominantly female viewers identify with gendered emotions and dilemmas portrayed in these genres. Our materials reveal how viewer pleasure is derived as well from additional textual elements and genres that resonate with other culturally meaningful experiences. The preceding quotations suggest that many viewers of the humanistic ensemble genre are connecting with the authenticity or realism of the characters and events on the program. The pleasure for viewers of other genres is described in these examples:

- I like shows that present the (for lack of a better word) weird side of life. "Twin Peaks" does a good job of this.

- ["Northern Exposure"] is such a gentle, relaxing show. It makes me feel good to be alive. It never fails to bring a smile to my face. ... What a great show.

The issue of viewer pleasure is also a component of the bond between viewers and producers, in that producers explicitly offer certain pleasures to the viewer for tuning in. One example has already been mentioned: the producer of "Northern Exposure" promising audience members that the "next two episodes are killers." Promises of pleasure are also routinely incorporated into promotional commercials for programs, revealing producers' perceptions of what they think their viewers want from television programs. An expert on commercials for daytime serials notes: "[Commercials] promis[e] viewers even more excitement, even sexier romances, and even better reasons to tune in" (Mazzurco 1989). Promotional commercials plainly cater to the viewer, illuminating, again, the interactive nature of the production of meaning on television—that is, that the audience is an active agent rather than a passive recipient in the viewing process.

Viewer pleasure is integral to viewers' claims to agency and to popularity. As seen in the following example, pleasure can register as intense viewer interest or indifference, spread by word-of-mouth to other viewers (see also our discussion next of the viewer-viewer bond). The form of this pleasure contrasts with our earlier discussion of agency that is publicly expressed in the form of letters and announcements and contributes to the viewer-producer bond. Viewer pleasure shared with other viewers and the agency this form of activity implies presumably are inaccessible to producers, whose rating systems measure only whether a television is on or off, not the level of viewer involvement or interest. As one bulletin-board member elaborates:

- I think television executives should do better surveys than just Nielsen ratings. After all there is a big difference between the shows you watch and the shows you LOVE, LOVE, LOVE! Because I am very busy, I try to look through the TV guide every day and circle the one or two shows that I really don't want to miss that day. Other times when I am not busy I sit there mindlessly flipping channels and watching whatever doesn't bore me to death, but somehow I don't think the Suits have ever figured out that there are very different levels of TV watching going on out there.

Our materials reveal the essential role different viewer pleasure plays in the satisfaction derived from the televisual experience, the varying forms viewer agency can take about that pleasure, and the role pleasure takes in generating attention and dispersing the popularity of particular televisual texts.

Viewer-Viewer Bond. Earlier research suggests that bonds are formed around the process of televisual viewing, transforming the experience from an individualized to a collective one (see Bielby and Harrington 1992; Lemish 1985). The viewer-character bond precedes and generates bonds between viewers. While this is most apparent in the face-to-face sharing of information, it can also be observed in the proliferation of informal social networks among viewers, such as fan clubs and videotape exchange networks (Bielby and Harrington 1992, pp. 40–41).

In the EBB materials, evidence for bonds between viewers is ample and varied. Evidence includes such things as the frequent exchange of addresses and videotapes that occurs on the network as well as the efforts by some members to connect or introduce other members to one another. For example, the detailed inside information provided regularly by the assistant director of "Northern Exposure" prompted others to post messages asking for information on the person providing the inside scoop. A person who communicates regularly with the director posted a message describing the qualifications of the director.

Another example involves the aforementioned episode of "Northern Exposure" in which portions were lost due to technical error. This prompted a flood of queries as to the events of the missing moments and a flood of detailed responses, including the following:

> **Kirsten:** Help came through. Be sure to check the post from Marilyn K. that came to my bulletin. Wasn't that an awful time for the film to freeze on us!

This remark illustrates nicely the role of facilitator assumed by some members of the EBB network and the existence of bonds between viewers.

Other evidence for the viewer-viewer bond is the presence of tangential conversation that occasionally occurs on the network. That is, although most of the dialogue focuses explicitly on television programs, there are infrequent instances when talk about television generates talk about other subjects. The most striking example of this is a long multiple-partied dialogue that initially focused on an episode of "L.A. Law" in which one female character kisses another. Debate about the incident sparked a complex dialogue on the meaning of homosexuality and bisexuality. Note the following excerpts:

- From what I understand, hostility towards bisexuals is not uncommon both within and without of the gay community. Bisexuals are accused of "straddling the fence."

- Bisexuality doesn't exist. ... We don't go around having both the mousse and the apple pie for dessert ... it's either one or the other.

- Bisexuality is more common than monosexuals like to admit; specifically, it's more common than homosexuality. If you have ever enjoyed it both ways, YOU ARE BI, no matter WHAT you call or think of yourself as. The "either one or the other" fallacy is an absurd misperception of a spectrum.

This debate about sexuality spurred a second debate about the place of homosexuality/bisexuality on television. The exchange indicates viewers' awareness of the constraints the medium places on the portrayal of fictional characters.

- If you are writing a script and you have a character walking around that has absolutely no preference, what kind of a character is that? How can you have someone in an ongoing series that has no sexual preference, regardless of whether or not they know it?

- From a writer's point of view I have to protest the notion of a character with such wishy-washy desires. Regardless of how confused the character appears to us ... there has to be something within him/her that is trying to get out.

This dialogue indicates that the EBB network functions as a basis not only for interaction about television but for interaction in general, which provides evidence for the generation and facilitation of viewer-viewer bonds.

In addition to the evidence just noted, we suggest that the most striking piece of evidence for the viewer-viewer bond lies in the examination of the bulletin-board network itself. Viewers subscribe to the EBB for the purpose of engaging other viewers in dialogue. It is a distinctly interactive medium and much more immediately accessible than other types of fan networks (such as pen pals, celebrity gossip, and numerous related systems). By becoming members, viewers can join a community of others interested in interacting about characters, story lines, production news, and so forth. This social network serves as a crucial point of reference for the subculture (Fine 1979). The EBBs facilitate and are, indeed, organized around the viewer-viewer bond, as one EBB member illustrated through the following message:

- I have talked about this show ["Northern Exposure"] to everybody I could to try to boost the ratings. I told all my friends ... both of them.

One might argue, however, that despite members' routine communication with one another, a bond has not really developed in that the messages are essentially anonymous. Anonymity is certainly the case for some messages; many times an entry is addressed to "All," meaning that anyone/everyone is invited to join the dialogue:

- Does anyone remember how Josh [a character on "General Hospital"] died? ... It's driving me crazy.

At other times, however, messages are addressed to a specific party, indicating that one member is directly engaging another member in a dialogue. In addition, personal information is often included in messages, indicating a bond between members:

- Hi Marta. How'd you do with your exam? ... The thought of Carly and Victor [characters on "Days of Our Lives"] being married for five minutes is dreadful.
- Louis—Hi! How've you been? Glad to see the ole soap plot's still going strong.

While we do not know for certain that these viewers were strangers to one another before subscribing to the EBBs, we suspect that the relationship was generated and facilitated by the electronic system itself. Relationships between members shift from "anonymous" to "intimate" as social bonds develop. Agency clearly underlies this shift and is instrumental in the formation of audiences from groups of viewers.

Viewers, Agency, and Audiences

Our work has contributed to audience studies by drawing upon the concepts of agency and popularity to explore issues about viewership. Using evidence from electronic bulletin boards, we captured viewer idioculture as it emerges naturally, unencumbered by observer probes, presence, or intervention. We gained insight into forms of viewer agency as it exists both privately for viewers themselves and publicly as feedback about viewers' interests for television producers, writers, and network executives.

By analyzing direct viewer-to-viewer interaction, we identified means through which viewers form the virtual communities that comprise audiences. We focused upon viewers' commentary, speculation, and gossip that emerge from viewers' expressed pleasures and displeasures with televisual texts. We examined how viewers interactionally organize around popular cultural texts through the diffusion of insights, opinions, and information to other viewers. We observed how diffusion of information is a crucial interactional element for the creation and existence of the idioculture of any given audience. In short, we examined the bases for audiences as interpretative communities that arise through social interaction.

By examining the content viewers identify to each other and the cultural resources they call upon to interpret televisual texts, we revealed ways in which cultural objects are established as popular. Viewers are very insightful about the elements that interest or disinterest them in the viewing process, including aspects of production, characterization, and expected pleasures from viewing. They also display effective agency in establishing social bonds with other viewers around these preferences and dislikes. Viewers actively seek out each other through simple queries and requests for information. Viewers also seek out each other for more complex interpretation, reflection, and evaluation of televisual texts as they relate them to larger social and cultural issues. That "reaching out" is crucial to the popular acceptance or rejection of televisual programming.

We have only begun exploring the links between viewership and audience formation. Viewers cooperatively and interactively call upon each other to make meaning of what they see. We provided evidence for the extent to which viewer interaction functions in a multitude of ways and carries multileveled responses. It remains to be examined how wider forms of viewer-to-viewer interaction contribute to audience formation, the interpretation of meaning, and the maintenance of popularity. Furthermore, we are curious about the extent to which viewer-to-viewer interaction overcomes anonymity, the extent to which true social bonds form among viewers, and the extent to which those types of bonds contribute to audience formation.

Our findings have implications for refining the concept of spectatorship as it relates to audience studies. Most approaches to spectatorship position the viewer theoretically in a manner that delimits the range of possibilities for textual readings. Work needs to be done on spectatorship that captures the diversity of meanings read at the moment of reception. Also unexamined is how the process of spectatorship is linked to the apparent social interaction that constitutes viewership. That is, if spectatorship is an individual-level process and viewership an interactional one, at what point should analysts attend to meaning?

Our analysis also has implications for study of the concept of agency. Earlier work examines agency as publicly identifiable feedback between viewers and producers of televisual series. We found evidence that its expression takes on forms that are not necessarily accessible to producers, writers, and executives and yet are instrumental in defining what is accepted as popular. Indeed, what is missing is knowledge of how producers accommodate to preferred, alternate, negotiated, or altogether rejected readings by viewers. Television's popularity and thus its commercial viability rest on this interaction. The forms of agency considered in our work suggest a far more dynamic interchange between producers' intentions and viewers' consumption. Scholars of audience studies need to rethink how the popularity of televisual programming is a reciprocal process between producers and viewers.

Audience studies has the potential for contributing to a broad theoretical agenda explaining the complex and dynamic relationship of audiences and viewers to televisual production. Ultimately, scholarship should attend to how creative personnel like producers must negotiate responsibility and control not only with those for whom they work (Becker 1982; Cantor 1980; Cantor and Cantor 1986) but with audiences' interests, tastes, and preferences as well. Viewer agency is a fruitful point of origin for examining the complex and dynamic negotiation among audiences of popular cultural objects like television.

References

Allen, R. C. 1983. "On Reading Soaps: A Semiotic Primer." Pp. 97–108 in *Regarding Television,* ed. E. A. Kaplan. Los Angeles: American Film Institute Monograph Series/University Publications of America, Inc.

———. 1985. *Speaking of Soap Operas.* Chapel Hill: University of North Carolina Press.

Ang, Ien. 1985. *Watching "Dallas."* London: Methuen.

———. 1989. "Wanted: Audiences. On the Politics of Empirical Audience Studies." Pp. 96–115 in *Remote Control: Television, Audiences, and Cultural Power,* ed. E. Seiter, H. Borchers, G. Kreutzner, and E.-M. Warth. London: Routledge.

Becker, H. 1982. *Art Worlds.* Berkeley: University of California Press.

Bielby, D. D., and C. L. Harrington. 1992. "Public Meanings, Private Screenings: The Formation of Social Bonds Through the Televisual Experience." Pp. 155–178 in *Perspectives on Social Problems,* vol. 3, ed. G. Miller and J. Holstein. Greenwich, Conn.: Jai Press.

Boden, D., and D. D. Bielby. 1983. "The Past as Resource: A Conversational Analysis of Elderly Talk." *Human Development* 26:309–319.

Brown, M. E. 1989. "Soap Opera and Women's Culture: Politics and the Popular." Pp. 161–190 in *Doing Research on Women's Communication: Perspectives on Theory and Method,* ed. K. Carter and C. Spitzack. Norwood, N.J.: Ablex.

Cantor, M. 1980. "Audience Control." Pp. 97–115 in *Prime Time TV: Content and Control,* ed. Muriel Cantor. Beverly Hills, Calif.: Sage.

Cantor, M. G., and J. M. Cantor. 1986. "Audience Composition and Television Content: The Mass Audience Revisited." Pp. 214–225 in *Media, Audience, and Social Structure,* ed. S. Ball-Rokeach and M. G. Cantor. Newbury Park, Calif.: Sage.

DuBrow, R. 1991. "Humanity Loses to Reality." *Los Angeles Times,* March 30, F1.

Feuer, J. 1984. "Melodrama, Serial Form and Television Today." *Screen* 25:4–16.

———. 1987. "Genre Study and Television." Pp. 113–133 in *Channels of Discourse,* ed. R. C. Allen. Chapel Hill: University of North Carolina Press.

———. 1989. "Reading *Dynasty:* Television and Reception Theory." *South Atlantic Quarterly* 88:443–460.

Fine, G. A. 1979. "Small Groups and Culture Creation: The Idioculture of Little League Baseball Teams." *American Sociological Review* 44:733–745.

Fine, G. A., and S. Kleinman. 1979. "Rethinking Subculture: An Interactionist Analysis." *American Journal of Sociology* 85:1–20.

Fiske, J. 1987. *Television Culture.* London: Methuen.

Grossberg, L. 1987. "The In-Difference of Television." *Screen* 28:29–45.

Hall, S. 1980 [1974]. "Encoding/Decoding." Pp. 128–138 in *Culture, Media, and Language,* ed. S. Hall, D. Hobson, A. Lowe, and P. Willis. London: Hutchinson.

Kaplan, E. A. 1983. *Regarding Television.* Los Angeles: American Film Institute Monograph Series/University Publications of America, Inc.

Lemish, D. 1985. "Soap Opera Viewing in College: A Naturalistic Inquiry." *Journal of Broadcasting and Electronic Media* 29:275–293.

Mazzurco, D. 1989. "The Network Promos." *Soap Opera Update* (October 23): 48–49.

Morley, D. 1980. *The Nationwide Audience: Structure and Decoding.* London: British Film Institute.

———. 1981. "The *Nationwide* Audience: A Critical Postscript." *Screen Education* 39:3–14.

Nye, R. 1971. "Notes for an Introduction to a Discussion of Popular Culture." *Journal of Popular Culture* 4:1931–1938.

Rosenberg, H. 1991. "Are the Nights of Yuppie Angst Really Over?" *Los Angeles Times,* May 28, F1.

Seiter, E., H. Borchers, G. Kreutzner, and E.-M. Warth. 1989. "Introduction." Pp. 1–15 in *Remote Control: Television, Audiences, and Cultural Power,* ed. E. Seiter, H. Borchers, G. Kreutzner, and E.-M. Warth. London: Routledge.

Shibutani, T. 1991. "Human Agency from the Standpoint of Pragmatism." Pp. 183–194 in *Verstehen and Pragmatism: Essays in Interpretative Sociology,* ed. Horst Helle, Frankfurt, Germany: Peter Lang.

Stone, A. 1990. "Cyberspace and the Limits of Social and Cultural Reality." In *Newsletter of the Sociology of Culture,* vol. 5, no. 2. Washington, D.C.: American Sociological Association.

Zimmerman, D., and C. West. 1975. "Sex Roles, Interruptions and Silences in Conversations." Pp. 105–129 in *Language and Sex: Difference and Dominance,* ed. B. Thorne and N. Henley. Rowley, Mass.: Newbury.

FIVE

Between the Public and the Private: The Domestic Uses of Information and Communications Technologies

DAVID MORLEY

Over the course of the last ten years or so, public debate in many of the advanced industrial countries of the West has often been focused on questions concerning the impact and role of new information and communication technologies in transforming both society at large and the family in particular. Public discourse, from governmental papers through business forecasting to popular journalism, abounds with images of the increasingly privatized family, shut off from public life, turned in on itself, within a culture of do-it-yourself home improvement and privatized leisure, connected to the wider world only through the electronic forms of satellite/cable TV and teleshopping.

This image has been articulated to both utopian and dystopian visions of various kinds. Moreover, this family itself is seen as increasingly fragmented internally—the multiactive cellular family whose home is a multipurpose activity center for the increasingly separate lifestyles of the individuals within it (see Tomlinson 1989). Thus Gunter and Svennevig (1987), commenting on the impact of new communications technologies, have asked whether we might see "a trend towards the increased acquisition of accessory equipment ... with each family member having access to a personal home entertainment system resulting in increased isolation of family members from each other" (p. 86).

This chapter has benefited from Roger Silverstone's comments on an earlier draft, for which I am grateful. Parts of the chapter draw on material previously used in a Brunel University Discussion Paper, "Families, Technologies and Consumption," written jointly with Roger Silverstone, Andrea Dahlberg, and Sonia Livingstone.

Much of this debate has been conducted within a frame of reference that takes technology as a (more or less) independent variable, which is then seen to have effects on both the family and society at large. Thus the new technologies are widely seen as portending both the transformation of relations within the family and the transformation of overall relations between the private and public spheres of society.

Of course, in this day and age, no one wants to be seen as a "technological determinist." Unfortunately, in practice, the premises of this position have not been abandoned in research, and, to some large extent, the field is still dominated by an agenda of how technology will/may change society. One might well draw a parallel here with developments in the more narrowly conceived field of media studies, which, over the last ten years or so, has gradually seen the abandonment of the theoretical problematic of the "effects of the media" in favor of a concern with a rather more complex set of issues. Central to these issues is how audiences (within the limits of their domestic and structural positions and with the limited set of cultural resources at their disposal, as a result of their social positioning) actively make use of and interpret the symbolic products offered to them by the mass media. In this connection, Stuart Hall has usefully drawn a simple distinction between the vertical dimensions of media analysis (concerned with questions of power and institutions) and the horizontal (concerned with the integration of media and other discourses of the everyday-life world) and argued that the key advance in media studies in recent years has been the recognition that one must study the way in which the former (vertical) dimension is mediated through the latter (horizontal). I shall argue that it is to those forms of mediation that we must address ourselves—not simply as applied to the consumption of mass media but rather as applied to the wider field of symbolic (and material) consumption practices through which a whole range of technologies are "domesticated." Different observers have pointed to the increasing centrality of the home as site of leisure activities (video, cable, and so on), of the growth of homeworking (computer, telephone services), and of interactive services (teleshopping, telebooking). But how much do we actually know about how these technologies are actually used behind the closed doors of the household? What do these technologies mean to their domestic users, and how are they incorporated into different household cultures? And further, to what extent are they used in the ways and for the purposes their designers and producers intended?

Clearly ICTs (information and communication technologies) play a fundamental role in connecting the public and private worlds; in so doing they also transgress the boundaries of the household unit. Thus questions arise as to how the use of ICTs is regulated in households of different types with different cultures and values. Further questions arise about how particular ICTs (which have the capacity both to integrate and to isolate the household) are used in households with stronger or weaker boundaries, and about the extent to which different types of social relations are mediated through various technologies in different types of households. Of course, over time, all of these technologies acquire particular meanings and significances through the particular ways in which they are used in domestic life. The issue then is exactly what these technologies mean to their users: How are different ICTs perceived and understood by different household members (for example, across divisions of gender and age)? Moreover, we have also to consider what role these private meanings then have in determining how (and by whom) these technologies are used and what the role of socialization is in developing and transmitting technological competencies, especially in relation to the construction and maintenance of different forms of gendered subjectivities.

This chapter arises from my involvement in a research project, designed to address these issues, based at Brunel University in England and conducted between 1987 and 1990 jointly with Roger Silverstone, Eric Hirsch, Sonia Livingstone, and Andrea Dahlberg. The project consisted of a loosely ethnographic study of technology use among twenty different families. In this chapter I shall take the opportunity to offer a number of theoretical reflections on some of the issues addressed in that project.

The Public and the Private

In attempting to develop an analysis of the domestic functions of communications and information technologies, we can usefully take as one of our starting points Bourdieu's (1972) analysis of the Berber house, in which he offers an exemplary model for the articulation of public and private space and for the articulation of domestic technologies within gender relations. While that analysis is, of course, culturally specific and clearly pertains to a preindustrial rural society, I would argue that a number of Bourdieu's insights remain pertinent to the analysis of these issues as they appear in urban and industrial societies.

In that analysis, Bourdieu formulates the relation between the domestic and the public as an "opposition between female space and male space, on the one hand; the privacy of all that is intimate, on the other, the open space of social relations." Bourdieu argues that the orientation of the house is fundamentally defined from the outside, from the point of view of the masculine, public sphere—as the "place from which men come out" so that the house is "an empire within an empire, but one that always remains subordinate" (Bourdieu 1972, 101).

My argument is that despite subsequent social and economic developments, in contemporary industrial societies the division between public and private remains fundamentally articulated to gender relations. Thus Gamarnikow and Purvis (1983) note that the private realm continues to be outside the boundaries of the social, equated not only with the feminine but also with the natural. Similarly, Fontaine observes that in our modes of social organization, we retain a fundamental opposition between the public and private spheres, in which "the former is [understood as] the realm of law and consists of the institutions of the state and the national economy, the latter is [seen as] the state of personal affection and moral duty" where there is a "well established association of women with domestic life and men with the public world of competition and power" (Fontaine 1988, 268; see Ardener 1981).

In his historical analysis, Zaretsky (1976) traces the process through which, as he puts it, with the transformation of the family from a productive unit to a unit of consumption, "capitalist development gave rise to the idea of the family as a separate realm from the economy, [and] created a 'separate' sphere of personal life, seemingly divorced from the mode of production." As a result of this development, Zaretsky argues that "The family became the major sphere of society in which the individual could be foremost—within it, a new sphere of social activity began to take shape: personal life" (p. 61).

In his analysis of contemporary patterns of consumption, Tomlinson (1989) addresses the cultural and ideological dimensions of what he argues to be the increasing centrality of the home—and associated concerns with home ownership and "home improvements"—within contemporary British society. He notes the familiar finding that for most people 80 percent of leisure time is spent in the home (see Glyptis 1989) and further notes the growth of consumer spending on (and in) the home. For Tomlinson, the central concern is with the development of the home as an autonomous or (increasingly) self-sufficient contained consumer unit. He argues that what we see in society is a continuing process of privatization, as home-based consumption represents a retreat from the public realm of community, and the private individual retreats into his (or her) house and garden. (See Docherty et al. [1987] on the shift from cinema to television as the primary mode of film consumption.)

Tomlinson argues that this represents not just a shift in patterns of consumption but also a crucial ideological shift in the cultural meaning of the home. The home has become increasingly the site for "an unprecedentedly privatised and atomised leisure and consumer lifestyle" (1989, 10). For him, the key shift is one in which "as the home fills up with the leisure equipment servicing the needs of the dispersed household members, it moves towards a new function. The Puritan notion of the home was as a Little Kingdom. The Victorian concept stressed Home as Haven: the late modern Elizabethan concept constructs the Home as Personalised Marketplace. It is where most of us express our consumer power, our cultural tastes" (Tomlinson 1989, 10).

Certainly I would agree with Tomlinson in giving a central place to processes of domestic consumption. However, he articulates this analysis of the centrality of the home in contemporary culture to a somewhat one-sided vision of the cultural significance of this growth in privatized consumption. In this sense he appears to offer a contemporary version of the "embourgeoisement" thesis that is prey to many shortcomings noted originally by Goldthorpe and Lockwood (1968).

The central point, then, concerns the articulations of a set of parallel oppositions—not only public/private but also masculine/feminine; not only production/consumption but also work/leisure. Our analysis of the uses of communications and information technologies must be integrated with an analysis of the shifting relations between these terms—and indeed must be concerned with the function of these technologies themselves in creating the possibility of such shifts. If we are to avoid the problematic "naturalization" of the domestic (and its assumed connections to femininity, consumption, and leisure), we must analyze its historical construction. In this connection King (1980), building on Thompson's (1967) work on the regulation of time in the development of industrial capitalism, offers an insightful analysis of the historical emergence both of leisure times ("the weekend") and leisure places (the home, the holiday cottage)—"a horizontal container for the consumption of surplus free time" (King 1980). King's analysis is principally concerned with class and the differential development of free time for members of different classes. I should like to extend that analysis by also considering the question of gender and the differential relations of men and women to leisure both as a temporal phenomenon ("after work," "the weekend") and as a spatial phenomenon (as sited routinely in the home or other places).

Brunsdon and Morley (1978) argue that while the domestic sphere is also a sphere of domestic labor (the reproduction of labor power), it has come to be centrally defined as the social space within which "individuality" can be expressed—the refuge from the material constraints and pressure of the outside world, the last repository of the human values that are otherwise crushed by the pressure of modern life. The central point, they argue (1978, 78), is that the workings of this private sphere cannot effectively be understood without attention to the specific role of women and their central place in the domestic sphere. As is noted in that analysis, the women and the home seem, in fact, to become each other's attributes, as evinced by Ruskin among others: "Wherever a true wife comes, this home is always round her" (Brunsdon and Morley 1978, 78).

However, the point is not simply a historical one; rather we see here an ideological construction of social domains and gender relations that retains a strong contemporary relevance—insofar as both the household itself and women's domestic labor within it continue to be conceived as the unchanging natural backcloth to the "real" world of activity in the public sphere. The further point is, of course, that men and women are positioned in fundamentally different ways within the domestic sphere. If for men the home is fundamentally a site of leisure and recuperation from work, for women—whether or not they also work outside the house—it is also a site of work and responsibility. As the overall social location of leisure moves increasingly into the home, the contradictions experienced by women in this sphere are correspondingly heightened (see Cowan 1989).

At the same time, I would argue that it is necessary to pay attention to the ways in which the private space of domestic life is socially constructed and articulated with political life. Zaretsky notes that historically "the early bourgeois understood the family to be the basic unit of social order—'a little church, a little state' and the lowest rung in the ladder of social authority. They conceived society as composed not of individuals but of families" (Zaretsky 1976, 42). In a similar vein,

Fontaine observes that in contemporary industrial societies, "households are also units in the political and economic organisation of society; as such they are part of the public domain. A legal address is an expected attribute of a citizen" (1988, 284). Thus, while the household enjoys privacy, which implies the right to exclude (unless the police have a warrant) and to enjoy autonomy of action, "that privacy is as much a matter of social definition as the effect of thick walls" (Fontaine 1988, 280).

Moreover, as Donzelot (1979) argues, the family does not have a unique or unambiguous status. For certain (e.g., juridical) purposes, it is private, while for others it is public. It is a site of intervention for various state welfare agencies, whose intention to regulate child-rearing practices within the family, for example, is legitimated by reference to the state's concern with the "proper" upbringing of future members of the national labor force (see Hodges and Hussain 1979). For Donzelot, the family is not simply a private institution but also the point of intersection of a whole range of medical, judicial, educational, and psychiatric practices; it is by no means a wholly private realm, somehow "outside" (or indeed setting the limits of) the social. In this sense the family is neither totally separate from nor opposed to the state; rather the "private" itself is a (legally, juridically) constructed space, into which the state and other agencies can intervene and the very privacy of which is itself constituted and ultimately guaranteed by these institutions. This is not to suggest that the "freedoms" of the domestic space are somehow illusory or ultimately reducible to their place within a history of regulation and power, in the way Donzelot himself at times seems to do. Rather it is to suggest that the latter perspective is a necessary corrective to any analysis of domestic processes that remains blind to the history and social construction of that space.

We need to be attentive in this context to the incorporation of communications technologies within preexisting social domains—in particular within different gender domains—and also to the particular role of communications technologies in the construction and reconstruction of these domains. Haralovich (1988) offers a fascinating account of the role of the suburban family "situation comedy" on American television in the 1950s in "the construction and distribution of social knowledge about the place of women" (p. 39). She is concerned with analyzing the interlinkages among factors such as the roles of television representations of lifestyles, government, economic and housing policies, and the consumer-product industries in defining the norms for a particular model of a "healthy" lifestyle (a single-family detached suburban home in a stable, nonurban environment) and in defining women's place within that domain as a "homemaker." Her argument is that television representations, in this respect, worked in close parallel to the material supports of housing policies, which were focused on organizing the interior space of the home so as to reinforce the gender-specific socializing functions of the family. Thus, she notes, in America in the 1950s, "the two national priorities of the post-war period—removing women from the paid labour force and building more housing—were conflated and tied to an architecture of home and neighbourhood that celebrates a mid-19th Century ideal of separate spheres for men and women" (Haralovich 1988, 43).

Thus we are returned to some of the concerns the earlier discussion of Bourdieu was designed to indicate. Certainly not all contemporary TV sitcoms are like the ones Haralovich analyzes (we now have the divorce sitcom, the single-parent sitcom, and so on), but the nuclear family continues to play a central role in television discourses—which in turn, I would argue, continue to construct and circulate social knowledge about the appropriate forms of gender relations and about the articulation of the domestic and the public spheres.

Technology and Gender

My argument is that we need a contextual understanding of the use and function of technologies as they are incorporated both within the social organization of the relations between the public and private spheres and within the domestic sphere itself. This is also to focus, initially, on questions of *how* rather than *why* in relation to domestic technologies. To transpose Lindlof and Traudt's argument (1983), it is also to say that the central theoretical and policy questions concerning the significance of the new technologies in the home cannot satisfactorily be framed, let alone answered, until a number of prerequisite questions concerning what the use of such technologies entails for all family members have been posed and investigated. In the first instance, this approach may lead us toward seemingly elementary considerations—such as the determining effect of the structure and size of the domestic space available to different families—that have been improperly neglected by researchers in this field to date. Thus, for example, it may be important to research the extent to which the aural barriers afforded by the consumption of various communication media (from the television to the Walkman) may function for members of higher-density families with more restricted physical environments as a way of creating "personal space" in lieu of physical spatial privacy.

However, the domestic sphere is not simply a physical space—it is also a socially organized space. Just as I argued earlier, following Bourdieu, that the public/private divide is closely articulated with gender relations, so again I follow Bourdieu's lead and turn to the significance of the gendered organization of domestic space within the private sphere as a fundamental determinant of the take-up and use of different technologies by family members. As Bourdieu puts it: "The opposition which is set up between the external world and the house only takes on its full meaning ... if one of the terms of this relation, the house, is itself seen as being divided according to the same principles which oppose it to the other term" (Bourdieu 1972, 104).

There is, of course, now a vast body of literature concerned with the function of gender as a fundamental principle of social and cultural organization that it is beyond the scope of this chapter to review. I shall take only two central points from that literature. The first is that one of the key concerns in this field has been the seeming invisibility of women and their activities in traditional sociology. The second (and related) point is that made by McRobbie and Garber in their analysis of girls' subcultures. They argue that this invisibility (within the public sphere of life on which sociological analysis has been traditionally concentrated) is itself structurally generated by women's particular positioning in the domestic sphere. Thus, they argue: "If women are marginal to the … cultures of work … it is because they are central and pivotal to a subordinate area, which mirrors, but in a complementary and subordinate way, the dominant masculine areas. They are marginal to work because they are central to the subordinate, complementary sphere of the family" (McRobbie and Garber 1976, 211).

That centrality, I would argue, is of great consequence in determining differential relations to domestic communications technologies for men and women. We can begin by briefly exemplifying this argument by reference to the significance of gender in organizing the domestic uses of one particular technology, in this case television, as that is one area in which these arguments have already been well developed. Hobson's work on housewives' television-viewing habits demonstrates that for the women she studied, their sense of home as a site of continuing domestic work and responsibilities leads to a quite distinctive form of television consumption: Viewing is, in the main, a fundamentally distracted and interrupted activity for them. At its simplest, this finding suggests that men's and women's differential positions in the domestic sphere—home as, fundamentally, a site of leisure for the one but, more contradictorily, a site of both leisure and work for the other—determines their differential relation to television.

Similarly, my own (1986) analysis of viewing patterns in working-class London households reveals the structuring effect of gender relations. In those families gender was consistently associated with distinctive viewing patterns, amounts and styles of viewing, and distinctive program preferences. Moreover, power and control over program choice were themselves seen to be a matter of gender relations; so too was the ability to sit and watch a chosen program without feelings of guilt. In that analysis I argued that the "gendering" of technologies is most apparent in relation to video and that, in the families I interviewed, videos were seen (like automatic control devices) as principally the possessions of fathers and sons, occasionally of daughters, but least often of mothers. In a similar vein, Rogge and Jensen (1988) refer to the world of the "new media" as principally a masculine domain. As Lull (1988) notes, the "masculinization" of the VCR:

> is a logical extension of the masculine roles of installing and operating home equipment. They are the family members who develop user competency. Many new technologies are "toys" for men [see Moores 1988] and they enjoy playing with them. So the responsibility becomes a kind of male pleasure. The operation of this equipment … is a function that men are expected to perform for their families. The responsibilities, pleasures and functions that men have with all these pieces of equipment gives

them some degree of control over them and over other family members along the way (Lull 1988, 255).

In her analysis of the use of home videos, Gray (1987) begins by noting that the differential cultural positioning of men and women in the domestic sphere is relatively independent of (and resistant to) actual economic transformations (such as male unemployment or women going out to work). Regardless of such developments, the domestic setting is still largely seen as a sphere of "women's work," and this, Gray argues, strongly informs gender-based views of new technologies such as video. Thus she follows both Cockburn (1985) in suggesting that new technologies have tended to reproduce traditional work patterns across gender, and Zimmerman (1981) in arguing that "old ideas" have largely become encoded in new technologies. From Gray's perspective, the use of all domestic technologies must be understood as being incorporated within the social organization of gender domains. The main structuring principle, she argues, is that technologies that are "used for one off jobs with a highly visible end product (e.g., electric drill, saw, sander)" are understood as masculine, while those "used in the execution of the day-to-day chores with an end product that is often immediately consumed (e.g., cooker, washing machine, iron)" are understood as feminine (Gray 1987, 5).

The use (or nonuse) of technologies is, as she argues, no simple matter of technological complexity. As she notes, while the women she studied did not use their domestic videos (or did not use particular functions, such as the time controls), relying instead on male partners or children, they routinely operated other extremely sophisticated pieces of domestic technology such as washing or sewing machines. The determining principle behind these women's felt alienation from the video seemed to have less to do with its technical complexity and more to do with its incorporation, alongside the television, into what they felt to be a principally masculine domain of domestic leisure—in which they felt they had no real place.

Appropriate Technologies: For Whom?

It is perhaps worth restating at this point the theoretical position being argued in relation to the gendering of technologies. I want to make clear that I am not advancing an essentialist argument that would interpret the empirical facts of different male and female patterns of use and involvement with technology as the inevitable result of the biological characteristics of the persons concerned. It is, in short, an argument about gender as a cultural category, not about sex as a biological category. Rather, I am concerned with the cultural construction of masculine and feminine positions, subjectivities, and domains and the articulation (or disarticulation) of technologies into these culturally constructed domains. Different empirical persons who are biologically male or female may, of course, inhabit the cultural domains of masculinity and femininity in different ways. However, the incorporation of technologies within these culturally defined patterns is the determining issue.

As Kramarae (1988) notes, a whole set of issues is at stake here concerning which machines are called technologies: of technologies not only as machines but also as social relations and communication systems; of the modes in which social relations are themselves structured and (re)organized by technological systems; and of the role the incorporation of technologies into gender domains plays in defining both the meanings of the technologies and for whom their use is appropriate. The question is how to move beyond the simple description of existing patterns. Thus Rothschild (1983) describes how the home computer can function to reinforce the gender division of labor, "mother using it for recipes and household accounts, children—boys more than girls—using it for games ... and dad using it both as an 'adult toy' and possibly for professional work" (Rothschild, quoted in Baines 1989, 6).

I shall return to the specific question of the gender determination of computer use at the end of this section. First, however, it is important to pursue the theoretical point about how such differential patterns of use might be explained. In this connection, Baines (1989) argues for the usefulness of Bush's (1983) concept of technological "valences," as concerned with the culturally defined attributes (rather than the mechanically defined "essential qualities") of technologies. Bush argues that we must see social values, including those of gender, as embedded in technologies, and this is a factor determining their social use: "Tools and technologies have ... valence(s). ... A particular technological system, even an individual tool, has a tendency to interact in similar situations in definable and particular ways ... to fit in with certain social [and specifically gender—DM] norms ... and to disturb others" (Bush 1983, 155, quoted in Baines 1989).

Rakow (1988a) argues against any tendency to assume that technologies produce homogeneous effects. Rather she suggests "we should assume that the same technology may be used ... by different people in different ways to different effects" (p. 59). As posed, her arguments have both the strengths and the weaknesses of the established "uses and gratifications" perspective in the study of the mass media (see Halloran's [1971, 20] well-known injunction: "We should get away from thinking about what the media do to people and start thinking about what people do with the media"). The strength of that perspective lies in its acknowledgment of the potential openness or polysemy of both media products and technologies; the corresponding weakness lies partly in a tendency to overestimate this openness—and to neglect the inscription of powerful dominant meanings through the design, structuring, and marketing of the products.

Rakow suggests that we should ask what role technologies play in constructing and maintaining gender relationships, seeing technology as "a site where social practices are embedded [that] express and extend the construction of two asymmetrical genders" (1988a, 57) and crucially examining "how certain values and meanings underlie the development of technologies, in particular, masculine and feminine assigned values and meanings about gender" (1988a, 60).

Gamarnikow and Purvis (1983, 5) suggest that "the public/private split is a metaphor for the social patterning of gender." Rakow's central point is that this articulation also implies technologies:

> Practices involving technologies are constituted ... in and through relations of gender. Who does what with a technology for what purpose is, at least in part, a cause and effect of gender. Consequently, not only a technology but also a social practice involving it are associated by gender. Men are more likely than women to be owners and operators of cameras that take pictures of women. Women have their pictures taken and may be more likely to have responsibility for maintaining family ties and history through photographs. ... Men speak, write and publish more in the public world of commerce, politics and ideas ... but women write the family letters and make the family telephone calls (Rakow 1988a, 67).

In a further essay, Rakow (1988b) extends her analysis of the mutual "implication" of technology and gender with particular reference to the telephone. She argues that the telephone is a technology that has been centrally implicated in managing the problems created by the physical separation of (feminine) activities in the private sphere from the predominantly masculine public sphere, the isolation of the home and of women in that domestic space. Indeed, she claims that the very history of the telephone "cannot be told without accounting for the gender relations within which ... [it] ... developed" (Rakow 1988b, 224). At an empirical level, the point is quite straightforward. As Mayer (1977, 23) reports, "The most important single factor [determining how many calls a household will make] is the presence of a woman." This is, of course, not only an empirical but also a cultural fact: The special role of the telephone in women's lives and the association of the telephone with women's talk ("gossip" or "chatter") is condensed in the well-known stereotype of the woman who talks "too much" on the phone. As Rakow (1988b) notes, both folklore and the phone companies' own marketing literature (after the initial period in which the networks seemed to disapprove of and discourage such social uses of the instrument) are replete with images of the woman user's "peculiar addiction" to the phone.

However, my concern is to offer an explanatory framework within which we might situate both the empirical facts and the cultural stereotypes. Maddox (1977) argues, quite simply, that women's particular attachment to the telephone as a mode of symbolic communication (which to some large extent replaces physical movement, but compare Cowan 1989) is to be explained by women's actual soc. position in relation to transport, housing, and public space. Maddox cites three principal reasons for many women's heavy usage of the telephone: their confinement to the phone while caring for children; their fear of crime in public spaces; and their physical separation from relatives, the maintenance of relations with whom they understand as being an integral part of their "job description." Both

Rakow and Maddox note that outside the home, women's other principal involvement with the phone has been as operators and telephonists, paid to mediate communications largely among men in the sphere of business.

The central argument is that the nature of many women's empirical use of this particular technology is an effect of their understanding of their gender-defined role, in combination with the social organization of space and the function of the telephone in managing physically dispersed social relations. Many women principally use this technology to discharge their responsibilities for maintaining family and social relations and for home-business transactions (calls to plumbers, dentists, babysitters, and so on). However, beyond this somewhat utilitarian perspective, Rakow (1988b, 207) also notes the important use of the phone for many housewives in alleviating their feelings of loneliness and isolation. In a similar vein, a number of housewives interviewed in the Brunel study were emphatic that the telephone was the key technology that they would hate to lose because they saw it (to use their recurring phrase) as a way of "saving their sanity" given their felt sense of isolation in their homes.

Video Games and Computers: Masculinized Technologies?

Skirrow (1986) offers an analysis designed to explore the articulation of gender and technology in the case of video games. She starts from the empirical fact that on the whole, these games are not played by women, and she accounts for this by means of an analysis of the extent to which the pleasure offered by these games are gender-specific. The issue is then the way in which the games fail to engage with (or are, indeed, more actively perceived as being at odds with) feminine cultural sensibilities. Once again, the argument is that the determining principle is the articulation of specific technologies with the social and cultural organization of gender domains. Thus Skirrow focuses on "the relationship between a technologised sexuality and a sexualised technology" (1986, 142). In this particular case, Skirrow argues that "video games are particularly unattractive [to women] since they are part of a technology which ... is identified with male power, and they are about mastering a specifically male anxiety in a specifically male way" (p. 138).

Skirrow's analysis is principally concerned with the question of how this particular technology has come to be identified with a masculine domain. It is not a matter of machine design and hardware, in her view; rather it is a question of the ways in which the software and its marketing (the games themselves, the advertising, the magazines) articulate the cultural meanings of the technology through a set of masculinized images. She notes that popular culture is marked by a clear split along gender lines; that the games industry relies heavily in its marketing strategies on realizing familiar elements of popular culture in its own specific form; and that "most of these borrowings are from popular forms that appeal to boys"—principally action, adventure, and horror genres in which the fundamental model is that of the single (masculine) hero "waging a personal battle against overwhelming odds" (p. 120). As she observes, most of the adventure games involve some kind of quest, and the narratives draw heavily on the models of the exotic thriller, the travel story, or science fiction—story genres that particularly appeal to boys and have strong emphasis on technology and technical inventions (somewhat in the James Bond mold) as the solution to narrative problems.

I want to suggest that the model offered by Skirrow can also be applied to understanding how (and why) the computer has primarily come to be seen (and used) as a masculine technology, and how attempts to market the home computer have largely ended up with its appropriation within the masculine subdivision of that predominantly feminine domain. Just as Moores (1988) argues that radio technologies were initially of interest primarily to technically minded male hobbyists (and just as Gray [1987] argues that video was certainly understood initially as a "masculine toy"), so Haddon notes that initial interest in home computers in the UK was primarily among "adult male electronics enthusiasts who read *Wireless World, Electronics Weekly,* etc. ... [who] wanted to explore the technology, how it worked" (Haddon 1988, 16). He notes the defensiveness of the men concerned about being seen as "playing around with toys" and their sensitivity about references to consumer electronics retailers as "adult (male) toy shops." Interestingly, Haddon's account of subsequent attempts to market home computers in Britain (via notions of user-friendliness and the provision of documentation and instructions designed for the nonexpert that deemphasized the computer's status as technology) can be read as a (largely unsuccessful) attempt to demasculinize the home computer and thus enable it to break out of this narrow market. However, as Haddon notes, the "nonexperts," who were the new marketing strategists' addressees, were still primarily implied to be "laymen" rather than women— whose involvement with home computers has thus far largely been confined to an indirect one in which, as part of their gender-defined responsibilities for the socialization of children, they are concerned with acquiring home computers to secure perceived educational advantage for their children.

This pattern of the masculinization of computer technology is no simple quirk of British culture. Similar patterns obtain in France, as reported in the work of Jouet and Toussaint (1987) and Jouet (1988), who note that the majority of users both of home computers and the Minitel system are men (by a ratio of 3:1 in their findings). The problem, of course, is to understand why this is the case. In this connection, Turkle (1988) offers an extremely interesting analysis of the seeming rejection of computers by highly able female students at MIT and Harvard. Turkle's term to describe this phenomenon is not, for instance, "computer phobia" but rather "computer reticence," which she characterizes as "wanting to stay away, because the computer becomes a personal and cultural symbol of what a woman is not" (Turkle 1988, 41).

Just as Skirrow is concerned with developing an analysis of the "gender valence" of the specific pleasures offered by video games as a means of understanding the social patterning of the use of that technology, Turkle attempts to develop an analysis of the motivating pleasures informing computer (and specifically "hacker") culture. Turkle argues that one of the key satisfactions offered by getting involved with computers is that the involvement with an abstract formal system (as opposed to the ambiguities of interpersonal relationships) often functions as a safe retreat into a protective world—"a flight from relationships with people to relationships to the machine" (1988, 45)—and she argues that this option (an intensive involvement with a world of things and formal systems) is particularly attractive to adolescent boys. However, beyond this, Turkle also argues that hacker culture is characterized by certain core values—a preoccupation with winning and risks or "dangerous" learning strategies in which the hacker "plunge[s] in first and tries to understand later" (p. 49)—that are heavily identified with masculine cultural traits.

However, Turkle takes the argument a stage further and offers valuable insights into the cultural processes in which the categories of gender act as filters that make particular technologies appear more or less appropriate to individuals inhabiting differently gendered modes of subjectivity. McRobbie and Garber (1976) and Walkerdine (1988), among others, have offered analyses of the processes through which adolescent girls, in particular, often feel compelled to reject subjects (and objects) that they view as gender coded in such a way as to compromise their sense of femininity (see the debates on "science and girls," "mathematics and girls," Walkerdine 1988). It is for the same reasons, Turkle argues, that many women reject computers—because they perceive them as culturally coded as masculine. And identity, of course, is always centrally about difference (see Saussure 1974)—especially when one is dealing with such an intrinsically relational binary opposition as that of masculinity/femininity.

Turkle is concerned with the social construction of the computer as a masculine domain, as seen "through the eyes of women who have come to see something important about themselves in terms of what computers are not" (1988, 41). As she observes, women look at computers and see more than machines; they see those machines as predominantly mediated through what they perceive as a heavily masculine culture—and as a result they wish to differentiate themselves from this culture because it would be threatening to their self-images to see themselves as "a computer science type," and they "don't want to be part of that world." In short, Turkle argues, "women use their rejection of ... computer[s] ... to assert something about themselves as women. Being a woman is [seen as] opposed to a compelling relationship with a thing [the computer] that shuts people out" (p. 50).

As mentioned previously, the focus of my analysis is on cultural rather than biological categories. I would also sound another note of caution. While I am convinced that gender is a vital dimension of the structuring of meanings and uses of technologies, it does not, of course, function in isolation. In the end, of course, our concern will be to develop a mode of analysis in which the function of gender categories can be integrated along with (and at many points, as they cut across) other structuring categories—such as those of age, class, and ethnicity. Moreover, as Ang and Hermes (forthcoming) argue, neither is gender alone a reliable predictor of behavior, nor can the precise way in which gender is implicated in behavior be determined (or understood) outside of the context in which the relevant practices take concrete shape.

Communications Technologies in the Domestic Sphere

In this section I shall focus on the role that communications technologies (and, in particular, broadcasting technologies) play in articulating the spatial and temporal relations between the private and public spheres (see Morley and Silverstone 1990). My argument is that it is necessary to contextualize the development of communications technologies within the broader historical frame of the changing relations between public and private domains in contemporary culture, and to denaturalize the now taken-for-granted and unobtrusive presence of various communications technologies within the domestic space of the household.

Moores (1988) offers an account of the troubled history of the introduction of radio into the home and argues that while radio was gradually accommodated into the living room—that space in the house designated to the unity of the family group—this accommodation was by no means unproblematic (see Boddy 1986 on initial anxieties as to whether the living room was the appropriate location of the television set). As Moores points out, radio's entry into the domestic sphere was "marked by a disturbance of everyday lives and family relationships" (1988, 26). Indeed, the initial enthusiasm for the medium came largely from young, technically minded men—who were fascinated by the machine as a technology—and it was often resisted by women, for whom the unattractive mechanical appearance of the early sets (and their tendency to leak battery acid onto the furniture), combined with the fact that their husbands dominated their use, meant that for many women, radio was at first an unattractive medium. As one woman respondent quoted in Moores (1988) noted: "Only one of us could listen and that was my husband [using the earphones—DM]. The rest of us were sat like mummies" (p. 29).

Thus, as Moores notes, radio signified something quite different for men and for women. For men, it was a craze, a miraculous toy (see Gray [1987] on video recorders as "women's work and boys' toys"); for women, it was, Moores argues, "an ugly box and an imposed silence" (1988, 30–31), as reception was so poor that anyone talking in the room made it difficult for the listener to follow the broadcast. It was only much later, with the development of loudspeakers to replace individual headphones and the design of a new generation of radio sets marketed as fashionable objects of domestic furnishing, that radio gained its taken-for-granted place within the geography of the house. Of course, its place in the living room has now largely been taken by the television set, with the radio(s) in most homes now banished to the kitchen or the bedroom for personal rather than collective use—an example of the "career" of a technology in a sense parallel to that proposed by Appadurai (1986). By extension, I would argue that similar processes can be observed in the contemporary entry of new communications technologies (e.g., video and computers) into the home—and that, again, entry there is likely to be marked by their differential incorporation into masculine and feminine domains of activity within the home.

The works of Boddy (1986), Spigel (1986), and Haralovich (1988) offer a useful model for the analysis of the development and marketing of contemporary new technologies. In a close parallel to Moores's analysis, Spigel (1986) offers an account of the problematic nature of the introduction of television in America in the early 1950s. She is concerned primarily with the role of women's magazines in presenting "the idea of television and its place in the home" (1986, 3) to their female readers—who were, of course (in their economic capacity), the key target group would-be TV advertisers wished to reach and, in their social (gender-defined) role, the group seen to be responsible for the organization of the domestic sphere into which the television was to be integrated.

Spigel argues that in the early 1950s, television was seen as potentially "disrupting" the internal arrangements of the home (just as radio had been regarded in the earlier period)—disrupting patterns of child rearing and marital relations, distracting housewives from the proper running of their homes, and necessitating a thorough rearrangement of the moral economy of the household. Indeed, from the industry's point of view, problems were seen as to whether TV, as a visual as well as an auditory medium (and thus, it was presumed, one that would require of its housewife viewers a degree of attention incompatible with the performance of their domestic tasks), could in fact be integrated into the patterns of daily domestic life. The introduction of TV into the home did not take place as an easy, unruffled insertion of a new technology into the existing sociocultural framework, not least because of concern that women would not be able to cope with the technological complexities of retuning the TV set from one station to another (there are similar recent debates about whether women can cope with video and computer technologies). The industry's primary response was to offer other products as solutions to the problems that television was seen to create; thus a wide variety of household appliances were marketed as "solutions" to dilemmas posed by the TV set. The crucial problem (from the advertisers' point of view) was how to bring the housewife into the unified space of the televiewing family. As Spigel notes, the electric dishwasher was marketed precisely as a technological solution to this problem—as it would "bring the housewife out of the kitchen and into the living room, where she could watch TV with her family" (1986, 8).

I wish to argue not only that our analysis must focus on how communications and information technologies come to be enmeshed in and articulated with the internal dynamics of the organization of domestic space (and particularly with reference to gender domains) but also that it must be situated within a broader analysis of what Donzelot (1979) has described as "the withdrawal to interior space." This is a process in which communications technologies themselves have played a key role in recreating, in contemporary terms, "the pleasures of the hearth" (Frith 1983), as their domestication has increased the attractiveness of the home as a site of leisure.

In analyzing all of these processes, I would emphasize the extent to which the preexisting social modes of organization of the home have exerted a determining effect on how communications and information technologies have been incorporated (domesticated) into everyday life. However, there are other dimensions to these processes. At the same time, we need to be sensitive to the various modes in which regulatory discourse has entered the domestic sphere and affected the development of these technologies (examples include current debates about censorship and scheduling policies in broadcasting; anxieties about the moral dimension of some interactive phone services; and concern over domestic video- and audiotape pirating). In all of these areas we must also pay close attention to the effects of the dominant images of the (nuclear) family and its healthy functioning held by producers and marketers and to the determining effect of these images on the policies of powerful institutions. However, there is more to the question than just the determining effects of domestic organization on the development of technology and of the impact of images of the domestic sphere held by policymakers.

Technologies of Communication and the Construction of Time-Based Public Identities

In analyzing the role of communications and information technologies in articulating the public and private sphere, we must attend not only to their spatial but also to their temporal dimensions. Of course, these two dimensions themselves can be transposed by these very technologies. Thus, as Giddens (1979) notes, the telephone recaptures the immediacy of interaction across spatial distance. Similarly, Pool notes that "the telephone seems to have effects in diametrically opposite directions ... [it] invades our privacy with its ring, but it protects our privacy by allowing us to transact affairs from the fastness of our homes" (1977, 4). However, beyond this capacity, many of those technologies are themselves heavily enmeshed in the structuring of social time. King (1980) argues that the development of both physical and symbolic technologies of communication has played a vital role in the standardization of time in industrial societies—bringing public (metropolitan) time into the previously differential rhythms of local and domestic modes of temporal organization. In a similar vein, Scannell (1988) has analyzed the role of broadcast communications technologies in the socialization of the private sphere and the significance of broadcasting's role in the domestication of standard national time. Scannell's key point concerns the role of communications technologies (especially in the form of national broadcasting systems) in organizing (both at a calendrical and at a quotidian level) the participation of the population in the public spheres of national life (whether through the occasional viewing of a royal wedding or the regular domestic ritual of watching the news as a structuring activity in the daily cycle of life in the home). As Scannell notes, modern mass democratic politics has its forum in the radically new kind of public sphere that broadcasting constitutes.

Cardiff and Scannell (1987), in their historical analysis of the development of British broadcasting, focus on broadcasting's crucial role in forging a link between the dispersed and disparate listeners and the symbolic heartland of national life, and its role in promoting a sense of communal identity within its audience at both regional and national levels. Historically, the BBC, for example, can be seen to have been centrally concerned with supplying "its isolated listeners with a sense of the community they had lost, translated from a local to a national and even a global level" (Cardiff and Scannell 1987, 162). As Cardiff and Scannell note, the audience has always been seen as composed of family units—as "a vast cluster of families rather than in terms of social classes or different taste publics." Brunsdon and Morley (1978) argue that the central image of much contemporary current-affairs and magazine-style programming is precisely the family—the nation as composed of families. In this type of broadcasting, the nuclear family is the unspoken premise of much program discourse: Not only is the programming addressed to a family audience, but this domestic focus accounts both for the content (human-interest stories) and the mode of presentation (the emphasis on the everyday aspects of public issues). What is assumed to unite the audience is the experience of everyday life as a nation of families. Broadcasting does much more than simply to make available experiences (the Soccer Cup Final, Wimbledon, and so on) that were previously available only to those who could be physically present. Beyond this function, the magic carpet of broadcasting technologies plays a fundamental role in promoting national unity at a symbolic level, linking individuals and their families to the center of national life and offering the audience an image of itself and of the nation as a knowable community—a wider, public world beyond the routines of a narrow existence, to which these technologies give symbolic access.

In a similar vein, in his analysis of the development of radio light entertainment, Frith observes that the radio did more than simply to make public events accessible by bringing them into the home; more important, "what was on offer was access to a community ... what was (and is) enjoyable is the sense that you too can become significant, by turning on a switch" (1983, 121–122). And thus, while domestic listening (or viewing) might be "a very peculiar form of public participation," it offers above all else a sense of participation in a (domesticated) national community. However, as Frith notes, the pleasures on offer were (and indeed are still) principally of a particular kind: The "quiet leisure" of broadcasting offers centrally "the pleasures of the hearth"—pleasures of "ordinariness" and "familiarity," a "community of the catch phrase" constructed around the central images of hearth and mother, family pleasure, and domestic life (see Moores 1988).

We must also, of course, pay close attention to the effect of broadcast schedules on the organization of domestic leisure time and the complex modes of interfacing between public and private modes of temporal organization (see Bryce 1987). My central point concerns the ontological significance for the viewing audience of modes of viewing, the motivation of which, as Rath notes, is not so much "'I see,' but 'I also will have seen' ... a formation of the collectivity around a shared visual perception ... [where] ... the spectator can feel part of this imaginary totality" (Rath 1988, 37). Here we approach another dimension of the articulation of public/private spheres, this time as between the nation and the family (or individual) viewing in the living room. In this connection, Hartley has argued that "television is one of the prime sites upon which a given nation is constructed for its members" (1987, 124), drawing on Anderson's (1983) concept of the nation as an "imagined community," the construct of particular discourses. The point lies in the central role of broadcast media schedules in regulating a simultaneity of experience for dispersed audiences (see Hartley [1987] on the function of newspapers as the basis of "mass ritual") and thus in providing them with a temporary authentication of their existence as members of a synchronized national community. As Bausinger (1984) notes, a variety of communications technologies (including the morning newspaper) can be seen to function in similar ways as articulating or linking mechanisms between the rituals of the domestic (private) sphere and the construction of the memberships of national (and other public) communities.

Technologies, Boundaries, and Domestication

It has been argued here that communications technologies play a crucial role in articulating the public and private spheres—thus the role of broadcasting in articulating the family and the nation into the national family. Insofar as the home and family in contemporary Western societies are considered to be a private shelter from public pressures, television and other communications technologies (e.g., the telephone) are problematic because they disrupt this separation of spheres. Similarly, technological developments such as the video and the telephone-answering machine can be seen as technical means for enhancing families' (or individuals') ability to regulate the transgression of their domestic boundaries. In the case of the video, this works by enhancing consumers' ability to manipulate broadcast schedules (by time-shift recording) so as to fit in more conveniently with domestic routines; it works in the case of the telephone-answering machine by enhancing users' ability to screen out unwanted interruptions into their domestic space. However, these technologies are also problematic: Their very capacity to break (and thus potentially transgress) the boundaries of the family means that they have always been seen as being in need of careful regulation—thus the long-standing concern over the danger that broadcasters will transgress standards of taste and decency in the most problematic sphere—inside the home.

Moreover, new technologies themselves create new anxieties and calls for regulation. Thus, as Paterson (1987) argues, the development of home video technologies in Britain quickly came to be seen as intensely problematic. The capacity of the video to offer individual family members (and particularly children) an increased freedom to view "uncertified" material became the justification for a whole new round of state interventions designed to regulate this field of activity.

Developments such as the proliferation of communication channels and cable and satellite networks offer the prospect of the fragmentation of the national audiences (and politics) that traditional broadcasting systems have created: the development of miniaturized and portable delivery systems; the further prospect of individualized consumption within the home (a double privatization).

Lindlof and Meyer (1987) push the point further, arguing that the interactive capacities of recent technological developments fundamentally transform the position of the consumer. As they put it: "With increasing adoption of technological add-ons for the basic media delivery systems, the messages can be edited, deleted, rescheduled or skipped past with complete disregard for their original form. The received notion of the mass communication audience has simply little relevance for the reality of mediated communication" (1987, 2). However, many of these arguments run the danger of abstracting these technologies' intrinsic capacities from the social contexts of their actual use (see Hymes's [1972] critique of Chomsky for a parallel argument). In understanding such technological developments, we could usefully follow Bausinger (1984) in his concern with the question of how these technologies are integrated into the structure and routines of domestic life—into what he calls "the specific semantics of the everyday." His basic thesis is that technologies are increasingly absorbed into the everyday ("everyone owns a number of machines, and has directly to handle technical products") so that everyday routines themselves are constructed around technologies, which then become effectively "invisible" in their domestication. The end result, he argues, is the "inconspicuous omnipresence of the technical" (Bausinger 1984, 346). The key point is to understand the processes through which communications and information technologies are domesticated to the point that they become inconspicuous if not invisible within the home. The further point is then to focus on the culturally constructed meanings of these technologies as they are produced through located practices of consumption.

References

Anderson, B. 1983. *Imagined Communities: Reflections on the Origin and Spread of Nationalism.* London: Verso.

Ang, I., and J. Hermes. Forthcoming. "Gender and/in Media Consumption," in J. Curran and M. Gurevich (eds.), *Mass Communication and Society.* London: Edward Arnold.

Appadurai, A. 1986. *The Social Life of Things: Commodities in Cultural Perspective.* New York: Cambridge University Press.

Ardener, Shirley (ed.). 1981. *Women and Space: Ground Rules and Social Maps.* London: Croom Helm.

Baines, S. 1989. "Approaches to Home Automation." Unpublished paper, Centre for Urban Regional Development Studies, Newcastle upon Tyne.

Bausinger, Herman. 1984. "Media, Technology and Everyday Life," *Media, Culture and Society* 6(4).

Boddy, William. 1986. "The Shining Center of the Home," in Philip Drummond and Richard Paterson (eds.), *Television in Transition.* London: British Film Institute.

Bourdieu, Pierre. 1972. "The Berber Home," in Mary Douglas (ed.), *Rules and Meanings.* Harmondsworth: Penguin.

Brunsdon, C., and D. Morley. 1978. *Everyday Television: Nationwide.* London: British Film Institute.

Bryce, J. 1987. "Family Time and Television Use," in Tom Lindlof (ed.), *Natural Audiences.* Norwood, N.J.: Ablex.

Bush, C. G. 1983. "Women and the Assessment of Technology," in J. Rothschild (ed.), *Machina ex Dea.* New York: Pergamon Press.

Cardiff, David, and Paddy Scannell. 1987. "Broadcasting and National Unity," in James Curran et al. (eds.), *Impacts and Influences.* London: Methuen.

Cockburn, C. 1985. *Machinery of Dominance: Women, Men and Technical Know-How.* London: Pluto Press.

Cowan, R. Schwartz. 1989. *More Work for Mother: The Ironies of Household Technology from the Open Hearth to the Microwave.* New York: Basic Books.

Docherty, D., et al. 1987. *The Last Picture Show.* London: Broadcasting Research Unit.

Donzelot, Jacques. 1979. *The Policing of Families.* London: Hutchinson.

Fontaine, J. S. 1988. "Public or Private? The Constitution of the Family in Anthropological Perspective," *International Journal of Moral and Social Studies* 3(3).

Frith, Simon. 1983. "The Pleasures of the Hearth," in James Donald (ed.), *Formations of Pleasure.* London: Routledge.

Gamarnikow, E., and J. Purvis. 1983. "Introduction" to E. Gamarnikow et al. (eds.), *The Public and Private.* London: Heinneman.

Geertz, Clifford. 1988. *Works and Lives: The Anthropologist as Author.* London: Polity Press.

Giddens, Anthony. 1979. *Central Problems in Social Theory.* London: Macmillan.

Glyptis, S. 1989. *Leisure and Unemployment.* Milton Keynes, U.K.: Open University Press.

Goldthorpe, J., and D. Lockwood. 1968. *The Affluent Worker.* Vol. 1-3. Cambridge: Cambridge University Press.

Gray, A. 1987. "Behind Closed Doors: Women and Video," in H. Baehr and G. Dyer (eds.), *Boxed in: Women and Television.* London: Routledge.

Gunter, B., and M. Svennevig. 1987. *Behind and in Front of the Screen: Television's Involvement with Family Life.* London: John Libbey.

Haddon, L. 1988. "The Home Computer: The Making of a Consumer Electronic," *Science and Culture* 2.

Halloran, J. 1971. *The Effect of Mass Communication.* Leicester, U.K.: Leicester University Press.

Haralovich, M. 1988. "Suburban Family Sit-Coms and Consumer Product Design," in P. Drummond and R. Paterson (eds.), *Television and Its Audience*. London: British Film Institute.

Hartley, J. 1987. "Invisible Fictions: Television Audiences, Paedocracy, Pleasure," *Textual Practice* 1(2): 121–138.

Hodges, J., and A. Hussain. 1979. "Policing the Family," *Ideology and Consciousness* (London), no. 6.

Hymes, D. 1972. "On Communicative Competence," in J. Pride and J. Holmes (eds.), *Sociolinguistics*. London: Penguin.

Jouet, J. 1988. "The Social Uses of Micro-Computers in France." Paper to International Association of Mass Communication Researchers Conference, Barcelona, July.

Jouet, J., and Y. Toussaint. 1987. "Telematics and the Private Sphere: The Case of the French Videotext." Paper to Data Communication Conference, Universite Libre de Bruxelles, May.

King, Anthony. 1980. *Buildings and Society*. London: Routledge.

Kramarae, C. (ed.). 1988. *Technology and Women's Voices: Keeping in Touch*. London: Routledge.

Lindlof, T., and T. Meyer. 1987. "Mediated Communication," in T. Lindlof (ed.), *Natural Audiences*. Norwood, N.J.: Ablex.

Lindlof, T., and Paul Traudt. 1983. "Mediated Communications in Families," in Mary Mander (ed.), *Communications in Transition*. New York: Praeger.

Lull, James (ed.). 1988. *World Families Watch Television*. Newbury Park, Calif.: Sage.

Maddox, B. 1977. "Women and the Switchboard," in I. de Sola Pool (ed.), *The Social Impact of the Telephone*. Cambridge, Mass.: MIT Press.

Mayer, M. 1977. "The Telephone and the Uses of Time," in I. de Sola Pool (ed.), *The Social Impact of the Telephone*. Cambridge, Mass.: MIT Press.

McRobbie, A., and J. Garber. 1976. "Girls and Subcultures," in Stuart Hall and Tony Jefferson (eds.), *Resistance Through Rituals: Youth Subculture in Post-War Britain*. London: Hutchinson.

Moores, Sean. 1988. "The Box on the Dresser: Memories of Early Radio," *Media, Culture and Society* 10.

Morley, David. 1986. *Family Television*. London: Comedia.

———. 1991. "Where the Global Meets the Local," *Screen* 32(1).

Morley, David, and Roger Silverstone. 1990. "Domestic Communication," *Media, Culture and Society* 12.

———. Forthcoming. "Communication and Context," in N. Jankowski and K. B. Jensen (eds.), *A Handbook of Qualitative Methodology and Media Research*. London: Routledge.

Nordenstreng, Kaarl. 1972. "Policy for News Transmission," in Dennis McQuail (ed.), *Sociology of Mass Communications*. Harmondsworth: Penguin.

Paterson, Richard (ed.). 1987. "Family Perspectives on Broadcasting Policy." Paper to British Film Institute Summer School, August.

Pool, I. de Sola (ed.). 1977. *The Social Impact of the Telephone*. Cambridge, Mass.: MIT Press.

Rakow, L. 1988a. "Gendered Technology, Gendered Practice," *Critical Studies in Mass Communication* 5.

———. 1988b. "Women and the Telephone: The Gendering of a Communications Technology," in C. Kramarae (ed.), *Technology and Women's Voices*. London: Routledge.

Rath, C. D. 1988. "Live/Life: Television as a Generator of Events in Everyday Life," in P. Drummond and R. Paterson (eds.), *Television and Its Audience*. London: British Film Institute.

Rogge, J. U., and K. Jensen. 1988. "Everyday Life and TV in West Germany," in J. Lull (ed.), *World Families Watch Television*. Newbury Park, Calif.: Sage.

Rothschild, J. (ed.). 1983. *Machina ex Dea*. New York: Pergamon Press.

Saussure, F. de. 1974. *Course in General Linguistics*. London: Fontana.

Scannell, Paddy. 1988. "Radio Times," in Philip Drummond and Richard Paterson (eds.), *Television and Its Audience*. London: British Film Institute.

Silverstone, Roger. 1989. "Television and Everyday Life: Towards an Anthropology of the Television Audience," in M. Ferguson (ed.), *Public Communication: The New Imperatives*. Newbury Park, Calif.: Sage.

Silverstone, R., E. Hirsch, and D. Morley. 1991. "Listening to a Long Conversation: An Ethnographic Approach to ICT in the Home," *Cultural Studies* 5(2).

Skirrow, G. 1986. "Hellivision: An Analysis of Video Games," in Colin McCabe (ed.), *High Theory/Low Culture*. Manchester, U.K.: Manchester University Press.

Spigel, L. 1986. "Ambiguity and Hesitation: Discourses on TV and the Housewife in Women's Magazines." Paper to International Television Studies Conference, London, July.

Thompson, Edward P. 1967. "Time, Work-Discipline and Industrial Capitalism," *Past and Present* 38.

Tomlinson, A. 1989. "Home Fixtures: Doing It Yourself in a Privatised World," in A. Tomlinson (ed.), *Consumption, Identity and Style*. London: Comedia/Routledge.

Turkle, S. 1988. "Computational Reticence: Why Women Fear the Intimate Machine," in C. Kramarae (ed.), *Technology and Women's Voices*. London: Routledge.

Walkerdine, V. 1988. *The Mastery of Reason, Cognitive Development and the Production of Rationality*. London: Routledge.

Zaretsky, E. 1976. *Capitalism, the Family and Personal Life*. London: Pluto Press.

Zimmerman, J. 1981. *The Technological Woman*. New York: Praeger.

SIX

Testimonies and Artifacts: Elite Appropriations of African American Music in the Nineteenth Century

JON CRUZ

I want to pose a very broad question: What is the relationship between social change and cultural perceptions of music? As we scramble to make sense of such an elusive question, we are compelled to ask additional questions: Which changes? Whose perceptions? What music? Immediately we find ourselves searching for case material. Invariably we confront social actors. Presumed definitions of music quickly recede as groups with interest-bearing accounts, each claiming some kind of investment in music, begin to occupy our attention. Music becomes less and less an isolated activity (practices), a particular aesthetic sensibility (tastes), an organizational product (goods or commodities), or an institutional element (norms). In pursuing our questions, we find that music loses its identity as a thing in itself. And the social relations that encircle it as well as shore it up, which are always presumed but frequently out of focus, become increasingly salient as music shifts from being a concrete fact to a historically circumscribed cultural field riddled with socially contentious meanings.

Around the middle of the nineteenth century, African American cultural expressions, primarily the slave narratives and the spirituals, took on new importance for white cultural elites. In the process of being discovered from above, African American voices were relocated on the cultural maps of reformers, social critics, educators, and social scientists. Hitherto part of African American oral culture, black voices were converted to literary forms. By 1850 the slave narrative, which fed into and off of the growing abolitionist movement, had become one of the most popular literary genres of the era. With the coming of the Civil War a decade later, the Negro spirituals were quickly "discovered" and incorporated into speeches, magazines, pamphlets, and books. As cultural texts, both narratives and spirituals were enlisted in the symbolic arsenal of abolitionists and other kindred cultural elites. The use of voices from the cultural and racial margins went beyond the criticism of slavery. Slave narratives and Negro spirituals also functioned as testimonies, helping elites refract their discomfort on a number of cultural fronts, which included the waning of traditional religious and political authority, the rise of middle-class politics associated with Jacksonian democracy, and the lockstep developments of industrialization, market society, and urbanization.

From midcentury up through the 1870s, the interest in African American expressions still retained ties to the social politics surrounding the legacy of slavery. But as the century came to a close, the moral and political associations that cultural elites brought to African American voices were eclipsed by the rise of social science and reconceptualized within an increasingly technical system of classification. By the 1890s professional folklore was helping to strip away the earlier moral and political debates concerning the problems of integrating former slaves in civil society. In the view of folklore (which helped to feed—inasmuch as it drew from—the new disciplines of ethnology, anthropology, and sociology), black voices were remapped and reclassified as cultural artifacts and relics. This transformation in cultural reception is important in that it marks some key shifts in the way in which racialized groups are constituted and traversed by the strategies of cultural appropriation from above.

Why did white elites discover such expressions? How did they tap these voices? What can the interest in African American music by elites tell us about elites and their shifting positions within the dominant culture? How does the appropriation of expressions from the cultural and racial margins shed light on social transformations that are quite removed from music? And how did the interest in and attention given to African American music help to install new conditions of reception within the larger cultural field in which African American music circulated as cultural material for elites? This essay explores some key features that characterize the motives of elite interest in African American music and analyzes the cultural implications this interest helped to promote. The interest elites brought to the musical practices and products of African Americans shares, to some extent, some of the aspects of "active audiences" (Ang 1991). Elites certainly had specifiable motivations that informed the ways in which African American music was recognizable and understandable. Audiences, however, do not simply exist; they come into being. To make this notion useful requires an interpretation of the development of interpretive formations. A historical assessment is required to understand the emergence of interpretive sensibilities. This essay is both a study aimed at this kind of analytical enterprise and an argument for the importance of such an approach in the cultural study of reception.

Most reception studies tend to consider the negotiations individuals and groups make of already well-defined cultural products: mainly the mass-produced economic staples of communication and media industries (e.g., television, cinema, radio, recorded music, and print material). There are important reasons for this kind of emphasis. The analysis presented here, however, backs up from this kind of starting point in order to look at how particular interpretive formations emerge and change. In the case of understanding white elite practices, it is not enough to begin with some a priori notion of what a musical text is. Rather, the focus is on how an interpretive map is actually generated in ways that enable distinct perceptions of black music to come into being. The emergence of interpretive formations as well as shifts in the practices of reception are sociohistorical problems. This orientation allows us to ask how strategically located groups were able to shape some of the cultural terrain upon which African American music was permitted to move. Examination of how white elites came to discover African American music in the second half of the nineteenth century and of how their interests in and interpretation of the Negro spirituals changed over time allows us to tap into a highly selective process of cultural reception. Moreover, it helps shed light on how groups within a relatively dominant cultural position come to use the cultural practices of subordinate groups in ways that help the former negotiate particular cultural tensions. Put another way, African American music was useful to elites engaged in struggles over social change. Responding to social tensions, white elites drew upon African American music to help frame their strategies of negotiating social change. In this regard, the object of analysis is not some notion of music defined a priori; it is concerned with the social relations the field of music refracts. Elite reactions to social tensions in the second half of the nineteenth century spill into the interpretation of the cultural practices of racialized groups at the social margins.

Focusing on elites, however, involves a shift away from more traditional orientations of analysis that privilege the meanings constituting music for African Americans. An investigation into the world of white elites, intellectuals, and cultural leaders is not an endeavor to account for the range of meanings that inform both the production and reception of African American music by African Americans. The focus here is on white elite interpretive and institutionalized formations. There is a long record of writings championing accounts of and insights into the meanings African Americans brought to and made as "publics" through music.[1] Scant attention, however, has been given to what white elites did with African American music as it became acceptable and useful.[2]

Cultural leaders, by definition, map the fields of interpretation. They struggle over cultural definitions, organize and mobilize intellectual perceptions that are effective in objectifying cultural realms, and make and refine parameters of meaning for other elites. Their activity is designed to establish proper modes of interpretation, and in doing so, elites establish the moral and intellectual properties that are demonstrated in acts of "cultural recognition" (Bourdieu 1984). Cultural elites shape the intellectual frameworks within which other intellectuals perform their acts of legitimized and legitimizing recognition. Elites are strategically—that is, socially and institutionally—situated in positions of cultural power in which they operate as intellectuals, spokespersons, and representatives for coordinated interests. Examining the activities of cultural elites also helps to assess the formation of institutional preconditions for other ensuing audiences.

Cultural elites and entrepreneurs discovered, gained access to, and made use of African American music, and music helped elites reflect upon conflicts in which they were engaged. To frame this problem, however, requires some clarification of the notion of *appropriation*. Roger Chartier's conceptualization of appropriation is helpful. Drawing on Norbert Elias and Pierre Bourdieu, Chartier suggests that "appropriation really concerns a social history of the various interpretations, brought back to their fundamental determinants (which are social, institutional and cultural) and lodged in the specific practices that produce them. ... Structures of the social world are not an object given. ... They are all produced historically by the interconnected practices—political, social and discursive—that construct their figures" (Chartier 1988, 13–14).

This notion of appropriation has a number of analytical merits. First, it suggests that we refrain from taking for granted the already objectified world of "things themselves," where cultural objects (such as African American music) appear already formed. Instead of beginning with the question of what an object is, we place emphasis on what kinds of meanings help make objects knowable and worthy of appropriation. In other words, we can assess how the constitution of cultural realities and the world of objects that fill such realities come to be. The task is to fathom the cultural sensibilities, strategies, and practices—the "common sense"—that groups use to objectify and construct their social world. Thus, looking at how groups appropriate the practices of others enables us to see how appropriation is also a cultural practice. This double-dimensional approach—of assessing the cultural appropriation of practices and of this process as practice—has the benefit of highlighting the complexity of socially embedded relationships that underwrite much of what we recognize as cultural action. We are thus better able to avoid the reification of culture. Second, we can be mindful of the problem of power and the unevenness and inequality of social relations. The fields within which cultural appropriations take place are not level. Some groups are able to develop practices of cultural appropriation that span large arenas of social life, absorbing and setting conditions for weaker forms located at more socially, politically, and economically marginalized sites. Being attuned to such socially rooted differences helps us assess how power is conveyed through the forms of attention to the cultural margins. Power relations enable groups selectively to appropriate and amplify certain meanings and practices and to screen out and silence others. Third, this approach provides ways to connect cultural forms to cultural formations without presupposing some essential, transcendental, and underlying structure that is presumably fixed. Yet it still allows us to retain the notions of unequal exchange, social asymmetry, and power that can be analyzed in the way group uses of cultural goods are always embedded in social relationships. Finally, this approach to appropriation enables us to avoid the pitfalls of determinism on the one hand (which poststructuralism brings so acutely to our attention) and the evacuation of historically and institutionally embedded social relations on the other (which poststructuralism plunges toward so easily). We need to be wary of *determinism,* yet we must retain the notion of *determinations.* Opportunities as well as limits mark the fields in which struggles over cultural representations and appropriations take place.[3]

Elite appropriations of African American music in the second half of the nineteenth century illustrate these analytical angles. The crisis over slavery generated tremendous political turmoil and led to an engulfing war. The lurch of expansion and the machinations of consolidating national boundaries were profoundly uneven events, with class, ethnic, and racial formations and corresponding political tensions emerging as regional characteristics. Burgeoning immigration and rapidly expanding industrialization produced gaping rifts in the social fabric and piecemeal realignments among institutions. Older patterns of cultural authority were increasingly challenged by the speed and magnitude of social development. It was a period of wrenching social conflict. Not surprisingly, the kinds of attention and interest cultural leaders paid to African American cultural practices varied greatly and changed over time.

From the 1830s to the 1860s, intellectuals affiliated with the antislavery movement found symbolic weapons in the narratives of slaves and former slaves. These eloquent black voices were important additions to the cultural arsenal of abolitionists. In the early 1860s, many of these same intellectuals began to discover the Negro spirituals. Like the narratives of a few decades earlier, the spirituals were counterpoised as evidence against the moral and political degeneracy of slavery. But the spirituals discovered in the context of the Civil War were also elevated to the most pure and eloquent expression of African Americans. These songs captured more than black voices; they served to refract in remarkably compressed form many of the crises induced by social change that plagued troubled elites.

The interest in black music continued after the Civil War. But these interests also changed substantially. Spirituals were initially attractive on distinct moral and political grounds. However, by the 1880s, the cultural ground had been transformed. Slavery had been eradicated. The aims of Reconstruction—to bring capitalist market relations and political democracy to the South—fizzled in less than two decades after the war. With the great antagonism of slavery gone, the abolitionist sentiment was transformed. Along with political disengagement, elites and intellectuals changed or withdrew their investments in the Negro spirituals. Other elites, however, were quick to reinvest in African American music. These new actors—folklorists and early cultural sociologists—were spurred by the novel appeal of an emergent social science. And they brought a very different sensibility to the interpretation and appropriation of African American music.

These cultural appropriations fan outwardly into many different forms. However, two general developments, each refracting the operations of different inter-

pretive formations with different interests, appear to be prominent: the politiciza-
tion of the Negro spirituals during the 1860s and the rise of professional folklore
analyses in the 1880s. These two modes of appropriation by professional publics
can be conceptualized as distinct cultural forms embedded in particular cultural
formations. The discovery of slave narratives and spirituals can be called a *testimony formation,* and the use of social science produced what I call *artifact formation.* Both are distinct formations, yet they overlap. We must view them in their
peculiar historical and cultural flow in order to assess their significant impact on
the larger cultural field in which elites made sense of African American music. To
talk of slave narratives and Negro spirituals as testimonies on the one hand and as
artifacts on the other is to acknowledge the cultural force organized and mobi-
lized in elite-based meanings. Each of these schemas of interpretation helped to
reconfigure the cultural location of African American music in American society.
Elite interests also impacted some of the ways in which African American music
was produced, enabled to circulate, and consumed. By no means do these two
modes account for all modes of appropriation, but examining how African American music came to be viewed from above enables us to reassess important cultural developments and their implications.

Discovering the Negro Spiritual
as Cultural Testimony

In the 1840s minstrelsy was one of the most pervasive forms of popular culture. As
a cultural practice, minstrelsy provided a framework for understanding African
Americans. In its appeal to different yet overlapping cultural sensibilities, minstrelsy charted race relations in several contradictory ways. Through its
caricaturization of slaves as childlike, docile, and happy, it legitimated and reinforced slavery and doubled as a form of cultural control. Yet as a representation of
the social relations of slavery, minstrelsy also provided images that joined with
reasons to block slavery's expansion into the western territories. In the North,
minstrelsy endorsed the racial divisions between white workers and free blacks.
Like many forms of popular culture, minstrelsy was more than a mode of entertainment; it also served as a social and cultural epistemology, a form of knowledge and knowledge making, that brokered the meanings of race, ethnicity, and
class throughout the nineteenth century (Roediger 1991; Saxton 1990; Boskin 1986;
Dennison 1982; Sampson 1980; Toll 1974).

Composing and transcribing slave recollections for publication marked the
first modern strategy by which elites were able to access black sensibilities
through print. This in itself was an important cultural transformation. But the
discovery, encouragement, and appropriation of slave narratives by abolitionists
also signaled a profound cultural break from minstrelsy, prompting a shift in the
way elites viewed African Americans in general and their cultural expressions in
particular. Serving different publics, both minstrelsy and slave narratives func-

tioned as competing claims for authentic representations of African Americans. Minstrelsy was an aestheticized caricaturization of racial difference; it served as a system of white representations of African Americans (and other races and ethnic groups), an important part of the symbolic infrastructure mediating institutionalized race and class relations. Minstrelsy produced a racial object—an image. Slave narratives, in contrast, were accepted as authentic voices of African Americans themselves; they were viewed as presentations by subjects, not cultural representations by others.[4] Slave narratives were objects produced by selves. Narratives such as those written by Frederick Douglass, Solomon Northup, and Moses Roper became extraordinarily popular (Starling 1981).

Like popular travel narratives, the slave narratives gave the reader an eyewitness account of a voyage into a personal realm of experience that a sympathetic abolitionist could appreciate, but only vicariously, through a politically and morally circumscribed reading. John A. Collins, general agent of the Massachusetts Anti-Slavery Society, writing to William Lloyd Garrison in 1842, expressed this interest when he claimed that "the public have itching ears to hear a colored man speak, and particularly a slave. Multitudes will flock to hear one of his class" (quoted in Gates 1987, xi). Ephraim Peabody, minister of Kings Chapel in Boston, called attention to how these texts "contain the victim's account of the working of this great institution [of slavery] (Peabody 1849, 63). In 1849 a review of Henry Bibb's narrative summed up the distinct link between these articulations and the political work of abolition: "This fugitive slave literature is destined to be a powerful lever. We have the most profound conviction of its potency. We see in it the easy and infallible means of abolitionizing the free States. Argument provides argument, reason is met by sophistry. But narratives of slaves go right to the heart of man" (quoted in Nichols 1959, 153).

The titles of slave narratives that began to emerge in the 1840s indicated that the texts were there to claim a truth and to witness a reality. Many titles included references to the author's life—as in "From His Own Mouth," "The Life of [Name]," or "My Life." These titles suggested the indisputability of experience; truth was framed in the account of who lived it. Titles such as Wilson Armistead's *A Tribute to the Negro: Being a Vindication of the Moral, Intellectual and Religious Capabilities of the Colored Portion of Mankind with Particular Reference to the African Race* (1848) and Lewis Clarke and Milton Clarke's *Narratives of the Sufferings of Lewis and Milton Clarke, Sons of a Soldier of the Revolution During a Captivity of More Than Twenty Years Among Slaveholders of Kentucky, One of the So-Called Christian States of North America, Dictated by Themselves* (1846) also reflected a critique of slavery as an institution purportedly erected on Christian foundations. Politically useful, the narratives aided the critique of slavery. Their transformation into documents, which in turn were catapulted into popular circulation in midcentury, was part of a larger shift in competing representations of African Americans. Traversed as they were by political, moral, and economic issues and ideologies, the motivations that made slave accounts meaningful are not easily separable. Nevertheless, black voices could be heard and read pretty much as they were, without the imposed mask of minstrelsy. Black voices—specifically those of men (African American women were largely ignored by the abolitionists, even though they were the first to publish narratives and collections of poetry and essays)[5]—were cultural and political weapons for white elites; by this criteria they became audible. In this manner, black voices helped to articulate particular social tensions Northern leaders were confronting in the growing antagonisms with the South. The uses and interpretations of hitherto unheard voices also produced a cultural template for identifying and pressing into service testimonies that could speak to social conflicts.

Social crises have the power to facilitate the compression of elaborate and complex discourses into simpler and more urgent forms. With the coming of the Civil War, the quest for more cultural ammunition grew. War had the effect of condensing the testimonies derived from black voices. On the eve of the Civil War, the Negro spirituals were being discovered, transcribed, and enlisted as new material in the literary battlefields. Samples of black spirituals were printed in magazines in the early 1860s. By the mid-1860s several collections were under way. The most notable collection, published in 1867 shortly after the Civil War, was William Francis Allen, Charles Ware, and Lucy McKim Garrison's *Slave Songs of the United States,* which contained 136 songs (Allen et al. 1867). The same year, Thomas Wentworth Higginson, a white abolitionist who commanded an all-black Union army regiment, also published a collection in the *Atlantic Monthly* (Higginson 1867). These songs were reprinted a few years later in his *Army Life in a Black Regiment* (Higginson 1962 [1870]).

In the introduction to *Slave Songs,* William Allen observed the "fresh interest" for slave songs, an interest "excited through the educational mission" being carried out on South Carolina's Port Royal Islands in 1861.[6] On the island the discoverers viewed the black inhabitants with a peculiar mixture of romantic zeal and benevolent patronage: "The agents of this mission were not long in discovering the rich vein of music that existed in these half-barbarous people, and when visitors from the North were on the islands, there was nothing that seemed better worth their while than to see a 'shout' or hear the 'people' sing their 'spirichils'" (Allen et al. 1867, i–ii). Since the vocal content was derived, in part, from Christian symbolism, abolitionists understandably viewed Negro spirituals as Christian texts. Such songs were certainly preferred, some becoming "established favorites among the whites, and hardly a Sunday passed at the church on St. Helena without 'Gabriel's Trumpet,' 'I Hear from Heaven To-day,' or 'Jehovah Hallelujah'" (Allen et al. 1867, ii).

Consider, by way of contrast, the kind of music slave owners preferred: "Many masters and overseers on these plantations prohibit melancholy tunes or words and encourage nothing but cheerful music and senseless words, deprecating the effect of sadder strains upon the slaves, whose peculiar musical sensibility might be expected to make them especially excitable by any songs of a plaintive character, and having any reference to their particular hardships" (Kemble 1863, 129). Particular musical forms and corresponding affects and emotions were meaningful to slaveholders insofar as the music's ascriptive function corroborated both the master's view of the contented slave and the slave's "particular hardships." If slaveholders sanctioned "cheerful music" and "senseless words," the abolitionists valued the "melancholy tunes" and those possessing a "plaintive character." Not all of black singing was sacred. Profane songs were present, but they did not command the same kind of interest for abolitionists. Song specimens that did not fit the image of "spirichils" were "intrinsically barbaric"; they were not associated with the civilizing touches of Christian culture. As Allen put it: "Still, the chief part of the negro music is *civilized* in its character—partly composed under the influence of association with the whites, partly actually imitated from their music. … On the other hand there are very few which are of an intrinsically barbaric character, and where this character does appear, it is chiefly in short passages, intermingled with others of a different character" (Allen et al. 1867, vi).

This early attempt to collect spirituals was intended to intervene in what amounted to scholarly neglect. As editors and collectors, Allen and his associates sought to capture and preserve cultural expressions that might soon be lost forever. The opening sentence of *Slave Songs* framed an urgent observation and stated the need: "The musical capacity of the Negro race has been recognized for so many years that it is hard to explain why no systematic effort has hitherto been made to collect and preserve their melodies" (Allen et al. 1867, i). Of course with slavery intact, the very social system that produced such melodies would ensure their continued production; such songs would not be in need of cultural preservation. However, with the Civil War came the prospect of slavery's eradication. It was against the backdrop of impending abolition that an elite-based recognition of cultural loss began to register.

The discovery of black culture spearheaded by abolitionists prior to and continuing throughout the Civil War could be construed as a cultural response to the conflicts over slavery. But another cultural dimension also fueled the discovery of cultural practices at the margins. The links between modernization and the romantic sentiments that helped frame the discovery of Negro spirituals suggest that there were other forces at work besides the antagonistic relations surrounding slavery. Frederick Douglass's observation that the spirituals expressed "the bitterest anguish" over their bondage and that "every tone was a testimony against slavery" is impeachable (Douglass 1855, 99). But this does not mean that the interests white elites brought to the spirituals were identical to the sentiments Douglass identified. Nor was the interest in the spirituals simply an example of how the Northern bourgeoisie's "cultural arm" used ideology to further the interests of capitalism. The selective strategies that informed the discovery and appropriation of black cultural practices cannot be reduced to an analysis rooted only within the framework of the political economy of slavery. Economic antagonisms were certainly important, but they do not in themselves offer the only account of the cultural meanings white elites brought to African American music. The cultural function of testimonies cannot be reduced to economic forces alone (Weber 1950 [1904]).

The turn to the cultural margins was actually part of a much more widespread reenchantment with racial otherness and the most marginalized social segments within a modernizing social order. Throughout the eighteenth and nineteenth centuries, European elites were rediscovering aspects of traditional society that were being rapidly overtaken by modernization (Burke 1978). As older feudal patterns gave way to capitalism and the rise of new nation-states based on postfeudal politics, some European intellectuals were caught up in reactions that took the forms of romanticism and nostalgia. Having already withdrawn from an older, more common—and in many cases Catholic—popular culture, elites were busy scrambling to retrieve a sense of tradition, and this retrieval took many forms. The search for nature, which doubled as a rejection of modern society and an antidote to malaise, was frequently carried out at the boundaries of civil society. In the European case these boundaries were peopled by the social vestiges of a precapitalist peasantry.

However, in the American case the boundaries were primarily racial. African Americans, Native Americans, Mexicans, and the Chinese marked the cultural and political lines of distinction between civil society and what was ethnologically problematic. This particular historical conjuncture was ethnically and racially complex. There were increasingly larger numbers of new immigrants from central and southern Europe who were non-Protestant Catholics and non-Christian Jews. For some elites the search for a noble savage was for an exceptionally American one, ideally a Transcendentalist of sorts. New European immigrants, so firmly tied to—and increasingly disgruntled with—their lot within the urban and industrial regimes, did not fit this need for a romanticized soul-searching cultural reference point at the margins. Nor did the Chinese or Mexicans. But slaves and Indians did. Enslaved African Americans shackled by the smug slave power, and Native Americans who marked the borders between civil society and the ever-receding wilderness, provided just the appropriate identity. Unlike the new urban working-class white ethnics, black and red noble savages were not viewed as threats to traditional Protestant cultural and political authority.

Market society brought antagonisms to preindustrial traditions of religiously rooted authority. Manufacturers and emergent industrialists were increasingly more powerful, setting conditions for more and more spheres of society. Industrialization—not race relations—was seen as the most corrosive force to cultural authority. In this case, the social movements associated with transcendentalism and associationism were quite important. In addition to harboring strong objections to slavery, both movements were deeply troubled by the encroachment of market society and the particular directions that it was perceived to be taking. Several decades before the outbreak of the Civil War, disenchanted Transcendentalists and Associationists had already launched attempts to resist and reject the dominant culture; the Associationists even attempted in the 1840s to carve out an alternative, autonomous community in the social experiment of Brook Farm. The retreat from mainstream society was to avoid market society. Transcendentalism provided its leaders with a conviction enabling a "revolt against the rationalism of their fathers." It also represented an attempt to found a "new religious expression in forms derived from romantic literature and from the philosophical idealism of Germany" (P. Miller 1957, ix). This revolt amounted to "the first outcry of the heart against the materialistic pressures of a business civilization. Protestant to the core, they turn their protest against what is customarily called the 'Protestant Ethic': they refuse to labor in a proper calling, conscientiously cultivate the arts of leisure, and strive to avoid making money" (P. Miller 1957, ix–x).[7] It was thus not so much the sentiments of antislavery as it was a growing disenchantment with market capitalism that helped to ground these social movements.

The nostalgia behind naturalism and romanticism complicates matters because it signaled a deep, pervasive, and complex response among newly emerging cultural elites as the rationalization of the West progressed. These larger and much broader ideologies had specific links to the crises associated with social change. And while romanticism and naturalism competed, they also overlapped. In the American case, romanticism, as Carey McWilliams has noted, "offered the simpler analysis of the malaise of American life." Modernization meant loss of contact with nature; it brought a new civilization that created barriers between individuals. In the new social order individuals were prevented "access to the roots of human genius and understanding in the intuitions" (McWilliams 1974, 231).

In the opening pages to *Walden*, Henry David Thoreau railed against the impoverishing impact that a money-driven society had upon its people. The virtues of self-reliance, so championed by Emerson, were trammeled under the widespread servitude to money and machines. As Thoreau put it: "It is very evident what mean and sneaking lives many of you live, for my sight has been whetted by experience; always on the limits, trying to get into business and trying to get out of debt, a very ancient slough, called by the Latins *oes alienum*, another's brass, for some of their coins were made of brass; still living, and dying, and buried by this other's brass; always promising to pay, promising to pay, to-morrow, and dying to-day, insolvent" (Thoreau 1910 [1854], 6). The frugal autonomy and success of self-sufficiency promised to one who followed Benjamin Franklin's sagely maxims was increasingly out of reach for the wage worker and petty entrepreneur of the midnineteenth century. Their lives Thoreau likened to slavery: "I sometimes wonder that we can be so frivolous, I may almost say, as to attend to the gross but somewhat foreign form of servitude called Negro Slavery, there are so many keen and subtle masters that enslave both north and south. It is hard to have a southern overseer; it is worse to have a northern one; but worst of all when you are the slave-driver of yourself" (Thoreau 1910 [1854], 6–7).

But freeing oneself from the grip of market society in order to "anticipate, not the sunrise and the dawn merely, but, if possible, Nature herself" (Thoreau 1910

[1854], 15) was a rather difficult task. As Thoreau's *Walden* states so elaborately and eloquently, one had to reject all the trappings and pressures of civil society in order to reconnect with nature. But the recipe for salvation in nature is ironic: The way in which nature is retrieved in the writings of Thoreau and other key transcendentalists is through an ostensibly political critique of modern cultural authority and civil society. One has to possess a keen and critical working notion of the very thing—modernity—that one wants to transcend. In other words, a working notion of "overcivilization" is necessary in order for one to know when one has transcended it and tapped nature. To grasp this spirit, and to live it as a civil religion, is to undertake a profoundly sophisticated intellectual journey.

In the romantic gaze of Higginson, the black soldiers under his command were able to bypass this task: "Their philosophizing is often the highest form of mysticism; and our dear surgeon declares that they are all natural Transcendentalists" (Higginson 1962 [1870], 71). They were not fully absorbed as partners into the institutions of utilitarian liberalism that created modern market mentalities. Slaves certainly did not have the "English and European manners and tastes" for which Thoreau had much "contempt" (Emerson quoted in P. Miller 1957, 371). Presumably as natural transcendentalists they had not been tainted by modernity or trapped behind a wall of civilization barring them from nature. African Americans were closer to nature. Viewed through a romantic lens, African Americans were virtuous for what they lacked. Higginson's reasoning reflects ties to a larger set of discourses on modern cultural distinctions that equate various races with states of nature and the relationship between race and civilization (Gosset 1963; Jordan 1968; Fredrickson 1971; Takaki 1990). In its benevolent and romanticist moments, such thought helped to construct the very meaning and value of the noble savage.

But Higginson's black troops were not just beyond the civilizing grip of the rational West; they also had the twin virtues of being feminine and oriental. Higginson could view his troops with the full panoply of attributes that were missing from the corrosive masculinity of vulgar market society:

> Yet their religious spirit grows more beautiful to me in living longer with them; it is certainly far more so than at first, when it seemed rather a matter of phrase and habit. It influences them both in the negative and the positive side. That is, it cultivates the feminine virtues first—makes them patient, meek, resigned. This is very evident in the hospital; there is nothing of the restless, defiant habit of white invalids. ... Imbued from childhood with the habit of submission, drinking in through every pore that other-world trust which is the one spirit of their songs, they can endure everything. This I expected; but I am relieved to find that their religion strengthens them on the positive side also—gives zeal, energy, daring. They could easily be made fanatics, if I chose; but I do not choose. Their whole mood is essentially Mohammedan, perhaps, in its strength and its weakness; and I feel the same degree of sympathy that I should if I had a Turkish command—that is a sort of sympathetic admiration, not tending towards agreement, but towards co-operation (Higginson 1962 [1870], 71).

In this romantic flight of association, ascription functions as description. Various attributes of exotic otherness were canvassed, retrieved, and compressed to fit the reflective moment Higginson composed for print. Not only are the soldiers Christian (that is why they sing spirituals); they are also other-manly, other-American, other-Western, and other-worldly. These features, elements of a romantic and antirationalist critique, also pointed toward the hollowness of the new social order so rejected by Transcendentalism. Market society and the increasing penetration of the cash nexus, vulgar Jacksonian democracy and its corresponding middle-class aesthetic as well as political mediocrity, the erosion of earlier forms of cultural authority, the dangers to civil society when egoistic masculinity masquerades as civil religion, and the Civil War—all of these are juxtaposed to all things desirable in the idealized spiritual realm that might mitigate the corrosive effects of modernity.

The logic of cultural discovery and the modes of appropriation that emerged in this era can be neither divorced from nor reduced to abolitionism. Indeed, the rejection of slavery, the anxieties unleashed by the unbridled pull of capitalist commerce, and transcendentalist disenchantment with the West join where abolitionism and antimodernism discover the Negro spirituals. In turning to African American expressions as cultural testimonies, Northern cultural leaders and intellectuals were able to frame a range of social antagonisms, conflicts, and tensions to which they were compelled to respond. These new interests helped to shift and reconfigure the interpretive ground upon which African American music was understood. Further, it marked a shift in the representations invoked to bring African Americans into a particular kind of focus. What was being sketched was a redrawing of the cultural and political map for the representations of African Americans by cultural elites. Transforming orality into cultural texts also enabled African American narratives and songs to circulate far beyond their more traditional and localized arenas of origin.[8] Both of these developments are major watersheds in the historical transformation of cultural forms and ensuing interpretive publics.

What I have been calling the *testimony* can now be summed up (albeit in a highly compressed manner). The testimony that draws upon the discovery of African American voices has three distinct but intertwined components: recognition, symptom, and function. First, it relies upon a recognition and reinterpretation of hitherto devalued or unrecognized cultural expressions. The slave narratives and Negro spirituals appear to have new positions of value—new cultural and political capital—on the maps of elites. The recognition is also symptomatic of a shift in interpretive sensibilities; in this case the attention toward the racial and cultural margins is constituted by tensions generated by social change (romanticism, antimodernism, antislavery, and so on). Finally, this recognition, rooted symptomatically in larger social tensions, is organized and rationalized in ways that transform the interpretation of cultural practices of African Americans servicing the mobilizing needs of groups and social fractions within the dominant culture whose members are pulled into social conflicts over the meaning and conditions of social change. Put briefly, the function of the cultural testimony, which frames the new meaning ascribed to black voices, is its capacity to service white meanings. As a cultural form, the testimony's power as an interpretive formation enabled elites to appropriate black cultural forms in order to transform them into a new cultural form that could serve crisis-driven interests. The testimony is actually quite removed from the ostensible interests of African Americans. This act of cultural appropriation signifies a social transformation of meanings: Meanings forged by African Americans as narratives and spirituals were reconstructed as meanings for elites within the dominant culture. In this manner, one cultural form (black voices from below) was transformed (from above) into another cultural form and in the process was recoded and enlisted to serve the needs of an elite social fraction. Thus as a cultural form, the testimony serves to articulate elite responses to social crisis through a reliance upon and use of the racial and cultural margins as political and cultural capital.

In the historical conjuncture surrounding the Civil War, political, ideological, and cultural maps were being drawn. These maps marked a new and different place for African American voices, a meaning-driven cultural and ideological relocation for their expressions, an understanding of African Americans that competed with minstrelsy. This was a moral, political, cultural, and material site where new veins of cultural ore were discovered and mined and where the promise of cultural payoff escalated strategies of investment for genuinely disenchanted intellectuals and political entrepreneurs. New kinds of cultural and symbolic capital were being mined, minted, and traded at the frontier of race relations—abolitionist-style. The raw material was the genuine and authentic voice of slaves and former slaves expressed through narratives and the Negro spirituals. The finished product, the testimony, circulated through speaking tours, pamphlets, magazine features, and newspaper articles and was drawn into sermons and political speeches. African American texts served as pretext in the context of the moral and political maneuverings against both slavery and market-centered modernization. The testimony was not simply a reified text of black voices valued in themselves; it was a new and distinct cultural form that functioned to broker many of the tensions unleashed by much larger social changes.

From Testimony to Artifact

In 1867 the preface to the collection of spirituals by William Allen and his colleagues raised the concern that there was no "systematic effort … to collect and preserve [Negro] melodies." Two decades later this challenge was met with the formation of a new intellectual discipline organized around an intensive search for folk culture. As a new cultural science, folklore was certainly attuned to—because it was a part of—an emergent sentiment of disenchantment with modernization. Professional folklorists inherited the concern for cultural authenticity that the romanticist strains of antimodernism embraced. Along with the larger enterprise of the cultural sciences at the end of the century, folklore was sympathetic and full of lament, but it was not hostile to modernization.

Folklore extended in a more systematic manner many of the same sentiments launched by the initial discoverers of the Negro spiritual. Indeed, it is entirely appropriate to view as proto-folkloristic the activities of Allen, Higginson, and others. As it took on more scientistic accents, the folkloristic appropriation of cultural practices marked a significant shift in interpretation. Traversed as it was by sentimentality and science, folklore was ambivalent. But its rationalist dispositions came to outweigh disenchantment, and folklore was, at the turn of the century, more than equally resigned to the triumph of modernization and market society. Unlike midnineteenth-century romanticism in general and American Transcendentalism in particular, scientific folklore was not designed to battle modernization. If Transcendentalism served as a rejection of modernization, professional folklore, along with the whole enterprise of social science, was symptomatic of an intellectual and cultural concession. Industrialization was here to stay. No social movement appeared effective to bring it to a halt.

As we trace the transformation of the reception of African American music from the abolitionists to the professional folklorists, what we see is the rationalization of nineteenth-century romanticist sentimentality. Abolitionists relied, in part, on the expressive practices of African Americans for purposes of social, cultural, and political critique of American society. Compelled by the new scientism, folklore managed to transform the romantic recognition of cultural loss into a systematic and objectified inventory of cultural activities, beliefs, products, and practices. In the process, the political thrust of romanticist antimodernism gave way to a new and powerful knowledge formation. The professionalization of American folklore scholarship was highlighted in 1888 by the rise of the American Folklore Society and the launching of the *Journal of American Folk-Lore*. Rallying around the concern to retrieve aspects of culture on the verge of being overshadowed by modern industrial society, the journal's editors promised to employ a "scientific character" in pursuing its "principal object," which was to collect "the fast vanishing remains of folk-lore in America." The first stated goal of the American Folklore Society was to collect "relics of Old English folk-lore"; second and third on the list of collection priorities were the "lore of Negroes in the southern states of the Union" and the "lore of the Indian tribes of North America."[9] From its inception until 1914, the journal published over 100 entries on African Americans, many containing treatments of music. With attention to the retrieval and classification of the cultural products of racialized groups, *American Folk-Lore* did more than publish articles and research notes on the study of African Americans and Native Americans; it entered into the flourishing development of the new American academic discourse on race, culture, and modernity.

Promoted in the early pages of *American Folk-Lore* was a neoromantic and sentimentalized framework accompanied by an increasingly dry, matter-of-fact, category-driven, and taxonomically inspired spirit intent on capturing the remnants of cultural practices disappearing in the march of progress. Compared to the moral intensity that surrounded the Negro spirituals as testimony, folklorist language refracted, even in its measured benevolence, a depoliticized, morally tepid scientism. Writing in *Forum* for a more general middle-class readership, Lee J. Vance summed up the new science's mission: "Folk-lore is concerned more particularly with the 'survival' of primitive or ancient ideas and customs in modern civilization" (Vance 1896–97, 249). It was not the meaning of the expressions that motivated this view of folklore; it was the concern over the very survival of culture itself. Vance was pleased with the new science: "The end of the nineteenth century [was] remarkable for the immense number of books devoted to the Folk—to people who have shared ... least in the general advance. These people are, first, the backward races, as the natives of Australia and our Indian tribes; then the European peasantry, Southern negroes, and others out of touch with towns and schools and railroads" (Vance 1896–97, 249). If the cultures of those "least in the general advance" were under threat of destruction, folklore's role was to intervene and its task was to preserve. Remnants, specimens, and artifacts were to be salvaged before they were banished by history.

In the pursuit of scientistic legitimacy, folklore objectified the notion of "folk" in a great range of forms. Virtually every sphere of premodern life could be grasped within a folk studies framework. Blending natural history with the study of folklore, Otis T. Mason could claim: "Without doubt, there is also a folk-speech, folk-trades and practices, folk fine art, folk-amusement, folk-festival, folk-ceremonies, folk-customs, folk-government folk-society, folk-history, folk-poetry, folk-maxims, folk-philosophy, folk-science, and myths or folk-theology. Everything that we have, they have—they are the back numbers of us" (Mason 1891, 103). All of these sites of folk life and popular culture were but remnants of a quaint irrationality. What folklore marked as objects of knowledge were cultural forms noted for their absence of fit in modern industrial culture.

What happened to the testimonial function of the Negro spiritual under this new intellectual orientation? What was at stake—more important, what were the shifting stakes—in the new interpretive formation? Most notably, the spiritual was stripped of its political and moral capital. It no longer functioned as a testimony for white elite political disenchantment. Drained of moral and political value, African American expressions became nostalgic objects viewed through the aesthetics of a new knowledge formation. And in this view they were *artifacts* that refracted a nostalgia for the present.

The fledgling Negro schools and colleges erected during and shortly after the Civil War were not exempt from these shifts in cultural appropriation. The transcriptions of spirituals were also later reincorporated into the musical instruction of former slaves at schools such as Fisk, Hampton, and Tuskegee where songs were made part of the educational curriculum. This, incidentally, was the cultural juncture in which the newly institutionalized Negro spiritual singers, such as the famed Fisk Jubilee Singers, emerge. Under tutelage, black students were guided in the retrieval of their musical heritage. Hampton Institute's director of music, F. G. Rathbun, noted in 1893 that Hampton was "the only institution in this country, I think, where this plantation and slave music is taught regularly and systematically to its students." According to Rathbun, Hampton Institute had by this time collected "over one hundred different songs" published in a volume entitled "Slave Songs" with "many more in manuscript as taken down from the lips of our students from various parts of the South year after year" (Rathbun 1893, 174).

However, it was no longer the testimonial function of the spirituals that Rathbun found most important. Gone was the capacity for the spirituals to reverberate across a range of anxieties, tensions, and problems that accompanied their appropriation three decades earlier. For Rathbun the spirituals were grasped in the framework of an emergent musicology: "The most striking attribute of the genuine 'spirituals' is their utter simplicity, being based entirely on three chords, or the tonic, sub-dominant and the dominant of the key, and I have yet to find one containing a modulation, either forward or backward; and as originally sung the harmony is often confined to open fifths and octaves, the third often being absent; but in rhythm they are especially rich" (Rathbun 1893, 174).

In the mid-1890s, Hampton started a "Department of Folk-Lore and Ethnology" section as part of the reportage included in its monthly publication, *The Southern Workman*. In a discussion reflecting the new interest in taxonomy, an article printed in 1895 (reprinted in Hampton Institute, 1976 [1895]) in *Southern Workman* drew a distinction among "Corn-Songs," "Dance-Songs," and "Shouts or Spirituals": "Words may differ, terms may differ in different localities or in the same locality from year to year, but the Negro must sing as he works, as he plays, and as he worships, and so these three classes of songs are always found."[10] Consider the text of the following song also printed in the *Southern Workman* article:

> *What in de worl' is de marter here*
> *Oh—oh, ho*
> *What in de worl' is de marter here*
> *Oh—oh, ho*
> *Fall out here and shuck dis corn*
> *Oh—oh, ho*
> *Bigges pil ever see sence I was born*
> *Oh—oh, ho*
> *Marster's niggers is fat and slick,*
> *Oh—oh, ho*
> *Case dey gits enough to eat*
> *Oh—oh, ho*
> *Joneses niggers is mighty po',*
> *Oh—oh, ho*
> *Don't know whedder dey gets enough er no,*
> *Oh—oh, ho*
> *I loves ol' marster an' mistis too,*

Oh—oh, ho
Case deys rich an' kin an' true,
    Oh—oh, ho
Po white trash I does despise ...

There is no discussion whatsoever of the words, what they address, and what might matter socially and culturally for the singer(s). Meanings for African Americans are neutralized. The song draws its significance from the framework of the taxonomy that gives it a new place within folklore: This is a work song and more specifically a corn song. It speaks the context of slavery—about owners and the owned and despising "po white trash." But what underwrites this historically embedded text's social references—the social relations of slavery—vanishes behind the eclipse of musicology and the accuracy of describing a performance that have come to matter more: "The rhythm sets the time of the work on which all are engaged, and the beating of the feet, the swaying of the body or the movement of the arm may be retarded or accelerated at will by the leader" (Hampton Institute 1976 [1895], 147). The song "Run, Nigger Run," presented as a corn song, is likewise treated. But the song's content—with lines like "Run, nigger, run patteroler'll ketch yer / Hit yer thirty-nine and ware 'e didn' tech yer"—engenders no reflection, other than being another example of "rhythmical combinations" (pp. 147–148). A similar technical neutrality blending with an interpretive aesthetic regarding the mechanics of form accompanies the discussions of dance songs.

These shifts in treatment, ostensibly more refined because they draw more consciously on the inner logic of scientific classification, signal a much larger interpretive transformation in which the social and institutional conditions of slavery as constitutive of the very production of African American articulations are overtaken by a new interpretive aesthetic that reworks the ground upon which authenticity is reconfigured and given a new legitimacy. However, in keeping with the legacy of the sentiments that put the Negro spirituals on the cultural map a few decades earlier, the shouts and spirituals are discussed as content-rich in the conclusion of the article. They still embody

> the emotional expression of the Negro reaching its highest development. In the Spirituals the length and breadth and depth and height of the American slave's religious and historical experience are laid bare. ... There is real poetry in the rude words, and harmony in the wild strains. ... It is not art, it is life—the life of the human soul itself, manifest in music and in words. ... No truer folk-music can be found in this or any other country, than the religious song of the black peasantry of the South (Hampton Institute 1976 [1895], 149–150).

Toward the end of the century, such descriptions had become routine, mechanical, and gratuitous. As a concluding remark at the end of the article, the homage to the spiritual and its reception as a statement about social relations functioned as an afterthought; at century's end it appeared not as an opening theme, which is what one would have observed a few decades earlier, but as a musical coda. What was earlier a romantic as well as politicized pretext was repositioned as a belated acknowledgment punctuating the conclusion of the scientific narrative. Overall, and in the context of the dominant culture's political resignation to modernization, the technical treatment of black voices was symptomatic of the rationalization of sentimentality.

The emergence of the American Folk-Lore Society, its journal, and related developments across the social sciences more generally are cultural examples of how antimodernist tensions, romanticism, and the new scientific spirit converged to reshape particular reception strategies of intellectuals who looked to the racialized cultural margins.[11] This shift in interpretation is what underlies the transition from cultural testimony to cultural artifact; it is also an example of a much larger epistemological and institutional process: the effects of the rationalization of social science upon domestic subcultures. In the process, black expressions were converted to artifacts, a remodeling that involves the realization of a cultural form by rendering it into a cultural object through the *objectifying strategies* of a particular group. In the hands of the new folklore, objectification was also a recasting of an older and earlier notion of authenticity: When this analytic framework met the Negro spirituals (and other kinds of songs, narratives, and folktales), it effectively repressed the politically informed interpretations and moral attachments championed by abolitionists. The abolitionists had recognized the slave narratives and the spirituals as African American responses to slavery; the cultural texts were allowed to speak to lived social relations within a larger social system. But under the gaze of folklore and early cultural sociology, the meaning of the spirituals was uncoupled from its initial moral and political moorings, and black culture and expressions were no longer grasped as part of a larger dialogue on the fate of African Americans after the dismantling of slavery. The elite reception of black voices, which by the turn of the century had become a largely academic endeavor, reflected the cultural and political separation and distance between an older reception based on cultural criticism and a new reception that embraced modernity.

As we move our assessment outward to consider the broader social and historical context, it becomes more apparent how the shift toward folklore and social science was tied to—and symptomatic of—new political and institutional reconfigurations. The abandonment of African Americans coincided with an intense redeployment of elite interventionist strategies targeting Northern urban white ethnics. Here the problems of labor control and industrial authority loo large. The years between 1873 and 1890 were economically depressed, and these were the years during which Reconstruction was challenged and eventually routed. Publications such as *Forum* and *North American Review* printed articles with revealing titles: "How to Quell Mobs" and "Is Our Civilization Perishable?"

for example. The title of Francis Walker's article, "Immigration and Degradation," clinched the growing threat of multiculturalism and its ties to labor antagonisms. These concerns were not just about race; they were also about the new ethnicity in labor and politics. White ethnics occupied the rank and file of wage workers. Labor unrest was widespread. In 1877 striking workers destroyed millions of dollars of property belonging to the B&O and Pennsylvania Railroad; in 1886 the Knights of Labor went on strike and the violence of Haymarket Square took place; and in the early 1890s the Homestead confrontation and the Pullman strike added even more to the notion that class strife was less an aberration than the pervasive norm of the new industrial order. The integration of white ethnics into the rapidly expanding industrial order had become a social crisis of great magnitude. Socialist mobilization threatened to shatter the ideology of American exceptionalism, and religious and economic leaders fretted over the extent to which the United States was vulnerable to the presumed degeneracy of European socialist politics. It is not surprising that in this incendiary climate of white-versus-white antagonism Reconstruction became increasingly expendable. After all, the rapid industrialization in the North was dependent upon white, not black, labor. Given such urgent concerns, an occupying army in the South and an ongoing commitment to Reconstruction were quickly seen as surplus energies. As the North abandoned the freed men, women, and families, a resurgent Democratic party reclaimed its role in redeeming the South. And with Northern withdrawal went the moral and political commitments to African Americans.

Abolitionist and antimodernist discourses helped to bring African Americans—partially, selectively, and temporarily—into the political and moral heart of the broader discourse on substantive egalitarianism. Such debates joined the deep apprehension toward modernization and the rapid encroachment of market society. But after the Civil War, the romantic and charismatic drawing power of the spirituals that had lured sympathetic elites succumbed to and became the catch of folklore. The shift in reception marked a splitting of meanings between those mired in the politics of slavery and cultural disenchantment, and those derived from the new epistemological relocation of black voices as objects of increasingly academic and neutralized discourses that constituted professional folklore and the formation of cultural sociology, ethnology, and anthropology. As folklore became increasingly rationalized, routinized, professionalized, scientized, and institutionalized, it distanced itself from the social and political crises—the contested conjuncture of slavery, antimodernism, market society, and erosion of traditional patterns of cultural authority—within which it was first constituted. Indeed, the abandonment of the moral discourses associated with the spirituals was coterminous with the collapse of Reconstruction and the withdrawal of Union surveillance of race relations in the South. In the transfer of political interests from slaves and freed African Americans to white laborers and new immigrants—in essence, a shift from race to ethnicity—the spirituals lost their initial symbolic capital. The disengagement of elites from the more open debate on race relations after emancipation and their migration toward a narrower, depoliticized, and neutral language of folklore are steps refracted precisely in the shift in the elite modes of appropriating black music—from testimony to artifact.

The discoverers of the Negro spirituals thus helped to spawn a major cultural transformation, but the cultural constructs and interpretive modalities they unleashed do not stop there. Indeed, they continue in the twentieth century and contribute to interpretations surrounding popular culture and American race relations. By the 1930s, even the federal government under the Roosevelt administration had entered the business of cultural collection and archiving. The efforts of John and Alan Lomax, who assembled collections under the auspices of the Library of Congress, exemplify the rationalization of folklore as it feeds into the state's official discovery and recognition of the cultural legacy of racial voices—and this certainly throws a different light on the meaning of "National Re-(dis)covery" during the depression years.

The spirituals (as I have quite narrowly delimited the topic—not as African American culture but as white-appropriated culture) were discovered and appropriated for different reasons. The discovery was not centered upon what the spirituals meant to African Americans—although from the discourses of abolitionists and even the ensuing folklorists, it would appear that the discovery was ostensibly an interpretive moment driven by what was perceived to be the marginal culture's intrinsic content and followed up by methods sanctioned by the new spirit of modern scientistic objectivism. On the contrary, discovery and appropriation centered on what the spirituals meant to the conflicts within the dominant culture. The spirituals helped to broker competing cultural and ideological currencies circulating and clashing within changing social conjunctures. Thus in the context of multiple publics exerting multiple claims, the spiritual genre can be seen as an epistemological problem;[12] it did not represent the same thing to the various elite fractions and cultural leaders over time within the dominant culture. And the meanings that the spirituals and black popular music were to have for white social fractions were certainly not the same for African Americans (Douglass 1855; Du Bois 1969 [1903]; Stuckey 1987). The spirituals were discovered and accessed by a set of strategic appropriations that enlisted elements of the cultural margins in larger discursive battles; these battles, which changed over time, extended quite beyond the actual content of black cultural texts.

How do particular interpretive publics with specific reception strategies come into being? What factors surround and ground their appropriation of cultural practices? To even begin to answer such questions involves rethinking how groups are historically, socially, and institutionally embedded. What applies to intellectuals and elites applies as well to subaltern groups. This analytical accent does not start from the view of audiences as preformed—as social aggregates assembled to receive some externally produced transmission. Instead, it seeks to highlight the interpretation of the development of interpretive formations. This orientation can help to restore the dynamics of social change to a more central place within audience studies and cultural analysis.

Notes

1. For examples, see Douglass 1855, Du Bois 1969 (1903), Hurston 1935, Stuckey 1987, Genovese 1974, Baraka 1963, Levine 1977, Webber 1978, Baker 1984. Important assessments of the role of black music and culture for white working-class Americans can be found in Levine 1977, Keil 1966, Erenberg 1981, Peiss 1985, and Lipsitz 1981.

2. The works of Epstein 1977, Southern 1971, and Lovell 1972 stand out among the few studies that delve into the issues of elite interests in black music. These are superb studies that marshal an abundance of material subjected to meticulous scholarship. Yet none confronts the kind of sociological questions that attempt to tie the strategies of elite reception of African American music to the crises of social change against the backdrop of modernization, nor do any chart the sociological impact these strategies have had on the ensuing canons of interpretation.

3. It is not my intention to resurrect the old assertions about mass culture and the elite domination of consciousness. Acknowledging the importance of preconditions of reception is not the same thing as invoking the argument that conditions determine reception. Elites cannot force worldviews upon people. Having the power to establish coordinated perspectives and institutional controls over some spheres of cultural production and interpretation does not automatically translate into a dominant ideology that finds a receptive home in every possible nook and cranny of cultural interpretation across social groups. As an ever-increasing body of cultural studies literature demonstrates, modes of reception, styles of interpretation, and the kinds of meanings people derive from cultural goods are diverse. Reception is not automatically beholden to some master class of symbol makers. The range of cultural meanings individuals and groups bring to or derive from cultural goods is far too sprawling and disparate to be symptomatic of a master narrative. Raymond Williams argued persuasively for rejecting cultural determinism. Yet Williams also insisted that we retain a notion of *determinations* (Williams 1977). Unfortunately, these two distinct theoretical moves are often conflated: The desire to avoid reductionism slips into a facile disregard for the conditions and limits imposed by social relations and institutional formations, and the result is a tendency within cultural studies that champions a desocialized pluralism that invokes yet evades the social.

4. The presumption that the narratives were autonomous constructs is problematic. Some narratives were written by former slaves, but others were co-written or were the product of ghostwriters. The bulk of the midnineteenth-century narratives were steeped in the abolitionist context and thus tied socially and politically to abolitionist currents. Nevertheless, they were viewed as presentations of individuals.

5. Gates 1988.

6. Port Royal, a major sea island of South Carolina, was annexed by the Union in late 1861 by a joint army and navy force. As a newly emancipated free zone, the island provided a foothold between the major Atlantic ports of the Confederacy.

7. Lewis Erenberg notes than an enormous concern with the "revitalization of self" took place in the 1920s as the new modes of mass culture enabled Victorian culture to be challenged (Erenberg 1981). Jackson Lears suggests that something like this was taking place

earlier, around the turn of the century, with elite antimodernists being attracted to orientalism and movements to revitalize craft and with revivalists concerned with the effects of technology on republican virtue. As Lears put it: "Behind this widespread plight some felt, was technological growth. Earlier republican moralists, though they distrusted material progress, had nevertheless often joined the national chorus of praise for machines and labor-saving devices. But after a century of staggering technological advance, craft revivalists had begun to fear that mechanization was unnerving even the most affluent Americans. ... Other craft leaders shared Adams's revulsion [with advantages]. They felt suffocated by the stale gentility of modern culture; they longed to flee the library and the cushioned parlor into 'real life'" (Lears 1981, 68–70). Perry Miller, however, pushes such concerns back even further, associating an antimodernist response with the transcendentalists who "in the 1830's became excited, or rather intoxicated, by the new literature of England and the Continent (and also by a cursory introduction to that of the Orient)" (P. Miller 1957, ix).

Clearly, there is a longer history of tensions that inform assessments of the cultural crises of modernity. But it may not be theoretically helpful to pursue these tensions by looking for some kind of point of origin where their first emergence might be seen. Perhaps the problem could be posed differently: Under what conditions do social groups experience a threat, real or imagined, to their solidarity? Inserting this question into historical contexts allows us to assess how social antagonisms engender and are engendered by the responses of groups to historical transformations. In this regard it is worth pushing the notion of antimodernism toward a wider framework that views the problems of crises from the vantage point of established social groups and classes whose cultural identities are challenged and threatened (Durkheim 1933 [1893]).

8. The significance of this transformation, which helped expand the circulation of African American music, is profoundly important for the larger musical public sphere and for ensuing developments of popular culture. This broader implication cannot be adequately addressed here.

9. See the introductory statement of intent in the first issue of *Journal of American Folk-Lore*, vol. 1, no. 1 (April-June 1888).

10. "Negro Folk Songs," *Southern Workman* 24 (February 1895), pp. 30–32. Quoted in Hampton Institute 1976 [1895], 146.

11. The rise of folklore gathering in the United States is important and deserves a fuller treatment. I touch upon only a few aspects here. The study of folklore, as it is professionally, rationally, and academically constituted in the American context, begins immediately with an intense interest in race. In the American situation, this is not surprising given the great significance of African American slavery and the series of national wars with—and in numerous cases the military destruction of—Native Americans. These two racialized groups figure prominently in the early formation of an American sensibility and culture. But not all dimensions of race and racialized groups mattered in the same way. African Americans and Native Americans were central to the cultural cataloguing objectives of folklore. But Mexicans and the Chinese immigrants, the two other distinctively raced groups in the United States at the time, did not receive the same kind of attention. The war with Mexico in 1848 and the annexation of Mexican territory were not a conducive backdrop for the emergence of romanticizing sentiments aimed at Mexican inhabitants. Mexicans had to be subjugated and absorbed into the juridical-legal apparatus of U.S. law (Barrera 1979; Montejano 1987). In the case of the Chinese, there were no grounds for nostalgia. The Chinese were relatively new. During the 1870s and 1880s, the Chinese had be-

come a national social and political problem. Though quite small in national numbers, they were symbolically central to late nineteenth-century xenophobia, and the animosity toward them served quite different political functions with regard to white working-class unionization and class conflict. The Chinese became objects of formal juridical-political exclusion precisely as early American social science began to emerge. In the years leading up to and following the 1882 passage of the Chinese Exclusion Act, Chinese immigrants were subjected to mob attacks, and some Chinatowns were literally razed by community-sanctioned acts of arson. No folkloristic forays into Chinatowns were likely in this antagonistic climate (Miller 1969; Lyman 1974, chap. 4; Chan 1991, 45–51; Fritz 1991).

12. This, I believe, is the case with any cultural practice or product that is part of a larger cultural form embedded in social relations and feeding into and from the social interests that mark its particular cultural location.

References

Allen, William Francis, Charles Pickard Ware, and Lucy McKim Garrison. 1867. *Slave Songs of the United States.* New York: A. Simpson.

Ang, Ien. 1991. *Desperately Seeking the Audience.* London: Routledge.

Baker, Houston. 1984. *Blues, Ideology, and Afro-American Literature: A Vernacular Theory.* Chicago: University of Chicago Press.

Baraka, Imamu Amiri. 1963. *Blues People: Negro Music in White America.* New York: W. Morrow.

Barrera, Mario. 1979. *Race and Class in the Southwest: A Theory of Inequality.* Notre Dame, Ind.: University of Notre Dame Press.

Boskin, Joseph. 1986. *Sambo: The Rise and Demise of an American Jester.* New York: Oxford University Press.

Bourdieu, Pierre. 1984. *Distinction: A Social Critique of the Judgement of Taste.* Cambridge, Mass.: Harvard University Press.

Burke, Peter. 1978. *Popular Culture in Early Modern Europe.* New York: Harper.

Chan, Sucheng. 1991. *Asian Americans: An Interpretive History.* Boston: Twayne.

Chartier, Robert. 1988. *Cultural History: Between Practices and Representations,* trans. Lydia G. Cochrane. Ithaca, N.Y.: Cornell University Press.

Dennison, Sam. 1982. *Scandalize My Name: Black Imagery in American Popular Music.* New York: Garland.

Douglass, Frederick. 1855. *My Bondage and My Freedom.* New York: Miller, Orton and Mulligan.

Du Bois, W.E.B. 1969 [1903]. *The Souls of Black Folk.* New York: New American Library.

Durkheim, Emile. 1933 [1893]. *The Division of Labor in Society,* trans. George Simpson. New York: Free Press.

Epstein, Dena J. 1977. *Sinful Tunes and Spirituals: Black Folk Music to the Civil War.* Chicago: University of Chicago Press.

Erenberg, Lewis. 1981. *Steppin' Out: New York Nightlife and the Transformation of American Culture: 1890–1930.* Chicago: University of Chicago Press.

Fredrickson, George M. 1971. *The Black Image in the White Mind: The Debate on Afro-American Character and Destiny, 1817–1914.* New York: Harper and Row.

Fritz, Christian G. 1991. "Due Process, Treaty Rights, and Chinese Exclusion, 1882–1891." Pp. 25–56 in Sucheng Chan, ed., *Entry Denied: Exclusion and the Chinese Community in America, 1882–1943*. Boston: Twayne.

Gates, Henry Louis, Jr., ed. 1987. *The Classic Slave Narratives*. New York: Mentor/New American Library.

———. 1988. *Six Women's Slave Narratives*. With an introduction by William L. Andrews. New York: Oxford University Press.

Genovese, Eugene D. 1974. *Roll, Jordan, Roll: The World the Slaves Made*. New York: Pantheon.

Gosset, Thomas F. 1963. *Race: The History of an Idea in America*. Dallas, Tex.: Southern Methodist University Press.

Hampton Institute. 1976 [1895]. *The Black Perspective in Music* 4, 2 (July): 145–151. Reprint of "Negro Folk Songs," *Southern Workman* 24 (February 1895): 30–32.

Higginson, Thomas Wentworth. 1867. "Negro Spirituals," *Atlantic Monthly* 19 (June 7): 684–694.

———. 1962 [1870]. *Army Life in a Black Regiment*. New York: Collier.

Hurston, Zora Neale. 1935. *Mules and Men*. Philadelphia: J. B. Lippincott.

Jordan, Winthrop D. 1968. *White over Black: American Attitudes Toward the Negro, 1550–1872*. Chapel Hill: University of North Carolina Press.

Keil, Charles. 1966. *Urban Blues*. Chicago: University of Chicago Press.

Kemble, Frances Anne. 1863. *Journal of a Residence on a Georgian Plantation, 1838–1839*. New York: Harper and Bros.

Lears, Jackson. 1981. *No Place of Grace: Antimodernism and the Transformation of American Culture*. New York: Pantheon.

Levine, Lawrence W. 1977. *Black Culture and Black Consciousness: Afro-American Folk Thought from Slavery to Freedom*. New York: Oxford University Press.

Lipsitz, George. 1981. *Class and Culture in Cold War America: A Rainbow at Midnight*. New York: Praeger.

Lovell, John. 1972. *Black Song: The Forge and the Flame*. New York: Macmillan.

Lyman, Stanford 1974. *Chinese Americans*. New York: Random House.

Mason, Otis T. 1891. "The Natural History of Folklore," *American Journal of Folklore* 4:97–105.

McWilliams, Wilson Carey. 1974. *The Idea of Fraternity in America*. Berkeley: University of California Press.

Miller, Perry. 1957. *The American Transcendentalists*. New York: Doubleday Anchor Books.

Miller, Stuart Creighton. 1969. *The Unwelcome Immigrant: The American Image of the Chinese, 1785–1882*. Berkeley: University of California Press.

Montejano, David. 1987. *Anglos and Mexicans in the Making of Texas, 1836–1986*. Austin: University of Texas.

Nichols, Charles. 1959. "Who Read the Slave Narratives?" *Phylon* 20:149–162.

Peabody, Ephraim. 1849. "Narratives of Fugitive Slaves," *Christian Examiner* 47 (July).

Peiss, Kathy. 1985. *Cheap Amusements: Working Women and Leisure in New York City, 1880–1920*. Philadelphia: Temple University Press.

Rathbun, F. G. 1893. "The Negro Music of the South," *Southern Workman* 22:174.

Roediger, David R. 1991. *The Wages of Whiteness: Race and the Making of the American Working Class*. London: Verso.

Sampson, Henry T. 1980. *Blacks in Blackface*. Metuchen, N.J.: Scarecrow Press.

Saxton, Alexander. 1990. *The Rise and Fall of the White Republic: Class Politics and Mass Culture in Nineteenth-Century America*. London: Verso.

Southern, Eileen. 1971. *The Music of Black Americans: A History*. New York: W. W. Norton.

Starling, Marion. 1981. *The Slave Narrative: Its Place in American History*. Boston: G. K. Hall.

Stuckey, Sterling. 1987. *Slave Culture: Nationalist Theory and the Foundations of Black Americans*. New York: Oxford University Press.

Takaki, Ronald. 1990. *Iron Cages: Race and Culture in Nineteenth-Century America*. New York: Oxford University Press.

Thoreau, Henry David. 1910 [1854]. *Walden*. New York: Longmans, Green.

Toll, Robert. 1974. *Blacking Up: The Minstrel Show in Nineteenth-Century America*. London: Oxford University Press.

Vance, Lee J. 1896–97. "The Study of Folk-Lore," *Forum* 22:249–256.

Webber, Thomas L. 1978. *Deep Like the Rivers: Education in the Slave Quarter Community, 1831–1865*. New York: Norton.

Weber, Max. 1950 [1904]. *The Protestant Ethic and the Spirit of Capitalism*. New York: Charles Scribner's Sons.

Williams, Raymond. 1977. *Marxism and Literature*. Oxford: Oxford University Press.

SEVEN

Intersections of Discourse:
MTV, Sexual Politics, and
Dreamworlds

SUT JHALLY

In my activities as both a researcher and teacher of popular culture, I have been influenced and guided, for good or ill, by two insightful observations. The first comes from Erving Goffman, in his brilliant book *Gender Advertisements:* "Perhaps the most negative thing that we can say about commercials is that as pictures of reality we do not perceive them as strange" (Goffman 1979, p. 25). That is, as something that purports to represent reality, advertising for the most part is perceived as a natural and unproblematic aspect of the landscape of contemporary social life.

The second comment, from an unknown source, concerns the way that the everyday environment in which we live is so taken for granted that it disappears from the frame of our active consciousness: "We're not too sure who discovered water, but we're pretty sure it wasn't the fish."

It was with these ideas in mind that I started a project that could help people (initially my students) obtain some cognitive and emotional distance from the world of images in which we are now immersed—to make the commercial culture in which we live strange and to pay attention to the sea of images that constitutes an important part of our contemporary environment—as well as provide a frame of reference for understanding that world. The resulting videotape, *Dreamworlds: Desire/Sex/Power in Rock Video,* acts as an illuminating case study of decoding behavior. This chapter tells the story of what essentially became a very widespread audience study concerning the interpretation of popular culture and, of equal importance, the struggle over intervening in that popular culture.

The text around which the interpretations are organized is the *Dreamworlds* video. The different audience groups include American high-school and college students, academics, feminist scholars, journalists, right-wing religious groups, university bureaucrats, lawyers, and members of the ordinary American public. The issues involved in the interpretations include questions of both content (gender images and sexual politics) and form (the use of video and visual imagery as tools of academic inquiry and cultural politics).

Background: Failure, Failure, Failure … Success?

I have been teaching large-lecture introductory courses on mass media and advertising in American universities since 1985. From the beginning, discussions of the cable channel MTV (Music Television) have formed an important part of my teaching for a number of reasons. First, MTV represents (or did in its formative years) the ultimate dream of network executives—a channel that featured nothing but advertising—and demonstrates the playing out of the logic of a commercial television system. It therefore acts as a condensed version of the system in total, representing both concretely and abstractly the essential core meaning of the broader system of institutions of which it is a part.

Second, by becoming the main marketing mechanism for popular music (and changing the way in which what we hear is chosen as well as the meaning we give to the products of the recording industry), MTV demonstrates in a very concrete way the indissoluble link between the material and the symbolic. It highlights the way in which issues of images and style are constitutive of broader cultural domains (such as music, movies, and fashion).

Third, and most relevant to this discussion, MTV has drawn renewed attention to other concerns—most visibly the issue of the representation of women in popular culture. From its inception, MTV has provoked widespread feminist criticism for its narrow and demeaning depictions of women. While this has not been the subject of much sustained academic work, the discussion of sexism and MTV has been and is prevalent within many journalistic commentaries.

It was within this context that I began to develop video material to use in my teaching, especially as regards highlighting the issue of sexism in the media—and to use MTV as a case study. Initially this took the form of bringing in different tapes with relevant videos recorded on them and playing them in class. My students were glad to have the chance to watch and listen to videos but looked at me blankly when I attempted to suggest that there was some systematic pattern to female representation, especially on those videos aimed at young male consumers. I concluded that the space between the videos, necessitated by physically changing the tapes, was too distracting.

When editing equipment became available for my use, I solved this problem by editing clips (of between one to three minutes) onto a single tape. When I presented this format to my students, a strange thing (at least from my perspective) transpired—they sang along with their favorite songs!

The next step was a vital one. Familiar images needed to be taken out of their normal context. Stripping the original music away seemed an obvious move at this stage because it seemed to act as a block to critical distance. Further, I replaced the music with a somber and slow soundtrack featuring the music of groups such as the German synthesizer band Tangerine Dream. The response of my students (for whom the images on display were very familiar and pleasurable) was not the enthusiastic identification of the previous attempt, but neither was it the spark they needed to really think about the images in new analytical ways. Although I had developed some structure to the sequence in which the images were presented, it was obviously not enough on its own to provide new frameworks of understanding. The second time I used the edited tape in a class, I talked over it as it played and attempted to provide additional structure.

Also, at this stage I was still including quite long segments from the videos, so that there was a fair bit of extraneous material from the viewpoint of looking at female representation. From a strategic marketing perspective, the use of female bodies within the videos is usually brief and fragmentary—short sharp shots of intense visual pleasure are presented at periodic points, a format designed to ensure the most intense type of watching and to discourage casual viewing—and rapt attention is required to ensure that the fleeting glimpses of concentrated sexuality are not missed. By reproducing this strategy, I was, I believe, making it harder to pay analytic attention to those images because they still appeared as short bursts of pleasure.

By then, I was moving to the idea of producing a more stand-alone piece, and I started systematically to collect and research music videos from the viewpoint of gender representation. I also was thinking of a video piece that would present, structured with commentary, wall-to-wall images without any extraneous material. To this end I produced my first complete piece of educational video around this material. Looking back on it, I now realize it was much too descriptive. I outlined the main ways in which women and sex are used in videos, the roles, behaviors, and activities the women engage in, and the camera techniques used; I ended with a focus on examples of explicit violence toward women and the way in which these women sent out signals that really meant "yes" even when they said "no." My ending made an implicit argument that images of this kind might cultivate attitudes that could legitimize rape.

Student reaction to this version was lukewarm. Even though I had decontextualized the images a great deal and provided a narrative that could aid the development of analytic frameworks of understanding, there was still something missing. It was interesting without being earth-shattering. Again, looking back on it, I now realize what was happening. Commercial images are directed at parts of the body other than the brain—their aim is emotional and sexual pleasure (or as close to it as is possible using visual imagery). I had produced a video exclusively for the head. People could thus get both messages without contradiction. The challenge was now to create an educational message that incorporated both emotional and intellectual strategies and to make the argument as explicit as possible. In the meantime I saw the movie *The Accused* (starring Jodie Foster and Kelly McGillis), which dealt with the real-life case of a gang rape that had taken place in a bar in New Bedford, Massachusetts.

The next version of my video was close to the final version. My narration had moved from description to greater analysis, and I tried to include humor and some sarcasm in my commentary to make it as entertaining as possible. The images were as concentrated as they could be—the wall-to-wall effect had almost been perfected (using examples from over 200 different music videos). The video was divided into seven parts and not only looked at videos of male bands but included segments dealing with female artists as well as the commercials that appeared between the music videos.

The vital new addition, however, was at the end of the video. After the discussion of women in videos saying "no" (but really meaning "yes") to male sexual advances in music videos, I asked the question of what would happen if these assumptions regarding behavior were applied to the real world. The next fifteen minutes of the video were spent cutting back and forth between the depiction of the gang-rape scene from *The Accused* and two rock videos: Sam Kinison's "Wild Thing," featuring Jessica Hahn being thrown about a mudless mud-wrestling ring as various rock stars—including Billy Idol and Steven Tyler—stand around and cheer the activities; and Mötley Crüe's "Girls, Girls, Girls," which featured many real-life Florida strip clubs and strippers. The audio portion from the rape scene was retained as an overlay to the music video images to demonstrate that when recontextualized within a brutal and violent sexual assault, the images and the soundtrack fitted perfectly. The rape soundtrack was a fitting accompaniment to the music video images, the two blending into one. The tape concluded with about one unedited minute of both the actual soundtrack and visuals from the Mötley Crüe video. Thus it ended with the material under consideration (music videos) presented as a whole but within a context totally different from MTV.

The last ten minutes of the video sought to ground the emotional wrenching just experienced within a more analytical frame. The relation between individual images and their place within a system of messages was addressed, as was the effect of commercial images of the cultivation of attitudes toward rape. The tape ended by presenting statistics pertaining to date rape and attitudes toward date rape on American college campuses and suggested that such violence and misunderstandings are not outside but inside our intimate relations and that images are related to the way in which we think about these issues (and ultimately, although not simply or directly, to our behavior).

Student reaction to this version was very strong. The video had the desired effect of disrupting the viewing of pleasurable (although largely unnoticed) images of popular culture. I will assess the reactions later in the chapter. The version just described was about seventy minutes long. I subsequently edited it to its present length of fifty-five minutes; this version had examples from 165 different videos.

Dreamworlds in its final version was completed in fall 1990. Seeking to get it into the hands of other teachers of popular culture, I invested a few thousand dollars of my own funds to produce 3,000 brochures describing the tape and used some professional association mailing lists to mail the information out to faculty in departments of women's studies and communication (broadly defined). The cost of the tape was set at $100 for institutional purchase and $50 for individual purchases. The Department of Communication at the University of Massachusetts handled the money that came in. I was reimbursed when there were sufficient funds. There was some interest in the tape from fellow academics, and by the spring semester (March 1991), about 100–125 tapes had been distributed in one form or another (either purchase or complimentary).

It was at this point that MTV Networks (a division of Viacom International Inc.) entered the picture and through its actions precipitated some quite widespread national (and international) media coverage of the tape. The end result was to dramatically increase the reach of the tape, and by May 1992, some 1,000 tapes had been distributed around the country for use in educational settings. Consequently, there has been a wide range of responses to *Dreamworlds*.

A Feminist Critique

The public controversy meant that the tape got into the hands of a number of feminist scholars, teachers, and activists, who recognized its value as a first-stage consciousness-raising effort and have used it effectively in that way. The great majority of responses from persons describing themselves or their work as feminist have been highly positive (including endorsements from *Ms.* magazine editor Robin Morgan and lecturer/critic Jean Kilbourne).

However, I was also coming under criticism from some feminists. The complaint was that *Dreamworlds* did not go far enough and that all young women got from it was victim imagery, which they knew about already. The same feminist response that denied the need to highlight victimization (for both males and females) also argued that *Dreamworlds* glossed over and misunderstood other very significant developments in popular culture—alternative, powerful images of autonomous women. In this regard Madonna is a key icon and was regarded as providing a different and alternative image. Popular culture is seen as a battleground on which important victories have already been won. This was a reaction to a brief comment I make in the tape to Madonna as fitting into the dreamworld without serious problems. In response to my reading some feminist critics saw Madonna as an artist refusing to speak from a position of victimization, and even though she appeared in the formal role of a stripper, hers was a different, more powerful presentation. One response even went so far as to suggest that my rejection of Madonna as a positive cultural development was part of "a finger-pointing frenzy" where women who express any form of sexuality are merely a figment of men's sexist imaginations. It was not just sexism I was against, it was sex itself, and the tape was accused of bearing an eerie resemblance to right-wings calls for censorship based on puritanical standards (although there is nothing said on the tape about censorship or morality).

On questions of strategy, I was called to task for reproducing the power and strategy of the original images in such a way that undermined the critique I was making. It was suggested that I examine more avante-garde and feminist filmmaking practices to ensure distancing, critique, and viewer displeasure. I was also encouraged to include a female narrator, as men (or rather, boys) must learn to take a woman's voice seriously.

What this critique indicated to me was that the meaning of the tape was not as clear-cut as some people seemed to think and that wider discourses were coming into play in how different audiences understood the tape. I will take this up in detail in a later section.

An Academic/Liberal Critique

Dreamworlds was presented at the opening plenary session of the Rhetoric and Ideology conference held at Temple University in April 1991. The tape came under heavy attack (as well as some lively defense) from commentators and the audience. (What was interesting was that the pop music critic of the *New York Times,* Jon Pareles, reproduced almost the same critique in his review of the tape [Pareles 1991], which indicates that there may be some convergence in liberal/academic analyses of popular culture.) There were five main issues raised.

First, there was the accusation of selectivity or nonrepresentation. One commentator argued that after viewing the tape she had watched MTV for a few hours and that my tape did not accurately represent the videos she saw—that the images I had reproduced were a small part of the videos on display during her watching. Jon Pareles conducted the same experiment and came up with a figure of one in six videos that used blatant sexist imagery. That is, the images I had used were not significant.

Second, the tape was accused of being extremely puritanical in its critique of commercial sexuality.

Third, it was argued that linking up the images to issues of sexual violence and date rape was misleading. The rape statistics had been overblown—anyway, young people were able to distinguish between fantasy (the videos) and other more real domains of socialization. MTV videos are an innocent world that people know and recognize as fantasy and that do not affect the way they live the rest of their lives.

The fourth claim was that by decontextualizing and recontextualizing, I had distorted the original meaning of the images. The meaning of them I argued for, as part of a male adolescent dreamworld, was not the meaning the images actually had for their consumers.

Fifth, *Dreamworlds* was a long way from reasoned and balanced discussion of the issues. It sought to push viewers toward a particular interpretation, especially through its visual strategies. Jon Pareles described it as using "smear tactics."

Measuring/Recognizing Significance

The question of *significance* is of course of vital importance for researchers of many subjects, but especially so for communication scholars. We seek, after all, to discover the social significance of symbolic and cultural forms. How we go about measuring that significance is at the heart of many theoretical and methodological debates. One measurement technique is content analysis, in which the number of appearances equates with significance. Obviously, this method is suggested in the critique advanced in the preceding discussion. However, there are assumptions built into such a methodology, the most important of which are (1) that frequency of occurrence equals significance and (2) that all single occurrences of different phenomena have the same significance. From such assumptions a theory of culture can be constructed by statistics.

I do not want to belittle what we can learn from such an approach (it must form part of any adequate analysis), but such a view has little to say about the semiotic difference among cultural phenomena and even less to say about the interaction between cultural phenomena and the audience. It has little to say of use on the process of the construction of cultural meaning. It is illuminating in this regard that Jon Pareles and my academic critics thought the best way to test my thesis was to watch MTV for a few hours. This indicates that they were unfamiliar with the world of MTV—they had to find out about it. It was a view from outside the sphere of significance of the target audience. (An alternative methodology may have involved speaking to young people about what they thought of the subject of sex and videos.)

I find it important that this criticism comes very rarely from the student viewers of the tape. When they see the images of *Dreamworlds,* they instantly recognize them as an important part of their world and their culture. Even when the images are on the screen for mere seconds, they register. This suggests that the images the tape refers to are an important and deep part of the discursive space in which young people live. They play a part in the construction and maintenance of gender identity. That discourse is certainly not the only important factor, but it has significance. It means something. (As a matter of interest and as a response to this criticism, I conducted my own informal content analysis of three different time periods on MTV; I sampled eighty-nine videos and counted six out of ten that in some way use the type of images that appear in *Dreamworlds.*) There is not space here to discuss this fully, but the question of *effect* is essentially the same as the question of significance. Significant stories of how the world works help us understand the world we live in. That understanding is one basis of behavior.

To the charge of distortion and decontextualization I plead guilty with no mitigating circumstances. The process of operating and struggling on the terrain of
commercial images requires new tools and new modes of address. The tape is an
attempt to create an alternative voice, to raise new issues to the level of cultural
debate. Balance, reason, and objectivity become possible when a debate already
exists. *Dreamworlds* is part of an attempt to create that debate and therefore must
articulate as powerfully as possible an alternative position. This means recognizing the rhetorical structure of modern image-based communication and using it
to say something about that world itself. If the tape distorts the meaning of the
original material, then the audience of viewers to whom it is directed will be
aware because they are intimately familiar with that world—they will reject
Dreamworlds as a work of false propaganda. If by decontextualization the tape
brings the meaning of familiar images to the surface level of consciousness, new
discussion can take place. The decision about whether the tape is unfair distortion will be made by the young viewers to whom *Dreamworlds* hopes to speak. I
will be happy to live by their responses.

Audience Reactions: Students

When I first showed the tape in its nearly finished form to my classes, I was worried most about one thing: What if they found it long and boring and it could not
hold their attention? This could have been an especially acute problem, as the tape
was shown originally in large darkened lecture halls (300 seats) with video projec-
tion. What was to stop viewers from treating this like a trip to the movies and
talking to classmates about their images?

I need not have worried. My strategy of creating a quite seamless flow of intense
images of sexuality meant that the tape could not be watched casually. The intensity and the force of the original images could be used back against the images
themselves. My editing (of already highly edited material) was very tight and left
no space for drifting off. The use of different music directed even more attention
to the visuals. Hooked visually, viewers could not ignore or tune out the narration.

In the reactions to the tape, some commentators have worried that I had essentially created the "best of MTV sexist images" and that it could simply reinforce
(rather than disrupt) the effect of the images. (There is a similar debate about
pornography and whether showing it even for critical analysis might, in some audiences, simply produce an additional opportunity to enjoy the original material.) That is, some men might find the tape arousing. This is a potential danger in
that the original music video images are indeed pleasurable (if they were not they
would not be used). I was very aware of this, but I saw this more as an opportunity than a threat. Young people would watch the images—I could get their attention. Could that attention then be directed against the images that were the focus
of the watching? My strategy was twofold: (1) to decontextualize by changing the

music, reediting, and adding narration; and (2) to recontextualize by relentlessly presenting one image after the other, by piling them on—to change initial pleasure into something different: overconsumption, a feeling of being full. The original images do their work in very specific contexts, and as already pointed out, they are fleeting. Could too many of these images lead to a different effect?

The tape has been shown at many colleges and universities across the United States, and many colleagues have sent me the written reactions of their students. I have the reactions of literally hundreds of students. I also have written reactions from my own students as well as the reaction of audiences of students for whom I have screened the tape at other colleges. The following comments are drawn from these reactions.

The positive reactions to the tape can be separated into two groups. The first is that of students who saw the video as giving them a way of looking at a familiar aspect of popular culture in a new way. Although differing in intensity, it was the majority reaction. Informal responses from colleagues who have used it in courses suggest that the response "I never thought about it before, but I will now" is the dominant reading. From my perspective this is also the "preferred reading."

- [The tape is] an interesting and effective way to present the material. We see these videos every day, but we don't realize how exploited women in the videos really are. It gave me more insight and allowed me to view the exploitation of women in media from a different perspective [observer?] instead of viewer, and as a serious problem.

- Sometimes the obvious is not as obvious as it seems until someone points it out to you directly. I've watched MTV for years, and I guess I've never really noticed how much women are exploited as sex objects and helpless children. The video *Dreamworlds* really opens my eyes to this. It angers me to be portrayed like that.

- The video is quite an eye-opener. Many of us have seen the videos used as examples but never really understood the impact that they have. There is a strong argument that the constant bombardment of the images of women as objects or just looking for and needing a man really affects many people's view of what is real and what isn't.

- I was really disturbed by this film. Not in the sense of the material presented. In the sense that I really wasn't aware of such a major problem. I watch MTV all of the time, and I enjoy seeing beautiful women in sexy outfits. Now that I am aware of such a problem I feel like a jerk for admiring these women. I thought the movie overall was an excellent presentation. After I see presentations of this kind, I wonder what the hell is going on in our society.

- This video was really powerful. It made me aware of the implications of images I was completely familiar with and had never seen as abnormal. It made me look at MTV from a different perspective.

- Shocked. Amazed. Confused. Disgusted. Enlightened. Any one of these terms could describe how I felt after I witnessed the video *Dreamworlds*. At first I was not sure where the subject was heading, but after about five minutes, I was hooked. Like most people my age, I watch MTV. But I never realized exactly what the music videos were saying. The way women were portrayed is nothing short of sexist. I had seen almost all of the videos shown, but I never gave them a second thought. But I will never look at a music video the same again.

A second set of reactions was also largely positive but broken down more along gender lines and featured female viewers becoming angry at the images of popular culture.

- The film was intense and had a great impact on me. I felt that the points discussed were very informative and aroused my interest. I was very angry at the images of women, especially ones that I had never realized before due to advertising's internalization of the social system.

- Being female, I felt like a victim, and the reality became very clear as I viewed the many clips. It was rather frightening and numbing to watch the shots, and I became aware how programmed or accustomed I was to seeing this not only on MTV but in ads on TV, magazines, and newspapers.

Far from female viewers seeing the tape as only confirming their victimization and thus as not having anything new to say to them (as some feminist critics claimed), some responses revealed the manner in which the images of femininity had been internalized and were quite central to the way in which identity was constructed.

- This was a very provocative, disturbing film. I am glad such a documentary exists and is being shown—such critique is necessary in a world where far too much goes unquestioned. On a personal note it made me rethink about my own life, and how I look at things and deal with others. As I am a woman, the film greatly disturbed me and made me question not only how I am presented but how I present myself. It clarified many of my own mixed emotions. So much of the time I feel completely torn: torn between the way I want to act (for myself in an intelligent, introspective way) and the way I feel I *should* want to act. ...

  The film made me think about how much time I spend on my exterior; how much advertising and videos really do affect one. When I went home that day, I cried for a bit and then proceeded to throw out every bit of cosmetic I owned, which sadly was quite a lot. While this gesture may seem a bit silly, I feel so much better for it— as I feel that I have made somewhat of a conscious choice not to involve myself in that world any longer.

- I walked out of class on Thursday stunned. I have always watched MTV (until recently) and in a way had viewed the women in the videos as a type of role model, as far as looks and appearance are concerned. Now I see how the "ideal" MTV woman shapes, twists, and corrupts the minds of developing children.

Feminist scholars who believe that young women do not need to be alerted about victimage are making a very dangerous political assumption. It results from overestimating the influence of feminist criticism beyond the narrow and often isolated domain of academia. As Naomi Wolf has demonstrated recently in her book *The Beauty Myth* (1991), the culture has responded forcefully to the real successes of the second wave of feminism by putting concerns about the body and sexuality at the heart of how women are encouraged to construct identity. An impossible standard of beauty (now achievable for the vast majority only through cosmetic surgery) keeps women in a constant state of anxiety and ill health. The power of the beauty myth comes from its *internalization* by women. To suggest that such a key ideological component of modern patriarchal culture is transparent and obvious (and hence does not need discussion) is folly of the most dangerous kind.

What is clear from these comments is that the power of images is much more apparent to those whom they affect the most. The argument for the effect of the images was much easier to make to females who felt themselves to be the intended victims.

There were also reactions that I did not expect and had not foreseen. Some women felt not only angry but also vulnerable and frightened of the social world they have to live in.

- At the end of the film I must say I felt vulnerable. It was frightening to see the direct similarities of the rock videos with the clip from *The Accused.*

- This film really hit home with me. I don't know if it made me as mad as it scared me. … I know I sound pretty harsh on this subject, but it also hits home with me in that I fall into one of the statistics mentioned at the end of the film and I know firsthand how destructive sex can be when displayed continuously like this.

For many viewers, the video had the effect of highlighting not simply the issue of images but also that of sexual violence and date rape. Frequent comments concerned a previous lack of awareness of the extent of the problems.

However, there were a number of negative reactions also. I did not expect a message directed to young people that argues their popular culture is concerned not only with pleasure but also with power and violence to escape strong criticism. I especially thought that male viewers would be defensive about their images. The main negative comments were divided into two types.

First there was the accusation of going overboard with the not so subtle techniques of flooding and intercutting. Sometimes these comments were made in the context of an otherwise positive evaluation of the tape.

- I found most of the points in your film thought-provoking and your statistics on rape shocking. But your presentation seemed more concerned with scaring me instead of teaching me. The end spoiled the rest of the film.

A very small number of responses accused me of selectivity.

- I think it looks a lot worse than it is when you string a bunch of videos together and bombard the audience with them. They don't have that impact when seen on MTV as they usually are. Also the same maybe 30 or so videos are sampled over and over. There are hundreds of videos and they don't all show sex in the way others do or sex at all.

(One instructor has made a virtue of responses of this type by showing the tape to students in TV production classes, who criticize it for its manipulative techniques. The response is used to draw students' attention to the political nature of all production and all communication.)

All in all, I would settle for this range of responses. In general, the tape has made commercial images strange for their consumers and has made them pay attention to the sea of images in which they navigate their daily lives. The tape has helped provide a certain critical distance from popular culture. Whether the responses were positive or negative, consumers of popular culture reacted (normally in a quite strong way) to the tape and had to think about the world they lived in and the effect of images on that world.

However, there were two other kinds of responses that I found interesting; these do not belong under the category of either positive or negative responses but more properly could be labeled "aberrant decodings." Viewers in the first group read the tape as arguing that rock video images cause rape, even though I had been very careful in explicitly establishing that this was not what I was saying. I did not want to deny the connection but wanted to link the two through the discussion of the cultivation of attitudes—rather than to make a simple direct causal link. My strategy of visual juxtaposition (especially in the use of the material from *The Accused*) was based on eliciting an emotional reaction to the material. For some viewers, this visual argument overwhelmed the accompanying audio narrative argument; they did not hear it or could not understand it within an appropriate frame.

In this regard the issue of context is crucial. In the instructions that accompany the tape, I am very clear that the tape should not be shown "cold" and that there has to be appropriate discussion of the relevant issues under consideration before the tape is screened. It is significant that these types of responses occurred in situations where there was not this opportunity to ground the issues and the meaning of the tape.

The second aberrant response was quite prevalent (across a range of other reactions also). For these viewers, the focus became the actresses, models, and dancers who appeared in the videos. My references in the tape to "the women of the dreamworld" were read as references not to the fictional world that videos create but to the real-life women who participate in their production. The issue became their willingness and their freedom to participate in the construction of the dreamworld. Consequently, the responsibility of the effects of the dreamworld was shifted to their shoulders. This response reflects a failure to abstract in any meaningful way from the representations on the screen. They are not representations—they are the real thing.

Public Responses: Sexual Politics in an Age of Right-Wing Moralism

Immediately upon publication of the first story concerning the tape in the general press (in *Newsweek*), I started to receive mail from members of the general public offering statements of support. A large amount of it came from people (mostly female) who were grateful for the raising of the issue of sexism, especially by a man.

As described in the press reports, however, the tape was also playing into some other discourses that were very disturbing. Here is one letter I received:

> I read the article about you in *Newsweek* and am pleased beyond words by any criticism of MTV. I believe you may be the head of a million-plus army who is outraged and appalled by the obscenity, profanity and pornography for the sole purpose of indoctrinating young minds. ...
>
> What a shame that the foundation this country is built on is represented by NEA [National Endowment for the Arts], MTV, Department of Welfare, filthy books and movies, et al.
>
> I noticed by the paper the other day that the Negroes are making up some new laws as they go along with the college administration fraudulently putting blacks above whites which is to "pay them back" for 300-some-odd years ago being sold into slavery by one of their kind.
>
> If the liberals feel sorry for the blacks, they are more than welcome to pay my share of the highly inflated, coerced taxes for DSS, ADC, abortions, federal housing, food stamps, et al. I can hardly pay my bills, but I am supposed to support these individuals.

Obviously, the writer of this letter thought that a critique of MTV must automatically put us on the same political side. MTV, for this writer, is a code word for liberalism or secular humanism. I also received letters of support from a group called Morality in Media, a right-wing watchdog group. Interestingly, other groups read my critique of rock video images as an attack on rock music, and I received yet more letters from anti–rock music groups. This came to a head when I learned from the producers of "Inside Edition," a tabloid news show, that the PMRC (Parents' Music Resource Center)—a group started by the wives of influential congressional leaders to lobby for labeling on record albums—had recommended my name to them as someone who could present the opposing view in a story on "the rock video girls." It has to be stressed that all of this reactionary positive support came not from viewing the tape but from the media stories on the tape.

Intersections of Discourse:
Closed and Open Texts

The literature on audiences from the perspective of cultural studies suggests that media messages do not have any one meaning—that not all people make the same sense of a message. The interpretation of a message depends upon what resources of interpretation we bring to its understanding. Social subjects are the point of intersection of a number of different discourses (or stories) about the world and ways to understand it.

Throughout our lives we are exposed to many different stories about how the world works. Depending upon our background and experience, we are influenced by many different factors. For example, our experience as males or females gives us different stories through which to make sense of the world. Similarly, our racial experience gives us different ways in which we understand the world—not because of any essential factor but because we are born into a world that, in general, positions blacks and whites at different places and provides them with different experiences. For both gender and race, natural distinctions are translated via culture into symbolic distinctions. Similarly, our social class experience gives us different ways in which we understand the world; these stem from differences of biology, culture, and education.

If we want to understand what effect the media have in terms of what meaning people give to a media message, we have to see how the media message interacts with the other stories that people have been told. They will make sense of the media story in terms of their background—what they bring to the message and how the message interacts with the other stories they have access to.

However, this is not a simple process. It is not merely a matter of saying that we make sense of messages in terms of what we bring to the message. The message also has power to influence how we make sense of it because all messages, especially media messages, are saying "Make sense of me this way—this is what I mean." The way a message is structured orients us toward an understanding of it. Thus the outcome is a result of an interaction between the message and the audience.

Again, it is not so simple as saying that there are messages and there are people and that it depends upon which side is more powerful. Complexity exists because the stories we use to make sense of the world—the stories that come from our experience, from our life history, from the factors that have influenced us—are in constant process. Because the stories are always in flux, the media can influence them. The media, especially the modern media because of their sheer presence in our daily lives, always are telling stories about race, gender, class, and so on. Their stories interact with our experience and the other stories in which we live to produce the meaning around those things. Because our understanding of ourselves is always a process that never stops—it continues every minute we are alive—we have to pay attention to the discursive environment in which we live to understand that process. To understand the effect of a media message, then, we have to understand the intersections of these different discourses—how the different stories fit together.

Looking at the media from this perspective requires us to make important distinctions about the nature of media messages and their interaction with other discourses. In an *open* message, the intersections of discourse are so loose and there are so many competing ones that the message is open to many different interpretations. The message is polysemic—it has many different meanings for the audience. In a *closed* message, the intersections of discourse are fairly tightly woven together; most people locate themselves at the same intersecting spot and thus produce shared meanings.

The process we as actors in the social world are engaged in is to try to produce closed communication messages. We do not want to be misinterpreted or misunderstood. We want to communicate because we want to affect the world, and we produce what we hope are appropriate texts. Whether a text is closed or open is not a property of the text by itself. It depends upon the other discourses available to people to make sense of it. It is thus a property of the context—of the other discourses that intersect with it.

What does the story that I have been telling in this essay—the story of the production and interpretation of *Dreamworlds*—tell us about this process? A great deal I believe.

First, from my perspective as the producer of an interventionist text designed to get young people who are the consumers of commercial images to look at them and understand them in new ways, for me the question of intersecting discourses was vital. The decision to use videotape as the medium of intervention was of paramount importance in this regard. Video allows a mode of address that young people are familiar and engaged with. Writing a book would not have had the same effect. (I have been approached numerous times at the University of Massachusetts by students who tell me they have seen *Dreamworlds* in some context other than my class and that they liked it. I have never had students approach me and say they have read one of my books and really enjoyed it. When I have screened the tape at other colleges, the rooms are normally crowded to overflowing. I am convinced a lecture by me on the same topic would not be attended to the same degree.)

Additionally, the decision to use nothing but the images of popular culture as the language of the tape involved both potential and risk. The positive aspect was that it would be easier to get attention beyond a surface level. The risk was that the pleasure involved in the identification would overwhelm any attempt at decontextualization/distancing. The language of camera movement and fast editing may not be able to provide a way of understanding the images themselves; this is the fear behind the calls of some people for me to explore more avant-garde and unconventional techniques. I deliberately chose the language and strategy I used because I wanted to be sure of making contact and speaking with the audience. MTV is the language of a modern image-based culture, and any attempt to have a voice in that culture will have to adopt that language, at least initially. For those engaged in cultural politics, this is not a choice—MTV is the language of the modern age. Such a strategy involves risk, to be sure, but there are no guarantees in politics. Texts may become open, and meaning may not be able to be pinned down as producers intended, but the guarantee of closed texts would mean confining the audience to those on the margins who already know the message—a politics of preaching to the converted.

The decision to use a male narrator also stemmed from this concern. Although I hoped many types of audiences would see the tape, I must admit that the person I had in mind as the prime target was a young male. I wanted to say something significant to him about his pleasure and its relationship with power. Using a female narrator would have risked losing him ("Not another woman moaning about fun images") before it even began.

I wish to remind the reader here of the process of making the final version of *Dreamworlds*. For the first few attempts, all of the potential problems actually occurred. The text was open long before it became closed. I believe that the present text is relatively closed; its dominant reading is one that I would accept. But it was the end result of a long period of failure—and it is still read in ways that disturb me.

The intersection of *Dreamworlds* discourse with that of sexual politics was certainly the most interesting aspect of the reaction. It highlighted for me both the potential and the danger of articulating a critique of commercial sexual imagery. It became clear to me that it is very difficult to distinguish among critiques of sexuality in contemporary culture. The dominant critique is a fundamentalist one— either the moralistic-based one from the Right or the politically motivated critique (although ultimately based on essential/natural notions) of radical feminists such as Andrea Dworkin. In such a view it is sexuality that is bad. If one believes that strongly, then a critique of commercial sex becomes a critique of sex. The right wing therefore saw the tape (at least as it was represented in press reports) as an ally in the fight against secular humanism. In the letter I quoted at length earlier, it was clear that the writer existed at the intersection of discourses connected with racism and sexuality and that the critique of MTV was somewhat like a code that conjured forth other things as well.

Similarly, a student at a southern university, for whom the Bible is a significant discursive context within which meaning is constructed, concluded a review of the tape in the following way:

> It is a sad state of affairs when by using a few commercial techniques and precise camera angles, promoters can make God's second greatest creation to look like trash and turn God's first creation into a trash collector.

In this regard, I have continued to view *Dreamworlds* as an open text and have struggled to close it in my preferred direction. In my subsequent discussions around it, I have tried very hard to pull it back to my meaning, not that of the fundamentalist Right. For instance, as the news story was breaking, I appeared (via telephone) on quite a few radio talk shows where I was obviously expected to be the moralistic and (by virtue of my university affiliation) expert protector of public virtue. Because the format limits radio talk to short bursts of two or three sentences at a time, I quickly developed a standard statement that my problem with MTV and commercial images in general was not that there was too much discussion of sex but that there was not enough! After a stunned response from the host, I would continue that the problem was not sexuality but the narrow definition given it by an advertiser-dominated media system whose function it was to sell us things. What we needed was more discussion by different and varied voices—more access and more democracy to break the authoritarian control of public space and media by corporate interests. As soon as I started to talk about the specific nature of the critique and the issues of democracy and access it raises, as well as those of the repression of other sexualities (primarily homosexual), I became for the fundamentalists the enemy again, for which I was thankful.

Conclusion: Texts, Audiences, and Madonna

The response of some feminists to *Dreamworlds* can be located similarly within the intersection of discourses surrounding sexual politics. For these feminists, there was a main area of concern: the right-wing attack on women's reproductive rights. In responses reflecting their marginal status within mainstream politics, some feminists saw the tape not as a tool in the struggle for a progressive sexual politics but only as a potential threat that right-wing individuals could use to further their attack. It might be well intentioned, but it could ultimately do more harm than good.

I believe it is this same context that leads to the appropriation of Madonna as almost a sacred feminist icon. The attack on abortion rights is a fundamental attack on women's control of their own bodies. From this perspective, Madonna is a powerful symbol of a woman in charge, controlling her body for her own sexual pleasure. My reading of Madonna's broader cultural meaning as being not that different from the image of other women who appear on MTV becomes an attack on an autonomous female sexuality.

So who is right? Is Madonna a "feminist" or a "bimbo"? From the viewpoint of purely textual criticism, I think the question could be argued both ways. If someone is armed with feminist theory and different views of other sexualities, then certainly Madonna could be read in a progressive way. If not, then Madonna's meaning is not so clear. Again the point is one of intertextuality—of the intersection of discourses. Madonna's genius lies in never being pinned down to a position—to negotiating brilliantly the line between the taboo and the accepted. She both challenges conventions and uses dominant sexual codes. (When she crosses the line and insists on explicit lesbian sexuality and uninhibited female pleasure and power, as in the video for "Justify My Love," she is banished from MTV.) The question then is not what academics make of her but how the culture makes sense of her. How do males make sense of her? How do females make sense of her?

The answer is ultimately to be found in empirical analyses of both texts and audiences and the interaction between them. In the absence of such evidence, I would be willing to argue for that reading of the tape as a dominant cultural reading—although certainly not the only one. Some of the initial empirical work on audiences and Madonna would support the *Dreamworlds* interpretation (see Brown and Schulze 1990).

At one level these questions could be seen as only of arcane interest to academics. However, for those of us who regard the academic world as inherently involved in cultural production, these are issues of high political importance. Our analysis of the relationship between texts and audiences will guide, in part, our discussions of cultural and social policy. If we believe that we can understand a good deal of how the society works by sitting in our offices and conducting sophisticated analyses of texts, we will be increasingly cut off from the "dirty" semiotic world of cultural life where knowledge and power intersect. Alternatively, if we deal only with what audiences say about their interaction with that world, we are in danger of floating off into the voluntaristic world of "uses and gratifications." It is only by examining the whole terrain of the semiotic world we inhabit—subjecting both texts and audiences and the cultural process in general to the greatest analytic scrutiny possible—that we can start to offer strategies of democratic resistance.

References

Brown, Jane, and Laurie Schulze. 1990. "The Effects of Race, Gender, and Fandom on Audience Interpretations of Madonna's Music Videos," *Journal of Communication* 40(2): 88–102.

Dreamworlds. 1990. Northampton, Mass.: Foundation for Media Education.

Goffman, Erving. 1979. *Gender Advertisements.* New York: Harper and Row.

Pareles, Jon. 1991. "Sex, Lies, and the Trouble with Videotape," *New York Times,* June 2.

Wolf, Naomi. 1991. *The Beauty Myth.* New York: William Morrow.

EIGHT

Reconceptualizing Gender: New Sites for Feminist Audience Research

CATHY SCHWICHTENBERG

In "The Technology of Gender," Teresa de Lauretis (1987) argues that the notion of gender as sexual difference has become a limitation to feminist thought, as have the derivative notions of "women's culture, mothering, feminine writing, and femininity" (p. 1). De Lauretis highlights a problem within feminist theory that continues to problematize the notion of gender in current feminist audience research. Although the concept of femininity has been politically imperative to the development of feminist cultural studies in the United States and Great Britain, sexual difference as the implicit assumption of gender has by now proved to be an impediment to further theorizing. Most crucially, if feminist audience research is to account for variantly gendered readings of self and culture, a stable notion of gender must be questioned. In this chapter, I provide a brief outline of the significance of sexual difference for feminist cultural studies, particularly in the pairing of gender and genre in feminist audience research. I argue that within feminist audience research, gender must be deconstructed and reconceptualized as contingent and multiple—a process rather than an a priori category. One avenue of approach may lie in a feminist culturalist revisitation of feminist literary theory—to begin where we began in a paradigm rapprochement, only with a more tentative and disjunctive account of the differences among women.

Since the 1970s, the field of feminist cultural studies has made major contributions to the project of theorizing gender without losing sight of women's lived experiences. In a variety of innovative ways, which have by now been well documented, feminist cultural studies has utilized theories and methods drawn from an interdisciplinary purview to become increasingly international as well as inter-

disciplinary (Long 1989; Schwichtenberg 1989a). The basis for many of the conver-
gent approaches that characterize feminist cultural scholarship in Britain and the
United States can be found in the paradigm intersection of the social sciences and
humanities. Currently, there is a wealth of exemplary work that broaches the divide by posing questions of feminine culture. Here, "feminine" culture refers to
those cultural artifacts and practices such as dance, gossip, teen magazines, and
fashion, as well as female-identified genres like the soap opera and the romance,
that enculturate girls/women in ways that express a "feminine" identity. Thus, the
social construction of femininity and its resistive forms of expression continue to
be priorities for feminist cultural studies.

Generally, there are at least two predominant strains of feminist cultural scholarship that oscillate between the humanities and social sciences paradigms, appropriating theories and methods from each to enrich conceptions of feminine
culture. On the one hand, there are those textual approaches attuned to reading
formations, hypothetical female spectators, or feminine cultural practices
(Brunsdon 1981; Byars 1987; Ellsworth 1986; Lewis 1987; McRobbie 1982; Modleski
1984; Schwichtenberg 1989b). Although many of these studies analyze specific media texts directed at female consumers, they nonetheless provide accounts, often
from the popular press, as to how these texts are read or used by female audiences. On the other hand, the feminist audience research approach is especially
attentive to women readers/viewers, whose responses to feminine artifacts or
genres are gleaned through ethnographies, questionnaires, or unstructured interviews (Ang 1985; Hobson 1982; Hudson 1984; Long 1986; McRobbie 1978, 1984;
Press 1989, 1991; Radway 1984). This approach focuses, in particular, on
girl's/women's perceptions of those forms that speak to their everyday experience.

Unlike 1970s *Screen* theory, none of the approaches constituting feminist cultural studies relies on textual analysis alone as a means to arrive at generalizations
about women's experience. The universal, ahistorical feminine subject of
Lacanian psychoanalysis has given way to a far more sociological conception of
women's experience through emphasis on feminine culture and its diverse
specificity. While gender continues to be theorized, it has assumed the more mod-
est parameters of local studies and specific audiences, whose responses are more
in keeping with patterns of enculturation as described by feminist psychologists
and sociologists of culture.

However, although progress has been made in our understanding of the construction of femininity as both enabling and constraining, more specific work
needs to be done; this is especially true in the area of feminist audience research,
which has had the tendency to unproblematically pair gender with genre. Feminist audience research has at its disposal the methods to particularize local struggles through the diversity of women's voices. This approach can be carried further
by focusing on those female respondents who do not conform to culturally prescribed identifications with feminine forms. For many women, the soap opera
and romance as well as other aspects of feminine culture fail to address their ex-

periences; rather, they derive pleasure from televised sports or participate in them or consistently identify with narrative heroes. Are these women to be regarded as aberrant "feminine" readers or participants in "masculine" culture? Are they gender blenders, or do they fall outside male/female definitions altogether? To examine such disparities between gender and genre would enable us to respond to the need to more stringently problematize and pluralize the notion of gender. Indeed, the a priori category of the "feminine" would by necessity become less pristine and more nuanced in the process of exploring those differences between and among women, particularly women's variant forms of identification.

One way to do this would be to problematize radically the notion of sexual difference without invalidating the coalitional politics that unite women as an oppressed class. However, as the cornerstone of gender distinctions, sexual difference has been a difficult concept to dislodge in both theory and practice. Sexual difference is based on Lacanian structural psychoanalysis and maintains a binary structure in which women's differences are posed in opposition to men's. The reliance on gendered binarisms results in women's separate but equal status or feminine essentialism, neither of which theorizes gender beyond the constraints of biological sex. While in the last decade many feminist theories have taken this critique to heart, Teresa de Lauretis (1989) reminds us that feminine essentialism need not rely solely on biologism but can also refer to "qualities (e.g., a disposition to nurturance, a certain relation to the body, etc.) or necessary attributes (e.g., the experience of femaleness, of living in the world as female)" (pp. 5–6) that are culturally assumed as "feminine." The cultural reproduction of sexual difference, which assumes such qualities or attributes, ostensibly excludes "others" who have variant sexualities/gender identifications and who do not accede to the male/female couplet—precisely, those straight, gay, lesbian, or bisexual "others" whether defined by sexual preference or multiple and overlapping gender identifications. For example, one could be a heterosexual woman with lesbian cultural proclivities, a lesbian with masculine cultural preferences, or a heterosexual woman who identifies as a gay male.

A thorough critique of sexual difference as an unconscious cultural reproduction suggests the need to forge ahead by posing gender as a process of negotiation with culture rather than as the assumption of necessarily feminine qualities, attributes, or identifications. Gender needs to be approached more tentatively as those differences within difference or perhaps through the notion of multiple genders. What form might some of these variant differences take if we are not to dismiss them as wayward variables? A key to this dilemma may reside in current studies that suggest a further rapprochement between humanities and social sciences paradigms. These studies provide provocative cues that direct our attention to alternative sites where "others" are given voice. Such a focus cannot help but enliven feminist cultural studies through empowering differences that articulate the need for a reconceptualization of gender.

In this context, lesbian readers/viewers provide a case in point as the persistent blind spot of feminist cultural studies, in both textual and audience formulations. As Sue-Ellen Case (1988/89) ruefully notes, lesbians have long been the "other" as "the skeleton in the closet of feminism" (p. 57). One area that has sought to correct this state of affairs has been feminist sociological research that utilizes ethnographic methods through participant-observation and interviews. Interestingly, research of this type, conducted by Wendy Chapkis (1986) in *Beauty Secrets* and Holly Devor (1989) in *Gender Blending,* also speaks to feminist literary theory across the divide and thus holds much promise for feminist audience research.

Chapkis's (1986) study, the more unstructured of the two, is a critique of the politics of appearance. As she forthrightly states, "Gender and sex do increasingly appear to be areas of fashion and style rather than biology and identity" (p. 138). *Beauty Secrets* is a personal and reflexive account as well as a sociological account of twenty-five women's responses to fashion, beauty, and the cultural standards that proffer a feminine ideal. As Chapkis notes: "Particularly important to me were the women who consented to be interviewed. Sharing secrets isn't easy. And their courage helped me to feel less exposed as I revealed my own. Though it has been impossible to include all the interviews [which suggests that she conducted more than twenty-five], this book reflects each of those talks. Many of my most 'original' ideas were formed during those sessions" (p. 195).

Thus Chapkis, a self-described lesbian, intersperses her book with reflections on her own experiences with beauty culture and also provides more academic passages that critique the ideology of beauty. Set off from these sections are a series of brief discussions by women identified as Ann, Paula, Joolz, Fran, and so on; included in the group are self-identified women of color, lesbians, differently abled women, heterosexual women, and a male-to-female transsexual. The women interviewed range in age and body type, and all make keen observations about their particular relationship to beauty culture. They speak for themselves, uninterrupted by Chapkis.

Particularly provocative is the commentary provided by Annelies (Chapkis 1986), a black lesbian who, in recounting her childhood experiences, describes herself as in search of a culture. Annelies describes her process of maturation as a coming to terms with her racial and gender identification. Early on, she associates acceptable femininity as applying only to white girls, since in all of the girls' magazines "everyone was blonde and blue-eyed" (p. 190). Annelies's inability to identify with girls is linked to her equation of whiteness with femininity. Her exclusion from a white femininity that "clearly didn't apply to me" is transformed into a virtue that "actually helped me escape from the pressure to conform" (p. 190). The following underscores Annelies's purposeful rejection of the "feminine," particularly in relation to girls' culture, as well as her disdain for rigid masculine/feminine demarcations.

On the street, I preferred to be harassed because of my cap, tie, and tough mannerisms than to have to listen to catcalls and whistles. It never bothered me to confuse people about my sex—"yes, sir, can I help you?" How little imagination most people have! Their ideas of male and female are so terribly narrow. The apology, "oh sorry ma'am," felt equally ridiculous. I am no more a ma'am than a sir. Those experiences made clear once more how everything was focused on being a girl or a boy. And yet I kept feeling that the divisions weren't appropriate to me (pp. 191–192).

Annelies names sexual difference as the boy/girl divisions, which "weren't appropriate" to her. She is engendered as neither one nor the other but as a third term—"other" than both. Neither girls nor boys provide Annelies with a youth culture, as she notes how she had "written girls off long ago" and had hoped boys would be "buddies" but found them "structurally annoying" (p. 192).

Annelies subsequently discovers within lesbian subculture a different and more empowering form of gender multiplicity in terms of style and cultural practices, which do not follow prescribed feminine or necessarily masculine ascriptions: "I found that there were in fact girls like myself with whom you could hang out, who liked to play chess, and who didn't talk endlessly about David Cassidy" (p. 192). She eschews "girl talk," assumed to be a feminine cultural practice, in favor of playing chess (often regarded as a masculine pleasure) with girls who do likewise. This leads to her discovery that "there were words for the feelings I had … it had a name—lesbian" (p. 192). This discovery is arrived at not by means of inclusion within feminine culture but by exclusion: "It was such a fine feeling of recognition; that means *me*. Particularly because most things *didn't* mean me" (p. 192). What means "me" is what culture didn't mean. To identify, Annelies had to think otherwise then assumed in order to arrive at gender as a negotiated process, concentrically defined through the multiple pleasures of style and practice. As Annelies reflects: "Another nice thing about the lesbian world was that people were into experimenting with clothes. Lots of other girls were walking around in sports coats and ties" (p. 192).

Throughout *Beauty Secrets,* Chapkis (1986) suggests the empowerment of gender play as the self-conscious excess or dissonance created through "gendered" costuming. As she puts it: "This element of parody and self-conscious creation of a gendered image distinguishes the new esthetic. It is exactly the awareness of gender as a social construct that makes the role playing play" (p. 137). Without eliding the politics of feminist struggle, Chapkis reassesses gender as a static category to instead pose gender as a process in which identification with elements derived from masculine or feminine culture is not a given. This destabilized identificatory process is echoed by feminist literary theorist Judith Butler (1990), who notes that "multiple identifications can constitute a nonhierarchical configuration of shifting and overlapping identifications that call into question the primacy of any univocal gender attribution" (p. 66).

Whereas Chapkis in *Beauty Secrets* explores gender play in the mix and match of styles described by her respondents, Butler (1990) provides a theoretical analogue for this in her discussion of butch-femme roles within lesbian subculture. Butler notes (p. 123) that the masculine/feminine interplay of butch-femme roles results in the destabilization of both terms, constructed through erotic dissonance in a figure-to-ground relationship in which a masculine identity may be the "figure" juxtaposed on the female body as "ground." Butler poses gender attributions as plastic and mutable. Sue-Ellen Case (1988/89) pushes this formulation still further to suggest that the individuals in the butch-femme couple inhabit the subject position together: "These are not split subjects, suffering the torments of dominant ideology. They are coupled ones who do not impale themselves on the poles of sexual difference or metaphysical values, but constantly seduce the sign system through flirtation and inconstancy into the light fondle of artifice, replacing the Lacanian slash with the lesbian bar" (pp. 56–57). In this context, assumed heterosexual gender attributions are only ever pure artifice as cultural codes that can be rearticulated and cut loose from their moorings in sexual difference.

Indeed, without losing lesbian specificity, these critiques of sexual difference place in relief a univocal conception of femininity as a problematic that applies to all women who have ever felt "differently" enculturated or engendered. Although aspects of feminine culture may be liberating for some, others may experience the gnawing feeling that "this doesn't apply to me," as did Annelies. The lack of a fit is key for those heterosexual women who are variantly gendered, but it is perhaps most pronounced for lesbians whose subjectivity is split between identifications that are at variance with the essentialist binarisms of culture. It is in this sense that lesbians are the aporia of feminist audience research. It is their absence that provokes a reassessment of the presence of gender as a given. They highlight the limits and limitations of gender as it is currently conceived.

Clearly, lesbians have much to teach us about the nuances and complexities informing gender. The strikingly similar conversations by Annelies, Chapkis, Butler, and Case all speak across the divide of sexual difference and research paradigms. At these intersections, there is a lesbian dialogue of intervention: theory with practice, humanities with the social sciences. Like Wendy Chapkis's (1986) social science research that speaks to literary theory, Holly Devor's (1989) sociological study of gender and the limits of duality also provides a key to the radical rethinking of femininity.

In *Gender Blending*, Devor (1989) provides an account of fifteen women (four heterosexual and eleven lesbian) who have been mistaken as men/boys throughout their lives. She calls these women "gender blenders," which she defines as "people [who] indisputably belong to one sex and identify themselves as belonging to the corresponding gender while exhibiting a complex mixture of characteristics from each of the two standard gender roles" (p. vii). Since Devor's study focuses on women who have been identified as "masculine" according to a standard gender schema, she arrives at her sampling through contacts within the feminist community of which she herself is a part. As Devor states: "I approached feminists on the assumption that women who were engaged in a critique of femininity might also be engaged in a rejection of femininity. I had, in fact, found much of my inspiration for this study from my observation of more than one feminist caught in the dilemma of 'becoming a man' in the eyes of others as the result of actions which she saw as a pro-woman rejection of femininity" (p. viii).

By means of structured in-depth interviews, Devor explores these women's experiences as gender blenders from childhood into adulthood, taking into account their relationships with parents, siblings, peers, and partners while also referencing occasions of mistaken identity throughout. On this issue, Devor notes that "my credibility as a researcher and interviewer seemed to be a deciding factor for many of them when considering whether or not to 'go public' about being mistaken for a boy or a man" (p. viii). As a result, many of the women interviewed were friends of friends or friends of other interviewees. Although Devor relies on word-of-mouth contacts, her demographics still yield an interesting cross-section: The fifteen women range in age from twenty-two to forty-one, are from both rural and urban backgrounds, and have attained varying levels of education. The most marked constants refer to race (only one black respondent) and to the male-dominated occupations chosen by the majority of the women interviewed (only four of the twenty-two jobs reported in their employment histories were dominated by women).

What is perhaps most striking about Devor's (1989) study is that all of the women in her sampling, although consistently misidentified as men, are self-identified as females who reject, in varying degrees, traditional femininity. As a case in point, virtually all of the interviewees grew up in traditional households where parental gender roles were clearly demarcated. However, rather than emulating her mother, each of these women very consciously rejected her mother as a role model, as well as the socially constructed feminine traits she embodied. As Devor notes: "The relationships that these women had with their mothers were generally not conducive to strong identification or role modeling. Their mothers, often full-time homemakers, were not perceived by these daughters as strong, competent, admirable figures whom they wished to emulate" (p. 65). Although I do not wish to pass judgment on "mothering," it is crucial to emphasize, as Devor's study does, that not all women accede to feminine culture through maternal role modeling. As long as gender oppression exists, there will be girls who consciously repudiate enculturated forms of femininity and opt for paternal identification as the more active and exciting of the socially limited two choices. Such findings not only suggest a more nuanced and overlapping conception of gender but also point with urgency to the need to deconstruct the asymmetries of sexual difference as that difference is configured within familial gender roles and patterns of enculturation.

Devor's research stresses the existence of females with a decidedly masculine identification and a propensity for masculine culture that nonetheless does not

mitigate their status as female subjects. They are female-identified but simultaneously identify with the culturally prescribed qualities and attributes of masculinity. As girls, Devor's respondents reveled in the tomboy sports, short hair, and
boyish apparel of early adolescence, only to confront puberty and feminine direc-
tives with anger or despair. As one respondent recounts: "In high school, I wasn't
allowed to wear pants so I wore the next best thing, tailored clothes. ... I wore
total camouflage clothes, dark green, navy blue, grey and brown. I never wore
dresses. I only wore skirts and knee socks and v-neck sweaters. Nothing frilly. ...
Tailored, I dressed tailored, in dull, dark colors" (p. 86). These female gender
blenders learned to develop a variety of survival tactics that they used to travel in-
cognito within the dominant culture, but they refused to relinquish an active,
masculine identity. According to Devor, "This reality flew in the face of society's
norms and expectations. Theirs was not an easy course to negotiate" (p. 87).

Gender is indeed a difficult process of cultural negotiation, as these female respondents discovered. Devor's (1989) study provides numerous detailed accounts
of how these women, thought to be men, were consistently excluded from the domain of feminine culture. For example, on the basis of aculturally coded expecta-
tion of feminine appearance, these women were often denied access to women's
washrooms. They were chased out, asked to leave, and in one instance, a respondent was confronted by airport security who refused to believe her protestations
until she pulled up her shirt. These gender-blending females also experienced
avoidance by other women when they walked down streets at night. On still other
occasions, Devor's respondents described the sex-identity mistakes made by service workers in stores, restaurants, and other public places to the extent that, in
one case, the "masculine-appearing" woman had to prove her identity to a bank
teller and bank officials who saw no resemblance between the woman and the
"Miss" on her green card.

In contrast, many of these women, mistaken as men, were accorded the male
privilege of being hired without question for jobs in male-dominated fields and of
feeling free to move unharassed within street culture. Since these women's sex-
role identification was as female, one might conclude that they felt disguised as
masculine as they traversed dominant culture; however, the reverse is true.

For Devor's (1989) gender-blending women, femininity was highlighted as a
narrow cultural category of appearance aligned with the notion of gender as performative, as an act. As Judith Butler (1990) observes, "'performative' suggests a
dramatic and contingent construction of meaning" (p. 139). Thus, when the
women in Devor's (1989) study were presented with the option of complying with
feminine markers such as dress and makeup to distinguish them more clearly
from men, they responded by describing femininity in dramatistic terms. As one
respondent notes in reference to her night out at the opera: "I really felt play acting. I think the gay movement's got the right word for it when they say 'in drag.' I
mean to this day I will refer to, if I go to the opera in a dress, I will say I'm going in
drag. But it's neat, as long as you recognize it as a costume, it's fine" (pp. 128–129).

Yet another respondent reflects, "If you want to be part of the gang, you wear the appropriate costume" (p. 128).

The women in Devor's (1989) study repeatedly described the assumption of femininity as costume, masquerade, or drag. For example, one woman's response to dressing up "real femme" resulted in her feeling "really self-conscious, like I'm in a masquerade and nobody else is" (p. 124). Another woman reflects that while she could assume feminine attire, she would "just look like a man dressed in drag" (p. 129). Yet another respondent expresses similar sentiments: "I know a way to be called Madam. If I dress up and put on high heels, or makeup, or things like that, they will call me Madam. But I'm not going to be a transvestite to myself" (p. 129). Likewise, another respondent: "The last time I wore a dress was when I was seventeen … I would just feel outrageous … I would feel like I was in drag … ridiculous" (p. 129); or as one woman put it, "because I don't go through the antics to make that female, it becomes male by default" (p. 127).

These provocative responses gleaned from Devor's study are suggestive of theoretical insights that until recently have been confined to feminist literary scholarship. For instance, Michele Montrelay (1978), Gayatri Spivak (1983), Mary Russo (1986), Judith Butler (1990), and Mary Ann Doane (1982) have all suggested the mutable cultural underpinnings of femininity as an exaggeration in which women act, perform, or play a part. Moreover, in reference to "drag," Judith Butler (1990) notes that "In imitating gender, drag implicitly reveals the imitative structure of gender itself—as well as its contingency" (p. 137).

Devor's (1989) gender-blending respondents were women, culturally identified as masculine, playing at femininity in the instances described. For them, sex and gender were dissonantly aligned, as was the feminine performance they found themselves expected to enact. Thus sex, gender, and performance were posed as radically disjunctive. Here, I will relate the positionalities of Devor's gender-blending females within the context of Judith Butler's (1990) plural account of gender. As Butler notes in reference to drag:

> We are in the presence of three contingent dimensions of significant corporeality: anatomical sex [female], gender identity [masculine], and gender performance [feminine]. If the anatomy of the performer [female] is already distinct from the gender of the performer [masculine], and both of those are distinct from the gender of the performance [feminine], then the performance suggests a dissonance not only between sex and performance, but sex and gender, and gender and performance (p. 137).

The experiences of the women in Devor's study assume urgent social significance beside Butler's deconstructive treatment of sex, gender, and performance. Butler's retheorization of gender as a complex process (contingent and negotiated) highlights the shortcomings of any essential bipolar schema, most clearly implicated in the concept of sexual difference. Similarly, as Devor (1989) observes in relation to her own findings: "Members of society can see two, and only two genders. All persons must be one or the other" (p. 153). In response to this, we might pose the notion of multiple genders as a useful corrective or, at the very least, recognize multiple identifications as the lived experience of "differences within differences"—a phrase that has been the clarion call for current feminist theory.

Indeed, when Wendy Chapkis's study (1986) and Holly Devor's (1989) empirical research are placed in dialogue with feminist theory, the discussion cannot help but yield promising results. Thus far, these results stress the need to further problematize all gender assumptions, whether in a masculine or feminine guise, as well as once and for all to exorcise the unconscious cultural reproduction of sexual difference from feminist cultural studies. Gender, far more protean than imagined, requires a rigorous examination of its contours within a variety of contexts that underscore its contingent and negotiated status. Such contexts, whether familial, subcultural, communal, interpersonal, or of spectatorship, open up feminist cultural studies to new sites where dissident voices speak those differences previously reserved for theory alone. Yet how might this be further accomplished methodologically?

While Chapkis's and Devor's works certainly suggest inroads for feminist audience research through empirical studies responsive to theory, similar kinds of studies can be undertaken that prioritize audiences and maintain gender as a problematic. For instance, an audience researcher could utilize discourse analysis as a means to code gender identifications as they emerge from respondents' commentary, rather than approach the audience group as gendered a priori. Another method might involve the placement of an ad in the gay press in order to solicit responses that describe how, for example, mainstream performers like Madonna or Bruce Springsteen are figured in gay/lesbian fantasy scenarios. Yet another approach could aim at the deessentialization of genres, the melodrama in particular, by exploring their ethnographic function and significance within gay subcultures. An elaboration of any of these albeit sketchy audience approaches could only prove enabling for a feminist cultural studies engaged in theorizing the notion of gender multiplicity from experience.

Finally, as Chapkis (1986) and Devor (1989) demonstrate, in order to understand the formation of gender within dominant culture, we must look to the margins where gender has always been a problematic negotiation—a process in flux. Only by bringing the margin to the center can we begin to interrogate gender attributions as the "common sense" of culture. Only by questioning the costume's fit can we locate our own theoretical blind spot. And only by giving voice to others can we challenge the "same difference"—and learn to think otherwise.

References

Ang, I. 1985. *Watching "Dallas": Soap Opera and the Melodramatic Imagination.* Trans. D. Couling. New York: Methuen.

Brunsdon, C. 1981. "'Crossroads': Notes on Soap Opera." *Screen* 22 (4): 32–37.

Butler, J. 1990. *Gender Trouble: Feminism and the Subversion of Identity.* New York: Routledge.

Byars, J. 1987. "Reading Feminine Discourse: Prime-Time Television in the U.S." *Communication* 9 (2/3): 289–304.

Case, S.-E. 1988/89. "Towards a Butch-Femme Aesthetic." *Discourse* 11 (1): 55–73.

Chapkis, W. 1986. *Beauty Secrets: Women and the Politics of Appearance.* Boston: South End Press.

Devor, H. 1989. *Gender Blending: Confronting the Limits of Duality.* Bloomington: Indiana University Press.

Doane, M. A. 1982. "Film and the Masquerade: Theorizing the Female Spectator." *Screen* 23 (3/4): 74–88.

Ellsworth, E. 1986. "Illicit Pleasures: Feminist Spectators and 'Personal Best.'" *Wide Angle* 8 (2): 45–56.

Hobson, D. 1982. *"Crossroads": The Drama of a Soap Opera.* London: Methuen.

Hudson, B. 1984. "Femininity and Adolescence." Pp. 31–53 in A. McRobbie and M. Nava (eds.), *Gender and Generation.* London: Macmillan.

de Lauretis, T. 1987. "The Technology of Gender." Pp. 1–30 in T. de Lauretis, *Technologies of Gender.* Bloomington: Indiana University Press.

———. 1989. "The Essence of the Triangle; or, Taking the Risk of Essentialism Seriously: Feminist Theory in Italy, the U.S., and Britain." *Differences* 1 (2): 3–37.

Lewis, L. 1987. "Female Address in Music Video." *Journal of Communication Inquiry* 11 (1): 73–84.

Long, E. 1986. "Women, Reading, and Cultural Authority: Some Implications of the Audience Perspective in Cultural Studies." *American Quarterly* 38 (4): 591–612.

———. 1989. "Feminism and Cultural Studies." *Critical Studies in Mass Communication* 6 (4): 427–435.

McRobbie, A. 1978. "Working Class Girls and the Culture of Femininity." Pp. 96–108 in Women's Studies Group (ed.), *Women Take Issue: Aspects of Women's Subordination.* London: Hutchinson.

———. 1982. "'Jackie': An Ideology of Adolescent Femininity." Pp. 263–283 in B. Waites, T. Bennett, and G. Martin (eds.), *Popular Culture: Past and Present.* London: Croom Helm.

———. 1984. "Dance and Social Fantasy." Pp. 130–161 in A. McRobbie and M. Nava (eds.), *Gender and Generation.* London: Macmillan.

Modleski, T. 1984. *Loving with a Vengeance: Mass-Produced Fantasies for Women.* New York: Methuen.

Montrelay, M. 1978. "Inquiry into Femininity." *M/F* (1): 83–101.

Press, A. 1989. "Class and Gender in the Hegemonic Process: Class Differences in Women's Perceptions of Television Realism and Identification with Television Characters." *Media, Culture, and Society* 11: 229–251.

———. 1991. *Women Watching Television.* Philadelphia: University of Pennsylvania Press.

Radway, J. 1984. *Reading the Romance: Women, Patriarchy, and Popular Literature.* Chapel Hill: University of North Carolina Press.

Russo, M. 1986. "Female Grotesques: Carnival and Theory." In T. de Lauretis (ed.), *Feminist Studies/Critical Studies.* Bloomington: Indiana University Press.

Schwichtenberg, C. 1989a. "Feminist Cultural Studies." *Critical Studies in Mass Communication* 6 (2): 202–208.

―――――. 1989b. "The 'Mother Lode' of Feminist Research: Congruent Paradigms in the Analysis of Beauty Culture." Pp. 291–306 in B. Dervin, L. Grossberg, B. O'Keefe, and E. Wartella (eds.), *Rethinking Communication: Paradigm Exemplars,* vol. 2. Newbury Park, Calif.: Sage.

Spivak, G. 1983. "Displacement and the Discourse of Woman." In M. Krupnick (ed.), *Displacement: Derrida and After.* Bloomington: Indiana University Press.

NINE

Textual Interpretation
as Collective Action

ELIZABETH LONG

The Ideology of the Solitary Reader

In her provocative book *Academic Writing as Social Practice*, Linda Brodkey explores and assails what she calls the image of "the writer who writes alone."

> When we picture writing we see a solitary writer. We may see the writer alone in a cold garret, working into the small hours of the morning by thin candlelight. The shutters are closed. Or perhaps we see the writer alone in a well-appointed study, seated at a desk, fingers poised over the keys of a typewriter (or microcomputer). The drapes are drawn. ... Whether the scene of writing is poetic or prosaic ... it is the same picture—the writer writes alone. ... And because such a picture prevails as the reigning trope for writing, we find it difficult to remember that the solitary scribbler tells only one story about writers and writing. In this story, writers are sentenced to solitary confinement, imprisoned by language. ... We know this story well, for there are moments when the solitude overwhelms us, when we do not understand the

I would like to thank Michele Farrell, Dorinne Kondo, and Sharon Traweek for their comments on many stages of this essay's evolution and Jane Gregory for her help with the archival research on Houston's early reading groups. The Rice University Center for Cultural Studies made it possible for me to begin this work and provided me with an audience for its first presentation. The National Endowment for the Humanities made it possible for me to complete not only this essay but also much of the research and writing for a book in progress of which this work is one component. I am very grateful for their support. (This chapter is based on "Textual Interpretation as Collective Action," in Boyarin, Jonathan, ed., *Ethnography of Reading*, Berkeley, Calif.: University of California Press, 1993, copyright © 1993 The Regents of the University of California, and is reprinted here with permission of the University of California Press.)

words we are writing, and when we cannot recall our reasons for doing so (1987, 54–55).

Brodkey claims that the image of the solitary scribbler is "taken from the album of modernism" and that it presents a hegemonic vision of writing by reifying only one moment of the writing process—the timeless freeze-frame of isolation and alienation. This "official story," according to her account, is replicated both in modern formalist literary criticism, which construes the autonomous and self-referential text as a "homologue of the alienated artist," and in academic studies of "composition," as a purely individualistic and cognitive affair (1987, 57–70). I would contend that modernism provides just one permutation of the ideology of the writer who writes alone, one that puts the spin of romantically alienated genius on a far older story (visually represented by some of the early images of solitary writers assembled here). Nonetheless, I agree with Brodkey that the image of the solitary scribbler is an ideological synecdoche that truncates our understanding of writing by overprivileging the moment of isolation. It also suppresses the social aspects of writing: reading other writers, discussing ideas with other people, and writing to and for others in a language the very grammar, genres, and figures of speech of which encode collectivity. As Raymond Williams puts it in "The Tenses of the Imagination":

> I am in fact physically alone when I am writing, and I do not believe, taking it all in all, that my work has been less individual, in that defining and valuing sense, than that of others. Yet whenever I write I am aware of a society and of a language which I know are vastly larger than myself: not simply "out there," in a world of others, but here, in what I am engaged in doing: composing and relating (1983, 261).

Our understanding of reading is, I argue, governed by a similarly powerful and similarly partial picture of the solitary reader. In reader-response theory, this isolated individual appears in several guises: the phenomenological reader of Poulet and Iser, the subjective or psychoanalytic reader of Bleich and Holland, the "ideal reader" spun out of textual strategies imputed by the academic analyst, and even, to a certain degree, the "resisting reader" who is a woman, although there at least the individual reader brings a social identity to her encounter with the text (Bleich 1975, 1987; Fetterley 1978; Holland 1968, 1975; Iser 1974, 1978).

The solitary reader also has a complex iconographic history, and I would like to summon it up briefly as indicative of some of the lenses through which we have envisioned reading as a cultural practice—lenses that have not always clarified the object of inquiry. The images that my account refers to do not, of course, intentionally portray the solitary reader; they are portraits of saints or scholars, surrounded by the symbolic attributes of serious reading and writing, or later, of women reading books and letters. I am interpreting them as *representing* a certain understanding of reading, an ideology if you will, much as the sex-differentiated pictures of boys and girls playing with toys on commercial packaging can be construed as representing a certain, unintended, construction of gender in the late twentieth century.

The first set of images represents a tradition that begins in early Christian art and continues through the nineteenth century. Here the reader, like the writer who writes alone, is withdrawn from the world and suspended from human community and human action. He is a scholar, surrounded by the symbolic attributes of serious research. Or he considers the book and his own mortality—the grim aspect of which can be transcended through the Word, which links each reader to another individual in a genealogy of immortal ideas, and, in its most serious and sacred aspect, harks back to that original author, the transcendent patriarchal God who was, in the beginning, the Word. These images represent the sacral aura of reading in a period of severely limited and, among Christians, mostly clerical literacy. The boundaries between reading and writing are blurred because both are privileges of scriptural authority, but such authority exacts its price: The scholar-anchorite is allowed at most a distant view of the sensuous delights of earthly intercourse (see Plate 1). Such images not only oppose reading to sociability and the vita activa but also privilege a certain kind of reading: erudite, ideational, analytic, and as morally and intellectually weighty as the tomes that inhabit these cells and are inhabited by their solitary readers. This is the visual topos of the serious reader, and, however diluted his lineage has been by secularization, mass education, democracy, and affirmative action, we as academics are all his heirs (see Plates 2 and 3).

The initial perturbations of these vast social transformations—which brought literacy to new constituencies of class and gender—were recorded in late medieval images of the Virgin Mary and the Magdalen reading, illustrations that began to appear in the psalters and books of hours destined for aristocratic and often female readers (see Plate 4). As the secular and private sphere of leisure expanded, images of women reading proliferated. Seventeenth-century Holland, where commercial expansion fueled an iconographic revolution that elevated the bourgeois interior as subject and what one might call "domestic realism" as genre, was a particularly fruitful site for early modern representations of the figure of the female reader. In such pictures, the solitary woman reads, encompassed by an interior that is no less timeless than the scholarly study but profoundly domestic. Her reading is inscribed within the family circle, and, as in the painting by Metsu, her "serious" reading is interruptable (see Plate 5). Usually, in fact, she reads a note, so her reading is ephemeral and circumscribed by the personal ties of affective relationships. If the male scholar transcends the world, the woman reader is firmly positioned in the mundane. In Vermeer's painting, the map of the world pulls us toward the distant horizon of Dutch mercantile adventures, while the woman preserves the heart of the home. But the letter seems to mediate between the two, bringing the outer world inside and enabling the woman to get beyond a purely interior life through her reading (see Plate 6).

By the eighteenth and nineteenth centuries, many images of women reading alone complement those of the serious male reader/writer (see Plates 7 and 8). Domesticity continues to frame these readers, but now it is less serene than sensuous, frilled, frivolous. The pictures celebrate the sheen and softness of the feminine sphere; they are as decorative as the women, and the books—grown tiny now—serve as the cultural decorations of a literacy at once leisurely and trivialized. The women themselves are less contemplative than languorous, narcissistically absorbed in imaginative literature that helps them while away the hours. Although upper class or solidly bourgeois, these readers provide the iconographic ancestry for our modern conceptualizations of escapist readers of mass market genres (Radway 1984).[1] Such women do not read to write but passively consume ... what?—perhaps the novels whose moral effects were so debated 150 years ago. When these women do write, it is not books but letters, as has been so delicately portrayed by Marie Cassatt. Thus the solitary woman reader/writer finds her ideological place in a binary opposition that associates authoritative men with the production and dissemination of serious or high culture, and even privileged women with the consumption and "creation" of ephemeral or questionable culture.[2]

Important distortions of either pole of real literacy are wrought by this gender dichotomization of icons of reading—the solitary male representing a simplistic image of even high cultural literacy, the image of the self-absorbed female delimiting women even as it trivializes the notion of culture as soft and inconsequential. Moreover, their very iconographic absence shows that access of certain class and racial groups to representations of reading has been even more circumscribed than their access to literacy itself. But rather than explore such issues, I would like to concentrate instead on some consequences of construing textual interpretation as a fundamentally solitary practice. All involve suppression of the collective nature of reading. Most of the essay will focus on one sociocultural form—the group of readers—that has been rendered all but invisible to academic analysis, so I will briefly point out some other theoretical and empirical repressions that are accomplished by the cultural hegemony of the solitary-reader image.

Theoretically, this trope locates reading securely in the realm of private life. This is problematic because of pervasive assumptions in social science that there exists a strict and exclusive dichotomy between public and private life and that significant social development and change occur only within the public realm. Such views privilege the level of large formal institutions and macrosocial processes, the development of which has, it is assumed, characterized the emerging contours of the modern world and similarly shaped the contours of social identity. Further, the most important locus of social change is also presumed to be large and organized aggregates of people, so here, too, the public realm is held to be paramount. If practices such as reading and other forms of cultural consumption are fit into this Procrustean dichotomy, they tend to fall analytically into the private sphere of solitary activity, which leads theorists to see them as epiphe-

Plate One: ANTONELLA DA MESSINA, ***St. Jerome in His Study*** (Reproduced by courtesy of the Trustees, the National Gallery, London)

Plate Two: JOHANNES VERMEER, **The Astronomer** (The Louvre, copyright © photo R.M.N.)

Plate Three: EDGAR DEGAS, ***Edmond Duranty in His Study*** (Private Collection, Washington, D.C.)

Plate Four: VITTORE CARPACCIO, ***The Virgin Reading*** (National Gallery of Art, Washington, D.C., Samuel H. Kress Collection)

Plate Five: GABRIEL METSU, **The Letter** (Courtesy of the Putnam Foundation, Timkin Museum of Art, San Diego, California)

Plate Six: JOHANNES VERMEER, ***Woman in Blue Reading a Letter*** (Courtesy of the Rijksmuseum, Amsterdam)

Plate Seven: JEAN-HONORE FRAGONARD, ***A Young Girl Reading*** (National Gallery of Art, Washington, D.C., gift of Mrs. Mellon Bruce in memory of her father, Andrew W. Mellon)

Plate Eight: JEAN BAPTISTE CAMILLE COROT, ***The Magdalen Reading*** (The Louvre, copyright © photo R.M.N.)

nomenal, marginal, or inconsequential—constituted by macro processes rather than, at least in part, constitutive of social identity and the sociocultural order. (See Anthony Giddens's work for one overview of this tradition and an attempt to destabilize this categorial framework [1979, 1984].) Jurgen Habermas, as well, has outlined a more interesting relationship between public and private spheres than the traditional dichotomy, although feminist critics take him to task for not pushing his critique far enough (Fraser 1989; Habermas 1989). There is an important self-alienated irony here, since as intellectuals most of us are moved to write not only by instrumental imperatives but by the conviction that our ideas may have effects on those who read them, a conviction that calls into question at least some of the previously mentioned distinctions and assumptions.

The theoretical location of reading in the private sphere or, most extremely, in the heads of isolated individuals (and obviously, like Brodkey, I do not mean to deny the immensely private aspects of reading but only their reification as the whole story) neglects two crucial aspects of its collective nature. The first aspect is the social *infrastructure* that is necessary, at the most concrete level, for enabling and sustaining literacy and sustained reading itself.

By the "social infrastructure of reading" I mean two things: foundationally, that reading must be taught and that socialization into reading always takes place within specific social relationships. Early images show mothers teaching children how to read, which substitutes a relational maternal lineage of literacy for the abstract paternal genealogy of books and ideas that assumes both adulthood and prior reading competence. Familial reading is both a form of cultural capital and one of the most important determinants of adherence to reading in later life.

Classrooms provide a more formal, public context for teaching reading and one that varies immensely depending on who the parties to the relationship are, which partially explains why reading rarely "takes" among certain groups of students. As Daniel and Lauren Resnick explain in their essay on "Varieties of Literacy," books and reading can be profoundly transformed in the school setting: "A test, as in school literature courses, for example, can change the context for even the best of literary texts from pleasure-giving literacy to functional literacy" (1989, 188). At its best, this social relationship can open up new ways of reading (symbols, structure, attention to intertextuality), while at its worst, it can produce "the deadly serious word" and a sense of thralldom to a deadening educational process. This atmosphere can so alienate poor students that they never feel the pleasure of the text, and it leads even good students to invent ways of reclaiming the autonomy of their reading from scholastic authority—by, for example, reading ahead so as not to read "for class."

Even beyond formal socialization into reading, the habit of reading is profoundly social. As midcentury American empirical studies of adult reading show, social isolation depresses readership, and social involvement encourages it. Most readers need the support of talk with other readers, the participation in a social milieu in which books are "in the air" (Berelson 1949; Ennis 1965; Mathews 1973; McElroy 1968a, 1968b; Yankelovich, Skelley & White, Inc., 1978).

In the second sense of the term, reading thus requires an infrastructure as *social base,* in much the same way as modern transportation requires a physical infrastructure of highways, airports, and fuel supplies. Robert Darnton's multifaceted study of the Enlightenment in France represents perhaps the best example of what it means to take seriously the social infrastructure of a literary movement—one that has been remembered as a constellation of philosophical giants who, through abstracted processes of dissemination, set in motion the avalanche of social revolution and cultural modernity. In a series of books and articles, Darnton anatomizes the complex web of commerce, law, literary patronage, and idiosyncratically responsive readers who in fact constituted the literary culture of the Enlightenment. In his analysis, mercenary Swiss typesetters and monopolistic Parisian publishers, corrupt censors, ill-paid peddlers, and cunning book smugglers working provincial byways and local fairs were the circulatory system that gave life to the Enlightenment.

More subtly, he argues that the content of the Enlightenment itself was much more complex and closely linked to popular forms and audiences than its representation in the twentieth-century academy indicates. Would-be *philosophes*, literary hacks, and readers who ordered erotica or scurrilous, crudely antiauthoritarian political pamphlets much more commonly than they did Diderot or Rousseau, or who, if they ordered Rousseau, read him as a manual for how to raise their children, such people—the bastards of literacy—created the political ferment and shift in moral sensibility whose development we have enshrined in a legitimate genealogy of great thinkers and the intellectual heirs who read them. Understanding the social infrastructure of reading, then, demands reconsideration not just of reading itself but of the ways we conceptualize culture and its impact on social change (Darnton 1974, 1979, 1982, 1984).

The hegemonic picture of reading as a solitary activity also suppresses the ways in which reading is *socially framed.* By this I mean that collective and institutional processes shape reading practices by authoritatively defining what is worth reading and how to read it. In turn, this authoritative framing has effects on what kinds of books are published, reviewed, and kept in circulation in libraries, classrooms, and the marketplace, while legitimating, as well, certain kinds of literary values and correlative modes of reading. Academics tend to repress consideration of variety in reading practices due to our assumptions that everyone reads (or ought to) as we do professionally, an approach that privileges the cognitive, ideational, and analytic mode. Further, recognizing the importance of the collective activity that determines the availability of books, privileges certain modes of reading, and valorizes certain books inevitably brings into view both the commercial underside of literature and the scholar's position of authority within the world of reading. Both raise questions about the politics of culture, including the role of the academy itself. This inquiry may partially explain resistance to scholarship that discusses issues of literary value in relation to historically contingent social relationships within the academy and questions of power and authority among the various elites and constituencies that make up the world of literacy.

For example, Fish's (1980) work on "interpretive communities," however contentious and nonsociological, demonstrates conclusively that textual interpretation among those Bourdieu (1984) calls "professional valuers" is dependent on shifting conventions or paradigms within a hierarchized academic community. It has aroused opposition that seems only partially explicable by his "bad boy" relativism (Bloom 1987; Hirsch 1987). Similarly, another crucial strand of this research into reading has investigated the social relationships among publishers, booksellers, popular and authoritative readers, and aestheticians that determine the fortunes of books vis-à-vis the literary canon (Davidson 1986, 1989; Eagleton 1983, 1984; Ohmann 1976, 1987; Smith 1988; Tompkins 1985). Again, the scholarly outcry that has greeted this work seems to a certain degree symptomatic of a desire to return literary debates to the realm of pure aesthetics unsullied by commerce or other sociocultural interests.

The ideology of the solitary reader, then, suppresses recognition of the infrastructure of literacy and the social or institutional determinants of what is available to read, what is worth reading, and how to read it. But perhaps most important, it has helped to frame our understanding of the cultural world so that the importance—historically and in the present—of groups of readers and their modes of textual appropriation has been invisible to scholarship. This lacuna also seems related to the prevailing analytic dichotomization of "culture" and "society" and to the related tendency to seek the sources of change either in an idealist conception of "great men of ideas" (the writer who writes alone) or in a materialist frame that locates innovation in abstracted forces of technological determinism.

The Practices of the Social Reader

The empirical and conceptual repression accomplished by the ideology of the solitary reader is most obvious when one begins to examine the relationship of groups of readers to those broad transformations of moral sensibility and social structure that have molded Western culture. Such work is being carried forward by a new generation of cultural historians, whose work promises to undermine some of the constraining conceptual frames previously mentioned. Darnton's scholarship exemplifies this orientation. Equally important are Natalie Davis's contributions. For instance, in her important essay on "Printing and the People" in sixteenth-century France, she discusses the ways that groups of readers made newly available printed material their own, in so doing becoming not merely vehicles for cultural dissemination but agents of cultural change, sometimes by becoming not just readers but writers as well. At the bottom of the social hierarchy, rural *veillées,* evening gatherings within village communities, began to feature readings from *Le Roman de la Rose* (which brought new ideas about women and love) and, perhaps more radically, from the vernacular Bible. Craftsmen, too, read in groups—often instructional books as well as the Bible—and, especially if they were printers, occasionally built up reputations as scholars and authors themselves. The most innovative reading groups were probably the secret Protestant assemblies, because, among other reasons, "they brought together men and women who were not necessarily in the same family or craft or even neighborhood" (Davis 1975, 214).

These groups, which Brian Stock calls "textual communities" (Stock 1983), not only empowered their members but also helped to create community, sustain collective memory, and challenge tradition.[3] Reading in such contexts can, in Davis's words, "provide people with new ways to relate their doings to authority, new and old" (1975, 214). Groups of readers clearly gave sixteenth-century Frenchwomen a new sense of their own competence, for Davis's work traces women authors, writing in some numbers on subjects from poetry to midwifery (this entry into print a bold contestation of received and often nonempirical medical authority), to participation in humanist circles that nurtured text-based disputation and conversation. Attention to such groups of readers enables the analyst to generate a much more complex and gender-balanced picture of the cultural currents contributing to the oral shifts of early modernity than does acceptance of the image of the solitary reader.

Reading in groups not only offers occasions for explicitly collective textual interpretation but also encourages new forms of association and nurtures new ideas that are developed in conversation with other people as well as with the books. Reading groups often form because of a subtext of shared values, and the text itself is often a pretext (though an invaluable one) for the conversation through which members engage not only with the authorial "other" but with each other as well. In such groups, reading becomes more communal than our image of the scholar-anchorite would have it and more active than the picture of reading as a leisured feminine pastime. I have claimed elsewhere that these groups occupy a social space that calls our received distinction between public and private into question and offer forums for critical reflection that have been crucial in negotiating the moral and ideological dimensions of social identity (Long 1986, 1988).

Two other historical examples demonstrate that the social and intellectual empowerment engendered by this form of cultural association has had consequences in the realm of social action as well as ideas and indeed constitutes a de facto demand to reframe the action/idea dichotomy by paying attention to culture less as a group of static and abstracted values than as ideas or beliefs articulated and sustained within concrete social practices. The first and more familiar is E. P. Thompson's account of Chartism and working-class radicalism. In *The Making of the English Working Class,* he shows that artisanal study groups and correspondence societies played a crucial role not only in the ideological ferment of reformism but in stitching together isolated groups of working men into a powerful social movement (1964).

Somewhat closer to home, and contributing to a reform movement of more ambiguous meaning, are the progressive-era women's literary societies and study groups. (Note the changing inflection of gender and class.) In studies by Karen Blair, Andrea Martin, and Megan Seaholm, it becomes clear that middle-class women formed reading groups at first for "self-culture"—that is, becoming in today's phrase "culturally literate" (Blair 1980; Martin 1987; Seaholm 1988). But the groups had unexpected consequences. Meeting to discuss Browning or English history brought these women out of the home (often despite resistance from husbands and pastors). Deciding on proper procedures gave them a sense of how to organize. Giving reports on the books they read brought them out of genteel silence. They discovered the eloquence of their voices and the strength of their convictions, and very quickly their study circles began addressing more public (although still appropriately womanly) issues of progressive reform: pure food and drug laws, protective legislation for women and children, and the establishment of public schools and libraries, parks, and clean water supplies, to mention a few of their urgent concerns (see Plate 9). The Houston Public Library was founded by one such group of women readers, who solicited funds from Andrew Carnegie and persuaded the city government to donate land and to budget annual operat-

Plate Nine: **Washburn House Reading Club, 1986** (Photo by Notman Photo Co., Boston, Smith College Archives, Smith College, Northampton, Massachusetts)

ing expenses (Hatch 1965). And an early twentieth-century reading group of black women in Dallas played a progressive role in developing their community as well, as the historian J. Mason Brewer acknowledged by dedicating his 1935 book *Negro Legislators of Texas and Their Descendants* to the Ladies Reading Circle of Dallas (see Plate 10):

> Because of their faithfulness and foresightedness
> in fostering a cultural program for the older women of their racial group,
> and because of the inspiration they have given the younger women
> of their community to read, study, and acquire culture (Brewer 1935).

My own work, of which this historical discussion is one component, centers on an ethnographic-like investigation of contemporary reading groups, male and mixed-sex as well as female, in Houston, Texas. Already, this scholarship has revealed a far more extensive, varied, and active population of book discussion groups than anyone might have (or has) predicted—at the most elementary level, illuminating and unsettling preconceptions about cultural practices that have been shaped by the ideology of the solitary reader. At the beginning of the project, no one—myself included—thought there would be more than six to ten groups

Plate Ten: **The Ladies Reading Circle of Dallas, Texas**, organized in 1892 (Anonymous photographer. Reproduced from *Negro Legislators of Texas and Their Descendants*, J. Mason Brewer. Dallas, Texas: Mathis Publication Company, 1935)

in all of Houston. A year later, after outreach efforts through contacts among known reading groups, a letter circulated to Rice faculty and staff, and calls to local bookstores and churches, approximately sixty groups were located.[4] By now, I know of between seventy-five and eighty groups, and in order to generate a complete census of reading groups in Houston, outreach continues through organizations (e.g., service groups, universities and their alumni groups, special interest groups), churches, and bookstores, with a special emphasis on finding groups that are unlike the typical reading group—white, upper-middle class, and female—and that thus may be more difficult to locate.

Groups meet in libraries, bookstores, cafes, and—most commonly—members' homes, and observing them covers the territory of middle- and upper-class literary culture in Houston. I have visited settings that range across the cultural spectrum: from a mystery-book store, the library in LaPorte (a small community by the water that draws science fiction aficionados from a twenty-mile radius), neo-Georgian mansions in the ever more gentrified West University neighborhood, and older mansions in the River Oaks and Memorial areas, to condominiums in inner-city Montrose (deemed by conservative Houstonians to be a den of homosexuals, artists, and left-wingers) and suburban apartments in the fast-expanding FM 1960 beltway area, under the pines north of Houston, that bear the signs of transience in their rented furniture and folding bookshelves. I have visited over thirty groups, some for several months. Typically this involves recording or taking notes on book discussions, often supplementing those observations with interviews of some or all of the members. For every group contacted, I generate an inventory of information about social composition, literary selection, and group procedures. The individual members of a smaller number of groups are also requested to complete a short survey about group participation, other leisure and organizational involvements, and demographic data, as well as a more open-ended question sheet about individual feelings vis-à-vis the group's literary choices, book discussions, and interpersonal dynamics.

This research has established the ways group participation constitutes social identity and solidarity, illuminated the moral and cultural dimensions of this process, and indicated the kinds of innovative positions people take up vis-à-vis the literary institution and their own experience—cases of personal insight and collective cultural or critical reflection. It is less easy to establish whether these processes give rise to important social effects because of two epistemologically significant constraints that implicate both positionality and its discursive framing. The first involves temporality. How can analysis give contemporary groups the analytic prestige that comes from linking their activities to broader social transformations or macrosocial developments, without knowing what the crucial and determining developments of our era are? Such questions raise the more general historiographical problem that human activity has tended to be valorized only if it is related to public policy or the sphere of public action, so at issue is not just where we stand in history, but what constitutes history or, indeed, social action.

Similarly, the study is grounded within reading groups and their activities. Most members see such activity as primarily cultural, placing it analytically (much as would most social theorists) on one side of a categorial divide that demarcates culture from society and politics. Examining this kind of cultural group and its uses of literature as a set of social practices (as this study does), constitutes one kind of effort to rework this distinction. So does questioning members about their social and political involvement beyond their reading groups. Such research strategies engage the issue of how to blur the boundaries between modes of activity whose separation (practical and theoretical) is one of the hallmarks of modernity. Thus, the study as a whole points to the need to remap analytically the definitional territory of "culture," "politics," and "society" and establishes a suggestive point of departure for that larger program. Examining the cultural practices of reading groups in relationship to critical thinking and transformational personal or group insight is not only an attempt to destabilize a familiar field of analytic distinctions, but also an implicit claim that a predominantly female and heretofore analytically devalued arena of human behavior that links cultural consumption to moral reflection is important for understanding sociocultural identity among the middle classes.

It is clear, for example, that the act of joining a reading group and deciding what its program will be provides an occasion for people to define who they are culturally and socially and to seek solidarity with like-minded peers. For many, joining a reading group represents in itself a form of critical reflection on society—or one's place within it—because it demands taking a stance toward a felt lacuna in everyday life and moving toward addressing that gap. This action, in turn, reveals both to participants and to the analyst some of the ways in which contemporary society fails to meet its members' needs, needs that correspond in patterned ways to their social situations.

Housewives with young children and technically oriented professionals provide stark examples of this process. Many women join reading groups during the time when they find themselves isolated in the suburbs with young children. They talk about their reading groups as providing a "lifeline" out of their housebound existence into a world of adult sociability and intellectual conversation. One such woman told of standing in line in a bank with her boisterous toddler and confessing to the woman ahead of her that she was at the end of her rope: no substantive talk, hadn't read a book for months, and so on. The other woman recruited her for a reading group. Technical workers like engineers find, conversely, that their workdays are filled with purely specialized information. An Exxon engineer who had led a reading group for three years said, "You may not believe that engineers read, but we do," and he told me about his co-workers' thirst for general and intellectually challenging reading. The group continued until corporate transfers dispersed the members.

Joining a group also demonstrates members' recognition of their own, often critical, position toward literacy or social values. Sometimes this positioning is explicit from the group's inception, as was the case with one feminist group that began by advertising meetings through the Unitarian Church (a local center of progressive social activity) and the *Women's Community Newspaper,* a publication that targets the feminist and lesbian communities. A science fiction group, contesting by its very existence the general devaluation of that genre, is similarly explicit about its literary values; it advertises in science fiction bookstores and in the programs for local and statewide "Cons" (meetings of science fiction aficionados).

Sometimes, however, the process of self-definition is more complex, as was the case for a group of by now avowedly traditional women. Three members started a reading group without an explicit social or literary program, but as the group grew in size, the members gradually recognized both that they were using the group to explore literature about women, in the main, and also that discussing such books revealed how much they shared certain deeply held convictions about womanhood. As one woman said: "We're all married to our first husbands, and we really believe in that. ... Everyone cared for her own children when they were young, and there's an open commitment to that. And an open wonderment at people who live differently—at people who have children and then leave them in other people's care, or who think they should leave their husband to find someone 'better.' ... We're fighting to hold the tide back" (MacBride 1988).

The interpersonal dynamics and modes of textual appropriation at work in many reading group meetings also make them occasions for engendering a particular kind of critical reflection that has transformative potential either for individuals or for the group as a whole. (The meetings can, in other words, be sites for cultural innovation, although this raises a set of questions about the conditions that enable these innovations to take root in people's lives—either personally or collectively—beyond the compass of the group.)

Reflection usually takes place through the lens of character, a category that links texts to individual members' lives. On the one hand, the centrality and ontological status accorded to literary characters in book discussions—they are the focus of most analysis and are often analyzed as if they were real people—serve as an indication that the group uses books and their interpretation primarily as "equipment for living" rather than as occasions, for example, of expert display or professional advancement. On the other hand, the social composition of most groups, in which members will typically have one or two close friends but feel comfortable acquaintanceship with the others, permits empathy and self-disclosure without the responsibility of deep involvement. Both factors allow members to reflect on life choices and orientations, using the books as a lens into the lives of the other group members, similarly using other members' personally associative interpretations of the literary characters as a lens into the books, and taking as much or as little from the discussions for their own personal insight as they are moved to do.

Such processes of self-definition through identification with book characters are often relatively complex. For example, one can feel close to but also disapprove of a character. One reader said in a discussion about the three heroines (or three aspects of one heroine) of the Latin American novel *The Girl in the Photograph,* "I found myself closest to the one who wanted to listen to music, yet I found her despicable. Of the three, she was the one I could most change places with." It later became clear that she despised this character because of political apathy, but her self-recognition in the mirror of the character enabled her to question whether she should become more politically involved: a reflective process implicating social action (My Book Group 1983).

Probably the most powerful example of this process was provided by a group I encountered before I had begun systematic research on this topic. The founders were women who had all been in the same sorority at the University of Texas and who all were then at home raising children. In the 1970s they decided that one of the social/literary movements "in the air"—a phenomenon they felt they should understand—was the women's movement. So they began to read feminist novels such as Jong's *Fear of Flying* or French's *The Women's Room.* In discussing these books, members would often isolate certain traits from fictional characters—as people do in reflecting on other people's character and choices—for fascinated examination. That examination, which also included examining other members' emotional responses to those traits, helped each individual expand and clarify her own aspirations. For instance, several members hated Erica Jong's heroine for her "narcissism and superficiality," but were intrigued with her idea that women might want sex without emotional involvement and admired her search for "selfhood." Similarly, many members of the group took Marilyn French to task for excessive anger and simplistic negative stereotyping of the husband in *The Women's Room,* yet felt inspired by the heroine's decision to return to school and forge a demanding and creative career for herself. In fact, one by one, the group members used these books and the insight and support of their group discussions to negotiate a passage for themselves out of a housebound existence and back into the world of professional employment (University of Texas Group 1980).

The process of living stories other than one's own may be crucial for confronting times of individual or social change, in part because it is then that such equipment for living is especially needed. Julie Cruikshank makes this point in her discussion of modern Native American Yukon women's refusal to abandon traditional storytelling during a time of irrevocable cultural change (Cruikshank 1984). Carolyn Heilbrun's discussion of reading about other women's lives in *Writing a Woman's Life* makes it clear that contemporary uses of literature among other women can be similarly motivated (1988).

In fact, gender is an occasion for much of this reflection—being arguably the dimension of social and personal change that has most deeply affected the American middle classes in recent years. It is certainly the issue that has challenged groups to engage in the most innovative working through of values and beliefs. A discussion of Ntozake Shange's *Cypress, Sassafras and Indigo* among a group of white women is one example of this process.

Despite reservations about the book's "hostility" toward whites and about individual characters' erotic choices—one tolerated battering from a lover, another became a lesbian—all endorsed the author enthusiastically for having created "powerful," "nurturing," "creative," and "sensuous" women. As one member said, "Being female was truly celebrated without any of the 'Be carefuls.'" The book describes in visionary terms rituals to mark women's menarche; the group members responded by describing their own unhappy experiences of their first periods and expressing a desire to experiment with some of the "earthy" potions and a magnolia bath Shange detailed. One member suggested, "Maybe we can have a female purification ritual next time," and others excitedly seconded the idea with "A menses celebration!" and "A celebration of the womb!" This theme surfaced again and again throughout a three-hour meeting (My Book Group 1984). Though unlike academic critical discourse, this discussion articulated the distressing consequences of our society's denigration of female sexuality and affirmed practices that might revalorize female embodiment and challenge the traditional dichotomy between spirituality and the (female) flesh. This example encompasses only one meeting, and indeed the group never acted *as a group* on these insights.

A more extended process of cultural innovation related to gender occurred in a book group of single people that was meeting at a classical-music cafe when I observed them. (The group still recruits new members through *Leisure Learning Un-limited,* a local compendium of noncredit courses in everything from canoeing to cooking.) The members were highly educated but proud of being very catholic in their tastes; one of the Great Books groups called them "the group that reads trash." They chose books by vote, and one of the more persuasive women in the group generally pushed for books about modern women's issues.

Resentment among the men about books they perceived as hostile to their sex finally came to a head when she sponsored a discussion of Lisa Alther's *Other Women,* a book about a woman who is deeply depressed, gets little pleasure out of men, and finds happiness through therapy and a lesbian relationship. Deeply offended by this "take" on gender relations, the men began teasing her every time she suggested another book: "Is this another book about women in pain?" This tactic silenced her for a while. But gradually she began to renegotiate her participation in the group by accepting women in pain as her literary genre of choice, saying, for example, "I know I'm always suggesting women-in-pain books, but this is much more interesting than most of them." By reformulating their derision as a literary category, she worked herself back into the group's conversation.

Then the men decided that women had no monopoly on pain and began a search for men-in-pain books that could serve as a moral equivalent to women in pain so that they would not be marginalized or silenced in turn. By now, both categories are a routine part of the group's generic mapping of modern literature. And, although "women in pain" is a recognizable, although trivializing, label for women's literature and has been from the nineteenth century on, in order to work themselves back into the group's conversation, the men had publicly to articulate something new about modern literature, modern life, and their own emotional makeup. By negotiating through their deeply felt differences about how each sex views the other to a common ground they agree on, the men and women in the group invented new cultural categories that articulate a new framework for literary and social experience (Bookpeople 1988).

What I want to stress here is neither the profundity nor scope of these discursive categories but the dynamic and collective nature of their constitution. A socially negotiated process of cultural reflection makes these groups—when they function well—sites for insight and innovation in the arena of identity, values, and meanings. Further, it is already possible to indicate several aspects of group organization and processes that are important determinants of reflectiveness within these groups.

First, the kinds of constituencies a group brings together affect both the reading choices and the nature of discussion. The degree to which the group must (and is willing to) work to adjudicate differences has seemed especially salient in ensuring open-minded discussion. The singles group, for instance, assembles a rather diverse group of people—more so than is the case for many neighborhood- or organization-based groups—so the task of finding common ground may involve more innovative cultural moves than would be the case for a more homogeneous group. But the group is not pure diversity; it is a heterosexual singles group and thus is willing to accede to both women's and men's refusal to be marginalized. The category "men in pain" might fare very differently in a lesbian group. Moreover, both men and women are willing to choose and discuss books about gender, since it is a category centrally implicated in the very constitution of the group itself. Thus, at play in each reflexive book discussion is a dynamic between differences and commonality—a dynamic that is also of necessity predicated on people's desire to continue meeting as a group, since that desire motivates people either to tolerate or to handle the difficulties of heterogeneity.

One must also consider the prior values that people bring to their groups. A feminist group with strong connections to the lesbian community provides the clearest example of how sociopolitical allegiances condition engagement with books. A sense of deep concern about feminist theory and praxis informs all the group's book choices, from Gerda Lerner's *The Creation of Patriarchy* to Margaret Atwood's *Cat's Eye*, and makes book discussions among the most focused and academic of any group in Houston. Even the informal talk about films, concerts, and other cultural events that takes place after the book discussions is suffused with a sophisticated awareness of the politics of culture, and judgments are rarely cast in a purely aesthetic mode. (I found the atmosphere of the group bracing—a slightly intimidating but exhilarating reminder that America's materialism and truncated politics is not a universal condition of the human species.)

Related to more literary values is the question of how reading groups gear into literary authority and the established hierarchy of taste. Local reading groups, for instance, often welcome visits from professors at nearby universities, eagerly soliciting their opinions on classics and new fiction or nonfiction. They also use course reading lists from their college-age children as authoritative sources on developments in literature. Personal booksellers are important as opinion leaders as well, often working with reading groups to set up an entire year's program of reading.

Even Cliffs Notes can provide discussion questions and thereby shape modes of textual appropriation. The ironic comments these notes often excite, however, show a refreshing distance from authority. For example, in one coed group discussion of *Huckleberry Finn,* a Cliffs Notes question about the symbolism of the river precipitated gales of laughter and a hilarious discussion about nature symbolism in college literature courses and everyone's favorite trick for getting A's. As one person said, "My favorite symbol was the ocean. It could mean death, sex, rebirth—you could do *anything* with the ocean" (Bookpeople 1987).

More generally, reading groups all operate within a commonly recognized hierarchy of taste that enshrines literary classics and "serious" modern books while denigrating genre books and other "trash." It should be pointed out that "trash" itself is not a fixed category but rather a contested boundary-marker for dividing the upper levels of literary value from those books not worth discussing; depending on the specific reading group, it may or may not include, for instance, bestsellers or best-selling authors, such as Michener or Uris, and some science fiction or mysteries. Shakespeare is never trash. Groups, then, do establish different relationships to this hierarchy but all recognize it—the historical sediment of the kinds of activities the new literary scholarship has begun to investigate under the rubric of cultural studies.

Equally interesting is the fact that the reading choices and value judgments of these same readers also demonstrate the limits of scholastic authority when it conflicts with the values that they hold dear because of their social location in the world beyond textual circulation. For example, many groups show irritation with some aspects of literary modernism, preferring a clear narrative structure and recognizably realistic characters over textual experimentation. Others refuse to entertain the literary merit of books that deal with certain subjects (one group will not read about incest) or that embody a realism they do not find morally elevating. Nabokov's *Lolita* and William Kennedy's *Ironweed*, for example, came in for harsh criticism by such criteria.

This stance seems only partially explained by the familiar category of "middlebrow," for the category is drawn from the domain of aesthetics or taste, while what is interesting about such readers' cultural behavior is precisely the limits of authoritative aesthetics vis-à-vis nonaesthetic systems of value. A Bourdieuian analysis of class fractions and cultural capital can account for some aspects of this phenomenon: Many of the readers have a strong sense of cultural entitlement that derives from their own position of educational and social privilege, so they can eschew with ease the pronouncements of the academy, which is to them just another fraction of the sociocultural elite. However, the behavior of these groups also implicates the link among cultural consumption, social experience, and social action, which has been undertheorized in the study of audience behavior as well as in the study of social change, each field's problematic being rooted in one side of the familiar culture/society dichotomy.

The complexity of groups' relationship to a literary authority that is itself both a carrier of critical discourse and a legitimating force for sociocultural distinction has ramifications for the analysis of their ability to be critical. Deference to the academy can encourage confrontation with difficult texts and disturbing ideas. Yet that same deference can shade into smugness, giving groups a warrant to indulge in self-congratulation about their authoritatively ratified taste. Similarly, rebellion against cultural authority can give rise to a critical iconoclasm that questions deeply held assumptions about criteria for literary worth or can encourage an attitude of facile know-nothingism.

Conditioning which of these responses to cultural authority will be enacted are the actual practices of selection and discussion. Many groups select by an informal process of suggestion and consensus that seems to give weight to those members who are either especially vocal or have established themselves as authoritative readers within the group by virtue of training, heavy reading, or the (usually informal) position as leader or core member. Other voices can be obscured in this process, which is the harder to criticize because of its very informality. However, most groups seem happy to give authority and the accompanying responsibility to certain members. For instance, one woman told me she didn't have the time to "read around and think about what the group might enjoy."

Choosing by formulating a program of several months' reading, however, usually involves a more self-conscious process of self-definition and more explicit mechanisms for ensuring democratic discussion about choice. Procedures of voting as a group on book selections or following a policy of strict individual choice appear to challenge groups' informal reading boundaries most deeply. A reading group in the FM 1960 area felt that a policy of individual choice had significantly expanded their range of selection. They cited mysticism, the black experience, and science fiction as subjects and genres they would never have taken on otherwise (FM 1960 Radio Area 1982). Similarly, the singles group previously mentioned found itself committed to reading science fiction and women-in-pain books because members voted as a group—and at meetings when new recruits joined the established group—rather than allowing the authority of the more literary core members to prevail.

Finally, the general quality of the group dynamics can encourage an atmosphere of trust that seems crucial for the sometimes tentative and exploratory openness (toward new ideas, about one's own feelings) that characterizes critical reflection in reading groups.[5] On the other hand, informal processes of social control can be extremely effective in silencing or stigmatizing members so as to enforce conformity. Joking and a lack of responsiveness appear to be the most often used enforcement mechanisms. For example, one member of my original book group was greeted with total silence when she proposed discussing a book by Shirley MacLaine; her suggestion simply vanished from consideration (My Book Group 1984). The humorously derogatory label of "women in pain" was intended to be another such silencing mechanism.

Both examples show groups falling short of attaining the "ideal speech situation" described by Jurgen Habermas (1979), in which an egalitarian group process enables people to mobilize communicative rationality in order critically to reflect on the presuppositions undergirding the instrumental reason that, in his view, has deformed the life world. Indeed, most groups do not approach that ideal most of the time because of power relations both within the groups and within the discursive world that frames their activities—for example, most are middle to upper-middle class and share the partialities of their social group. Also, most accept distinctions among the spheres of literature, society, and politics that inhibit some varieties of critical thinking, although those same distinctions underwrite the existence of reading groups as sites of cultural reflectiveness. However, an almost Habermasian Enlightenment ideal is at play in most groups' understanding of what makes a "good discussion," and those good discussions are remarkable for the ways they mobilize texts in the service of multileveled and often creative reflection. This reflection bridges the world of books and the world of social experience, which may be taken as a text for purposes of analysis, but presents possibilities for action that cannot be reduced to either reading or writing.[6]

In conclusion, I return to the image of the isolated reader. Unseating the ideology of reading as essentially and only a solitary activity challenges the hegemony of an associated model of how culture works, a conception I call the "trickle down" model of cultural dissemination. It holds that innovative ideas and values originate with transcendent high cultural figures and are delivered by abstracted processes—and in diluted form—to the lower (and in this model, relatively passive) levels of the sociocultural hierarchy.

Understanding that this model, like the image of the solitary reader, is at best a partial one in turn opens up for scholarly exploration the immense variety of ways that reading practices—like other kinds of cultural "usage"—contribute to the formation of sociocultural identity. The groups discussed in this essay are at the same time one aspect of this kind of negotiation, in which people figure both as products and producers of culture—and, I would contend, are emblematic of the general process of cultural dissemination or invention itself.

Notes

1. The cover art of Radway's *Reading the Romance* is an ironic comment on this point.

2. Feminist literary theorists have already traced many implications of the dichotomy between male and female authorship and between serious or high culture versus ephemeral or questionable culture in their considerations of women writers. The parallels between female readership and female authorship are striking. See *Writing and Sexual Difference* (Abel 1982) and note the book cover for a representation of that related iconographic dichotomy.

3. This process clearly brought cultural capital and social distinction, but its importance does not seem exhausted by the Bourdieuian notion of cultural usage.

4. The book page editor of the *Houston Post,* in fact, refused to consider running an article about book groups because of that assumption of their scarcity. Ironically, he eventually did run a story on reading groups after I discussed some findings from my project (including the large population of groups) with a book discussion group that included a *Post* reporter.

5. The discourse of academic critical thinking presupposes participants' immersion in certain debates and familiarity with a process of hammering out one's views in agonistic or even polemical encounters; it is structured, in other words, in very particular ways. I would contend that nonacademics can be critically aware without being immersed in the same debates or comfortable with the same styles of thinking; critical questions may be both framed and expressed differently, although to be "critical," such nonacademic discou must also challenge assumptions and taken-for-granted views.

6. Indeed, the link between cultural consumption and social action seems relatively clearly established by historical evidence about reading groups. How it operates in the present and how it might best be theorized are questions addressed by several orientations in cultural studies. Bourdieu, for example, has presented an extremely systematic study of cultural consumption and social distinction that adumbrates issues of individual mobility

and collective repositioning within the sociocultural hierarchy, the latter offering at least the possibility of substantive change of the hierarchy itself. However, his survey research tends not to focus on actual groups or collectivities, and he is less attuned to popular forms than to hegemonic processes. Perhaps more important, processes of insight, identity formation through identification, and other ways by which people forge themselves through culture seem less interesting to him than the strategic acquisition and deployment of taste, so the very category of "action" seems somewhat truncated in his analysis (Bourdieu 1984).

Perhaps more promising are those initiatives under the loose rubric of "Birmingham School of Cultural Studies" that also understand cultural consumption as social practice but focus on popular forms through historical and ethnographic research (Davidoff 1987; Hall 1980; McRobbie and Nava 1984; McRobbie 1991). This work, my own study, and "process-oriented" studies of sociocultural change like those of Lynn Hunt and George Lipsitz—which begin with everyday life and thereby integrate culture, memory, and social action a priori—have begun to offer insights into the way people use culture to define themselves and thereby remake both themselves and their social world (Hunt 1984; Lipsitz 1988, 1990).

References

Abel, Elizabeth. 1982. *Writing and Sexual Difference.* Chicago: University of Chicago Press.

Berelson, Bernard, with the assistance of L. Asheim. 1949. *The Library's Public: A Report of the Public Library Inquiry.* New York: Columbia University Press.

Blair, Karen J. 1980. *The Clubwoman as Feminist: True Womanhood Redefined, 1868–1914.* New York: Holmes and Meier.

Bleich, David. 1975. *Readings and Feelings: An Introduction to Subjective Criticism.* Urbana, Ill.: National Council of Teachers of English.

———. 1987. *Subjective Criticism.* Baltimore: Johns Hopkins University Press.

———. 1988. *The Double Perspective: Language, Literacy, and Social Relations.* New York: Oxford University Press.

Bloom, Allan David. 1987. *The Closing of the American Mind: How Higher Education Has Failed Democracy and Impoverished the Souls of Today's Students.* New York: Simon and Schuster.

Bookpeople. 1986. Meeting. Fall.

———. 1987. Meeting. February.

———. 1988. Meeting. February.

Bourdieu, Pierre. 1984. *Distinction: A Social Critique of the Judgment of Taste.* Cambridge, Mass.: Harvard University Press.

Brewer, J. Mason. 1935. *Negro Legislators of Texas and Their Descendants.* Dallas, Tex.: Mathis Publication Co.

Brodkey, Linda. 1987. *Academic Writing as Social Practice.* Philadelphia: Temple University Press.

Cruikshank, Julie. 1984 (May). "Life Lived Like a Story: Women's Lives in Athapaskan Narrative." Canadian Ethnology Society Annual Meetings. Montreal.

Darnton, Robert. 1974. "Trade in the Taboo: The Life of a Clandestine Book Dealer in Prerevolutionary France." In Paul J. Korshin, ed., *The Widening Circle: Essays on the Cir-*

culation of Literature in Eighteenth-Century Europe. Philadelphia: University of Pennsylvania Press.

————. 1979. *The Business of Enlightenment: A Publishing History of the Encyclopedia, 1775–1800.* Cambridge: Harvard University Press.

————. 1982. *The Literary Underground of the Old Regime.* Cambridge: Harvard University Press.

————. 1984. *The Great Cat Massacre and Other Episodes in French Cultural History.* New York: Basic Books.

Davidoff, Leonore, and Catherine Hall. 1987. *Family Fortunes: Men and Women of the English Middle Class, 1780–1850.* Chicago: University of Chicago Press.

Davidson, Cathy N. 1986. *Revolution and the Word: The Rise of the Novel in America.* New York: Oxford University Press.

————. 1989. *Reading in America: Literature and Social History.* Baltimore: Johns Hopkins University Press.

Davis, Natalie Ann Zemon. 1975. *Society and Culture in Early Modern France: Eight Essays.* Stanford, Calif.: Stanford University Press.

Eagleton, Terry. 1983. *Literary Theory: An Introduction.* Minneapolis: University of Minnesota Press.

————. 1984. *The Function of Criticism: From The Spectator to Post-Structuralism.* London: Verso.

————. 1990. *The Significance of Theory.* Oxford: Blackwell.

Ennis, P. H. 1965. *Adult Book Reading in the United States: A Preliminary Report.* National Opinion Research Center. National Opinion Research Center Report, no. 105.

Fetterley, Judith. 1978. *The Resisting Reader: A Feminist Approach to American Fiction.* Bloomington: Indiana University Press.

Fish, Stanley Eugene. 1980. *Is There a Text in This Class? The Authority of Interpretive Communities.* Cambridge: Harvard University Press.

FM 1960 Radio Area Group. March 24, 1982.

Fraser, Nancy. 1989. *Unruly Practices: Power, Discourse, and Gender in Contemporary Social Theory.* Minneapolis: University of Minnesota Press.

Giddens, Anthony. 1979. *Central Problems in Social Theory: Action, Structure and Contradiction in Social Analysis.* Berkeley: University of California Press.

————. 1984. *The Constitution of Society: Outline of the Theory of Structuration.* Berkeley: University of California Press.

Habermas, Jurgen. 1979 [1976]. *Communication and the Evolution of Society.* Translated by Thomas McCarthy. Boston: Beacon Press.

————. 1989 [1962]. *The Structural Transformation of the Public Sphere: An Inquiry into a Category of Bourgeois Society.* Cambridge, Mass.: MIT Press.

Hall, Stuart, et al. 1980. *Culture, Media, Language: Working Papers in Cultural Studies, 1972–1979.* London: Hutchinson.

Hatch, Orin Walker. 1965. *Lyceum to Library: A Chapter in the Cultural History of Houston.* Texas Gulf Coast Historical Association. Publication Series, vol. 9, no. 1.

Heilbrun, Carolyn G. 1988. *Writing a Woman's Life.* New York: Norton.

Hirsch, Eric Donald, Jr. 1987. *Cultural Literacy: What Every American Needs to Know.* Boston: Houghton Mifflin.

Holland, Norman N. 1968. *The Dynamics of Literary Response.* New York: Oxford University Press.

————. 1975. *Five Readers Reading.* New Haven, Conn.: Yale University Press.

Hunt, Lynn Avery. 1984. *Politics, Culture, and Class in the French Revolution.* Berkeley: University of California Press.

Iser, Wolfgang. 1974. *The Implied Reader: Patterns of Communication in Prose Fiction from Bunyan to Beckett.* Baltimore: Johns Hopkins University Press.

————. 1978. *The Act of Reading: A Theory of Aesthetic Response.* Baltimore: Johns Hopkins University Press.

Lipsitz, George. 1981. *Class and Culture in Cold War America: A Rainbow at Midnight.* New York: Praeger.

————. 1988. *A Life in the Struggle: Ivory Perry and the Culture of Opposition.* Philadelphia: Temple University Press.

————. 1990. *Time Passages: Collective Memory and American Popular Culture.* Minneapolis: University of Minnesota Press.

Long, Elizabeth. 1985. *The American Dream and the Popular Novel.* Boston: Routledge and Kegan Paul.

————. 1986. "Women, Reading, and Cultural Authority: Some Implications of the Audience Perspective in Cultural Studies." *American Quarterly* 38(4): 591–612.

————. 1988. "Reading at the Grassroots: Local Book Discussion Groups, Social Interaction, and Cultural Change." Paper presented at American Sociological Association meeting, Atlanta, Georgia, August 1988.

MacBride, Elizabeth. 1988 (Summer). Personal communication.

Martin, Theodora Penny. 1987. *The Sound of Our Own Voices: Women's Study Clubs, 1860–1910.* Boston: Beacon Press.

Mathews, V. H. 1973. "Adult Reading Studies: Their Implications for Private, Professional and Public Policy." *Library Trends* 22(2): 149–176.

McElroy, E. W. 1968a. "Subject Variety in Adult Reading I: Factors Related to Variety in Reading." *Library Quarterly* 38(1): 164–166.

————. 1968b. "Subject Variety in Adult Reading II: Characteristics of Readers of Ten Categories of Books." *Library Quarterly* 38(2): 261–269.

McRobbie, Angela. 1991. *Feminism and Youth Culture: From "Jackie" to "Just Seventeen."* Basingstoke: Macmillan.

McRobbie, Angela, and Mica Nava. 1984. *Gender and Generation.* London: Macmillan.

My Book Group. 1983. Meeting. April 5.

My Book Group. 1984. Meeting. June 4.

Ohmann, Richard M. 1976. *English in America: A Radical View of the Profession.* New York: Oxford University Press.

————. 1987. *Politics of Letters.* Middletown, Conn.: Wesleyan University Press.

Radway, Janice A. 1984. *Reading the Romance: Women, Patriarchy, and Popular Literature.* Chapel Hill: University of North Carolina Press.

Resnick, Daniel P., and Lauren B. Resnick. 1989. "Varieties of Literacy." In Andrew E. Barnes and Peter N. Stearns, eds., *Social History and Issues in Human Consciousness: Some Interdisciplinary Connections.* New York and London: New York University Press.

Seaholm, Megan. 1988. *Earnest Women: The White Woman's Club Movement in Progressive Era Texas, 1880–1920.* Dissertation, Rice University. (Ann Arbor, Mich.: UMI 1989).

Smith, Barbara Herrnstein. 1988. *Contingencies of Value: Alternative Perspectives for Critical Theory.* Cambridge: Harvard University Press.

Stock, Brian. 1983. *The Implications of Literacy: Written Language and Models of Interpretation in the Eleventh and Twelfth Centuries.* Princeton, N.J.: Princeton University Press.

Thompson, E. P. 1964. *The Making of the English Working Class.* New York: Pantheon Books.

Tompkins, Jane P. 1985. *Sensational Designs: The Cultural Work of American Fiction.* New York: Oxford University Press.

University of Texas Group. 1980 (November). Interview.

Williams, Raymond. 1983. *Writing in Society.* London: Verso.

Yankelovich, Skelly & White, Inc. 1978 (October). *Consumer Research Study on Reading and Book Purchasing.* Book Industry Study Group. BISG Report no. 6.

TEN

Romance and the Work of Fantasy: Struggles over Feminine Sexuality and Subjectivity at Century's End

JANICE RADWAY

The March 1989 issue of *Romance Writers Report,* the official publication of the Romance Writers of America, is entitled "Beat the Press: Countering Negative Publicity with a Positive Image."[1] No fewer than thirteen different articles in this issue provide concrete advice to the magazine's readers on how to counter the stereotyped image of the romance writer as someone who needs "bubble baths, provocative negligees, and wine to 'get in the mood' to write a love scene."[2] The editors note in their introduction to the section that "some of the horror stories about how romance writers are treated by the media may make you smile, grimace, tear out your hair, or let out a primal scream." "Bear with us," they advise reasonably, "keep reading and you may find some specific suggestions for dealing—gently, but firmly and professionally—with the idiots."[3] The abrupt and wry change in tone here signals to readers that the editors feel as embattled as they undoubtedly do and that the editors intend not only to be hardheaded in their suggestions but to be clear about their opinion of those who would consign them to the ranks of silly amateurs. Among romance writers' opponents one writer lists "nosy reporters," "holier than thou 'literary' authors," and "certain types of feminists."[4] This issue of *Romance Writers Report* is important not simply because it constitutes a powerful and coherent defense of the genre by its writers, sometimes in the terms of feminist discourse, but also because it urges us to see that the romance is now, and has been at least for the last fifteen years, a principal site for the struggle over feminine subjectivity and sexuality and, I would argue, over feminism as well.

What I intend in this chapter, therefore, is to review the nature of the struggles that have been conducted at this site and to show that just as feminist discourse about the romance has changed dramatically in a short time, so too has the romance changed as writers have resisted the efforts of the publishing industry to fix the form in the hope of generating predictable profits. Writers have responded instead both to their culture's habitual tendency to dismiss their efforts and to changing attitudes about women and their roles by playing significantly with the fantasy at the heart of their genre. Romance writers have learned to protest in terms like Ann Maxwell's that "romances aren't an inferior form of fiction best suited to beginners and bimbos." They also have seemed to gain confidence in their efforts to claim sexuality for women and to imagine it in a less linear, less goal-directed way, organized now not genitally but polymorphously in elaborated and extended fashion.[5] Equally significant, they have also attempted to imagine a feminine subjectivity that might support such an active sexuality.

My own book, *Reading the Romance,* was only one intervention in this complex and ongoing struggle to redefine feminine subjectivity and sexuality.[6] My objective was to place the romance with respect not only to the discourses of patriarchy but also to those of feminism. Although I tried very hard not to dismiss the activities of the Smithton women and made an effort to understand the act of romance reading as a positive response to the conditions of everyday life, my account unwittingly repeated the sexist assumption that has warranted a large portion of the commentary on the romance. It was still motivated, that is, by the assumption that someone ought to worry responsibly about the effect of fantasy on women readers. It is true that *Reading the Romance* ends with a deliberate and strategic equivocation about the romance's final effects. Indeed, the conclusion attempts to entertain seriously the possibility suggested by the Smithton readers that romances might empower women in important ways. Nevertheless, that conclusion still repeats the familiar pattern whereby the commentator distances herself as knowing analyst from those who, engrossed and entranced by fantasy, cannot know. At some level, then, my analysis remains related to those endless newspaper stories about the rising popularity of the genre that began inevitably in the 1970s and early 1980s with a passage of supposedly "lush" and "lurid" prose juxtaposed without commentary to the rational, clear analysis of the knowing, authoritative investigator. Despite the fact that I wanted to claim the romance for feminism, this familiar opposition between blind fantasy and perspicacious knowing continued to operate within my account. Thus I would now link it, along with Tania Modleski's *Loving with a Vengeance,* with the first early efforts to understand the changing genre, a stage in the debate that was characterized most fundamentally, I believe, by suspicions about fantasy, daydream, and play.[7]

This first volley in the battle over female sexuality waged at the site of the romance was occasioned by the sudden increase in the genre's popularity in the early 1970s. Indeed, the sheer ubiquity of the commentaries and their tone of moral outrage might have led an uninformed observer to conclude that the romance constituted some wholly new threat to the integrity of women. In fact, romance even then had enjoyed a long history and had been closely associated with the interests and pleasures of women. What made the genre newly threatening in the 1970s was that it had developed its narrative in a more openly and explicitly sexual way and that it appeared simultaneously with a revivified women's movement. The romance thus constituted a double challenge. On the one hand, to a traditionally patriarchal culture, it appeared as threatening evidence of the impact of the so-called sexual revolution of the 1960s upon respectable women. There was thus an underlying uneasiness about the insatiability of romance readers (whether for the books themselves or for the sexual excitement they represented) that explained the level of vituperation heaped upon everyone connected with the genre. In an article in the *Village Voice,* for instance, Walter Kendrick referred not only to romance readers "chirping for more" from "frighteningly prolific" romance writers but went on to observe that the romance was itself "escapist, masturbatory, [and] exploitative." He continued, "It's a typical mass-produced American product, catering to a public so dull and timid that even when it dreams, it can conceive only what it's dreamt before."[8]

On the other hand, to feminists like Ann Douglas, the romance constituted evidence of a backlash against the women's movement. "Popular culture is out to get the so-called liberated woman," she wrote. "Mass culture increasingly specializes in dominance games, fantasies in which women lose and men win. It is important that such fantasies are popular among women as well as among men, and that they are fantasies." She argued that the extraordinary disjuncture between their lives and those fantasies ought to "provoke ... serious concern for their women readers."[9]

Policing, it seems to me, was the real work enacted by conservative, leftist, and early feminist critiques of romances and their readers. Whatever the distinct differences among these discourses and, their political projects, all were built on the distinction between a cold-blooded, pragmatic, and rational realism and a seductive, illusionary fantasy life that could lead to complacency if not to a wholly relished decadence. Anxiety about the dangers of fantasizing underwrote this urge to discipline: These commentators not only rebuked romance readers for neglecting their real tasks—whether cleaning the house and tending the children or challenging the patriarchy—but also laid down a moral vision about what women ought to be doing with their lives. The stern, disapproval of these first early critiques evokes the authoritarian and adult disapproval of the parent for the silly, self-indulgent games of the pleasure-seeking child. The move perpetuates what Allon White has called "the social reproduction of seriousness," a set of practices (carried out principally in the institution of the school) that serves to underwrite the familiar oppositions between the serious and the frivolous, the rational and the sentimental, the public and the private.[10] All of these, of course, can be seen as variations of a conceptual division central to post-Enlightenment bourgeois thought, that between the real and the unreal, the latter coded always as fictional, chimerical, or imaginary and therefore without efficacious impact on the real world. By relying on this familiar conceptual armature, the early critics of the romance located it within the domain of the nonserious and therefore constructed the reading of it as a fantastic, entirely suspect escape.

When placed in the context of these early efforts to cope with the burgeoning evidence that many women led active fantasy lives outside the approved norms and conventions, Tania Modleski's *Loving with a Vengeance* and my own *Reading the Romance* take on the appearance of transitional events in the struggle over the genre. Both books in fact share a desire to take romances and romance readers seriously—without automatic scorn and derision for their ongoing interest in a fantastic portrayal of heterosexual romance. They thus demonstrate a certain distance from the jeremiads of Kendrick and Douglas by elaborately demonstrating that the fantasy of the romance is closely connected with the social and material conditions of women's lives in a patriarchal culture. Modleski noted, in fact, that it was an important part of her project "to show that the so-called masochism pervading these texts is a 'cover' for anxieties, desires and wishes which if openly expressed would challenge the psychological and social order of things." She went on to observe that "for that very reason, of course, they must be kept hidden; the texts, after arousing them must … work to neutralize them."[11] Although her interest in and knowledge of psychoanalysis led her to attribute powerful and positive effects to the fantasies embedded in romances and soap operas and she thus came very close to rethinking the opposition between fantasy and the real, she ultimately continued to privilege a separate order of things where "true" feminist change would have to occur. In concluding her argument about soap operas, for instance, where I believe she was at her most radical, she challenged the opposition only to reinstate it in the end:

> It is important to recognize that soap opera allays *real* anxieties, satisfies *real* needs and desires, even while it may distort them. The fantasy of community is not only a real desire [as opposed to the "false" ones mass culture is always accused of trumping up], it is a salutary one. As feminists, we have a responsibility to devise ways of meeting those needs that are more creative, honest, and interesting than the ones mass culture has supplied. Otherwise, the search for tomorrow threatens to go on, endlessly.[12]

What is projected here is a vision of a world where utopian fantasy might stop, where tomorrow would come finally, where fullness and equality would be achieved definitively. Itself a utopian vision, this one works by imagining that others would no longer need *their* fantasies.

The final passage of my book is little different from this one, repeating as it does this same desire to see the need for the romance wiped out: "Interstices still exist within the social fabric where opposition is carried on by people who are not satisfied by their place within it or by the restricted material and emotional rewards that accompany it. They therefore attempt to imagine a more perfect social state as a way of countering despair." However, instead of resting content with this observation and thus acknowledging the reality of these fantasies, I extended my argument:

> We who are committed to social change [must not] overlook this minimal but none-theless legitimate form of protest. We should seek it out not only to understand its origins and its utopian longing but also to learn how best to encourage it and bring it to fruition. If we do not, we have already conceded the fight and, in the case of the romance at least, admitted the impossibility of creating a world where the vicarious pleasure supplied by its reading would be unnecessary.[13]

Once again, a romance commentator had registered her discomfort with fantasy and insisted on devaluing it by seeing it only as a symptom of problems in the real world. I will argue shortly that this attitude toward fantasy has changed significantly in the academic feminist community and that, when taken further, might provide the basis for a new politics of the romance that could ally feminist critics with romance writers and readers in the project of defending daydreams like the romance as a space where important critical and utopian work gets done.

To return to the struggle, however, it should be noted that romance writers and their editors neither ceased producing the genre nor remained unaware or unaffected by the seemingly endless dismissals of it. Indeed, during the late 1970s and early 1980s, romance production boomed as news of Harlequin Enterprises' success with the publication of these novels in a series format made its way through the publishing industry. In the midst of consolidation and further incorporation, the industry was itself looking for ways to use profits from paperback houses to subsidize the less financially remunerative production of hardback houses that had been grouped together within single corporate conglomerates. The romance looked like a particularly attractive proposition to these new corporate entities because the audience appeared to be readily identifiable and thus could be surveyed for its preferences and because sales could be predicted with a fair degree of accuracy. This sort of reasoning led Simon and Schuster, owned by Gulf and Western, to create Silhouette romances in 1980 that then began to challenge Harlequin for domination of the field. Within three years, sixteen more series had been introduced, and by 1985 40 percent of all mass market paperback books published in the United States were romances.[14] In that same year, the genre boasted 20 million readers and chalked up a half billion dollars in sales.[15]

The expansion of romance publishing could not have occurred, of course, if editors and publishers had not been able to identify and even to create many more romance writers. The fact is, however, they were able to do this with very little effort. As more and more women chanced to pick up one of these books at the local mall bookstore or at the supermarket, many of them were moved either by the experience of reading itself or by the increasing publicity about the success of favorite writers like Janet Dailey and Kathleen Woodiwiss to try their own hands at plotting out such a story. The editors assisted by creating house guidelines capable of advising the novice on appropriate characters, tone, and goals for such stories. A cottage industry developed as a consequence, aided by the proliferation of home computers. The production end of this industry was simultaneously matched by the equally vital development of an advisory apparatus designed to serve romance readers. Since virtually no "respectable" magazine or newspaper ever reviewed category romances, committed readers found it increasingly difficult to make choices about what to read when faced with a steadily growing list of titles every month. In response to this felt need, many amateur newsletters and a few more professionally produced magazines appeared with the express purpose of reviewing romance fiction.

These developments soon triggered efforts to organize this largely amateur industry, a move that was fueled by the desires of writers to share their experiences and their problems and by the needs of editors to provide a stable supply of adequately conceived and written stories. These desires were first institutionally coordinated and articulated in 1981 when the Romance Writers of America organization was founded in Houston, Texas, by two writers with the help of several prominent editors in the industry.[16] The organization immediately began to publish a newsletter and to organize an annual professional conference. The newsletter, which was initially dominated by a highly personalized and conversational, even chatty tone, focused first on romances themselves rather than on the activity of writing and publishing them. However, it soon developed into a bimonthly professional magazine complete with current marketing information, advice about how to deal with agents and editors, and material on how to integrate a writing career with home and family responsibilities.

Many of these new romance writers in fact clearly conceived of their decision to write as the act of embarking on a professional career. This conceptual move was deeply affected, I believe, by popular media discourses on the middle-class women's movement and by gradually changing attitudes about the acceptability of work for married women. Feminism, it seems to me, first made its way into romances through the career aspirations of the middle-class writers of the genre. Evidence for this can be found in a range of places. In the December 1981 issue of *Romance Report* (the initial title of the organization newsletter), the editors included a short article on an academic study that claimed romances were "moving 'feminist' messages to women who never read a Friedan, Steinem or Greer treatise on the role of women."[17] The headline "Romance Survey—Finally! A Survey in Our Favor" graphically portrayed the editor's sense of embattlement with those who were dismissing both them and their work. The article not only publicly and approvingly linked the romance to feminism but also went on to praise Carol Thurston's claim that paperback historical romances portrayed androgynous heroes and heroines, challenged the value of the macho male, and made new suggestions about women's possibilities. The editors of the publication, at least, were not constructing themselves as traditionalists or conservatives defined simply in opposition to "women's libbers" or "feminists." Nor were they claiming, as they had previously, that all they were writing were harmless escape stories. Rather, they constructed themselves as women actively participating in social change by narrating pleasurable fantasies about newly imagined individuals and relationships. Like their academic sisters, romance writers also seemed to be sensing that fantasies had validity—that they too could be real and thus might have an impact on other aspects of daily life.

Further evidence exists to suggest that at least some romance writers were beginning to redefine themselves in terms they took to be feminist. The first study of a regional chapter of the Romance Writers of America, for example, conducted by Catherine Kirkland in 1984, detected significant sympathy for the goals of the women's movement. In her dissertation, "For the Love of It: Women Writers and the Popular Romance," Kirkland reported that of the sixty-two members of the New Jersey chapter of the RWA participating in her study, "most seem[ed] to espouse the socially visible goals of the contemporary women's movement and were likely to call themselves feminists (albeit 'quiet' feminists) and to see little disparity between their work and the most obvious principles of equal rights, equal pay, and self-determination."[18] Her study documents the complex social, material, and conceptual transformation that took place as romance readers began to take on the identity of "romance writer." Passages such as the one that follows testify to the discursive conflict experienced and enacted by women who were attempting to think of themselves as autonomous professionals even as they retained the highly valued relationality and responsibility of their traditionally feminine roles. One writer responded to Kirkland: "I don't think many feminists have read the new romances. Because I consider myself a feminist. Well, anybody willing to work this hard at something—it cuts into your family and everything. It's the same as when I was selling advertising; it's my job. And if I wasn't a feminist, I wouldn't be able to lock myself into my room and ignore everybody on Saturday."[19]

What this writer's comment reveals is an attempt to claim the term "feminist" for romance writers and an effort to define it meaningfully in the context of a particular group of women's shared experiences. The fact that this definition is undoubtedly somewhat different from the definition of feminism simultaneously being elaborated in the academy or among political activists should not lead to the unfortunate practice of ranking them against each other as more or less pure versions of a reified feminism, a move I myself have been guilty of in the past.[20] Rather, what we should note here is that just as romance writers and their critics were struggling over the right to define what feminine subjectivity and sexuality would look like, so too were they beginning to struggle over the appropriate way to define and to live out feminism. We will see shortly that the stories romance writers penned in response to their understanding of at least some versions of feminism (those that had been caricatured in the media) attempted to refute the assumption that the search for independence among women implied both distaste for men and little need or desire for intimacy. Their project, it would seem, was to construct a feminist position for white, middle-class, heterosexual women that would manage to envision for them autonomy and success as well as inti-macy, relationality, and the opportunity for a restorative, limited dependence upon a man.

Before discussing the changes produced in the romance from 1980 to 1985 as a consequence of these cultural and professional developments, I will discuss briefly two academic studies of the romance genre that broke significantly from the ear-lier conceptual framework of the critical discourse on romances. It is especially intriguing to me that these two academic discussions of older romances map the itinerary of a reading process that was just then being configured more clearly and explicitly by romance writers obviously experimenting with the form, a de-velopment I will turn to in a moment. The articles are Alison Light's "'Returning to Manderley'—Romance Fiction, Female Sexuality and Class" and Cora Kaplan's "*The Thorn Birds:* Fiction, Fantasy, Femininity."[21] Both articles are deeply in-formed by psychoanalysis and both therefore make an effort to treat the subject of desire and the activity of fantasy not only seriously but with approbation. Conse-quently, the authors make important efforts to break down the conceptual dichot-omy that has operated for too long to dismiss women's fantasies as irrelevant to or counterproductive for the processes of social change.

Alison Light first developed the argument persuasively in her introductory re-marks to her study of the complexity of subject positioning in Daphne du Maurier's *Rebecca*. She argued explicitly that feminist critics' cultural politics must not become "a book-burning legislature," nor should feminists fall into the traps of moralism or dictatorship when discussing romances. "It is conceivable," she wrote, "that Barbara Cartland could turn you into a feminist. Reading is never simply a linear con job but a ... process which helps to query as well as endorse social meanings and one which therefore remains dynamic and open to change."[22] She continued with a call for critical analysis:

> I think we need critical discussions that are not afraid of the fact that literature is a source of pleasure, passion *and* entertainment. This is not because pleasure can then explain away politics, as if it were a panacea existing outside of social and historical constraints. Rather it is precisely because pleasure is experienced by women and men within and *despite* [emphasis added] those constraints. We need to balance an under-standing of fictions as restatements (however mediated) of a social reality, with a closer examination of how literary texts might function in our lives as imaginative constructions and interpretations.[23]

Light's point, clearly, is that fantasy accomplishes important work both indi-vidually and socially. She goes on to demonstrate through a remarkable reading of *Rebecca* that this is done through the narrative construction of multiple subject positions, all of which can solicit the reader's identification. She argues, too, that the process of imaginary identification is itself an activity with real consequences both within the process of fantasizing and in its potential generalization or carryover to other activities. Although Light does not say so explicitly, this carryover can (and I would insist does) occur because those other activities construct a subject in exactly the same way the romance does by positioning the reader within discourse. The subject positions taken up within the activity of reading or by engaging in any other so-called fantasy are not incommensurate with those taken up in and through other practices because all practices are discursively produced. Thus any position constructed for the reader by a romance could potentially continue to operate for her by empowering her to refuse other discursive positionings she might earlier have willingly adopted. I should add here, however, that while such carryover and continuity are possible, they do not always necessarily occur. Still, what Alison Light's article accomplishes more than anything else is the dissolution of that sharp boundary between fantasy and the real that had been maintained so assiduously in earlier work on the genre.

In a complex argument I cannot do justice to here, Light defines fantasy as the exploration and production of desires that may be in excess of the socially possible or acceptable. She demonstrates that in du Maurier's novel, Rebecca emerges "as an aristocratic mix of independent and 'essential' femininity, a strong physical presence, a confident and alluring sexuality."[24] Light suggests that the unnamed narrator and the reader who cannot but identify with the position from which the story is told want to be like Rebecca but dare not do so because her sexuality is presented as deviant and overnatural. What saves the heroine, finally, is her middle-classness. Light makes the crucial point, however, that once the identification with Rebecca has been set in motion, "its effects can never be fully contained nor its disruptive potential fully retrieved."[25] Rebecca then becomes a figure who exposes the narrator's and reader's still unfulfilled desires for an active and searching feminine sexuality. Her murder reveals subsequently that successful heterosexuality is a construct—that correctly passive femininity must be learned. Rebecca's ceaseless return, however, enacted because the narrator feels compelled to remember her, demonstrates that "the girl and Rebecca need each other in order to mean at all"—that "it is their difference from each other that gives each meaning."[26] Light explains that for the girl in *Rebecca,* the narrating of the story is therefore "both a making safe and opening up of subjectivity, a volatile disclosure which puts her 'self' at risk. Rebecca acts out ... what the girl also desires."[27]

Thus she concludes with the observation that whereas du Maurier's novel exposes the fundamentally divided nature of subjectivity and the fact that feminine sexuality is itself an unstable formation, most romances offer a triumph over the unconscious, over the resistance to fullness, coherence, and identity that lie at the heart of psychic life. As she says, "Romance offers us relations impossibly harmonized; it uses unequal heterosexuality as a dream of equality and gives women uncomplicated access to a subjectivity which is unified and coherent and still operating within the field of pleasure." It thus provides important opportunities for reader empowerment because it makes possible the imaginary experience of "control of the uncontrollable." The fact that romance reading is a repetitive ritual suggests in the end that such control is always an illusion and that what the stories finally offer is not closure but postponement of fulfillment. "The activity of reading repeats the compulsion of desire and testifies to the limiting regulation of female sexuality."[28]

Cora Kaplan develops many of these same themes in her discussion of the hugely popular 1977 novel *The Thorn Birds* and suggests, in fact, that even traditional romances may not manage so finished and coherent a subjectivity. Drawing on her own reading experience of *The Thorn Birds, Gone with the Wind,* and other similar romances, Kaplan parallels Light by arguing that such fantasies speak to women "in the register of desire" by constructing a particular version of feminine subjectivity and sexuality. As with Light, what is innovative about Kaplan's treatment of these issues is her willingness to draw on her own pleasurable experience of the novels and of her refusal to draw a rigid boundary between that kind of passionately engaged reading and her subsequent analysis of it. Kaplan and Light "know," in effect, not only because they can mobilize psychoanalytic discourses but also, and perhaps more important, because they have themselves been seduced by the romance fantasy. I am here redefining "knowing," now no longer conceived as rationality qua rationality but rather as a complex process of understanding involving the body, affect, and cognition. Kaplan, in fact, moves easily back and forth in her article between a description of what it is like for a woman viscerally to engage certain characters, themes, and narrative developments and a psychoanalytic account of what that experience might achieve for her. Her claim is that "a psychoanalytic theory of fantasy not only takes 'pleasure seriously' but places the ability to think about pleasure at the center of what constitutes us as human subjects."[29] Thus she is able to develop the argument that Colleen McCullough's romance is "a fantasy about both history and sexuality imagined from the woman's position" that speaks to "the contradictory and unreconciled feelings about femininity, feminism and fantasy which mark out that position for, at the very least, first world white female readers."[30]

Again, I cannot discuss every aspect of Kaplan's complex treatment of this novel, but I do want to make a few observations about her analysis of the reading process to show how it enriches Light's account of the instability at the center of the form and because some of her crucial claims seem to have been corroborated both by later developments in romance writing and by expressed reader preferences for particular kinds of narratives. Kaplan makes an initial distinction between the narrowly focused series romance such as the Harlequin or Silhouette and longer "blockbuster romances." She suggests that, unlike the series books, these latter novels do not ask the reader to identify with a single female character. Rather, Kaplan observes, "they invite ... the female reader to identify across sexual difference and to engage with narrative fantasy from a variety of subject positions and at various levels." "*The Thorn Birds*," she goes on, "confirms not a conventional femininity but women's contradictory and ambiguous place within sexual difference."[31]

Kaplan secures her point by demonstrating that the reader of *The Thorn Birds* is asked by the very process of the narration to identify first with the heroine, Meggie, and then with the unlikely hero, the priest, Ralph de Bricassart. Indeed, she is able to show that the otherwise inexplicable multiplication of plot devices in the novel is necessary to "construct a complex fantasy, a series of scenarios in which the reader's position vis-à-vis Ralph and Meggie is constantly shifting. Until the sequence reaches its penultimate moment" she concludes, "it is fair to say that the reader oscillates from the woman's position to the man's position—*represented as poles of subjectivity rather than fixed, determinate identities.*"[32] The story offers the woman reader what Kaplan calls "a liberated derepressed version of the seduction fantasy," a version in which the daughter (Meggie) seduces the father (Ralph) rather than the more familiar reverse pattern. Her larger point is that in all romance reading, the reader "not only identifies with both terms in the seduction scenario, but most of all with the process of seduction itself."[33]

This view of the reading process complicates the significance of the fact that the consummation of any romance relationship is postponed interminably and exquisitely throughout most of the narrative. To conclude the representation of desire and seduction too quickly in an act of fulfillment or achieved wholeness would be to preclude the possibility of moving around within the fantasy, of mobilely assuming quite different subject positions—the active seducing partner and the more passive desired object. What Kaplan is able to show is that although romances are quite obviously fantasies about heterosexual relationships, they are also daydreams about the possibilities opened up by the contradictory, unfinished construction of feminine sexuality in patriarchal society. Her work, together with that of Alison Light, suggests that not only has the struggle over feminine sexuality played itself out across the romance, with different voices making contending claims about the state of the sexuality thereby produced, but that the struggle is played out within the romance as well in the form of an imagined alternation between the different subject positions of desiring subject and object of desire. If that alternation is conventionally stopped in the romance so as to fix one pole rather than the other for the reader, the very fact that the oscillation precedes the fixation at least holds out the possibility that it might, under some circumstances, be permitted to go on indefinitely.

Before demonstrating that this kind of oscillation between subject positions persists in recent romances and is actively being played with even now, I should point out that both Alison Light and Cora Kaplan are careful not to isolate romance as primal fantasy from more broadly social concerns. For instance, Light anticipates the charge that she is retreating into subjectivism. She manages to defend herself by exploring the complex process through which primal fantasy is wedded to social concerns through the intersection of sexuality and class in *Rebecca*. Similarly, Cora Kaplan admits that "fantasy, with its aggrandizing narrative appetite, [always] appropriates and incorporates social meaning, structuring through its public narrative forms the historically specific stories and subjectivities available." She demonstrates this by describing the precise ways in which race figures in the narrative of subjectivity and sexuality at the heart of *The Thorn Birds,* claiming finally that as the foundation of sociality and identity, fantasies are also "scripts that define otherness and exclusion."[34] In my view, it is their awareness of the intersection between fantasy and the social that enables both Alison Light and Cora Kaplan to suggest a politics of the romance different from that elaborated in earlier discourses about the genre. Recognizing that fantasy is itself at the heart of the process of subject construction and reconstruction, both feel little compulsion to disparage it, to erase it, or to deny it to others. What they do suggest, however, is that because fantasies always necessarily are bound to popular representations, those articulations or links between the primal and the social might be exposed, analyzed, and perhaps even loosened or changed altogether. As Cora Kaplan concludes: "Our priority ought to be an analysis of the progressive or reactionary politics to which fantasy can become bound in popular expression. Those narratives, which include of course issues of sexual difference, as well as of race, class and the politics of power generally, *can* be rewritten."[35]

Recent developments in romance writing and reading suggest, in fact, that processes of reconceptualization have already been proceeding apace. The changes produced in the genre are contradictory, which indicates that the struggle to rethink and to rearticulate feminine subjectivity and sexuality goes on. Some of the most important changes in the genre have been extensively chronicled by Carol Thurston in *The Romance Revolution: Erotic Novels for Women and the Quest for a New Sexual Identity.* Although Thurston does not employ a psychoanalytic perspective to make sense of the appearance of thousands of sexually explicit series romances in the 1980s, she does concern herself with changing portrayals of female sexuality. She argues in fact that these new romances "mark the first appearance of a large and coherent body of sexual literature for women, providing the opportunity to learn to use sexual fantasy and to explore an aspect of their identities that patriarchal society has long denied women."[36] She thus takes issue with the same earlier discourses on the romance criticized by Light and Kaplan and suggests, too, that fantasy is an integral component of human life, although the definition she gives of it in her account is narrower and exclusively sexual.

In general, Thurston claims that these stories are progressive, even feminist, because they attempt to imagine a more active, highly elaborated version of feminine sexuality in which the entire body is eroticized and even conversation is libidinally charged. She, too, claims the romance for feminism, although she also makes clear throughout her account that she will have nothing to do with a feminism that she believes sacrifices intimacy and relationality to female autonomy and independence. The language and tone of the following passage give some indication, I think, of how earlier versions of feminist discourses have been received by some women. Thurston herself, like some romance readers and writers, apparently fears that feminism implies not only loneliness but the adoption of a threatening male-identified subjectivity:

Contrary to the voices of doom warning that romance novels are the opiate of the female masses, operating both to subvert the women's movement and to condemn addictees to a derivative, vicariously experienced life, these tales of female becoming appear to have played the role of unsung and often maligned heroine to the feminist movement's macho and often sadistic hero reaching millions of women most feminist writing, whether fiction or nonfiction, has not.[37]

Clearly this fear of becoming wrongly gendered seems to overpower Thurston's syntax and larger argument, although her choice of metaphors also suggests that indeed she finds feminism's macho hero more than a little seductive. My own reading of romances written between 1980 and 1989 suggests that a similar anxiety about gender construction is widespread in the culture and that a need to think through the sources of and solutions to this anxiety has underwritten the plot structures of many recent entries in the genre. In fact, as Thurston has herself demonstrated, the basic conflict motivating the romance has changed substantially since the early 1970s. Where previously an innocent, virginal, and lower-classed heroine had to be awakened to her sexuality by an aristocratic, powerful, and experienced hero, now, more often than not, a career woman must learn that she can combine her much-prized independence with both sexual and emotional intimacy. The question the new erotic romance addresses is less one of how a girl becomes a traditional woman than how to think of autonomy and relationality together within a single adult individual. A passage quoted by Thurston from Mareen Bronson's *Tender Verdict* is illustrative: "'Anna Provo thought of her limitations. She believed she was inadequate outside of anything but law. Who wanted a woman who wouldn't have children? Who could deal with her hot temper, her single-mindedness about her family and career? It was unreasonable to expect anyone to tolerate her lack of maternal instincts, her busy schedule.'"[38] The hero of the story, of course, effectively persuades Anna Provo that indeed she can be loved, that even feminist women relish the care and attention of a man. This sort of story suggests that women will not be ungendered by assuming positions of agency and relative power in the public sphere but rather will be able to combine that subject position with the more traditional one of passive object to male attention.

Lest I leave the impression, however, that all such romances give greater weight to the desires represented by traditional femininity and indulge in detailed self-doubt by women about adopting newer roles, I should note that it is equally common to come across sentiments like these quoted by Thurston from Moeth Allison's *Love Everlasting:* "'How dare he call her hysterical. How dare he imply she wasn't a whole woman if she didn't marry him. It was an insulting proposal that sounded as if she were some poor stupid slob who'd made a hash of things and needed a man to take care of her.'"[39] The emotional weight of passages like this one pushes the other way. As much as the new romance heroines are overwhelmed to discover the joys of intimacy, so do they passionately cling to their independence, often extracting from the heroes lengthy assurances that their men will be happiest if the heroines continue to pursue their career objectives.

The intensity of both sorts of passages suggests that feminism has profoundly unsettled accepted thinking about gender construction at century's end and necessitated myriad efforts to rethink it—if still always within the parameters of an unquestioned heterosexuality. Indeed, I see great ambivalence at the heart of recent romances as the genre's writers attempt to think through the apparent contradiction between a more active and autonomous feminine identity and traditional assumptions that relationality and connectedness are not only woman's work but woman's desire as well. What we see in recent romances, I think, is evidence of a halting, exploratory, often contradictory effort to reconstitute gender, built upon that same instability of and oscillation between subject positions that Light and Kaplan found to be at the heart of *Rebecca, The Thorn Birds,* and even more traditional earlier versions of the genre.

In fact, one of the most significant developments in the form also discussed by Thurston in *The Romance Revolution* is the tendency to devote increasing amounts of time and energy to the hero's point of view. When she conducted her survey in 1982, Thurston discovered that her respondents most wanted to see detailed sexual description in a romance, followed closely by a narrative that rendered the thoughts and feelings of the hero. By 1985, however, the hero's point of view topped the list of most-desired story features with more than three-quarters of her sample expressing a preference for a narrative structure permitting access to the emotional lives of both the heroine and the hero. Because romance editors and publishers themselves detected this change in reader preference, they began to permit much greater flexibility in the rendering of point of view. Indeed, as Thurston notes, one publishing house even went so far as to institute a once-a-month romance "from his point of view" in its Rapture Romance line.

It would be easy enough to attribute this development to a craving for variety in the wake of increasingly repetitive romance production. That explanation, however, would be too simplistic. In fact, this move might fruitfully be seen as a more deliberate and direct offer of the male-gendered point of view to readers who had always briefly inhabited that subject position in romances but who are now demanding that it be more fully imagined, more fully clothed for experimental wear. The independent career heroine, it seems, is still not enough to capture the reader's attention and identification. Thus in many recent romances, readers are asked to identify not only with that new heroine but with a powerful man who is not only *not* threatened by her independence but convinced that she can combine it with intimacy, connectedness, and love. This hero may therefore provide further possibilities for experimenting with subject position and equally supply needed reassurance that assumption of greater agency by a woman will not threaten her essential gender identification. It is thus understandable that the point of view now shifts frequently even in sex scenes. By narrating at least part of a sexual encounter from the hero's point of view, the writer of this restructured romance manages to demonstrate to the reader not only that the heroine is indeed desired precisely as an object but also that the hero too can be overpowered by an active, openly sexual woman who is well aware of her own desires both for pleasure and for power. None of this repositioning, however, threatens heterosexuality, which remains unquestioned in mainstream mass market romance.

Thurston demonstrates the new approach with an exemplary passage from Nora Roberts's 1984 romance *A Matter of Choice:*

> "Her aggression both unbalanced and aroused him. ... She was undressing him swiftly, her lips following the path of her busy hands until his mind was totally centered on her. Shivering thoughts, quick tastes, maddening touches—she gave him no time to focus on only one, but insisted he experience all in an enervating haze of sensation. ... She was driving him beyond the point of reason, but still he couldn't find the will to stop her and take command. This time there was only response. It poured from him, increasing her strength and depleting his. Knowing he was helpless excited her."[40]

Thurston cites this passage in order to argue that "the erotic heterosexual romance by the early 1980s was portraying a female sexuality that was no longer repressed or made obtuse and mysterious ... forbidden to the heroine by the double standard."[41] "Erotic romance heroines today," she continues, "are full partners with the men in their lives, including shared sexual initiatives and satisfaction."[42] I do not dispute Thurston's claim but rather would enlarge it to suggest that what such fantasies are doing is offering not only different visions of female sexuality but different subject positions for their readers to take up and to try on—that is, different ways of inhabiting a feminine self now no longer constructed solely as the object of another's gaze. The romance is straining, I think, to remap gender divisions, or more accurately, to rethink the construction of masculinity and femininity, since the two basic categories are always retained and seen as necessarily related.

I am suggesting, then, that if the contemporary popular romance is any indication, feminist discourses of the 1960s through the 1980s have had a significant impact on white middle-class women. Not only have those discourses combined with other material and social developments to move such women increasingly into the paid labor force and to begin to change child-rearing practices, but they have also profoundly affected women's strategies for self-representation and self-construction. They seem to have created both the desire for and the possibility of imagining new subject positions for women, positions that differ substantially from that fixed single positionality finally secured and offered to the reader by the conventional ending of the pre-1970s genre. Recent romances suggest that women are not limited to dreaming only what they have dreamed before, as Walter Kendrick claimed, but are, in their fantasies, attempting to move even more freely back and forth between the subject positions of the desiring subject and the desired object and, even more radically, exploring the possibility of coding those po-

sitions not solely complementarily but equivalently and alternatively as potentially masculine and feminine. This move seems not insignificant to me. In fact,
its effects could be cumulative, perhaps even transformative in the long run.

To give an indication of how unsettling such fantasies can be to the romance
narrative and to point to the obstacles still working to block a more radical reor-
dering, I conclude with a brief discussion of Jude Deveraux's fascinating 1987
novel *The Princess*. Deveraux is one of the top-grossing romance authors now
writing, and her work appears frequently on the *New York Times* paperback best-
seller list and has repeatedly been included in Literary Guild catalogues. This particular novel is built on the improbable premise of a World War II encounter between a kidnapped princess from the fictitious European country of Lanconia
and an intelligence officer of the American Navy. The plot is too complicated for
easy summary here, but I should note that the sexual play and experimentation
with subjectivity are centered around Princess Aria's prolonged masquerade as a
free-spirited working-class American girl. Not only is the reader asked by the narrative to move back and forth between the more traditional, strait-laced, and sexually repressed princess and her double, the exuberant, openly sexual Aria who at
one point dresses and dances as Carmen Miranda, but the reader is also asked to
spend whole chapters inside the head of J. T., the Navy hero who also masquerades. This sort of oscillation continues for more than 335 pages of misunderstand-
ing until J. T. finally rescues the princess from the hands of someone trying to
usurp her throne. What is interesting about the final resolution, however, is that it
seems entirely forced after the elaboration of several almost carnivalesque scenes
in which gender expectations are significantly rattled even as hero and heroine
momentarily find each other.

In the first idyllic scene, Deveraux describes the relations between hero and
heroine who have until that point been actively trying to avoid each other. This
scene is set in an out-of-the-way valley of Lanconia where the inhabitants are engaged in habits and rituals portrayed as centuries old in origin. The women train
as white-robed warriors alongside the men, both sexes engage in agriculture; in
this society, "quite often the men [take] care of the younger children and it [isn't]
unusual to see a fifty-year-old man trailed by three four-year-olds."[43] This state of
affairs is depicted entirely favorably, and both hero and heroine express their approval. Class distinctions are momentarily broken down in the scene, too, as the
princess shares a simple meal with the valley's citizens. Of course, the idyll does
not last very long, and J. T. and the princess return to the world of the court and
its class and gender hierarchies. They also return to their characteristic antipathy
toward each other.

Another similar carnivalesque scene occurs somewhat later when J. T. is responsible for the arrival of a group of war orphans in Lanconia (a country, for
reasons too complicated to explain, with almost no children of its own). J. T. de-
livers the orphans during a ceremonial parade, and the royal family has no choice
but to abandon its traditional roles and positions and to join happily in the busi-

ness of washing and dressing the children. J. T. and Aria, the reader is told, "personally bathed fourteen kids." The happiness and chaos of the scene then dissolve into passionate sex between hero and heroine. Surprisingly, however, they separate abruptly once their passion is spent, and they remain apart for the final twenty-eight pages of the novel. It is almost as if Deveraux cannot bring herself to resolve her play with various hierarchies or to close off the open-ended possibilities for the princess by returning her to the traditional heterosexual mold. Return her she does, however, on the last page, after one final protest by Aria at J. T.'s effort to claim her as his wife. That protest is characterized by her effort to continue speaking to her subjects as their ruler. When J. T. finally declares his love, he also tells Aria she won't have to abdicate because her people have asked him to return. The people acclaim him "king" to Aria's unheard protests that he can only ever be "Prince Jarl." The last two brief paragraphs in the book provide the only information we are given about Aria's feelings at this moment, and they seem curiously unsatisfying and oddly anticlimactic:

> "Come on, baby, let's go home," J. T. yelled. "I brought some members of my family with me. We're going to bring this country of ours into the twentieth century."
>
> She slipped her arm around him, forgetting she was in public and that she was a princess. "Ours," she said, smiling. "Our country."[44]

In two brief paragraphs, American superiority has been proclaimed and restored. Lanconia has been set inexorably on the road to modernization, and gender symmetry has been reestablished. Primal fantasy is here once again wedded to dominant social narrative as traditional order is maintained. But it seems to me that the desires generated by the prolonged masquerades, by the carnivalesque play with hierarchies, and by the fascination with instability in this novel (and in others like it) are profoundly in excess of that last narrative move. Closure, then, may be futile and perhaps even fleeting at century's end if such desires insist on demanding a new logic—if they continue to search through the romance form for more appropriate modes of expression and more satisfying routes to fulfillment.

Notes

1. *Romance Writers Report,* vol. 9, no. 2 (March 1989).

2. Anne Bushyhead, "The Ten Interview Questions You *Don't* Want to Be Asked—And How to Answer Them," *Romance Writers Report,* March 1989, 23.

3. Editorial headnote for Olivia Hall, "Cover Story—Learning Curves," *Romance Writers Report,* March 1989, 18.

4. Anne Bushyhead, "Ten Interview Questions," 23.

5. Ann Maxwell, "Writing—and Defending—Popular Fiction," *Romance Writers Report,* March 1989, 26.

6. Janice A. Radway, *Reading the Romance: Women, Patriarchy and Popular Literature* (Chapel Hill: University of North Carolina Press, 1984).

7. Tania Modleski, *Loving with a Vengeance: Mass-Produced Fantasies for Women* (Hamden, Conn.: Archon Books, 1982).

8. Walter Kendrick, "Falling in Love with Love," *Voice Literary Supplement,* August 3, 1982, 34.

9. Ann Douglas, "Soft-Porn Culture," *New Republic,* August 30, 1980, 28.

10. Allon White, "The Dismal Sacred Word: Academic Language and the Social Reproduction of Seriousness," *LTP: Journal of Literature, Teaching, Politics* (2), 1983, 4–15.

11. Tania Modleski, *Loving with a Vengeance,* 30.

12. Ibid., 108–109.

13. Janice Radway, *Reading the Romance,* 222.

14. Carol Thurston, *The Romance Revolution: Erotic Novels for Women and the Quest for a New Sexual Identity* (Urbana: University of Illinois Press, 1987), 16, 63–64.

15. Ibid., 16.

16. I want to thank Catherine Kirkland for first introducing me to the Romance Writers of America and to their *Romance Report* (original title of the newsletter that evolved into the *Romance Writers Report* magazine).

17. "Romance Survey—Finally! A Survey in Our Favor," *Romance Report,* vol. 1, no. 5 (December 1981), 19.

18. Catherine Kirkland, "For the Love of It: Women Writers and Popular Romance," Ph.D. dissertation, University of Pennsylvania, 1984, 260.

19. Ibid.

20. Janice A. Radway, "Reading Is Not Eating: The Theoretical, Methodological, and Political Consequences of a Metaphor," *Book Research Quarterly* 2 (Fall 1986), 18.

21. Alison Light, "'Returning to Manderley'—Romance Fiction, Female Sexuality and Class," *Feminist Review* 16 (April 1984), 7–25; Cora Kaplan, "*The Thorn Birds:* Fiction, Fantasy, Femininity," in Kaplan, *Sea Changes: Essays on Culture and Feminism* (London: Verso, 1986), 117–146.

22. Alison Light, "'Returning to Manderley,'" 8.

23. Ibid.

24. Ibid., 13.

25. Ibid.

26. Ibid., 17.

27. Ibid.

28. Ibid., 23.

29. Cora Kaplan, "*The Thorn Birds,*" 126.

30. Ibid., 120.

31. Ibid.

32. Ibid., 139 (emphasis added).

33. Ibid.

34. Ibid., 132.

35. Ibid., 146.

36. Carol Thurston, *The Romance Revolution,* 88.

37. Ibid.

38. Ibid., 97.

39. Ibid.

40. Ibid., 145.
41. Ibid., 140.
42. Ibid., 142.
43. Jude Deveraux, *The Princess* (New York: Simon & Schuster, 1987), 335.
44. Ibid.

ELEVEN

Democracy and the Constitution of Audiences: A Comparative Media Theory Perspective

IAN ANGUS

Genuine democracy requires widespread public participation in the processes of deliberation and decisionmaking. For this reason, the ideal case of Greek face-to-face participatory democracy retains an appeal, even though it seems unrealizable in a large-scale industrial society. Relations of immediate reciprocity such that each can speak and listen in turn, combined with access to relevant social knowledge, ideally guarantee that deliberation and decisionmaking cannot be monopolized by powerful interests. Democratic theory and practice therefore rely on a normative conception of communication. Even in a complex society where representative procedures must supplement citizen participation, the ideal of reciprocity seems essential to rule by the people.

Freedom of speech in its classic form was fundamental to democratic societies because it intended to guarantee both widespread access to relevant social knowledge by banning government censorship and widespread ability to articulate opinion and engage in decisionmaking. In contemporary capitalist societies, democratic theory must address two main sources whereby reciprocity is attenuated: the monopolization of access to relevant social knowledge and the inability of listeners to transform themselves into speakers. Both of these may be posed as questions of the extent to which an audience also produces and circulates social knowledge and engages actively in the process of deliberation and decisionmaking. The tendency of the most significant contemporary communication systems is to produce audiences without this capacity. Audiences tend to remain simply audiences; that is, communication systems tend to sever audiences from reciprocal production of social knowledge and engagement in decisionmaking. Even if projected advances in communication technologies were to allow for inputs and plebiscites on various public issues, as C. B. Macpherson has argued, we must recognize "an inescapable requirement of any decision-making process: somebody must formulate the questions" (1977, p. 95). It is this fundamental nonreciprocal component of contemporary media of communication that is problematic for democracy. For this reason, a critical theory of society dedicated to the recovery and extension of democracy must analyze the role of audiences in contemporary communication systems.

This issue for a democratic theory of audiences is not limited to coverage of news and politics in the usual sense. A genuinely democratic theory requires that the very definitions of what is newsworthy and what is political emerge from the process of reciprocal communication. It implies a focus on the constitution of audiences in the whole of cultural production. In a real sense, the audience is the key mediating link between cultural production in general and the possibilities of participatory democracy. The articulation of the classic principle of reciprocity in contemporary conditions of cultural production suggests that democracy is not merely a matter of political institutions but a whole way of life that is uniquely and newly endangered by the constitution of audiences and that can only be recovered and extended by being diffused throughout the entirety of cultural production.

Any cultural object can be viewed from the perspectives of its production, its audience, and its critical evaluation. Cultural production today is increasingly monopolized by the cultural industries, whose replication and transmission of the productions selected for promotion crowd out locally produced and nonprofit cultural forms. Yet, in this situation, the plurality of audience interpretations of any given mass media text is often presented as evidence that the audience is always "struggling to establish its own meanings" and is not a simple dupe of media moguls. The latter may well be so, but the polysemy of mass media texts is a condition for their commercial success, especially in a culturally diverse world characterized by transnational media flows, and doesn't go any distance at all toward proving that the audience isn't hindered from wider social action by the mass media. The assumption that texts must transmit a univocal meaning in order to play an ideological role is a caricature that serves to let virtually everything off the hook.

It is much easier for the new pluralist apologists to celebrate the "ingenuity of people" to use the products of mass culture in diverse ways (despite their control by increasingly fewer hands) than for critical theorists to define precisely the constraints that foreclose political alternatives. Such celebrations leave the larger context of cultural production and reception undisturbed: The globe is being carved into competing free trade zones reinforced by political and military power legitimated, in large part, by a transnational cultural system in which consumption is promoted as the model of social life. In short, the plurality of audience interpretations of a given cultural production is often interpreted in an ideological way as a pluralism that tends to legitimate monopoly by the cultural industries. Moreover, insofar as the standpoint of the critic is conflated with that of an "audience member" with "just another interpretation," the mere fact of plural interpretations is taken to be sufficient apology for the current cultural system. Critical cultural studies is in the process of being tamed by liberal pluralism, which (as we all used to know) is the ideological veil for the endemic exploitation inherent in the capitalist social form.

I am suggesting that a tamed legitimating circle encompassing monopolized cultural production, plural audience interpretations, and a decapitated critical sense is a pervasive tendency in contemporary cultural studies. Insofar as no one can claim today that there is widespread democratic access to production of cultural products through the mass media, the *plurality of audience responses* is the key term through which this ideological legitimation operates. But it is important to notice that the audience responds in a plurality of ways to the *content represented* in the media; it does not have the option of being in a plurality of relations to the medium itself. For this reason, the perspective of comparative media theory can offer cultural studies a renewal of its critical edge.[1] It claims that any audience study that does not theorize plurality simultaneously with constraint is ideological and looks for that component of constraint in the social relations constituted by media of communication.

In the present analysis, I focus on the formation of the audience to argue that a new political principle must be advanced in order to extend democracy in industrial capitalist societies. This principle suggests that every lack of reciprocity in a medium of communication must be compensated by the "right to speak" in another forum of equal social significance—a forum in which one is likely to be heard. This amounts to a reassertion of the principle of reciprocity in a context in which it is impossible to rely primarily on face-to-face communication to guarantee democratic participation. Such a reassertion requires that the different characteristics of media of communication—such as speech, writing, radio, television, and so forth—be identified and clarified in a comparative fashion. The perspective of comparative media theory suggests that democracy must now be addressed through the social relations that various media institute and emphasize because "the people"—as an effective or passive political force—are constituted through the media of communication that predominate in a society.

The radio broadcast was discussed in this manner by Jean-Paul Sartre as an indication of the predominance of what he called "serial" social relations that inhibit the possibility of collective action:

> But the important point is not whether a particular radio listener possesses his own transmitter and can make contact, as an individual, *later,* with some other listener, in another city or country: the mere fact of *listening to the radio,* that is to say, of listening to a particular broadcast at a particular time, establishes a serial relation of *absence* between the different listeners (1982, p. 271, emphasis in original).

Listeners are grouped together through the medium of the radio broadcast and have relations only through it. Consequently, it is impossible for them to act collectively; their action can only be the sum of individual actions, so that the meaning of this sum is not an intended outcome of any member. As Sartre continues, "My impotence does not lie only in the impossibility of silencing this voice: it also lies in the impossibility of convincing, *one by one,* the listeners all of whom it exhorts in the common isolation which it creates for all of them as their inert bond" (pp. 272–273). The speaker-listener relation and the listener-listener relation are constituted simultaneously by the broadcast such that the audience's seriality inhibits the collective political action that democratic participation requires. It is important to notice that this perspective of comparative media theory does not deny that each listener may interpret the content of the broadcast in a relatively unique manner. The emphasis here is on the constitution of social relations, not only the circulation of opinions and interpretations.

This theoretical investigation of the role of the audience for a contemporary democratic theory begins with a historical situating of the problem of the audience in the contemporary postmodern cultural condition that shows why the notion of "plural interpretations" now takes on such a key legitimating role. Second, it undertakes a transcendental inquiry that illuminates the conditions under which "audience effect" can be posed as a problem. Finally, the theoretical strategy of comparative media theory is explicitly introduced in order to articulate the political principle of reciprocity in contemporary conditions such that the "right to speak" can have real efficacy as a "right to be heard."

The Audience in Postmodern Theory

The contemporary postmodern cultural field exhibits a remarkable duality with respect to the role of the audience: On the one hand, cultural theory has focused on arguing for an expanded capacity of the audience to engage in active interpretations after the decline of classic modern cultural theory. On the other hand, the notion that there are a plurality of audience interpretations of any text has come to play a key legitimating role insofar as it appears to render moot the issue of the centralizing of media ownership, which in consequence has constricted access to cultural production. Understanding this duality is fundamental for a contemporary theory of the audience. In order to develop a critical cultural theory of audience reception, it is essential to theorize the plurality of interpretations along with constraint. Indeed, if there is no relevant constraint, there is no need for a critical theory. We can begin the characterization of the dual role of the audience in postmodern culture by sketching the conception of "writing" that has been developed primarily in France.

The concept of *écriture* (writing) was developed in order to theorize the new space opened up by the death of the author. As Michel Foucault noted, the notion of an author refers to the status of a discourse within society and culture and therefore to the question of its legitimation. Modern cultural production utilized the concept of the author (which is the aesthetic counterpart of the epistemological priority of the subject in modernity) in order to unify cultural productions and to mediate their relation to the whole cultural totality. Foucault described an author as "a point where contradictions are resolved." This resolution is accomplished through the definition of the author as a level of quality, a coherence, a style, a historical figure, and a principle of unity (1977, pp. 123, 128). It is through this resolution of tensions and contradictions that the author's works became integrated as a whole into culture.

The central feature of the modern unified conception was the encompassing of specific works, through the mediation of the author, into the totality of culture that educates the taste of the audience to promote a reasonable authority that can guide national politics. The classic representative of this position within the English language is Matthew Arnold. The sense of the impossibility of assuming a unification of culture—a concept that was previously axiomatic—is ubiquitous nowadays. This sense of our unique historical moment lies behind the many discussions of the "post-ness" of contemporary culture. Let us take as exemplary here George Steiner's account of contemporary "post-culture."

> The loss of a geographic-sociological centrality, the abandonment or extreme qualification of the axiom of historical progress, our sense of the failure or severe inadequacies of knowledge and humanism in regard to social action—all these signify the end of an agreed hierarchic value-structure. Those binary cuts which organized social perception and which represented the domination of the cultural over the natural code are now blurred or rejected outright. Cuts between Western civilization and the rest, between the learned and the untutored, between the upper and the lower strata of society, between the authority of age and the dependence of youth, between the sexes. ... The line of division separated the higher from the lower, the greater from the lesser: civilization from retarded primitivism (1971, p. 81).

In this loss of the hierarchic value-structure that we may call the "unified classic modern conception," it is neither the individual cultural productions nor the social context that is lost but the "passing-over," or *Aufhebung* (Hegel)—the moment of passage of the individual work toward totality that connects particular to universal and origin to goal. Modern cultural theory accomplished this passage with the concept of the author. It is this key component of the modern cultural synthesis that is rejected in the emergence of the concept of *écriture*.

The unlamented death of the author indicates a shift in the relation of literary discourse to society in which, as Roland Barthes described it, "writing can no longer designate an operation of recording, notation, representation, 'depiction' (as the Classics would say); rather, it designates exactly what linguists, referring to Oxford philosophy, call a performative, a rare verbal form (exclusively given in the first person and the present tense) in which the enunciation has no other content (contains no other proposition) than the act by which it is uttered." Writing thus exceeds every paternity of the text by an author, every fixture of meaning by an anterior cause, and liberates a territory of intertextual quotation and polysemic play of meaning within the wider field of discourse in general. Barthes thus calls writing a "pure gesture of inscription" that "traces a field without origin" (1977a, pp. 145–146).

The notion of "text" that replaces the classical notion of "work" within the postmodern concept of "writing" is a central notion in the postmodern cultural field because it expresses the removal of the author's mediation and consequently liberates a plurality of interventions and interpretations. The only place where this multiplicity can now be focused is with the reader. As Barthes phrased it, "The reader is the space on which all the quotations that make up a writing are inscribed without any of them being lost; a text's unity lies not in its origin but in its destination" (1977a, p. 148). Thus, a certain priority passes over to the audience in the fixing of meaning. However, even this certain priority of focusing in the audience is not guaranteed or absolute since it can be reconfigured in another context.

It is at this point that we can locate the emergence of the duality of the role of the audience in a contemporary postmodern cultural field. On one hand, the audience appears as the locus of the fixture of meaning—and this seems to call for a critical theory of the procedure of fixation by locating the audience in the context of the social formation as a whole. On the other hand, the death of the author appears to lead to a general leveling of the activities of inscribing, reading, and criticizing a text. In this sense artist, audience, and critic now represent only temporarily different punctuations of a discourse. Continuous quotation and reinscription of textual meaning within the discursive field appear to multiply writing, and the meanings it conveys, without limit. In this eventuality there seems to be no fixture at all—and therefore no need for a critical theory because there appears to be no locus of constraint.

Although the argument for the death of the author begins by elevating the audience, it proceeds toward a leveling of the three positions of inscriber, audience, and critic. But I do not want to simply accept this concept of writing as an adequate description of the postmodern cultural field. My purpose in prefacing it with a longer historical reflection has been to insinuate some reservations about the extent to which the respective roles of inscriber, audience, and critic can be adequately formulated in these terms. Let me suggest these reservations quickly: First, from the standpoint of the inscription of meaning in a text, the writer does not wish to say just anything at all but desires to fix meaning—even though this fixture is not such as to preclude active interpretations. The textual reformulation of the writer as the "first reader" does not capture this desire at all. Moreover, the suggestion that this desire to fix meaning is simply an authoritarian, reactionary gesture does not account for the appearance of new writers from hitherto repressed classes and groups who, no less than any others, do not wish their readers to be totally unconstrained in confronting their work. Second, with respect to the role of the audience, a simple textual polysemy released by active interpretation neither suggests an emancipatory move nor describes how it is possible. The conflation of social criticism into plural readings proposes an extremely attenuated notion of criticism. Third, regarding the role of the critic, it may well be important to transform the critic from a separate individual into a relation to textual practice that can be occupied by a diversity of subject positions, but in the formulation based on the idea of writing, there is no justification of such a critical relation—which is collapsed into the activity of every reader. In fact, the leveling of the activities of inscription, reading, and criticism seems to occlude the vital functions of each. Yet there is something central to postmodern culture captured by the elevation of discourse that the leveling of these activities opens up.

How then are we to understand the claim for the audience in *écriture?* In the first place, the audience emphasis constitutes the historical polemic of *écriture:* It is through the liberation of the audience that the hegemony of the author is overthrown. But the focus on the destination of a text also undercuts any specific audience interpretation or effect by placing it within an ongoing stream of textuality the ultimate meaning of which cannot be fixed because it is of indefinite extension—there can always be another discursive intervention that modifies the stream as a whole. In this sense, the historical priority of the audience is a polemical prologue to an undifferentiated postmodern cultural stream.

Ultimately, in the postmodern cultural field the relations of writer, reader, and critic are leveled and the evaluative component (on which the initial claim for liberating the audience rests) is undermined. Without the classical distinctions among a creator of meaning, a receiver of meaning, and a dispassionate evaluator of meaning, the argument that the focusing of meaning has any privileged location is undercut. Since the discourse on a text is another text, the reading of a text is a production of meaning. To quote Barthes again, "the distance separating reading from writing is historical" (1977b, p. 162). The notion of textuality is an attempt to reduce this difference to its minimum. Through the reduction of the author to a scribe, the critic and reader are elevated; their activities are not so much different in principle as temporary punctuations of a continuous stream of discourse. The emergence of this continuous stream of discourse is possible due to the death of the unifying function of the author who previously accomplished both its internal structuralization and its connection to the wider totality of culture.

The interplay of these polemical and historical components has been repeated by many other writers after Foucault and Barthes: It is claimed that the death of the author's sovereignty is a liberation of the audience, but it simultaneously involves a leveling of subject positions within *écriture* that makes any evaluative and therefore genuinely critical approach to a text impossible or arbitrary. The overthrowing of the author ultimately overthrows the basis for evaluating any type of fixture in audience interpretations and thereby occludes the whole question of the status of a discourse within society and culture in the postmodern world. Ironically, the very means used to overthrow the ideological conception of classic modern culture becomes the main ideological underpinning of postmodern culture. In the criticism of constraints on the audience by the work, it has come to seem as if there are no constraints within the pure stream of textuality.

The initial polemical insistence on the interpretive activity of the audience serves to introduce a leveling of positions within the stream of discourse. This leveling then undermines the possibility of an analysis of the means of fixture and thereby a critical and evaluative component to discourse. Such an evaluative component would have to be located (in a manner analogous to that used in classical modern cultural theory) in the passage from specific cultural productions to the social context as a whole. Since the mediating term "author" is lost, such a passage is rendered impossible. Thus, the audience in postmodern culture occupies a dual role due to the historical conditions of its emergence. In its polemical relation to modern cultural theory, it promotes a liberation of plural interpretations. In its relation to the newly uncovered postmodern cultural field, the plurality of audience interpretations serves to suggest that a critical theory, which would focus on constraints on interpretations, is unnecessary. Of course, it will be conceded, since no audience can actually engage in all possible interpretations of a given text, the plurality is factually limited. We could thus engage in an interminable argument about the extent of the actual multiplicity of interpretations by a given audience: In the first place, one could show their predominantly apologetic tendency; in the second place, one could show their "in principle" open plurality. The problem is that both positions would be correct within the context of the undifferentiated stream of discourse. This kind of sidetracking of inquiry by capturing it within insoluble dilemmas is characteristic of how ideology, in this case pluralist ideology, functions.

The postmodern shift necessarily puts the audience in a dual role because its apparently liberating effect derives from the polemical point of its emergence, not from its intrinsic character. Thus, the plurality of audience interpretations can be properly situated as the key apologetic and legitimating component after the full emergence of the postmodern cultural field. The apologetic direction of liberal pluralism is peculiarly suited to the postmodern cultural field and can be expected to arise spontaneously. It is the task of critical cultural theory both to account for this spontaneous ideological tendency and to provide a theoretical vantage point from which it can be challenged. A theory of the transition from classic modern culture to postmodern culture locates the evaluative question precisely at the "point of passage" from specific cultural productions to the social formation as a whole—neither in a supposed loss of totality nor in the simple plurality of interpretations. The shift from author to text describes the emergence of a postmodern cultural field through the revision of the relation of literature to society—stated another way, of the relation of the reading/writing medium of communication to the social context as a whole.

A genuinely critical theory of the audience can only be established through analyses that uncover the relationship between plurality and constraint. Investigations of this type would intercede in the supposedly undifferentiated stream of discourse at two key locations: first, to uncover the means by which a fixture of meaning occurs in the audience; second, to clarify its relation to the social formation as a whole. Investigations of specific cases in this style depend upon the prior theoretical issue of how the audience is constituted as such.

The Metaphysical Space of "Audience Effect"

The preceding characterization of the postmodern cultural field through the analysis of the shift to *écriture* has shown that investigation of the audience is crucial to contemporary critical theory. Moreover, it has shown that the notion of plural audience interpretations takes on a key legitimating role in postmodern culture. To displace this ideology adequately, a critical cultural theory must formulate precisely the relation between plurality of interpretations and social constraint.

In this section, I present a transcendental reflection on the emergence of the metaphysical space within which the concept of the audience has been articulated. This reflection focuses on the conditions under which a question of audience effect emerges, which I will call "metaphysics." This intellectual strategy opens the social formation as a whole to critical inquiry, whereas it is simply presupposed and therefore uninvestigated by audience studies of the pluralist type. Whereas the analysis of the preceding section was concerned with the current cultural condition through a transformation of the concept of writing, the present one is concerned with the institution of the audience through the metaphysical interpretation of a transformation of orality.

The problem of a message's effect on an audience arises as soon as there is a suspension introduced between speaking and replying. In conversation there is a continuously reestablished reciprocity because each participant is, in turn, both speaker and audience. This allows a checking of audience reception through the speech that it motivates and, thus, through the further audience reaction to this motivated speech. This process of mutual checking of speech act and audience effect occurs through the production of further speech that refers continuously backward and forward to the exchange that enables the conversation to continue.

Interruption of this reciprocity separates production from consumption—speech act from audience effect—and therefore raises the problem of their relationship. Because of the suspension of an immediate relation of reciprocity, the scope of communication is expanded in space and time, thus instituting the possibility of a culture dispersed throughout various forms with different relations between production and consumption. This expansion raises the general question of the various types of mediated relationships that are possible and predominant between communication acts and their effects. Specifically, the problem of audience effect arises when the meaning of a communication act is stretched between its production and its effect—in conditions in which the direct reciprocity of mutual checking is suspended.

Such a separation can be introduced from the outside—from factors external to the act of producing and consuming the communication act itself. For example, although conversation allows reciprocal turn-taking, a speech in a public arena does not. Reciprocity is transformed into the understanding of the speech, internal evaluation of it, and, possibly, heckling. If one is socially recognized as being allowed to do so, there may be the possibility of making another speech in rebuttal. But this is another speech, with the same features of relationship between speaker and audience, not an immediate reciprocity in the same communication act. In fact, it is often precisely because of such immediate nonreciprocity that political bodies devise rules that institutionalize the right to reply. Audience response is suspended, though not altogether nullified, because a given communication act does not occur alone but in the context of a socially organized plurality of communication acts. Nevertheless, once reciprocity is pushed outside a given communication act, institutional rules and procedures are required to reestablish a certain kind of reciprocity through the right to produce similar and related acts. At this point, exchange can only be established by producing more similar communication acts, not by continuing in the same act. Basic features of political regimes can be delineated by the different ways they deal with this issue. Democracy, for example, is the attempt to push the right of reply prior to decisionmaking to its furthest extent.

The turn-taking of conversation can be called a single communication act because the structure of each intervention is formed by the prior and subsequent reciprocity from which the specific intervention gains its meaning. One public speech and a subsequent rebuttal, in contrast, must be regarded as two separate communication acts because the structure of a speech is independent of the existence or nonexistence of a rebuttal. Thus, the very constitution of the audience of the first speech means that reciprocity is possible only through subsequent speeches. Whereas the reciprocal turn-taking of conversation includes a before-and-after reference to other parts of the same communication act, the mutual referencing of separate acts (such as speeches) is established at a higher, more inclusive level that can be called a "discourse." The suspension of reciprocity thus simultaneously constitutes an audience and splits the communication act into a plurality of acts. This splitting of a continuous communication act into several chronologically related acts originates the problem of the effect of a message that cannot be checked through the continuous process of the same communication act. It motivates the institutionalization of rules concerning the right to reply— the right to add another communication act. The very constitution of an audience poses an issue for democratic theory of another forum in which the broken reciprocity can be repaired.

The external transformation of conversation into speech-making is an institutional transformation within the oral medium of communication. This is by no means a negligible transformation. Such external social and institutional forces contribute to the meaning of any specific communication act. Some political regimes do not, after all, institutionalize the right to reply or, perhaps more important, the right to initiate speech. Often, only some positions of influence are allowed to produce relevant speech and have the right to make pertinent replies. It is the considerable merit of democracy to base its political theory on the principle of an institutional right of everyone to initiate and reply. In practice, this principle is probably always curtailed to some degree. To this extent, democracy may be a regulative ideal capable of greater degrees of approximation but not of final actualization.

Such a transformation of conversation into speech-making with an audience is a result of external institutional forces. The suspension introduced between speaking and replying is not inherent in the medium of communication that we can call "orality" but depends on social, economic, and political forces acting upon orality and giving it a particular sociohistorical form. This distinction between speech-making and conversation determines the point at which Aristotle's investigation of rhetoric emerges and finds its place in the ethical-political determination of political regimes: "Rhetoric falls into three divisions, determined by the three classes of listeners to speeches. Of the three elements in speech-making—speaker, subject, and person addressed—it is the last one, the hearer, that determines the speech's end and object" (1984, pp. 31–32, 1358a–b). Rhetoric in the classical sense emerges precisely because of the suspension of turn-taking and allows the classification of speeches by their different relations to an audience. Rhetoric can thus be defined as "the power of observing the means of persuasion on almost any subject" (1984, p. 24, 1355b). Rhetoric emerges through the constitution of the audience at the point where the reciprocal checking of conversation is suspended from outside; consequently, the problem of the persuasive force of a speech can be posed independently of its content.

The emergence of an independent concern with persuasion involves a simultaneous reformation of the concept of truth, the internal content of which can now be conceptualized apart from its persuasive force. In Aristotle and in ancient Greek philosophy generally, this was conceptualized as the distinction between dialectic and rhetoric. Dialectic was concerned with the discovery of truth, rhetoric with its persuasive dissemination. This distinction is applicable not only to questions of truth but to all use of language. Searle, for example, distinguishes in similar fashion between the "sense," or propositional content, of an utterance and its (illocutionary) force (1970, pp. 30–33). We may say, in a general way, that language has both a semantic, descriptive dimension and a pragmatic, active dimension. This distinction between the "inherent content" of an utterance and its "effect, or force," has persisted in various forms precisely because it is constituted by the emergence of the audience.

It is not the specific forms in which this distinction can be made that concern us here but rather the suspension of reciprocity from which emerges a space in which this distinction can and must be made. This space can be called "metaphysics" insofar as it opens up the possibility of a foundational discourse centered on an internal truth distinct from its persuasive effects.[2] Although the notion of truth is key to this metaphysical space, nevertheless it simultaneously involves a related (though devalued in relation to truth) conception of persuasion. The suspension of reciprocity institutes rhetoric as a concern with the persuasive means of accomplishing an audience effect in the same moment that it formulates a distinction between the internal content of an utterance and its external effect—dialectic and rhetoric.

Let us now make a preliminary conclusion based on this analysis of the suspension of reciprocity. The problem of audience effect as it emerges within metaphysics is parasitic on the central organizing notion of the internal content of an utterance. Thus, any investigation of audience effect that takes place within this distinction and therefore inquires into persuasion—defined as distinct from inherent content—presupposes that effect is a function of factors external to the communicative act itself. Insofar as the separation between truth and persuasion determines the space of investigation, the formation of the subject positions of speaker and audience are thrust outside the communicative act.

Rhetoric, of course, has investigated the strategies of speech that have commanded a persuasive energy on an audience. Nevertheless, the actual effect of these persuasive strategies depends on the audience itself. Rhetoric presumes that the communicative act has an audience already there prior to the utterance. The constitution of the audience through the suspension of reciprocity expels the formation of the audience outside the communication event. The effect that emerges from the impact that the persuasive strategies have on an audience is thus defined outside the communicative act itself. Investigation of the audience in this manner will necessarily become essentially a positive, empirical description of an audience whose main features are presupposed prior to the communicative act. Thus, the process of communication under investigation will be denied a constitutive function in forming its audience.

The same point can be put in a slightly different way: The metaphysical distinction between internal content and persuasive effect locates persuasion ambiguously: Is persuasion located in the style (formal, metaphorical, and so on) of the speech or in the actual persons persuaded? Both? Neither? Perhaps persuasion should be located in the *connection between* the speech act and its audience. But this connection cannot be properly investigated within the metaphysical space because the separation of all persuasion from internal content necessarily undercuts the possibility of thinking of these two components as together. We may say that the primary distinction relegates the secondary one to irrelevance. Because the rhetorical study of persuasion is instituted by the distinction between internal content and external effect, it cannot investigate the actual locus at which persuasion occurs—between internal and external, or at the point of their connection. The Aristotelian formula "speaker, subject, person addressed" leaves the formation of the "person addressed" outside the communicative-rhetorical-persuasive act, at the same moment that it is concerned with the effect on this already formed person. Similarly, this formula leaves out the formation of the "speaker" as well. This is because the "subject" is already understood on the basis of the prior mode of internal content. But it is precisely this formation of the relation between speaker and audience that is the main effect of a speech act. It is the key concern of persuasion after metaphysics.

In sum, the suspension of reciprocity institutes a distinction between internal content and external effect that, in turn, requires that the effect of this content be investigated in relation to an audience formed outside the given communication. The key question is thus this relation between a specific communication act and the social context in which it occurs. This prior formation of the audience is either left uninvestigated (within traditional rhetoric) or shunted off to be covered by an entirely separate social theory (social scientific audience studies). A dilemma must arise: Either the audience is presumed to be preformed, in which case the communicative act is investigated simply as representational and denied any constitutive power, or the communicative act is regarded as constituting its audience effect, in which case it is seen as all-powerful. Avoiding this dilemma requires that the instituting metaphysical distinction between inherent content and rhetorical force be held up to scrutiny. This dilemma with regard to the formation of subject positions corresponds to the dilemma pointed out in the previous section with respect to the theoretical plurality but factual limitation of audience interpretations. Both cases seem to pose an unsatisfactory alternative between extensive plurality and factual limitation: It seems impossible to theorize plurality and constraint simultaneously.

Democracy as Reciprocity

Within the closure of metaphysics, every expression is subdivided into internal meaning/content, or sense, and external persuasive force. Any investigation of audience effect within this framework remains caught within this duality that creates an insoluble dilemma at each level of the inquiry. In this context we can appreciate the radicalness of Marshall McLuhan's claim that the content of a medium is its users, or that internal sense is entirely present in persuasive force (Molinaro et al. 1987, pp. 427, 443, 448; Marchand 1989, pp. 34, 114, 167, 255). This view and other apparently paradoxical formulations aim to provoke a questioning of the metaphysical distinction that has set up our separation between content and effect, or dialectic and rhetoric. Even more important, it focuses attention on the notion of a "medium" of communication—a notion that is outside this metaphysical framework and can serve to unsettle it.

The present inquiry takes up the issue of the audience in a postmetaphysical space in order to develop its role in a contemporary democratic theory. To do so, it must undercut the distinction between internal sense and external persuasive force. The strategy for this effort centers on the "external" materiality of the medium of communication. This is not the relative, secondary externality of persuasive effect, which is constituted in opposition to internal content. The material externality of the medium of communication undercuts the sense/force, or content/effect, of the expression as a whole and pertains to the structure and consequences of the communicative act itself. This radical externality opens up the possibility of undercutting the metaphysical distinction between internal content and persuasive force by subjecting it to a more fundamental axis of investigation. Moreover, whereas the metaphysical tradition and the dependent conception of rhetoric have been formed by the focus on speech—from which the very term "audience" (hearers) is formed[3]—this inquiry centers on the comparison between different media of communication. In this respect, the fact that the previous discussions are based on transformations in the media of writing and orality respectively serves us well.

It was noted previously that rhetoric came into being as an external transformation of the medium of orality such that the reciprocal turn-taking of conversation was suspended. This suspension is the condition for the emergence of the question concerning audience effect. If we wish to formulate generally the limits within which all interpretations are constrained, our analysis will necessarily depend upon the formation of the audience—the entire social and institutional complex of the social formation. This entirety may be expected to be present empirically in audience interpretations and to limit pragmatically the polysemy of the text. We may formulate the conclusion of this inquiry in general terms: The suspension or reciprocity within a medium of communication pushes the constraints on interpretation outside the given communication act and, thereby, to the social formation as a whole. In the most general terms, this is where the interplay of constraint and plurality that fixes meaning must be located.

There is a different form of suspension introduced when we compare the reciprocal turn-taking of conversation to writing. This is not an external institutional transformation of orality but a transformation to a different medium of communication altogether. The relation between writer and reader is analogous to (but not the same as) the relation between speaker and audience. Because the materiality of the medium of communication is different, writing is not a transformation of the social and institutional setting of orality but a transformation of orality itself, of the medium in which the communication act occurs. In the case of writing, there is instituted a separation between producer and consumer within the medium itself—which is analogous to (but not the same as) the separation introduced into orality by its institutional transformation into speech. This internal separation in writing may be called the *context of the medium*. It inaugurates a different type of suspension of reciprocity that puts into play an internal set of social relationships within the writing-reading, or literate, complex.

We may go even further to observe that writing is not necessarily a transformation of speech at all. One may write, as Ricoeur says, instead of speaking (1981, p. 146; 1976, p. 25). One may write where there is no need, desire, or possibility of speaking. In this sense, writing is simply another medium of communication that allows communication acts of a different type. There is a plurality of communication acts here too, but it is not the simple plurality of acts of speech-making in the same oral medium of communication. Every speech act occurs in relation to a plurality of speech acts (interorality). Also, for example, every act of writing occurs in relation to other acts of writing (intertextuality). It would not be meaningful otherwise. But there is also a plurality of media of communication in relation to the materiality of expression. It can only be addressed by putting the various media in relation to each other by discussing the context of the medium in a comparative manner. This perspective can be called *comparative media theory*.

These two forms of suspension of reciprocity are based in the plurality of media of communication. The first refers to external institutional transformations within a medium. The second refers to the plurality of media of communication themselves. It was stated previously that the fixture of meaning in the audience in the first case is dependent on the social formation as a whole. When we add the notion that the social formation as a whole consists not merely of one medium of communication but of a plurality of media that interact with—or "translate"— each other, this fixture can be seen to be dependent on the general interaction of media. For example, the fixture of meaning in the audience for a book is established, in the first place, in relation to other forms of writing and the different institutional relations that this implies. But, in a second and larger sense, the fixture is dependent on the relation of writing to the whole social formation—which can be defined as the interaction of all existing media of communication. When we consider the medium of writing thematically, the social formation stands as a background constituted by the interaction of all media of communication except writing. (Writing is exempt from the background because it is the foreground focus.) We have here a dual externality: There is an externality "internal" to the medium—other forms of writing, other forms of orality, for example—that is based on institutional influences on the medium. Also, there is a more general Externality that we can designate with a capital *E*. This Externality refers to the media environment in the social formation—the plurality of media of communication, their interactions, and the translations in and out of the medium in question.

The question concerning the audience emerges at the site of the suspension of reciprocity—a suspension that takes two forms: one oriented to the external institutional transformation of a medium of communication and another pertaining to the External formation of the institutional complex itself. Thus there are two kinds of fixture of meaning in the audience: The first pertains to the *mirroring* of all external social differences in different interpretations of a given meaning/content. Here we will expect to see the influence of other social variables affecting the plurality of audience interpretations. The second fixture pertains to the very *formation* of these social differences through the media environment. After metaphysics we cannot simply presuppose a formed audience and must therefore venture into the Externality of the totality of the media environment.

It is in the interplay between these two e(E)xternalities that the connection between expressed content and audience effect can be formulated—a connection that evaded metaphysics. The medium of communication is a medium precisely insofar as it *establishes connection,* and in that sense, there is a presumption toward (some kind of) reciprocity in the very idea of a medium. A medium of communication is neither internal sense nor persuasive force but the establishment of the ground of their connection. For orality, it is the space that allows speaking and hearing; for writing, it is the paper behind the marks of a pen; for video, it is the tape and recording/playing apparatus. Even more precisely, the medium of writing is the connection of pen with paper enabled through the alphabet. Metaphysics consists in asserting a definite complex of a dominant medium of communication in order to stabilize an internal meaning/content whose external effect can then be posed. The question concerning the audience is circumscribed within the metaphysical space as long as it accepts this stabilization. The shift toward the comparative theory of media of communication is a postmetaphysical inquiry that formulates the fixing of meaning by situating the audience within the social formation in a double sense. From this perspective, both the conceptions of pure interpretive plurality and single injections of meaning/content are ideological deformations. Human expression is the establishing of connection. Connection itself can only be theorized through the medium of communication by which it is instituted. In this sense, communication is the ground of social relations, a ground that establishes the interplay of plurality and constraint within a social formation.

Let me illustrate with respect to the current social role of the commercial use of video technology—the medium of television. The first fixture of meaning refers to the institutional complex of television in relation to the other (discarded or marginalized) possibilities of video. Constraint at this point is focused through the political economy of television that consists in delivering audiences to advertisers (Jhally 1987, chap. 3). The plurality of audience interpretations can be expected to mirror the social differences of the entire social formation. But this mirroring is "focused," or thematized, through the necessity that the audience as a whole must fill the social role allotted within the political economy of television. Anything else will spell the quick demise of this audience, and its plural interpretations of the previously selectively produced fare, in the face of the commercial imperative. The second fixture of meaning refers to the internal social relations of the medium of television in relation to the Externality of other media. In this connection, it is the one-to-many relation of a centralized source broadcasting to a plurality of isolated receivers that is most important. Constraint, with respect to this plurality of interpretations of television content, consists in the fact that *any content whatever* on this medium connects the audience into this social relationship with the centralized information source. At this point, the relevant comparison is with other media of communication that allow for more participatory social relations and less centralized sources of information (see Angus 1988, 1989). The institutional complex of the medium provides the constraint through which audience interpretations mirror wider social differences. It is with respect to the External context of the medium that the role of the social relations within the medium are placed in relation to the social formation as a whole and that the necessary constraint upon the audience by this subject positioning can be formulated. The ideological role of television in contemporary society operates in both these dimensions. In each case, it is the interplay of plurality and constraint that enables cultural studies and the focus on audiences to be incorporated into a critical theory of communication.

The analysis of the ideological functions of contemporary communication systems aims to reinvigorate democratic theory. Insofar as reciprocity in communication is built into the very idea of democracy, critical theory must analyze failures and suspensions of reciprocity. An audience is constituted by just such a suspension of reciprocity. It is not that an audience is entirely passive with regard to the content of the medium. It is merely that its active response is expelled to another communication act. Reciprocity can thus be salvaged to the extent that there is a political right to produce other communication acts. One may be compensated, as it were, for being an audience by the right to initiate and reply in another forum. But this right to speak in another forum requires a forum of equal social significance if it is to be able to counterbalance the nondemocratic suspension of reciprocity. Since an entirely face-to-face democracy is no longer viable, a principle of equal compensation for the constitution of an audience would amount to a reassertion of the democratic participation in a context dominated by cultural industries.

Every medium occurs in the context of two e(E)xternalities: the institutional context of the medium and the media environment. To the extent that the suspension derives from the first externality, equal compensation takes the form of the traditional right to reply—to reply to a news editorial, for example; to produce another speech in a political forum; or to gain access to television for minority opinion. This right is recognized in democratic theory, and it would make a great deal of difference to contemporary society if it were fully put into practice. Nonetheless, the present analysis suggests that there is a further issue with regard to the right to reply that has not been addressed at all and that stems from the second Externality.

An example: To the extent that one becomes an audience for television, one has a right to compensation in another medium of equal social significance. The right to reply on television deriving from the first externality is not sufficient to address the fact that all television (no matter who is speaking) reinforces the one-to-many structure that constitutes the audience in their mutual seriality and absence. This Externality can only be addressed by compensation in another medium that, rather than reinforcing the television audience, would institute a different set of speaker-audience relations. The problem, of course, is that there is probably no other medium to equal television in social effect. This compensation would thus have the effect of requiring institutional support (of the type of the first external-ity) for other media, such as public meetings, art shows, guerrilla video, and so on. The upshot of this principle is thus to require that audiences be compensated for the monopolization of cultural production by pervasive media such as televi-sion. The effect of this compensation would be to reduce this monopoly—not only to produce more access to television as it exists or to produce better television but to reduce the monopoly that the medium of television holds over cultural production. In the long run, such a principle would undermine the ability of any medium to effectively control cultural space. It would be a democracy not only of citizens but of media themselves. This is the only long-run means whereby we can transform the contemporary media environment in a democratic direction.

New political principles are hard to come by, but something such as this is needed to reform the democratic tradition so that it can deal with the contempo-rary proliferation of media. This chapter has attempted in a tentative way to ad-dress this issue through the problem of audiences. Let me end by stating the prin-ciple of the second Externality in a general form: The creation of any audience in any medium, insofar as it suspends the reciprocity on which democracy depends, requires the compensation of that audience by the subsidizing of other media in which that audience can attain active expression in such a manner that the social decisionmaking process can be influenced to the extent of the suspending me-dium. It would take this much to establish the reciprocity on which participatory democracy depends. If it seems too much, then let that serve to measure the dis-tance we have to go.

Notes

1. The perspective I refer to as "comparative media theory" is known in communication studies primarily through the work of Harold Innis, Walter Ong, Marshall McLuhan, and Eric Havelock. Its key component is the analysis of each medium of communication as in-stituting a distinct set of social relations that enters into a complex relationship with other media in the "media environment." "Culture" is thus understood as a specific configura-tion of this media environment. The common concept of "communication" as referring to the content of representations is thereby set aside in favor of one that ties it much more closely to social and political theory. I have sketched this perspective in several other essays (Angus 1988, 1989, 1992, forthcoming).

2. This short account of the emergence of the metaphysical space is obviously rather al-lusive and truncated. The concern here is to show how the traditional notions of rhetoric,

persuasion, and audience effect are circumscribed within this space despite the fact that its key instituting moment is the discourse of truth, or "philosophy." This chapter thus investigates the audience after the end of philosophy. A more complete account would need to distinguish between the discourse of truth interpreted as foundational and the discourse of truth "as such." Such a distinction would show how philosophy can continue in a postfoundational, postmetaphysical space.

3. On the centrality of speech to the formation of the metaphysical tradition, see the work of Jacques Derrida (especially 1978a). The discussion of the rhetorical tradition in this chapter indicates a support for this claim independent of Derrida's account. Nevertheless, for other reasons, I do not regard this claim as fully justified.

References

Angus, I. 1988. "Oral Tradition as Resistance." In M. Lupul (ed.), *Continuity and Change: The Cultural Life of Alberta's First Ukrainians*. Edmonton: Canadian Institute of Ukrainian Studies.

_____. 1989. "Media Beyond Representation." In I. Angus and S. Jhally (eds.), *Cultural Politics in Contemporary America*. New York: Routledge.

_____. 1992. "Mediation and New Social Movements." *Communication Theory* 1 (2): 71–83.

_____. Forthcoming. "Orality in the Twilight of Humanism: A Critique of the Communication Theory of Harold Innis." *Continuum: An Australian Journal of the Media*.

Aristotle. 1984. *Rhetoric*. In W. Roberts (trans.), *The Rhetoric and Poetics of Aristotle*. New York: Modern Library.

Barthes, R. 1977a. "The Death of the Author." In S. Heath (trans.), *Image, Music, Text*. New York: Hill and Wang.

_____. 1977b. "From Work to Text." In S. Heath (trans.), *Image, Music, Text*. New York: Hill and Wang.

Derrida, J. 1978a. *Of Grammatology*, G. Spivak (trans.). Baltimore and London: Johns Hopkins University Press.

_____. 1978b. *Writing and Difference*, A. Bass (trans.). Chicago: University of Chicago Press.

Foucault, M. 1977. "What Is an Author?" In D. Bouchard and S. Simon (trans.), *Language, Counter-Memory and Practice*. Ithaca, N.Y.: Cornell University Press.

Jhally, S. 1987. *The Codes of Advertising*. New York: St. Martin's.

Macpherson, C. B. 1977. *The Life and Times of Liberal Democracy*. Oxford: Oxford University Press.

Marchand, P. 1989. *Marshall McLuhan: The Medium and the Messenger*. New York: Ticknor and Fields.

Molinaro, M., C. McLuhan, and W. Toye (eds.). 1987. *Letters of Marshall McLuhan*. Oxford: Oxford University Press.

Ricoeur, P. 1976. *Interpretation Theory: Discourse and the Surplus of Meaning*. Fort Worth: Texas Christian University Press.

_____. 1981. "What Is a Text? Explanation and Understanding." In J. Thompson (ed. and trans.), *Hermeneutics and the Human Sciences*. Cambridge: Cambridge University Press.

Sartre, J.-P. 1982. *Critique of Dialectical Reason*, A. Sheridan-Smith (trans.). London: Verso.
Searle, J. 1970. *Speech Acts: An Essay in the Philosophy of Language.* Cambridge: Cambridge University Press.
Steiner, G. 1971. *In Bluebeard's Castle: Some Notes Toward the Redefinition of Culture.* New Haven, Conn.: Yale University Press.

TWELVE

Reflections upon the Encoding/Decoding Model: An Interview with Stuart Hall

The following interview was recorded at the University of Massachusetts in February 1989. The aim of the discussion was to take another look at Stuart Hall's influential "Encoding/Decoding" essay (Hall 1980) in order to consider some of the problems that still confront those involved in audience research. Those interviewing Stuart Hall (SH) were Ian Angus (IA), Jon Cruz (JC), James Der Derian (JD), Sut Jhally (SJ), Justin Lewis (JL), and Cathy Schwichtenberg (CS).

SJ: We'd like to start off in the most general way by talking about the "Encoding/Decoding" piece and the context within which it was written. Could you say a little bit about the theoretical, political, and cultural context and how that affected the emphasis and thrust of the model?

SH: Well, I think that the piece has a number of different contexts which it is worthwhile identifying. The first, in a sense, is a kind of methodological/theoretical context, because the paper was delivered to a colloquium which was organized by the Centre for Mass Communications Research at the University of Leicester.

Now, the Centre for Mass Communications Research was a traditional center, using traditional empirical, positivistic models of content analysis, audience-effects survey research, et cetera. So the paper, although you may not realize it, has a slightly polemical thrust. It's positioned against some of those positions, and it's positioned, therefore, against a particular notion of content as a preformed and fixed meaning or message which can be analyzed in terms of transmission from sender to receiver. It's positioned against a certain unilinearity of that model, one-directional flow: Sender originates the message, the message is itself pretty unidimensional, and the receiver receives it.

Now, do you see that the implication of that model is that all communication is perfect communication? The only distortion in it is that the receiver might not be up to the business of getting the message he or she ought to get. But if he or she was intelligent enough and wide-awake enough, obviously there is no problem about meaning: Meaning is perfectly transparent, it's a message the receiver either gets or doesn't get. The communicator wants to get the message through, so he or she wants to know what the blockages are to the perfect transmission of meaning.

So the positioning of the early encoding/decoding paper is partly to interrupt that sort of transparent notion of communication, to say: "Producing the message isn't quite as transparent an activity as that." The message is a complex structure of meanings, which isn't as simple as you think it is. Reception isn't the open-ended, perfectly transparent thing at the other end of the communication chain. And the communication chain doesn't operate in a unilinear way.

That's one context. The second context is obviously a political context: If you read the paper, there is a notion running through it of working against the grain of a rather overdeterminist model of communication. It is the notion that meaning is not fixed, that there is no overall determining logic which can allow you to decipher the so-called meaning or the ideological import of the message against some grid. The notion that meaning is more multilayered, that it's always multireferential. Those new models are being set to work in the paper. And that, of course, reflects the beginnings of structuralism and semiotics and their impact on cultural studies.

In terms of that larger theoretical context, it really has to do with the impact of early Barthes—the Barthes of *Elements of Semiology* and *S/Z*—and the whole Levi-Straussean recovery of the model of Saussurian language. Now, this has political implications because, as you can see, there is also an argument with Marxism going on. There is an argument with the base-superstructure model, with the notion of ideology, language, and culture as secondary, as not constitutive but only as constituted by socioeconomic processes. There is the opening up of a notion of politics to culture. The political questions also have to deal with the construction and reconstruction of meaning, the way meaning is contested and established. Those processes are not secondary to some other determining groundwork but have to be given a relative autonomy or efficacy of their own, which is specific. That part of it is not political in the narrow sense; it isn't a political project coming out of the paper. It has a bearing on how one thinks about political questions.

Finally, it has a context in relation to a debate about Marxism itself. The model which I outline in the opening paragraph of the paper is drawn from another paper of mine which was written at the same time, "Notes on the Reading of Marx's '1857 Introduction,'" which is Marx's most, in my view, elaborated and most interesting methodological text (Hall 1974). And I'm reading that as a way of contesting the overstructuralization of Marxism which is going on in Althusser. Althusser quotes the "1857 Introduction," and I go back to the "1857 Introduction," and what I hear is half of the move which Althusser says Marx made towards the structuralist model, but only half of it. I don't hear that absolutism which is Althusser's *Reading Capital* [Althusser and Balibar 1971]. I don't hear a theoretical practice which is divorced from real structures and relations. Also, I don't hear a notion of capital which is grounded in an entirely determinist logic stemming from what is called "the relations of production." What I find in the "1857 Introduction" is a very interesting model which I think has not been sufficiently understood: a model which is elaborated from the notion of the circuits of production. Production, consumption, realization, reproduction—the expanding circuit. And it's grounded on the notion of a circuit of production. Marx, of course, gives a kind of privileging to the moment of production. But what I don't hear is what had become a sort of fetishized version of Marxism: Production determines everything else. Because if you read the "1857 Introduction" carefully, you will see that he says consumption determines production just as production determines consumption.

This provides a model of what I call "articulation," an understanding of the circuits of capital as an articulation of the moments of production, with the moments of consumption, with the moments of realization, with the moments of reproduction. He says if you have to start this model analytically somewhere, you've got to start with production.

JL: I think many of us found the essay an important break that dragged us out of the confines of the uses-and-gratifications and effects schools of research you've referred to. Reading the piece there is a clear feeling that we are on the dawn of a new era, particularly in terms of looking at audiences and decoding. In Umberto Eco's essay [Eco 1972] of about a decade earlier, where he talks about semiotics of decoding in a different way, he also in some ways anticipates the dawning of a new era—an era which doesn't develop. Almost nothing really happens. Actual research in the area, David Morley's work [Morley 1980] being an obvious exception, was not forthcoming. Is that something you've been disappointed by?

SH: I don't think so, not really. The encoding/decoding model wasn't a grand model. I had in my sights the Centre for Mass Communications Research—that was who I was trying to blow out of the water. I didn't think of it as generating a model which would last for the next twenty-five years for research. I don't think it has the theoretical rigor, the internal logical and conceptual consistency for that. If it's of any purchase, now and later, it's a model because of what it suggests. It suggests an approach; it opens up new questions. It maps the terrain. But it's a model which has to be worked with and developed and changed.

Morley's work is not quite the encoding/decoding model: As he reflects on his own practice, he shifts it. It wasn't a model which was specifically designed to be the point of reference of a long period of empirical work. It's only once I had written it that I saw that if you were going to contest an old model of audience research and open up a new one, then somebody's going to try and put it into effect. And then, with Dave Morley, we had the real problem: How the hell do you actually test this with some actual folks? Because if you look at the encoding/decoding paper, you will see these hypothetical decoding positions sketched out—I think I created a lot of problems for myself there. They are what I call ideal-typical or hy-pothetical-deductive positions. They're not yet empirical positions. They are de-coding positions; they are not sociological groups. It's very possible for an indi-vidual or group at one moment to decode in what I call the "hegemonic codes" and at another moment to use oppositional codes. It is simply to give some flesh-ing out to the notion that decoding is not homogeneous—that you can read in different ways and that is what reading is about.

JD: Your recounting of the context of forms of representation going on at the time you wrote this echoes in some ways Eco and also Baudrillard's view that we've gone through three stages of representation: one purely realistic or empiri-cal; the second one of not reflecting reality but good ones or bad ones—as in Marxism, with its idea of false consciousness; and a third one—and this is some-thing Eco brings up in his *Travels in Hyperreality* and Baudrillard does in *Simula-tions*—that representation has been displaced or has disappeared by the emer-gence of simulacra. I was interested in this, because at one point in this article you do say that reality exists outside language but is constantly mediated by and through language. And then you say "The dog in the film can bark but it can't bite." But I'm wondering now, when we have simulacra like Reagan where clearly the bark was worse than the bite—where it seems fantasy and spectacle are dis-placing these realities of representations—whether you minimize this power of simulacra?

SH: I would put it slightly differently. I've shifted in my notion of what repre-sentation is. I think the encoding/decoding model is grounded in a rather unproblematic notion which exists separate from and outside discourse. I proba-bly still think that, but I'm damned if I can tell you where it is. And I think I know why I can't tell you where it is, because since we can only know the real through language, through conceptualization, how the hell would I be able to tell you where it was? Because I can only do that inside language. I think that is the prob-lem of the "1857 Introduction" in a curious way; when Marx says of course real structures exist, we can only think about them—where else—in the head. And forever after that he says thought can only be articulated on the real; it cannot be just a reflection of the real. I think in the 1857 manuscript there's already a notion of the real as having some existence which can only be produced discursively. So I don't think there's an unproblematic notion of the real or the empirical in "En-coding/Decoding," but it still has a slightly unproblematic status. And therefore when representation is used in the paper, it is still a little bit like the real exists and then representation represents the real. I'm already far outside of that notion of an unproblematic reality against which the distortions of representation could be measured. I really have never been much attracted by the full-blown notion of false consciousness. I've always thought that there is something deeply troubling and wrong about it, including the fact that nobody confesses themselves to being in false consciousness. It's always somebody else.

JD: Well that's a symptom of it; if you're not aware of it, you're surely the victim of it.

SH: Yes, of course. Absolutely. So you can't win with false consciousness. Now the question is: How far has one gone with opening up the notion of representation as itself constitutive—as the effect of a practice, but not as a practice to which some real origin can be signified? How much has one blurred or opened up the notion of representation in the direction of the simulacrum? And at that point I do hesitate before the full-blown Baudrillard position. And I do that for two reasons. One is because Baudrillard is a master of the provocative overstatement. I don't think that he believes literally almost anything he says. But he is positioning himself still against an unproblematic notion of representation and of the clear separation between the media and real life, and he's just saying that the relations are much more complex than that. So I take it slightly as a polemical position. But my hesitation is based on more than that. Let me take the metaphor that you used. It is true that with Reagan the bark was perhaps bigger than the bite; but there was a bite as well, and the rest of the world bloody knows it. So I cannot subscribe to a theoretical position which says we are simply in nothing but reflections of one another's discourses. I just don't think that is an account of what the whole of the world is like—I think it may be an account of how some Americans now feel at the edge of their world, but I don't think that the whole of the world is like that.

IA: I'd like to ask a question related to this. You talk about a circuit, a circuit of meaning which you call "the articulation of linked but distinctive moments." Now it seems to me that encoding/decoding model focuses the emphasis on the distinctive moments. And the term "articulation" comes up only three times that I can notice. And then in your more recent work you connect articulation explicitly to linkage. I wonder if you would see, in retrospect, what appears to me as a tension between a semiotic model of encoding/decoding, which seems to focus on the distinctive moments, and a tendency in articulation, coming from a model of totality, to focus on the relations between the moments? Do you see a tension between those?

SH: I have to be honest, I don't. Because, analytically, if you're going to talk about articulation, you have to identify the separate moments in order to talk about what is related to what. But I don't talk about it as if those moments have any self-sufficient character. So it's always production and consumption in a relation. You have to know, analytically, why consumption and production are different in order to talk about how they're articulating. You have to recognize difference at each point. So the fact that I spend some time talking about the encoding moment and the decoding moment does not preclude looking at the relations between them. I call encoding and decoding the two different but related practices which connect what can be analytically identified as two separate moments.

The only point at which I'm slightly bothered by what you say is something which may be true. Of course there is a notion hiding away in there somewhere of complex totality, the Althusserian notion of complex totality—that is to say, of the articulation of differences, and that is the Saussurian model: Language is an articulation of differences, so you have to identify the differences to know what is articulating them. Language is an articulation of differences. The economy can be thought in the same way; that's really the thrust of *Reading Capital* [Althusser and Balibar 1971]. And I guess that is the notion of a complex or overdetermined totality, not an underdetermined one. And it is right to say that the encoding/decoding model is therefore trying to think the circuits of communication as a complex, overdetermined totality. But I have to put the question back to you, because I don't think the semiotic model quite so sharply or totally contrasted with the notion of a complex, overdetermined totality. So I don't see that distinction, though I may be just blind to it.

IA: I think there is one. If you take the sense in which Marx means production is consumption, consumption is production, when I eat I am consuming the products of labor, and I am producing myself as a future laborer, as the laborer of tomorrow. So consumption and production are analytically moments but analytically separate moments of the same activity, in the same place, at the same time. So the distinction is conceptual and analytical. Now, if you apply that to an encoding/decoding model, it seems to me that the major difference is that encoding occurs in some sorts of institutions by some people; it can be complicated, but basically it occurs with some people in some places. And decoding occurs somewhere else, at another time, by other people. And that seems to me to be an important difference with regard to the conception of totality.

SH: I think I disagree with that, and I'll tell you why. I disagree with it because I don't think the analogy can be with the individual. That is what makes it sound as if it happens in the same place, at the same time. But if you think about it in terms of the circuits of production in general, production can take place in Taiwan, consumption can take place in Manhattan, and delay in reinvestment may not take place in the next ten years. So, as a general model for the framework of the relations of capitalist production and consumption, the moments are very different. Each is sustained by some condition. You have to understand the conditions in Taiwan which allow for production. Then you have to understand the relations which articulate the investor in Tokyo with the production in Taiwan. Then you have to understand the relations of consumption in mass consumer society, in the supermarket down the road. Then you have to understand how that profit goes back via London to somebody who is reinvesting in Tokyo, who will reinvest in Taiwan.

I think the model in Marx excited me precisely because it seemed to be a model over space, over time, and to relate to apparently disconnected practices, each of which could break down. If the production in Taiwan breaks down for its own internal reasons, that makes it impossible to produce the goods which will be sold in the supermarket. So I was looking at it more as a model of a system as a whole.

And I think the problem might be that if you look at it individually, the body grounds it all in the same place. So the production and consumption seem to be happening within the same entity. But if you think of it in terms of an economic system or an ideological system, then they don't have to happen in the same place. They're part of the same practice in an absolutely global sense: The sum of production is related to the sum of consumption, which is related to the sum of reproduction. But I don't think in any other way do they have to be part of the same internal practice, which would lead me to a stronger notion of totality than I think I derive from the "1857 Introduction."

SJ: I'd like to get your thoughts on the critique made by Justin [Lewis 1983] in his article on the model. One reading of the article could argue that contained within the model are two levels of signification: signification in general of the social, cultural, and political world; and a secondary level of signification connected to the encoding practice. This reading argues that the encoding process here merely acts in terms of reproducing or not reproducing the broader systems of meaning, rather than being a part of the primary constitutive process. Would you agree with that reading, and if so would you still support it, or do you think that is a misreading of the argument in the paper?

SH: No, I think it is an accurate reading, and I think that there are two levels of signification which are identified in the paper. They're not as clearly differentiated as they should be. At one level I'm talking about the continuous process of signification of the cultural/ideological world which is always signifying and resignifying—that's an endless process. And there's a point where I use encoding and decoding to speak about the specific practice of making television programs. So I leap from one analytic level to another. And the encoding/decoding model is really about the latter.

I simply take the cultural/ideological ground as something which always exists. In that sense it's an Althusserian paper; it suggests that there will always be ideology, just as there will always be economy and politics. These are the three instances of any social formation. And therefore there will always be discourses in the society which are the means by which people make sense of the world, give meaning to the world. That never stops. That is the field of signification. That's what Althusser would call "signification in general," like ideology in general. Then, within that, I now want to talk about what is specific to producing a television program, rather than writing a book, or writing a text, or punishing somebody, or hanging them, all of which are discursive practices. What is specific about the activity of producing a television program? So there is, I think, a confusion in those two levels of signification by not specifying them properly.

The encoding model is an attempt to talk about a new way to do media studies within this larger world. Now, you quite rightly say that there is a notion of reproduction, whereby the encoding/decoding process, as a particular moment of symbolic production by the media institution, reproduces the larger ideological world. And I don't think that, and I don't think I ever thought that, but I think it is a reading which could be quite legitimately made from the paper. And I'll tell you why. Because it has the notion of reproduction in it, and the notion of reproduction is almost impossible, in the English language, to separate from mere repetition. So when I say "reproduction," it sounds as if all that is happening is the already given dominant ideology kind of pops into the program and out into the decoding.

O.K., you might then say, "Why use the notion of reproduction?" Well, that is located in contestation with another discourse. It's located in contestation with the discourse coming from film theory, and from *Screen,* and from that absolute position which talks about every meaning as a production. There are no anterior conditions. Each meaning is a total act of production. It's the high, Brechtian moment in *Screen* theory. Production, production, production. Each speech is a production. And what I want to say is that each speech is not a production in that sense, because it is on the ground of the already given meaning. If you have to say something new, it is because it is transforming the meanings which are already there. So each act of signification transforms the given actualized state of all the significations already in existence. Each time I say "Englishness" I do something to the entire map of Englishness which existed before me.

JL: If I understand you correctly, you're saying that rather than having a notion where you have a world of signification in general, which produces, like concrete blocks, signs which the media then act upon and reproduce, we have two notions: signification in general, and specific signifying practices within media institutions.

SH: And everywhere else.

JL: So these specific practices engage with signification in general in much the same way that signifying practices within other ideological state apparatuses do?

SH: Absolutely. I'm only doing it with media studies because I'm talking to media people, but we could talk about any literary text or any bureaucratic piece of writing or any set of rules—anything that is a kind of recodification of something which already exists. What is important about that is the "always already"—being there, as it were. And I want to hold on to that for two reasons. First of all, because I want to get rid of the notion of any originating moment, I simply bury the question of where this all started. It may have started in the Garden of Eden, but I don't know. After that we are in history already; therefore we are in discourse already. So what the media pick up on is already a discursive universe.

The encoding moment doesn't come from nowhere. I make a mistake by drawing that bloody diagram with only the top half. You see, if you're doing a circuit, you must draw a circuit; so I must show how decoding enters practice and discourses which a reporter is picking up on. The reporter is picking up on the presignified world in order to signify it in a new way again. And I really create problems for myself by looking as if there is a sort of moment there. So you read the circuit as if there is a real world, then somebody speaks about it and encodes it, then somebody reads it, then there's a real world again. But of course, the real world is not outside of discourse; it's not outside of signification. It's practice and discourse like everything else is.

IA: So the two levels of signification would be better understood as universal and particular rather than as levels of fundamentalness of reality.

SH: It is not at all the second. It's just an analytic distinction between ideology in general and specific ideological practices, or our discursive ideological configurations, or whatever you like.

CS: You've cleared up the confusion by situating the model within Althusser and the idea of a general ideology and a specific ideology. Is there a reason why you did not have that in the original paper?

SH: It wasn't a paper which gave its full credentials. So, for example, the "1857 Introduction" and Marx are not mentioned in the original paper at all. So I'm only gradually showing my hand. In a colloquium of the Congress of European Mass Communications Research, you would have closed minds if you said, "This is founded on the Althusserian notion of the overdetermined, complex totality." They would have left the room at that point. So I think it's probably the second; maybe it's a bit of both. I'm reading and contesting Althusser because my own thinking is very influenced by Althusser, but I'm never a doctrinal Althusserian.

Now, perhaps, if I were writing a definitive version of "Encoding/Decoding" for a collection of papers, perhaps I ought to footnote or recognize more directly the impact of working with or arguing within the Althusserian problematic.

SJ: Let me pose a general question. What exactly do you mean by the terms "preferred meanings" and "preferred readings" in the text? Where is the preferring process located? Is it in the text? Is it in the wider social/political culture? And on the side of decoding, what are the consequences, both theoretical and political, of putting preferring on one site on the circuit?

SH: Preferred reading is another problem in the text, and the slippage between preferred meaning and preferred reading is what does the damage. Because preferred reading appears to put it on the decoding side, whereas preferred meaning is on the encoding side, not the decoding side. Why is it there? Well, it is there because I don't want a model of a circuit which has no power in it. I don't want a model which is determinist, but I don't want a model without determination. And therefore I don't think audiences are in the same positions of power with those who signify the world to them. And preferred reading is simply a way of saying if you have control of the apparatus of signifying the world, if you're in control of the media, you own it, you write the texts—to some extent it has a determining shape. Your decodings are going to take place somewhere within the universe of encoding. The one is trying to enclose the other. Transparency between the encoding and decoding moments is what I would call the moment of hegemony. To be perfectly hegemonic is to have every meaning that you want to communicate understood by the audience only in that way. A kind of dream of power—no blips on the screen, just a totally passive audience. Now, my problem is that I don't believe that the message has any one meaning. So I want to get a notion of a power and structuring in the encoding moment which, nevertheless, does not wipe out all the other possible meanings. All that I mean to say is that a statement by the BBC about the Falklands war is not entirely open-ended. They want you to read this message in a certain way. The element of preferred reading is the point at which power intersects with the discourse. And it is both outside and inside the message. It's not just that they are powerful because they control the means of production; they try to get into the message itself, to give you a clue: "Read it in this way." That's what I mean by preferred reading. It's an attempt to hegemonize the audience, which is never entirely effective and usually not effective. Why? Because they cannot contain every possible reading of the text. The very text which they encode slips from their grasp. You can always read it in another way.

So a preferred reading is never fully successful, but it is the exercise of power in the attempt to hegemonize the audience reading. That's all it is. I just don't want to suggest that the text is infinitely open, with no elements within it.

Let me take a text which is not from the media. Take the very complex texts of a Shakespeare play. We know, now, after three or four hundred years, that a Shakespeare play can be produced and read any way you like. There are hundreds of readings of King Lear. But Shakespeare wouldn't be satisfied to have hundreds of readings of King Lear. He wants you to see Lear in a particular way. He wants to make it seem that you can't read it any other way; you have to see Lear as the besieged father. If you choose to read him as a stupid old man who can't tolerate the fact that his daughters bring a lot of people home, that's an odd reading, that's an aberrant reading; he doesn't want you to read it in that way. So I think not only is there a will to power in the practice of signification, of encoding, but I think that one can see those elements lodged in the text itself.

SJ: So in this sense you could say that the preferred reading is the intention of the producer at the encoding site?

SH: I don't want to reduce this to the intention of the producer, because the producer in the BBC is constrained by his institutional setting.

JL: Obviously, as you say, TV programs are not like the "bean" that Roland Barthes talks about at the beginning of *S/Z*, a bean whose physical ambiguity could, ultimately, signify the whole world. They contain preferred meaning, shaped by structures of power. And, invariably, within media institutions those structures of power relate to dominant meanings within the society. However, how does the conception of preferred meaning work for texts that not only don't work within that dominant meaning system but work against it? TV messages that have a preferred reading, textually, that is opposed to a preferred meaning, in the dominant sense, in the society, as a whole? How do these kinds of messages work in terms of this model? It seems also to me to have consequences in terms of the three responses: the dominant, the oppositional, and the negotiated.

SH: Yes, it's perfectly true, what you are saying. If there is a homogeneity in the preferring, it's only what you can detect in terms of a pattern of preferrings over a long period of time. So you can say that, on the whole, over the output of a long period, you would tend to get the hegemonic message more frequently.

But, of course, the media produce all sorts of other things. Britain has a whole channel, like Channel 4, which is institutionally dedicated to minority voices as well as all kinds of minority programs and oppositional programs. So the encoding side itself is a much more contested and variable space than comes through in this model. This model does make the media institutions sound rather homogeneous in their ideological character, and they're not. It's not sufficiently attentive to that.

I don't think the encoding model, as it's outlined here, has a sufficient notion of why it's a contested and contradictory space, even in the media institutions themselves. It treats the institutionalization of communication as too one-dimensional, too directly articulated to a dominant ideology.

JD: I'm just wondering that if you could go further, in the sense that you're deferring the meaning as well, you're always predicating this interpretation on difference, on it being different from another, and it deferring, always already deferring. So I'm just curious whether or not you could put this into a Derridean scheme of intepretation?

SH: The reason why preferring cannot stop or fix the text is because meaning is infinitely deferred (in the Derridean sense). So that's already the ground on which I'm working. But is the text just a set of open, semiotics things which can be decoded in any way? Well, not quite; there's a bit of power in there. Somebody has to control the means to signify the world. A lot of people out there who don't have any other way of knowing about the world depend on its being signified to them.

So, in that sense, the model takes the Derridean notion of deferring of difference for granted. That is the nature of textuality, already, and it simply asks, "How can we prevent this model from being the infinite playfulness of language?" It's not quite that, because power needs something out of language. It needs something out of the shaping of the maps of meaning which the population is going to use to understand events.

I use ideology as that which cuts into the infinite semiosis of language. Language is pure textuality, but ideology wants to make a particular meaning. I want to break the chain of meaning here. I want it to have this meaning, not every other meaning. So, politically, I slightly separate those two out. I think it's the point where power cuts into discourse, where power overcuts knowledge and discourse; at that point you get a cut, you get a stoppage, you get a suture, you get an overdetermination. The meaning constructed by that cut into language is never permanent, because the next sentence will take it back, will open the semiosis again. And it can't fix it, but ideology is an attempt to fix it.

IA: So your notion of preferred is, in fact, much closer to Derrida's notion of erasure. It's the point at which the play of differences must be erased in order for a center to be constituted, and it's around that center that makes the text.

SH: Absolutely, absolutely. It is what requires you to come to the end of a sentence—that's my metaphor. You have to come to the end of a sentence in order to make any meaning at all. You are then under the illusion that that is all you have to say. But, actually, the next somebody will say something else. The next sentence deconstructs it.

IA: So is one of the tasks of the critic to kind of pull apart that preferring process, to open up the play, to turn ideology back into language?

SH: Absolutely. That is why this kind of critical work on encoding/decoding is always a deconstructive practice. It opens up the text to the variety of meanings or appropriations which were not legislated for in the activity of its encoding.

JD: But in your article on Thatcherism you go to great pains to distinguish yourself from a purely deconstructive position. You say reconstruction is necessary against political movements such as Thatcherism.

SH: Yes, I'm not a pure deconstructionist in the sense that I don't think that just that moment of deconstruction is the only one there is. I think that I'm, in that sense, a Gramscian—that every moment of deconstruction is also a moment of reconstruction. That reconstruction is no more permanent than the previous one, but it is not just pulling the text apart. And the reason I say that is because it's positioned in relation to a very specific context. It's positioned in relation to what I regard as the entirely depoliticized, formalist way in which deconstruction has been appropriated in America.

I think the American appropriation of deconstruction has robbed it of its political bite—has made it into a kind of intellectual playground. And it doesn't matter a damn what you do with deconstruction; it's to show how bloody clever you are at pulling apart the presuppositions of every text. But the point is also to produce some new texts (although those new texts are not forever). You can't get out of the fact that to say something is to pull apart an existing configuration of meaning and to begin to sketch out another configuration.

SJ: Can we move on to discuss the three decoding positions (preferred, negotiated, and oppositional) and the adequacy of those positions?

SH: I think that the decoding side is less well formulated and worked out than the encoding side in the paper. What I tried to do was to follow through the notion that there is no one fixed meaning, and, consequently, there never can be one fixed reading, based on a notion of a set of ideal typical positions. So there's a position of ideal transparency and perfect equivalence between the two moments, where the reading more or less perfectly corresponds to the way in which the text was preferred.

Then, there's the opposite of that, a systematically oppositional reading which may or may not understand what was preferred but constantly gets out of the very same text exactly the opposite—looks at, for instance, the exercise of law and order as an exercise of oppression, of resistance, looks at the same pictures and sees the other side.

The problem, if you translate those two positions into politics, is that you get back into a very determinist position. You have either the false consciousness of a perfectly transparent reading or the perfect revolutionary subject of the always oppositional subject. So I want something in between. So I simply talk about the negotiated code. And the negotiated code is in the paper as one position, but, of course, it's not one position at all. And if you look at a rather similar model, which is in the long introduction to *Resistance Through Rituals* [Hall and Jefferson 1976], you will see that what we call the "negotiated space" is filled out by a number of different positions in relation to subcultures. So the truth is, negotiated readings are probably what most of us do most of the time. Only when you get to the well-organized, fully self-conscious revolutionary subject will you get a fully oppositional reading. Most of us are never entirely within the preferred reading or entirely against the whole grain of the text. We are boxing and coxing with it. So that strengthens the notion that these are ideal typical positions. I simply say, "The spectrum is like that."

None of the positions in decoding are intended as sociological descriptions. It is an open-ended model. Audiences are clearly moving between the three positions; so they're positionalities, they're not sociological entities. It remains for empirical work to say, in relation to a particular text and a particular section of the audience, which readings operate.

JL: Can I just make a comment on that in relation to my own experience working with these concepts in decoding? One of the problems I had, when looking at the way in which people read specific pieces of TV news in relation to these three responses, involves the assumption that there is already a preferred meaning: one which we then negotiate with, agree with, or oppose. Now, I kept finding things were going on in the readings that I hadn't anticipated. News items that I had thought were quite clearly about one particular thing, and were preferred in a particular way, were repeatedly read by viewers as being about something entirely different.

This relates to a question that Dave Morley asks in his critical postscript to the "Nationwide" [British television program] study. He says, "Where is the preferred reading?" Is it already inscribed in the text? Is it in the analyst's reading of it? Or is it in the audience's reading? Now, he is very enigmatic and teasingly leaves the question open. And I wonder whether that was because he felt it might be the wrong question. In other words, is it our role, as researchers, not to presuppose a preferred meaning, but to begin by opening up the text as far as we can and then see how it is closed down by people in the audience? This enables us to use empirical evidence to locate and specify those textual moments that, for particular types of viewers, determine (or fail to determine) a program's meaning.

SH: Preferring on the decoding side means something different from preferring on the encoding side. I can, as it were, deprefer your preferring and reprefer mine. I can say, "You wanted me to read it in that way, but I don't read it in that way." Therefore the element of closure can never work, which doesn't mean that it's not made. That's why preferring is the attempt which power makes to secure the message to one meaning—which it can never succeed in doing. But I do say, and I guess I still think, that the text will bear within it—as well as the real signifiers which can support—a different reading. It does contain what I can only call the "indicative" signifiers which try to imprint inside the message itself in which it could be decoded.

JL: Yes, but how do we find out what those indicative signifiers are? Do we assume that we, as analysts, can somehow discover them? Or do we say that the way we discover them is to see how the audience constructs its own preferred readings and, having done so, look back at the text and see how the text actually forced them into those positions, in negotiation with their own ideological worldviews? We can then say there is a preferred reading, or a set of preferred readings, because we have seen how the text actually does prefer certain kinds of meanings.

SH: No, I can't make the move that way because that would suggest that the decodings are too closed, you see. I think the decoding can reread the text right against the grain of the text, so I don't think that you can use the decoding which the audience makes to say what is the preferred meaning in the text.

JL: How, then, do we discover the preferring moments?

SH: Well, I think you can only do that by a certain kind of textual analysis.

IA: Which is already a decoding on our part.

SH: Yes, of course it's already a decoding; that's what I said to you before. As soon as you've given an account of the text, it is a kind of reading. I think you have to make that risk of analysis, and I say that because I don't think that this is an arena in which you can have a fully objective scientific method—because I don't think that there is any science which can account for meaning. So you have to risk trying to read as much as you can, as neutrally as you can get, what seems to be the shaping that the text has received as a consequence of passing through a particular site. That's all. I think that part of your account has to be quite openended, quite neutral. It's the sort of necessary objectivity. I don't believe in true objectivity, but it's the moment of research where you try as much to suppress your own reading of it in order to reconstitute the text as a researchable object. But I do think that there is no way in which you can do that without recognizing that you are already inside meaning.

JL: I still have, I suppose, an analytical problem. My feeling is that despite the great distance that textual analysis has come, two people, both very skilled in textual analysis, can come out of the same film and argue with each other, at great length, about what the film was actually about. I think we're still exploring how texts work. Given that, doesn't decoding research become more subtle, more sophisticated, if we have an idea about a preferred meaning that exists within the text, but that we then play with during decoding? In other words, we've gathered decodings, we've seen how that idea seems to be working, and then we actually construct and nail down a preferred reading, rather than nailing down the preferred reading before we've done any decoding research at all.

SH: Well …

JL: Because what if we're wrong? Which we may well be. We simply end up with a number of aberrant decodings.

SH: It's the same problem that you have with the notion of preferred reading, I think. And I don't know that I can answer you in any different way. I think there are dangers on either side, you see. I think that if you have a preferred reading, you already prestructure the decodings that you're likely to get. That's, I think, your worry about it. If you don't have a preferred reading, I think you are in the illusion of objectivity. I think you're in the commitment that the text can mean anything. I don't know how to hold a position in between those two, because there doesn't seem to be any space in between those two.

But, still, I see we're not outside the philosophical problem. Because however tentative and open-ended it is, it is a kind of reading. It's a reading where you stop yourself short of saying "This is what it means." You're halfway up the road to saying "This is what it means." If you settle for that, I would settle for it too.

JC: So if there are limits, then, around meaning, if meaning isn't simply up for grabs at any point in time, then it seems to me that a lot of the issues you have been raising in your work presuppose taking the analytic risk of specifying what is historically specific at any given point in time. So my question in terms of the encoding/decoding model is one that leaves us with the problem: Either we recognize that chasm between discursive practice, on the one hand, and the assumed real, or we deny that and just go with discursive analysis and smuggle in notions of the real when we take that risk, that step of specifying what we think is an appropriate reading. I'm speaking of the role of the analyst here. What comments do you have on that? There are some limits, there are problems of historical specificity that shape, that force the researcher into specifying, giving name to the real, even though there are moments and movements that deny the real. How do we get around that problem without just simply focusing on texts?

SH: I suppose in the end the position dodges or ducks the question of any fixed or verifiable distinction between the real and the discursive, or between the discursive and the extradiscursive. I don't know where that extradiscursive is. I regard the extradiscursive as a kind of wager. It's a kind of bet that the world exists, which cannot be proven in a philosophical sense. I don't know how one would prove it. What I certainly don't give the discursive, the extradiscursive, or the real is any ultimately defining determinacy.

I suppose, nevertheless, I simply can't think "practice" without touching ground, with each practice always touching ground as the necessary but not sufficient element—its materiality, its material registration. Somewhere. What that, however, pushes me to is what I would call the historically real, which is not philosophically real but which has a good deal of determinacy in it. So the historical structures may not be long lasting, they may not be forever, cannot be transcendental, but while they're going, they do structure a particular field. And, therefore, they do mean that any piece of research is already located in a historical moment, in a historical conjuncture. The questions that the researcher has do not come from some objective science but from some particular set of concerns. There are notions about what political and historical conjuncture we are in that shape the research. All of those factors are there.

That is the Gramscian appropriation. And that's why I give attention, through Gramsci, to what I call the conjuncture—to the specific articulation of moments, to what is particular and peculiar to a specific historical moment, to the way in which the particular balance of forces between different social elements defines a terrain of movement and practice at any particular time. This conjuncture does not proceed as a result of an abstract analytic or scientifically defined reality. In that sense there is no science of history which can guarantee, but there is a kind of recognition that the reading is located somewhere historically. This conversation is being conducted in a particular place, at a particular moment in history; and the conjuncture has some shaping effects on how that research will be done, and how the questions will be asked, and what will be done with the research.

So I suppose in moving away from the real or the extradiscursive as a kind of transcendental signifier outside of the system, I try to reintroduce it back as an element of tendential structuration. So there is no reason why the fact that the English have dominated the rest of the world for three hundred years should mean that every time one reaches for English identity it sees itself as superior to the rest of the world. But there is a bloody good historical reason why that should be so. And the tendency in the culture will be always for Englishness to mean that; and if you want it to mean something else, if you want it to mean the black kids in the photography group I work with, you have to do a heck of a lot of ideological work to shift the word, the concept, from that tendential structuration to some other one.

In that sense I remain attached to certain origins of my own thinking in hermeneutics. The promise of semiology is to make hermeneutics as scientific as it possibly could be, which is an impossible project. What it will not deliver is the science of meaning, like the third law of thermodynamics. But it does say that you've got to do something more in orderly scientific work than just "Well, this is my guess, and I feel that about the text." You have to go as far as you can in suggesting that this is something which is grounded in the operations of language. You can give some account of that which isn't just solipsistic, internally the result of subjective prejudice. But the notion that what you produce is *the* meaning, scientifically validated—obviously, you see from what my interpretation of what meaning is, I can't hold that position. The objectivity of social science research is always in quotation marks. It's the aspiration to theory, but it stops before theoretical practice. All research is theorized, but it is not theory with a capital *T.* It is the activity of theorizing, of going on thinking, rather than the end point of the production of a final theoretical model.

IA: Stuart, if we look at the range of possibilities for decoding, it seems to me that there are two other alternatives, both of which are, for various reasons, unsatisfactory. There is, on the one hand, the traditional hermeneutic route, in which we distinguish between an initial understanding of the text and the interpretation by a given reader. This is problematic because it presupposes a common core of meaning in all interpretations. It's bad old essentialism.

If one rejects this, then one falls into the other problem of being unable to really distinguish an aberrant decoding from an oppositional decoding—or between understanding a text and oppositional readings. In this case, just thinking that the text is about something completely different seems like an oppositional practice. The question is, somehow we need a way around both these alternatives; we have to understand the practice of decoding or reading in a way that gets around both of these positions. The only way of talking about this that I can see is to start talking about "interpretive communities." The advantage of using such an idea is that practices of reading are placed within a social and institutional context, a context which is different from institutions of encoding. Is this a way of probing that makes sense to you? And what do you think of the term "interpretive communities"?

SH: I guess I don't see yet or am only just beginning to see the distinction that you make between understanding and interpreting. I think you're probably right that these are two analytically separable moments, but I certainly am not aware of thinking of them as two different activities. So it's a sort of hyperbole when I talk about contesting the meaning—as if you read it, and you know that that's the preferred reading, and then you say, "I don't like that, so I will read it in a different way." It's only in the course of my having to persuade my audience that this can really be different that I talk about it in those separate moments. You sort of see what it's trying to say to you; in the same moment you can't really understand it in that way, but you're already understanding it in another way. So as a practice, those moments are not analytically separate; they're analytically separable in my text just because it's an analytic text and it's exactly like the circuit. You have to give them some specificity in order to talk about their articulation, but in reality they don't exist. They only exist already in articulation.

I know that this is slightly problematic in that there's another problem lurking in there, namely: Are there forms of understanding which are more intuitive, which are not so ideologically structured, so ideologically driven, forms of knowledge which can't be so clearly related to the codes? And I guess I don't know yet what I think about that, but I think that is there. So I may have skirted over some problems in taking understanding and interpretation as part of a single whole. But certainly in the paper it's taken as part of a single whole.

Now, as far as the point that you raise, then, about trying to stop short of the opposite of that, I do think that interpretation is one of the best ways of trying to move the ideal-typical aspect of the decoding model into empirical research. That is what audiences are. They share certain frameworks of understanding and interpretation. They share certain frameworks of reading. Reading in that sense is not simply the lonely "uses and gratifications" individual. It's not purely subjective reading. It's shared. It has institutional expression; it relates to the fact that you are part of that institution.

Your readings arise from the family in which you were brought up, the places of work, the institutions you belong to, the other practices you do. And that is really what I think, although the term "interpretive communities" is not used. That is really what governs Morley's research—trying to identify certain very distinctive interpretive communities which share some decoding frameworks in common and to contrast them loosely against one another. That's why Morley's research is just the first stages of the empirical application, extension and development of that model. We don't use the term "interpretive communities."

Tony Bennett's work on Bond now talks about "reading formations"—which is another way of talking about the fact that interpretive communities share the tools of reading the text, and that these are not purely solipsistic, individualized things. I think that's an interesting way to go. I think Morley's work after this period, which looks at the family, is another way of looking at a particular interpretive community, which because of the domestic nature of television is absolutely crucial. It has the extra added advantage of bringing in very centrally to the whole decoding activity questions of gender, which of course are backgrounded in this model. So I think one could work with the notion of interpretive communities or reading formations very effectively, although there are problems with identifying those sociologically. But, still, I think that it's one way to go.

CS: I have a question about interpretive communities. To some extent that's a term that's been coined in reader-response criticism by, for example, Stanley Fish. And Frank Lentricchia takes Fish to task on the basis that Fish's interpretive communities are simply academics on the U.S. eastern seaboard. So I'm just wondering how you respond to that in terms of the kinds of audience research done by Bennett and by Morley, and then by reader-response approaches. Do they contest each other?

SH: Yes, first of all Fish: I think the criticism is probably right. Each of us has our own preferred interpretive community, some of which we live in all the time and mistake for the rest of the world. And that's a problem in academic life all the time.

Reading competencies, if they exist, are like language competencies, which we all know are fundamentally social. There's no point in having a language just for you. So inside your head you can speak to yourself without the language. The moment you get a language, you're in a social situation. And I think reading is a social activity of that kind. So then one wants to say, "Well, what are these groupings?" They're not necessarily given by sociological analysis because they are not coterminous with classes or anything like that. Within any class there are a number of them. So how do you break it down in a way that is sensitive to the fact that what you are trying to study are the readings? You can't break it down by professions or by any of those given sociological categories because interpretive readings may overcut a number of them. Discourse and ideology have their own specific structures, which do not correspond to an economic or social structure in a simple way. So interpretive communities is simply that.

SJ: Could you talk a little bit more about how we go about investigating these activities in an empirical fashion? And, connected to that, why has there been so little audience-based critical research? Do you think it's an important direction in which to go? Do you think this is a vital next step that needs to be taken, or are there other productive areas that we could develop? And, related to this, could you talk about the problem or issue of pleasure, which has obviously had a wide currency in recent critical work that claims to be about the audience?

SH: Why wasn't there more work of this kind? I think there are a couple of reasons. First of all, during this period, a great deal of cultural studies is really very closely related to communication studies. So content analysis and "effects" kinds of audience research were still very much a dominant preoccupation in cultural studies. But, as you know, very shortly after this (when the encoding/decoding paper was written), things were about to shift. The encoding/decoding paper was written on the edge of the shift which Barthes makes from the interpretation of the codes into the notion of textuality, and then later into the notion of desire and the pleasure of the text. And it's therefore the moment of a movement in cultural studies from communication studies to literary theory, to the cinematic text, to psychoanalysis, to feminism, and to the beginnings of poststructuralism. And I think that that has been very important in shifting away from the empirical work which people wanted to do, and away from developing the encoding/decoding model, into other types of concerns. I think there are problems with it, as I've clearly said, but I don't think it's only that. It has something to do with the co. juncture.

Immediately after completing the encoding/decoding paper, we tried to get funding for the exercise of making it a more empirically applicable model. Now this is an institutional question—we couldn't get any. You could have gotten money overnight to do an enormous audience-effects survey. Anybody would have funded it if you wanted to do it. But nobody would fund attempts to look at decoding. Finally Dave Morley became attached to the Centre [for Mass Communications Research], and then we got a little bit of money which enabled Dave to work part-time on the "Nationwide" project. There was also Charlotte Brunsden's work—she was beginning to work on domestic serials and soap operas, and so on, within a more feminist perspective. And we constituted a little research team. That's why the "Nationwide" project is so flimsy—it's done on a shoestring, and therefore it couldn't really define empirically the interpretive communities. It had to shortchange that and say, "Well, we have a guess that those three might become useful ones to look at." A lot of the problems are the result of the unwillingness of funding bodies to pursue this institutionally.

If somebody now said, "Well, cultural studies is a big operation these days, which we're willing to fund"—would I go back to the encoding/decoding model? I think I would not. That's not because I don't think it has some purchase in it: in the field of communications research, in the study of the institutions of communication, in the study of the networks of communication, and in the study of audiences. I think the model still has purchase in those areas. So my hesitation is not because I don't think the model can yield further developmental work (although I insist on what I said earlier—if you're going to work with the model, you have to change the model and develop it). It's not a question that the model can now be practically and empirically applied. You have to work on the model as well as work on its empirical application. I think that still has something to deliver in communication studies.

And I think it also has something to deliver in the area that you asked me about, namely, reception studies. A similar sort of model has been developing in the question of how to understand the audiences for particular literary texts. And although the model isn't exactly the same, I think the encoding/decoding model has something to give to that kind of work.

But I think that, for me, a lot of the theoretical and philosophical underpinnings of the model have been somewhat dismantled or deconstructed by the movement in poststructuralism because textuality—Barthes's notion of textuality—is no longer amenable to the identification of those clearly distinguished analytic moments of encoding and decoding. I can only describe this spatially. It flattens out my circuit. Instead of a circuit, which has a clearly distinctive movement around, of an expanded kind, it kind of lays reading and the production of meaning side by side. It makes it lateral rather than a circuit.

In the notion of decoding, I'm trying to control the question of reading, to give it a bit of structure so that we can find out about it. But in the high point of textuality, the idea of textuality in Barthes, especially in *Pleasure of the Text*, there is no control over it any longer. Why? Partly, because the model is then decentered from somewhere else; it's decentered, if you forgive the spatial metaphor, from down below. Because not only have textuality and interpretation been given a much wider, expanded meaning laterally, but the questions of the unconscious, of psychoanalysis, and of feminism have come into the model. And at that moment you ask: What is the play across the text of meanings, which are not amenable or accessible to interpretive codings of a semiotic kind—what is the semiotics of the unconscious, or the semiotics of gender positioning, alongside the semiotics of political ideology? Well, you now have a much more fractured notion of what the text now means. You have a much more fractured notion of what interpretation means. My model is quite cognitive. It's not true, I think, to say at the center of the decoding/encoding model is the Cartesian subject; it's already a decentered subject. But it's still a sort of cognitive decentered subject; it's still a subject with a lot of interpretive codes going on. But it's not yet a subject with an unconscious. When it becomes a subject with an unconscious in which textuality also involves the pleasurable response, or the pleasurable consumption of the text, it's very hard to know, empirically, how you then go about finding that out in some observable, behaviorally identifiable way.

One of the problems of this later development in critical theory is that it expands our understanding of just how complex meaning really is, and how many different sites of determination are involved in it. So we know a lot more about it, but actually we are less secure in giving that an empirical and demonstrably empirical moment of research. And that is one of the reasons that one of the problems just now is that everybody nowadays is, surprisingly after thirty years, a literary critic.

We have made a surreptitious return to the undisciplined literary reading which this whole exercise was designed to firm up. We got into it because we weren't satisfied by just everybody sitting around Leavis's table saying, "This is what the text means, isn't it?"

The image of Leavis is of the perfect interpretive community, sitting in Downing College, Cambridge. As the result of the highly selective educational system of England, weeding out all of those other interpretive communities, finally at Downing College you would get the eight ideal readers, and, of course, they would produce a common reading, the common informed reading. They would know exactly the point at which *The Portrait of a Lady* stops being a good text and starts being a bad one. And we would all agree and that would produce the consensus, the ideal reading. And in a funny kind of way, not in that consensual way, we've gone back around to people trusting their intuitive understandings of the text and giving that a kind of authenticity, a kind of validity. It's a long way of answering your question, but it does undermine the certainty that I would now have that I could pick up the encoding/decoding model and go out and identify the audience, look at the encoding, and look at the decoding.

So if anybody thinks that the encoding/decoding model has enough purchase on a particular problem that confronts them now, to pick up this mantle, rework and try out, I would love to see them do it. I, perhaps, wouldn't do that because I'm trying to puzzle about another set of problems. But somebody else might be at the point where they can get something out of it. Theorizing and theoretically informed empirical research must work amongst a number of paradigms and construct its own paradigmatic point of departure. So I certainly wouldn't want to say, "Don't try to use it." I'd love to see it applied and I do think that even in its own time it didn't get a good run for its money. At the time I would have loved to have done a properly constructed test of the model and see what it delivered, and whether I could have developed the model better in the light of that. We didn't have that chance.

References

Althusser, L. 1971. *Lenin and Philosophy.* London: New Left Books.
Althusser, L., and E. Balibar. 1971. *Reading Capital.* London: New Left Books.
Barthes, R. 1967. *Elements of Semiology.* London: Jonathan Cape.
———. 1974. *S/Z.* New York: Hill and Wang.
———. 1975. *The Pleasure of the Text.* London: Jonathan Cape.
Baudrillard, J. 1983. *Simulations.* New York: Semiotexte.
Bennett, T., and J. Woollacott. 1987. *Bond and Beyond: Fiction, Ideology and Social Process.* London: Macmillan.
Brunsden, C., and D. Morley. 1979. *Everyday Television—Nationwide.* London: BFI.
Eco, U. 1972. "Towards a Semiotic Inquiry into the Television Message," *Working Papers in Cultural Studies,* no. 3, CCCS, University of Birmingham.
———. 1987. *Travels in Hyperreality.* London: Picador.
Fish, S. 1980. *Is There a Text in This Class? The Authority of Interpretive Communities.* Cambridge: Harvard University Press.
Gramsci, A. 1971. *Selections from the Prison Notebooks.* London: Lawrence and Wishart.
Hall, S. 1974. "Marx's Notes on Method: A 'Reading' of the 1857 Introduction," *Working Papers in Cultural Studies,* No. 6, CCCS, University of Birmingham.
———. "Encoding/Decoding," in S. Hall et al., eds., *Culture, Media, Language.* London: Hutchinson.
Hall, S., and T. Jefferson, eds. 1976. *Resistance Through Rituals.* London: Hutchinson.
Lentricchia, F. 1980. *After the New Criticism.* Chicago: University of Chicago Press.
Lewis, J. 1983. "The Encoding/Decoding Model: Criticisms and Redevelopments for Research on Decoding," *Media, Culture and Society,* no. 5.
Marx, K. 1971. "1857 Introduction" and "1859 Preface" to *A Contribution to the Critique of Political Economy.* London: Lawrence and Wishart.
Morley, D. 1980. *The Nationwide Audience.* London: BFI.
———. 1986. *Family Television.* London: Comedia.
Saussure, F. de. 1974. *Course in General Linguistics.* London: Fontana.

About the Book and Editors

In recent years, the academy has resounded with the collapse of traditional theories of representation and interpretation. Whole canons have been called into question, new fields of inquiry have opened up, and disciplinary cracks have appeared throughout the humanities and social sciences. The question of how history, culture, and society are to be interpreted has become critical.

These radical new developments have caused many scholars to reconsider a category that once seemed straightforward—the audience. As researchers from different fields have interrogated the meaning of things, the roles of the reader, viewer, or listener have been brought to the surface. What is an audience? How is it constituted? What role do audiences play in the construction of meaning? How do audiences interact with messages or "texts"?

Viewing, Reading, Listening explores these questions with essays from a range of fields—such as cultural studies, communications, sociology, literary criticism, and women's studies—and a variety of perspectives. The aim of this collection is neither to define the field nor to promote a new unified theory of the audience, but to provide a snapshot of transdisciplinary issues emerging in audience research and cultural reception. As Cruz and Lewis suggest, this book provides the reader with a map of new developments in the field rather than leading the reader in any one direction.

The collection covers a diversity of sites of cultural reception, from TV viewers to book-readers, to fans of music and music videos. Some of the contributors deal with theoretical questions, and others present findings from their empirical research. All the contributions come from outside the traditional canon of audience research and share theoretical concerns that can be broadly located within a cultural studies perspective.

This book is essential reading for those interested in audience studies and in the questions it raises.

Jon Cruz is assistant professor in the Department of Sociology and the Asian American Studies Program at the University of California–Santa Barbara. **Justin Lewis** is associate professor of communication at the University of Massachusetts–Amherst.